Origins of the
Popular Style

Origins of the Popular Style

The Antecedents of Twentieth-Century Popular Music

PETER VAN DER MERWE

CLARENDON PRESS · OXFORD

Oxford University Press, Walton Street, Oxford OX2 6DP
Oxford New York Toronto
Delhi Bombay Calcutta Madras Karachi
Petaling Jaya Singapore Hong Kong Tokyo
Nairobi Dar es Salaam Cape Town
Melbourne Auckland
and associated companies in
Berlin Ibadan

Oxford is a trade mark of Oxford University Press

Published in the United States
by Oxford University Press, New York

British Library Cataloguing in Publication Data
Van der Merwe, Peter
Origins of the popular style
1. Popular music—History and criticism
I. Title
780'.42'   ML3470.V36 1988
ISBN 0-19-816305-3 (paperback)

Library of Congress Cataloging in Publication Data
Van der Merwe, Peter
Origins of the popular style/Peter van der Merwe
p.cm. Bibliography: p
1. Popular music—History and criticism. I. Title.
ML3470.V.36 1988
780', 42'09—dc19 87-28794   CIP   MN
ISBN   0-19-816305-3 (paperback)

Typeset by Pentacor PLC, High Wycombe, Bucks.
Printed in Great Britain by
Courier International Ltd

PREFACE

THIS book began in the late 1960s with an interest in what was then contemporary popular music. If I had foreseen the work this would involve me in, I would probably have abandoned the project then and there. But fortunately a blithe ignorance of the scope of the subject carried me on, digging further and further into the past, and with every spadestroke discovering even deeper roots. Eventually it was clear that all the essential features of twentieth-century popular music were already in existence by 1900, if not long before. By then the whole subject had grown so enormously that it seemed best to leave the twentieth century alone for the time being and confine myself to these origins. Hence this book.

It has certainly not been an easy book to write, and I am deeply grateful to the friends who have sustained me by their help, advice, encouragement, and patience in putting up with my clumsy attempts to explain what it was all about. More directly, I am indebted to Andrew Tracey, for his invaluable help in transcribing some of the African musical examples, David Rycroft and Gerhard Kubik, for reading the section on African music, and most of all to Richard Middleton and Paul Oliver, who, through the offices of the Oxford University Press, read through two previous drafts of the whole book. Without their advice and criticism this would certainly have been a far inferior work.

P. v.d. M.

PREFACE TO THE PAPERBACK EDITION

I have taken advantage of this paperback edition to correct numerous misprints, put right a few factual errors, and make some minor changes and additions to the text. Except for these trivial alterations the book is as it was when I sent it off to the printers about five years ago.

Subsequent research has convinced me even more of the basic unity and continuity of nineteenth-century music. I am now less inclined than I once was to see 'parlour' and 'serious' music as radically separate things. The real odd-men-out were the heavy Germans, whether of the Brahmsian or Wagnerian persuasion. But, since I intend to deal fully with this question in my next book. I shall say no more about it here.

ACKNOWLEDGEMENTS

I am grateful to the following for permission to reproduce copyright music examples.

ABKCO/Westminster Music Limited: 'Honky Tonk Women' (Ex. 61(*a*)) 1969, international copyright secured.

Carlin Music Corp.: 'Hard Headed Woman' (Ex. 143 (*b*)).

Columbia University Press: 'Captain Holler Hurry' (Ex. 35) © 1963.

Empress Music Inc.: Titon, *Early Downhome Blues* (Ex. 8(c)) © 1930, © renewal effective 1958.

Famous Music Corporation: 'It's Always You' (Ex. 61 (*b*)) © 1941, renewed 1968.

Harvard University Press: Exx. 74 (*c*) 'The Noble Skewball', 77 'Frankie and Albert', 87 (*b*) 'Jimmy Rose', 154 (*b*) 'Mister Frog', all taken from Scarborough, *On the Trail of Negro Folk-Songs* © 1925 by Harvard University Press, and 1953 by Mary McDaniel Parker.

Jewel Music Publishing Co. Ltd. London: 'Susie Q' (Ex. 43) and 'Sweet Little Sixteen' (Ex. 70).

Macmillan Publishers, London and Basingstoke: Mossi Song (Ex. 10 (*a*)) © 1954.

Martinus Nijhoff Publishers, Dordrecht, The Netherlands: Watutsi Song (Ex. 27) © 1973.

University of Missouri Press: Exx. 11 'Show Pity, Lord!', 66 (*b*) 'Get Along Home, Cindy', 74 (*b*) 'Rye Whiskey', 113 'Andrew Bardeen', all taken from Randolph, *Ozark Folksongs*, vols. 3 and 4, © 1980 by the Curators of the University of Missouri. Also 'Cowboy's Challenge' (Ex. 115).

Venice Music Inc.: 'Long Tall Sally' (Ex. 81) © 1956.

Warner Bros. Inc.: 'Sweet Georgia Brown' (Ex. 126) © 1925.

CONTENTS

A NOTE ON THE MUSICAL EXAMPLES

THE preparation of the musical examples has inevitably involved many delicate compromises. Among the rival claims to be considered are brevity, the convenience of the reader, and fidelity to the original; and this last sometimes raises the question whether the fidelity should be to the music as *heard* or as *annotated*. The most difficult cases are the African examples, but even British folk music presents problems. In general, I have stuck close to conventional notation, but with the following modifications:

1. Note values have been made to reflect the rhythm as faithfully as possible: for instance, | ♫♩ ♪♪ | instead of | ♫♫♩ |. This may take a bit of getting used to, but it is remarkable how much more vividly the rhythm leaps to the eye. In some of the examples, taking a hint from Gerhard Kubik, I have replaced the conventional bar-line with short strokes above and below the stave, thus allowing, for instance, | ♩ ♪♪| ♫| instead of | ♩ ♫|♫♩|. This type of bar-line has been used in all the African examples.

2. Notes which are about a quarter-tone sharp or flat are adorned with little arrows, pointing upward or downward as the case may be. Sometimes, when the inflection is consistent, the arrow appears above an accidental in the key signature.

3. In a very few examples special key signatures (perhaps they should rather be described as 'mode signatures') have been used. In such cases the sharps, flats, or naturals apply to every octave, as in a conventional key signature.

4. Glides between notes are indicated by a straight line almost connecting the notes.

5. In the African examples the time signature merely indicates the number of pulses in the African 'bar'. Nowadays such time signatures are usually given as a simple number, generally 12 or 8. For the sake of familiarity, I have given them in the form $\frac{12}{8}$, $\frac{8}{8}$, etc. These should not be confused with conventional European time signatures. The African $\frac{12}{8}$, for instance, carries no implication that the pulses are to be parcelled up into triplets.

6. Pieces in unmeasured rhythm have no time signature of any kind.

Where examples have been taken from a printed source the original notation has been standardized along the above lines. There are also numerous other modifications, either to save space or to help the reader. Some of these are merely notational—a matter of whether the stem of a note goes up or down, whether it is notated as D♯ or E♭, etc. The main modifications are the following:

1. *Transposition*. All the examples have been transposed, where necessary, to the pitch where they are easiest to read. This usually means that the tonic is C, A, or G. In every case the transposition is given in the List of Musical Examples at the end of the book, to the nearest semitone where the transposition is from a recording. Where the transposition has already been done in the original notation I add the words 'in the original notation'.

2. *Reduction*. Examples that originally appeared on two or more staves have been squeezed onto one, not only saving space but often making them easier to read as well, if one does not mind a few leger lines. Sometimes the example has been further reduced, by replacing the accompaniment with chord symbols, leaving out the middle parts, etc. The rule is that big notes are to be taken literally and little notes provide an indication of the harmony. Further, wherever the reduction is not self-evident, it is explained in a note. Accompaniments added to originally unaccompanied songs have been omitted without comment. Examples quoted in their entirety are designated '(complete)', though in the case of songs this applies only to the tune, not the words.

3. *Words*. In general the words of songs are given, except:
(*a*) where they are unobtainable;
(*b*) in general, when they are in a non-European language which is likely to be intelligible to very few readers (though even here they are often retained when the fit of the words to the melody is of some interest);
(*c*) where they are only an addition to a traditional instrumental tune.

4. *Change of rhythmic values*. In a few cases where the notes fit the words very badly they have been changed, but only on the lines of replacing ♩ with ♫ , etc. In each case there is a comment to this effect. The notation of the few medieval examples has been modernized. In 'Blin' Man Stood on de Way an' Cried' (Ex. 73(*d*)) the note values have been doubled for easier comparison with the adjacent examples. Otherwise the original note values have been retained, though they may be expressed rather differently: ♩. instead of ♩♪, 𝅗𝅥 instead of ♩ ♩, etc.

5. *Expression marks*. Unimportant marks of expression have been omitted, particularly in nineteenth-century 'parlour' and Romantic examples.

6. *Repeat marks*. Where repeat marks are used to save space, the repeat may not always be quite literal. Where the variations are of any consequence they are indicated by small notes.

INTRODUCTION

Even that vulgar and Taverne Musicke, which makes one man merry, another mad, strikes mee into a deepe fit of devotion, and a profound contemplation of the first Composer; there is something in it of Divinity more than the eare discovers.

Sir Thomas Browne[1]

THE conviction that the traditional materials of music have been used up has been with us for a long time. As Dorothy Sayers's detective hero, Lord Peter Wimsey, put it as long ago as 1929:

'Well, what can you do with the wretched and antiquated instruments of our orchestra? A diatonic scale, bah! Thirteen miserable, bourgeois semi-tones, pooh! To express the infinite complexity of modern emotion, you need a scale of thirty-two notes to the octave.'

'But why cling to the octave?' said the fat man. 'Till you can cast away the octave and its sentimental associations, you walk in fetters of convention.' (*Strong Poison*, p. 97.)

Composers of the kind described as 'serious' were inclined to agree with Lord Peter, and even to concede that the fat man might have a point. As long as they stuck to the diatonic scale, the familiar chords, regular bar rhythms and the rest of it, their music had a tiresome way of sounding as though it might have been written before 1900. Try as one might to be modern, one walked in fetters of convention.

Such was the predicament of the serious composer. Meanwhile, non-serious composers, whose indifference to musical theory often took the drastic form of complete ignorance, continued to use those hoary old formulas, and yet somehow their music was of the twentieth century. No one could mistake a Noel Coward waltz for a Strauss one. Think what one might of Gershwin or Cole Porter, one could not accuse them of sounding like Schubert or Hugo Wolf, Massenet or even Puccini. As for jazz, it was as typical of the 1920s as cloche hats or bathtub gin.

Some people, of course, put it all down to novel rhythms. 'Jazz', said Ernest Newman, 'is not a "form" but a collection of tags and tricks,'[2] no doubt primarily rhythmic. I wonder whether he really believed it himself. Certainly anyone who paid any real attention to popular music

[1] *Religio Medici*, section 9.
[2] *The Sunday Times*, 'The World of Music', 4 September 1927.

must have realized that it spoke a *language* that was subtly but unmistakably different from the classical language. It was not a superficial matter of performing styles. It was not a question of jazzing the rhythm or adding a note or two to conventional chords. No, it went far deeper than that.

It is this something that distinguished the languages of popular and classical music, this elusive quintessence, which is the subject of this book. The period covered is from primordial antiquity to about 1900, by which time all the essentials of twentieth-century popular music were already in existence; though with several sallies into the present century, sometimes to follow a trend to its conclusion, and sometimes in search of an appropriate musical example.

And that ought to be all there is to it, except that experience has shown that this is a book which is apt to be misunderstood. I must therefore carefully explain what it is not.

It is not concerned with superficial stylistic features—such things as pitch, tempo, loudness, instrumentation, and in general all the devices by which the popular music trade gives Golden Oldies a specious appearance of novelty.

It is not a work of criticism. The space a particular musical genre receives has nothing to do with its artistic worth. Some excellent music receives only cursory mention, while a great deal of attention is paid to some styles, like the Victorian parlour ballads, which consist mainly of rubbish.

In spite of the emphasis on the evolution of styles and idioms, this is not a revival of the Sir Hubert Parry gospel of musical progress. Musical styles certainly evolve, but whether they get better is another question. I have a great deal of sympathy with whoever it was who described the history of music from the eighteenth century to the present as 'downhill all the way'. The word 'primitive', as used here, has no pejorative connotations. When applied to musical forms and styles, it simply means earlier (from the Latin 'primus'), not in point of time, but in point of development. And even when this implies simplicity, or even a certain crudeness, these are not necessarily faults.

This is not primarily a book about American music. It is a book about a kind of music in which American influence has been very great, but that is not quite the same thing. If one were to write a history of the art of salesmanship, the United States would no doubt figure largely in it, but for all that the subject would be salesmanship, not American salesmanship. There is a great deal on American music, partly, to be sure, because it is so important, but also partly because it needs a great deal of explaining. The European tradition of popular music—what I have called 'parlour music'—is equally important, but much more familiar in its essential language.

I make no claims to deal with the music of Latin America and the Caribbean, except where it touches on the United States. A really comprehensive treatment would include these areas, but, heaven knows, the scope of this book is great enough already.

The term 'the popular style' is a label, not a description. 'Style' is really a less pretentious synonym for 'basic musical language'. As for 'popular', it is seriously misleading. In the ordinary sense of the word the popularity of the music discussed here is almost irrelevant. To be popular, whether in the sense of 'generally liked' or 'of the people', is an evanescent quality. If history follows its usual course the popular idioms of today will become the learned idioms of tomorrow, and the antiquated academicism of the day after tomorrow. In short, the term 'popular' is an infernal nuisance, but there seems no alternative to it.

However one defines it, my 'popular style' is a product of Western Europe and its colonies, and in particular of the English-speaking world. I do not claim to describe the popular music of other parts of the world, though it may sometimes share many of the features discussed here. This is another good argument against the word 'popular'; I can only repeat that it has been adopted, like most musical terms, for want of a better one.

This is not a work of sociology. Its intent is solely musicological, with certain exceptions in the chapters on the American and European backgrounds, which were brought in only for what light they could throw on the complex, puzzling, and important subject of the music itself. There is nothing wrong with the socio-economic-political approach to the arts—I only wish someone would do a good study of 'serious' music along those line—but it does seem to have rather monopolized the treatment of the popular arts. It is, moreover, extremely difficult. Once one gets beyond platitudes, it is so easy to fall into the kind of speculation that can neither be proved nor disproved. In this book I have tried to confine myself to problems that are at least theoretically capable of solution.

Finally, I must disclaim any indiscriminate enthusiasm for popular music in general. Reviewing the popular music of the twentieth century as a whole, most people would probably agree that some of it is excellent, some unbearable, and most of it very indifferent. What the good, bad, and indifferent share is a musical language, and that is the concern of this book.

One further point. This book, in a strange and indirect way, is almost as much about classical as popular music. For a whole variety of reasons, an analysis of popular music over the past two hundred years casts light on the serious music of the same time. After all, it could hardly be otherwise. Highbrow and lowbrow lived in the same world; quite often they were the same person. Inevitably, serious music has constantly reacted to popular music, even if this has increasingly meant being as unlike it as possible.

WORDS, WORDS, WORDS

Working on this book has given me a new respect—if that is the word—for terminology. Much of it, as the reader will see, has been specially invented, but even commonplace, well established terms raise endless difficulties. They are too broad, or too narrow, or too vague, or misleadingly precise, or offensive to somebody. Very often, a name refuses to be just a name and acquires laudatory or pejorative overtones, if it has not been burdened with these from the start. It is probably no use protesting that no such connotations are intended in this book. 'Classical', for instance, simply denotes a particular stylistic tradition, the antithesis of 'popular' (as used 'amongst less educated people', according to Percy Scholes[3]). As far as I am concerned, the most rubbishy product of the dreariest hack of a symphonist or opera composer is 'classical' if it is in the classical style. The same goes for the neologisms that I have reluctantly had to create. The term 'parlour music', again, simply denotes a style, which, by the way, has not very much to do with parlours. It is not intended to be derisive or facetious; and if it is rather a misnomer that is probably an advantage, since an obvious misnomer is the less likely to be taken with misleading literalness.

The great trouble with loaded terms is that they lead to endless arguments about definitions and applications, which are really disguised squabbles about values. Because 'Classical', in the narrow sense, carries more prestige than 'Romantic', it is felt to be a compliment to describe Beethoven and Schubert as Classical composers, so that when one comes to define the word 'Classical' the definition must be framed to include them. Similarly with 'folk' and 'popular'. Although I hope that my terms are clear, and have even gone as far as including a glossary of them at the back of the book, I believe that far too much fuss is made about definitions in general. Sir Karl Popper has some interesting remarks on this point:

In science, we take care that the statements we make should never *depend* upon the meaning of our terms. Even where the terms are defined, we never try to derive any information from the definition, or to base any argument upon it. This is why our terms make so little trouble. We do not overburden them. We try to attach to them as little weight as possible. We do not take their 'meaning' too seriously. We are always conscious that our terms are a little vague (since we have learned to use them only in practical applications) and we reach precision

[3] *The Oxford Companion to Music*, p. 193.

not by reducing their penumbra of vagueness, but rather by keeping well within it, by carefully phrasing our sentences in such a way that the possible shades of meaning of our terms do not matter. This is how we avoid quarrelling about words. (*The Open Society and its Enemies*, vol. 2, p. 19.)

Would that workers in the humanities could say the same!

Part One
The Historical Background

I must repeat that the general history in this section is purely a background to the music, particularly in the case of the United States, where the wealth of detail may give the misleading impression of an attempt at comprehensiveness. And, just as the general history serves merely to explain the music, the music is selected merely for its contribution to the popular style. Nothing as absurd as a complete treatment of African or European music has been attempted. It may be wondered why there is no mention of the American Indians. Even in South America, where native musical traditions undoubtedly were important, it is often difficult to distinguish their influence from that of Africa. In North American it would be next to impossible. In any case, no such influence seems to have occurred to past observers; so perhaps we can thankfully leave them out of an account that is already quite complex enough.

I. EUROPE AND THE NEAR EAST

1. THE OLD HIGH CULTURE

ANTIQUITY

'THE Old High Culture.' With this ringing phrase Alan Lomax describes the chain of settled communities that existed some three or four thousand years ago from the Nile to the Pacific, while northern Europe was still the domain of wandering and illiterate tribes.[1] The title is certainly deserved. North Europeans take a perverse delight in depicting their remote ancestors as even more barbarous than they really were, but it is after all true that civilization, however you define it, spread northward from these Asian lands. *Musical* civilization, at any rate, certainly did.

For our purposes it is fortunately not necessary to go further east than Persia. There was a musical trade between Egypt, Mesopotamia, and Persia from very early times, and the movement towards a common musical culture was greatly accelerated when they all became part of the Islamic empire. The common style that developed is usually called 'Islamic' or 'Arab', though in fact it transcends religious, ethnic, geographical, and linguistic boundaries. Perhaps it is best just to call it the Near Eastern style, remembering that this is a Near East that can stretch as far east as India and as far west as Morocco.

The music of these ancient civilizations has long since vanished into silence and dust. We have a few maddeningly sketchy accounts by contemporaries; a handful of tunes in primitive notation; numerous depictions of instruments and musicians; and a few of the instruments themselves. We know far, far more about instrumentation than any other aspect of ancient music. We know that the Egyptians of the Old Kingdom liked the sound of flutes and harps, and that everywhere from Egypt to Persia the sound of plucked strings was popular. We know that the sound of reed pipes and drums of various sorts was relished in Mesopotamia, and that these tastes were introduced into Egypt around

---

[1] *Folk Song Style and Culture*, pp. 29–30.

1500 BC. Apart from such facts we are more or less reduced to guesswork based on documentary and iconographic evidence, and, more particularly, on a comparative study of the musical traditions springing from these ancient civilizations.

By patiently piecing together such fragmentary evidence, one can deduce in fair detail how Near Eastern music around the beginning of the Christian era probably sounded, and how it dispersed to surrounding cultures. But this question of dispersal is a tricky one. It is all too easy to form a mental picture of everything emanating from one central spot, a sort of musical Garden of Eden, and to forget the yet more shadowy but doubtless well-developed traditions of surrounding cultures. And there is always the danger, attendant on all historical thinking, of smoothing out the past into a homogeneity it never possessed. There was not, of course, a single Near Eastern style, originating at a single point, but a family of styles of diverse origins, constantly converging and diverging and generally interacting. All we can hope to summon up is the family likeness uniting them.

Let us begin, then, with our most solid pieces of evidence, the instruments. Mesopotamia seems to have been the birthplace of the bow harp, roughly describable as a bent stick with a sound-box at one end and several strings strung between this and the other end. It probably developed out of the musical bow, which is still a widespread instrument in Africa. Another very early Mesopotamian invention was the lyre. Later on the lute made its appearance in the same area, or perhaps a little to the north or east. 'Lute' is the conventional designation of the instrument, but in fact it would be more accurate to describe this ancestor of the whole guitar and fiddle family as a primitive banjo, with a skin stretched across the sound-box and the strings, played with a plectrum, tied onto the broomstick-like finger-board.

The reed pipe was another Mesopotamian development. A silver double pipe from Ur has actually come down to us from about 2500 BC, though the reed crumbled to dust long ago, and it is therefore debatable whether it was single or double.[2] The harps, lyres, lutes, and pipes of Mesopotamia spread into Egypt, and later into Greece, and, mainly through the Greek influence, to Rome. Via the Roman empire they then made their way into northern Europe.[3] From Egypt the same instruments spread south and westward into black Africa, where some of them survive to this day: the lyre family in East Africa, and the lute, in something like its original form, in the more northerly parts of West Africa.[4]

[2] See Baines, *Woodwind Instruments and their History*, p. 199.

[3] See Bruce-Mitford, 'Rotte (ii)', *The New Grove*, vol. 16, p. 261.

[4] The remarkable resemblance between ancient Mesopotamian and modern African lutes can be seen by comparing the reconstruction of the former in Collon and Kilmer, 'The Lute in Ancient Mesopotamia', p. 27, with photographs of the latter, for instance that on p. 23 of Van

The early, narrow-bore reed pipes must have made a pungently nasal sound, whatever their exact construction, and it is likely that the prevailing vocal tone was similar. In all probability, the singing style regarded as typically Oriental by the European was widespread in the ancient Near East as well. With the nasality goes a tendency to seek expression not in dynamic changes but in graces of the shake or mordent type, glides, and microtonal inflections. There is also often an intense but somehow withdrawn emotional tone, with a suggestion that the singer is singing to himself, or at any rate listening intently to his own voice. This last feature is well conveyed by the habit of covering an ear with one of the hands, as shown by ancient Egyptian artists and widely practised by folk singers today.

As far as we can tell, the melodic organization of this ancient music was similar to that of the modern Near East and India. There were pentatonic, diatonic, and chromatic scales—this we know from ancient Greek writings—and music generally seems to have been organized around complex modes or melodic types, like modern Indian *rāgas* or Arabic *maqāmat*. There was probably a certain amount of harmonization, based on fifth or fourth chords, as in African and archaic Italian folk music; and that is about as specific as we can now be on the subject of ancient harmony.

One harmonic effect that was certainly known to the ancients, however, was the drone. Although drone-like effects are common in many parts of the world, the systematic exploitation of drones seems to have been an invention of the Near East, whence it spread eastward to India, northward and westward into Europe, and southward into Africa.

The ancient Near East probably delighted in rhythmic intricacy. All the cultures that have come under Near Eastern influence—Islamic, North African, northern Indian, medieval European—show this characteristic. In particular, they all have the hemiola, the mixture of $\frac{3}{4}$ and $\frac{6}{8}$ time, either in alternation or in simultaneous cross-rhythm.

THE ARAB WORLD OF THE MIDDLE AGES

Whatever its exact nature, the Near Eastern style began to percolate into surrounding areas at a very early date. The Romans carried it into their empire; among other things, they introduced the lyre to northern Europe, where it gradually assumed a Germanic form. Later on there was some Byzantine influence on western Europe, and Egyptian culture influenced black Africa, in music as in other things. The real heyday of Near Eastern influence, however, came with the rise of Islam and the Arab world. Muslim conquests imposed Islamic rule on much of North,

Oven, 'Music of Sierra Leone'. The main difference is that the strings of the ancient lutes were tied to a tailpiece, whereas the African ones are usually fixed to a bridge like that of the guitar.

East, and West Africa, on Spain, and on the southern tip of Italy. In Europe the Islamic tide eventually receded, but not before leaving deep marks on these areas. Meanwhile the Islamic world was achieving a cultural eminence far in advance of anything in Europe. During the period from about 1100 to 1400 the Arab influence in Europe left few arts or sciences untouched. As well as music, the visual arts were greatly affected, in particular architecture and the minor decorative arts. Philosophy, science, and even theology were indebted to the Arabs, as were warfare, story telling, cookery, medicine, and manners generally.[5]

There was an influx of Arab instruments into Europe during the thirteenth and fourteenth centuries:

The stricter observance of the distinction [between loud and soft music] may have owed much to late thirteenth-century interest in Arab music-making. There had been nothing particularly Arab about either the provenance or the usage of the earlier 'Gothic' instruments, but now, towards the end of the thirteenth century, there appeared a fresh group of instruments, this time obtained direct from the Arab civilization. It included some of the principal stringed instruments of Arab chamber music, as the lute, and the Moorish fiddle *rubebe*; also the Saracen military band equipment, with long metal trumpets, the small Oriental kettle-drums *nakers,* and the band shawm . . . With the advent of these came also the Oriental strict distinction between loud and soft instruments and music . . . (Baines, *Woodwind Instruments and their History*, p. 231.)

Loud music, played on shawms, kettledrums, and a pair of long, straight trumpets, made its way into Muslim-influenced Africa as well as Europe. Soft music was played on various combinations of lutes, fiddles, and flutes in heterophony, that is, all simultaneously playing variations of the same melody, often with a discreet drum accompaniment. This also established itself in East Africa and the savannah regions of West Africa, especially in the form of a duet between fiddle and lute accompanied by some relatively quiet percussion instrument.

In both Africa and Europe many of these new Asian instruments were specifically designed to produce drones, such as the 'loud music' trumpets, fiddles and lutes with drone strings (the latter preserved in the modern banjo), and the bagpipes.

Along with the instruments went the Near Eastern singing style. In Africa it can be found in approximately the same areas as the Near Eastern instruments, and there is every indication that it prevailed in medieval Europe as well, at least among the upper classes.[6]

No sooner had the Islamic influence reached its height, around 1300, than it began to recede with the first stirrings of the Renaissance. In one way, the Renaissance was itself the outcome of Oriental influences.

[5] See the two editions of *The Legacy of Islam*.
[6] See Jander, 'Singing', *The New Grove*, vol. 17, p. 339.

Europeans, and especially Italians, took Arab science, Arab thought, Arab culture, Arab financial methods, and with them started a train of developments which have gone on to this day. In another and more familiar sense, it was a revival of European nationalism. The intricate, part-Oriental Gothic architecture gave way to the neo-classical style, the Catholic church faced the revolt of home-grown Protestantism, and medieval music yielded to a new style, blander in tone, simpler in rhythm, mellow and symmetrical. For a long time, however, this change of fashion affected only the upper reaches of society. The peasants continued to make music in the medieval style, just as they continued to build their cottages along Gothic lines. But as decade followed decade and century followed century, the tastes of the upper classes gradually filtered down and the old ways died out. This dying out followed a predictable pattern. It was most rapid in the cities and in those regions which were closest to the Renaissance influence. The countryside, economically backward areas, inaccessible places like islands and mountains, and the eastern and northern extremities of Europe were longest to cling to the old ways.

This explains why so much that is Oriental in character lingered on in the folk music of Scotland and Ireland. The poverty that sent millions of emigrants across the seas kept these countries relatively free of sophisticated fashions. Situated in the north-western corner of Europe, they kept up styles that had once been current over the whole continent. These folk styles were taken across the Atlantic, and the same poverty and inaccessibility that protected them in the old country continued to preserve them in such places as Newfoundland and the Appalachian mountains. Describing the performance of a Newfoundland folk-song, a collector mentions the 'strident, nasal manner of singing, similar in effect to Oriental or Indian voice production'.[7] Writing of the United States, Alan Lomax describes 'Southern backwoods singing' as 'mostly un-accompanied, rubato, highly ornamented and solo; the voice "oriental", high-pitched and nasal, produced out of a tense body and throat'.[8] A. M. Jones gives much the same description of the Afro-Arab style: 'The Islamic tradition can at once be recognized by the very nasal and stringy quality of voice that is invariably used. But added to the nasal vocalization there is the very frequent use of mordents to embellish the melody notes.'[9]

This African style, too, was taken across the Atlantic. Late nineteenth-century commentators remarked on it. 'This girl here, so tall and straight, is a Yaloff,' writes George Washington Cable in his description

[7] Peacock, *Songs of the Newfoundland Outports*, p. 570.
[8] Lomax, *The Folk Songs of North America*, p. 153.
[9] *Studies in African Music*, vol. 1, p. 207.

of ante-bellum New Orlean dancing. 'You see it in her almost Hindoo features, and hear it in the plaintive melody of her voice.'[10] Another writer describes an 'exceedingly nasal and undulating' singing style, in terms that would equally well apply to the West African savannah, Cairo, Bombay, or for that matter some archaic Irish styles.[11]

Black and white American folk styles therefore had much in common. Both were heirs to an ancient tradition, apparently no more than vestigial in the West. An observer of 1900 might have regretted the imminent passing of these quaint and precarious survivals; it is hard to imagine him predicting any important role for them in the coming century. How very wrong he would have been!

[10] 'The Dance in Place Congo', p. 523. 'Yaloff' means Wolof, the principal tribe of Senegambia.
[11] See Jeanette Robinson Murphy's remarks in the section 'Arabic Influences' in ch. 16 below.

2. EUROPE

THE European musical background presents unique difficulties, partly because it involves unique developments, both musical and social, and partly because anyone brought up in the European tradition is likely to find the very familiarity an obstacle to a clear view. The traditional attitudes of the musical establishment have not helped. To the naïve 'music lover' there are only two kinds of music that really count. One is classical music, produced by geniuses, invariably isolated, towering figures who are misunderstood by their contemporaries, starve in garrets, and probably die young. The other is folk music, which is mysteriously evolved by illiterate peasants untouched by the nastiness of urban civilization. Nothing else is of any consequence. This view, though admittedly a caricature, is not far from that held in sober earnest by many good people; and it is also not far from that set forth in almost every book on 'serious' music up to about 1960.

Since that time those two heirlooms from the Romantics, 'the genius' and 'the folk', have become rather battered and ragged around the edges. The stocks of not-quite-geniuses like Telemann, Cherubini, or Saint-Saëns have risen considerably (though here one may suspect an element of barrel scraping) and there is a healthy tendency to treat undoubted geniuses as human beings, with digestive systems and bank balances. Popular music has become a respectable subject of study, and attempts are made to dispel the mystical nineteenth-century aura attached to folk music.

Nevertheless, the old muddle dies hard. In an attempt to kill it off, let us put ourselves in the position of an ethnomusicologist from, say, Micronesia trying to make sense of the musical customs of nineteenth-century Europe. After extensive field-work in the countryside and towns, the concert halls, and the slums, he might well decide to categorize European music according to the three criteria of musical literacy, social class, and aesthetic status. The first of these is simple enough. At one end stands the musician who cannot read music and is even unaware of the existence of musical notation; at the other, the musician capable of composing or following an orchestral score. Obviously, musical literacy makes a world of difference, for good or ill, to one's attitude to music. It is also worth noting whether our illiterate musician can think in harmonic terms or play an instrument capable of chords, such as the piano or guitar. If he cannot, he passes the old, puristic test for a folk musician. If he can, he falls into an interesting and important intermediate category, of great importance in the development of popular music. At the other end of the spectrum, too, there are important gradations. Next to the fully-trained musicians, and far outnumbering them, there are local bandmasters, rustic choirmasters, village organists, and the like, whose defects of technique would tend to give a popular or folk-like quality to their compositions or arrangements. Indeed, it is often hard to say whether a particular characteristic —the absence of modulation in eighteenth-century glees, for instance— is a defect or a legitimate, intentional effect.

The second of our criteria, social class, is also fairly straightforward. In the nineteenth century, and even more so in earlier periods, each class had its own style of music. The aristocrat maintained his own band; the bourgeois went to concerts; the lower orders got their music at taverns where it was laid on as part of the entertainment, and the poorest of all were driven to make their own music if they were to have any at all. There was a very clear financial restraint on rising above one's musical station, as it were. The aristocrat might, if he felt like slumming, indulge himself in a musical tavern, but the proletarian could never attend a symphony concert. He simply could not afford the price of a ticket, and even if he could, he would probably have been thrown out for not wearing the proper clothes.

The real difficulties begin with the third criterion, that of aesthetic status. Our ethnomusicologist would have noticed that the status of musical types varied greatly in the eyes of the cultivated music lover; and these status distinctions grew greater with time, until by the end of the century the art of music had been divided into perfectly separate categories, soon to be designated 'highbrow' and 'lowbrow'. It is important to notice that this was not in any simple sense a class distinction. The tastes of the upper classes were as likely to be lowbrow as highbrow—more so, if anything, in England. At the other end of the social scale, lower-class music was regarded as lowbrow only if it belonged to the same basic type as that of the bourgeoisie. Music-hall songs were lowbrow but rural folk-song was not, even though agricultural labourers were even poorer than the frequenters of music-halls. This was not only because the rural poor had come to be romanticized; a far more fundamental reason was that rural folk music was outside the mainstream of urban culture. In an aesthetic sense it was 'classless', just as a Scottish accent is classless in the south of England.

In fact, as social class distinctions came to diminish with the spread of wealth and education, so aesthetic class distinctions widened, and what began as a matter of aesthetic class—good versus bad, serious versus frivolous, heavy versus light, idealistic versus commercial—eventually developed into a difference of musical language. Starting from around 1790, the classical tradition gradually pulled away from a mass of middle- and lowbrow music. The latter, which I call 'parlour music', covered an enormous spread of social class and artistic pretension. It was enjoyed by dustmen and dukes, burglars and bishops. Between it and folk music lay a wide territory where folk and commercial popular music interacted: a world of itinerant semi-professional musicians, rustic dance bands, broadside ballads, and the like. Scholars now point out that much of 'folk music' really belonged to this world. (Some deny that there is such a thing as 'folk music' at all.) They cite the ballad singer who refreshed his memory with a printed or handwritten text, the supposedly naïve folk artists who were actually sophisticated performers, and the many commercially composed songs in the repertories of folk singers.[1]

Conversely, the bourgoisie were never averse to plundering the repertory of the 'folk'. In particular, Scottish and Irish melodies enjoyed a prolonged and remarkable vogue. The 'Scotch tune' or song became all the rage in England around 1680, and maintained its popularity for over two hundred years—indeed, its day is still far from done.[2] Irish folk music, though known in England from the sixteenth century, did not really catch on until about 1800; but then it rivalled or even overtook its Scottish counterpart, with the Americans even more enthusiastic than the English.[3] There are many fascinating parallels between this vogue and the later one for Afro-American music. In each case the 'Scotch', 'Irish', or 'nigger' music was often so bowdlerized and sophisticated as to be hardly recognizable. Indeed, much of it was completely bogus. In each case musical indebtedness went along with social hostility. And, as we shall see, there were many musical parallels between the Celtic and Afro-American styles, not all of them coincidental.

One could put it all down to the charm of the exotic, but I believe this would miss half the truth. These styles were popular because they were mildly exotic, it is true, but at the same time homely and familiar. The foreign styles fashionable among cultivated music lovers in the English-speaking world, first Italian and later German-Italian, never completely established themselves. There was always a hankering for something

---

[1] See Harker, 'Cecil Sharp in Somerset: Some Conclusions' and 'The Making of the Tyneside Concert Hall' (especially pp. 28–30, which gives an interesting account of the life of an eighteenth-century itinerant musician); and also Palmer, *The Book of English Country Songs*, pp. 2–5, for a description of the semi-professional 'singing men' of the English countryside.

[2] For a full discussion of the Scotch tunes and songs, see Fiske, *Scotland in Music*, ch. 1, 'The Scotch Song Comes to London'. This stimulating book is a study of the influence of Scotland and Scottish music on composers outside Scotland.

[3] See Hamm, *Yesterdays*, ch. 3, ' "Erin, the Tear and the Smile in Thine Eyes"; or, Thomas Moore's *Irish Melodies* in America'.

with more of a tang to it. But why Scottish and Irish? Why black American? Why not English and white American? No doubt the motives were similar to those that led the same people to import their 'serious' music and musicians from Italy and Germany. No doubt, too, there was an element in it of the condescending affection appropriate to subject peoples. As a matter of fact, English and white American tunes did get smuggled in, under the guise of these mildly exotic products.

At the other end of the spectrum parlour music melted into the lighter classical forms such as opera and ballet. Nor was any great stylistic distinction made between sacred music and the more solemn secular types. The same basic homogeneity of style overrode class distinctions: 'The Eton Boating Song' and 'Oh! Mr. Porter' (Ex. 110 (a)) may be worlds apart socially, but they speak the same musical language.

SOME THOUGHTS ON THE GREAT MUSICAL SCHISM

The divorce between classical and popular styles was a very gradual affair. As always, we must be on our guard against reading present-day attitudes into the past. When Bernard Shaw, on receiving for review 'Herr Meissler's waltzes arranged for the flute, The State Ball Album, The Children's Ball, and M. de Faye's arrangements of Braga's Serenata', protested 'My good sirs: do you think that di Bassetto regards this sort of thing as serious music?'[4] he did not mean what we should now mean by the term. The chasm that now separates the popular musician from his 'serious' colleagues was then only a small but perceptible rift, though it is from just such usages as Shaw's that our present-day term 'serious music' is derived. The dances, marches, drawing room ballads, and popular songs were regularly augmented by arrangements from more pretentious music. In the days when most musical entertainment was necessarily home-made, arrangements of all kinds had an importance which it is now difficult to imagine. Knowledge of orchestral music was obtained, not through putting a record on a turntable or switching on the radio; nor, except for a favoured few, by any sort of regular attendance at concert halls or opera houses. It was obtained by playing arrangements, usually for the piano but often for other instruments, or for voices. Recent studies suggest that it was by such means that an enthusiasm for opera was diffused among the Italian people, 'largely outside the opera house, through workers' choral societies and amateur bands and even through itinerant puppeteers . . . ',[5] and similar processes were at work all over Western Europe and the United States.

---

[4] 'The Popular Musical Union', *The Star*, 13 April 1889, p. 4. Reprinted in *Shaw's Music*, vol. 1, p. 605. 'Corno di Bassetto' was Shaw's pseudonym in his early days as a music critic.
[5] Rosselli, *The Opera Industry in Italy from Cimarosa to Verdi*, p. 163.

Some of these arrangements were of surpassingly bad taste, like the notorious one of Handel's 'Hallelujah chorus' for two flutes, or the transformation of the main theme from the slow movement of Beethoven's Seventh Symphony into a Chorus of Monks. The quadrille, one of the most popular of nineteenth-century ballroom dances, was noted for its frequent use of arrangements, and by the late nineteenth century it had become a fashionable joke to draw them from sources as bizarre as possible: the most celebrated and probably the funniest of these exercises being the one Chabrier concocted out of themes from Wagner's *Tristan*. It has often been remarked that the quadrille was one of the precursors of the 'classical' rag, and there is a direct link between arrangements such as these and the later practice of 'jazzing the classics'. With Chabrier's example in mind we can better understand the ancestry of such things as George L. Cobb's 'Russian Rag', 'interpolating the world famous "Prelude" by Rachmaninoff' (1918).[6]

Deplorable as such productions might be, they at least showed that popular musicians had nothing against drawing inspiration from their more pretentious colleagues. The reverse was gradually ceasing to be true. Haydn and Mozart put tunes of a deliberately popular sort into their symphonies, drawing indiscriminately on rural folk music and the new urban popular style.[7] The first generation of Romantics continued to use popular material, but they were beginning to grow a little self-conscious about it, and after their day a certain mild edginess relentlessly turned into outright distaste. As soon as a turn of melody, harmony, or rhythm had attained the status of a cliché in parlour music, highbrow composers instinctively avoided it. Certain melodic features common in Chopin and Liszt during the years 1830–50 faded out of 'serious' music after the mid-century, though they continued to flourish in popular music. A little later the same thing happened to the Romantics' lush chromaticism. As soon as it became the property of every parlour balladeer the 'serious' composer abandoned it for ostentatious dissonance, modal diatonicism, parallel chords, and so on—it hardly mattered what, provided it was clearly non-popular.

This, I believe, was the immediate cause of the Great Musical Schism. No doubt there were many remoter ones. Popular music was undoubtedly vulgarized by the growth of commercial interests and the mass migration to the cities. Classical music, as it ceased to be the diversion of a small upper class, was acquiring its present overtones of culture and uplift. Composers, far from being mere skilled craftsmen, were beginning to see themselves as rather superior beings: in Britain they stood a chance of being knighted. Then, too, the heady whiff of progress

[6] See Lamb, 'Quadrille', *The New Grove*, vol. 15, pp. 489–91, particularly p. 491.
[7] See Rosen, 'The Popular Style' (*The Classical Style*, section VI, ch. 1), especially pp. 329–37.

was in the air, bringing with it the charms of the 'advanced', or even 'avant-garde'.

The upshot was that by the end of the century three types of music could be recognized. There was the basic nineteenth-century style, so ubiquitous and commonplace that no one thought of giving it a name— my 'parlour music'. There was 'serious', 'good', or 'classical' music, which was rapidly becoming predominantly the music of the past. And there was folk music: a notoriously confusing category.

What exactly is folk music? Is it even, as one school of thought holds, a meaningless term invented by 'bourgeois' commentators?[8] Now, there is undeniably a great deal of mythology attached to the whole idea. Both those slippery fellows, the 'folk', and their supposedly pristine culture, have a way of eluding rational definition. The category 'folk music' does, however, have a certain validity for particular cultures at particular stages of development, distinguishing what is neither 'art' music nor music commercially produced for a mass audience. But even this would not be worth bothering about if there were not also a stylistic difference. In this book I use the term freely of British music and cautiously of American music. In discussing Africa I have avoided it altogether. It is a convenience, nothing more.

[8] This is the argument of David Harker in *Fakesong: The Manufacture of British 'Folksong', 1700 to the Present Day* (published 1985).

3. BRITISH FOLK MUSIC

THE features that most distinguish European 'folk' from 'art' music are the following:

1. *Lack of harmony*. In general European folk music is non-harmonic, at least as regards the older styles. There is a tradition of instrumental accompaniment in the south, and here and there one finds traces of ancient harmonic practices of a completely non-classical kind, in Iceland or Sardinia for instance. Whether such practices survived in Britain, and, if so, whether they had any influence on vocal harmonization in the United States, are interesting questions. The Copper family of Sussex is known for its two-part unaccompanied vocal harmonies, but this style gives a strong impression of being derived from eighteenth-century glee singing.[1] Apart from such isolated and problematical survivals, the only harmonic effect of any importance in British folk music is supplied by drones.

2. *Modal variety*. In Britain the commonest folk modes are the major (but with no harmonic implications) the mixolydian, the dorian, and the aeolian; or to give them their sol-fa names, the doh, soh, ray, and lah modes. The classical minor is not found, because it makes sense only in a harmonic context. There are also occasional appearances of the phrygian and lydian, or me and fah modes. This summary is, however, a gross simplification of the reality. Actually, the modes can shade into one another, or appear together in the same piece; and then there are the pentatonic and hexatonic modes which resist classification because they lack certain notes. It is pointless asking whether a tune built on the notes C D E G A is major, mixolydian, or even possibly lydian. There are also modes which resist classification because it is doubtful which note, if any, is the tonic.

3. *Flexible intonation*. Classical intonation is foreign to folk music. Generally speaking, and certainly in Britain, folk musicians sing the third, sixth, and seventh of the scale relatively flat. These folk intervals can in fact be anything between the orthodox major and minor, and often different inflections will appear in the same piece, a third or seventh, say, being flatter in the eighth than in the second bar. The same variable intonation is encountered in fiddle playing, and in Irish fiddling and piping notes

[1] See for instance the songs at the back of Copper, *A Song for Every Season*.

are often decorated with glides, or 'bent', as the jazz musician would say.

4. *Repetition and variation.* Except for certain rhapsodic styles found especially in southern and eastern Europe, European folk music is firmly based on the repeated cycle. The cycle can vary in length from the two bars of children's chants to melodies taking a minute or longer. And along with the repetition goes variation. In a song, the tune will automatically be changed to fit the words of each new verse. In instrumental music the changes are likely to be more deliberate, sometimes amounting to variations in the classical sense. The degree of variation differs between performers and musical cultures, but *some* element of variation is always there. Cecil Sharp described how impossible it was to get folk singers to reproduce a tune exactly. He would ask them to sing it again in the same way so that he could write it down, and they would, quite unconsciously, change a note or two. In some traditions, for instance the singing of parts of Scotland, the degree of variation becomes quite astonishing.

Beyond these points it is difficult to generalize, even about specifically British folk music. One salient British characteristic is the sharp rhythmic contrast between singing and dance music. The lone singer, untrammelled by any accompaniment, is free to play with the rhythm as much as he likes. Notes can be added to or removed from a phrase, dwelt on or shortened. When such liberties are taken to extremes, the result is a complete absence of bar rhythm. When they are used in moderation, the result is a $\frac{3}{4}$ bar in the midst of a $\frac{4}{4}$ tune (or the other way round), a syncopation, or some such slight irregularity. Sometimes a song will be sung against the background of a regular triple- or common-time beat, but with a rubato to accommodate the words to the tune, so that certain notes arrive slightly before or after their due moment. Earlier collectors usually ignored these rhythmic subtleties, but one can find them in the more precise notations of recent collections. For instance ♩ ♪,

♫♫♩, and ♩ ♩ ♩. ♪| ♩ may actually be closer to ♩♩, ♫♫♩| ♩ and ♩ ♩ ♩ ♫| ♩ respectively.

In the Celtic regions singing is often used as dance music. In these dance songs rhythm is paramount, just as it would be with instrumental dance music: here there is no question of lengthening or shortening bars, though there may well be syncopations. Words are very much subordinate to melody, and will probably consist of improvised nonsense, stock verses jumbled about in any order, or meaningless syllables—'diddling', as it is expressively known in Scotland.

Whether dance music is vocal or instrumental, it will be in duple or triple time, arranged in phrases of four or eight bars. The rhythms might be notated as $\frac{4}{4}, \frac{2}{4}, \frac{2}{2}, \frac{3}{4}, \frac{6}{8}, \frac{12}{8}$, or $\frac{9}{8}$, all of which basically come down to beats arranged in either twos or threes and individually divided into two or three pulses. In other words, the basic rhythms of British folk dance are the same as those familiar in classical music.

STANZA FORMS

Non-dance songs in the English language are closely tied to their texts. There is an intimate connection between stanza and tune types, which, because of its interesting consequences in North America, is worth discussing in some detail here.

Usually the stanza consists of two, four, or eight lines (the differences are largely a matter of notation), which are straightforwardly set to an eight- or sixteen-bar tune:

> Said my lord to my lady, as he mounted his horse:
> 'Beware of Long Lankin that lives in the moss.'[2]

> Of a' the maids o fair Scotland
>   The fairest was Marjorie,
> And Young Benjie was her ae true-love,
>   And a dear true-love was he.[3]

> As I roved out one morning,
> All in the blooming Spring
> I overheard a damsel fair
> Most grievously did sing,
> Saying 'Cruel were my parents
> Who me did sore annoy
> They would not let me tarry
> With my bonny Irish boy.'[14]

(More examples of this type are Exx. 62, 63, 73(a) and (b), 74(a), and 75.)

This simple scheme is often varied by the devices of refrain or repetition. Inserting refrains after each line of a couplet gives us an old and popular ballad type:

> There were twa sisters sat in a bow'r,
>   Binnorie, O Binnorie;
> There cam a knight to be their wooer,
>   By the bonnie mill-dams o' Binnorie.[5]

In twentieth-century Hebridean singing the refrain is treated as a chorus, giving a call-and-response effect,[6] and it seems probable that this was the

---

[2] 'Long Lankin', Vaughan Williams and Lloyd, *The Penguin Book of English Folk Songs*, p. 60.
[3] 'Young Benjie', Bronson, *Traditional Tunes of the Child Ballads*, vol. 2, p. 408.
[4] 'The Bonny Labouring Boy', O Lochlainn, *Irish Street Ballads*, p. 18.
[5] 'Binnorie; or, The Cruel Sister', Bruce and Stokoe, *Northumbrian Minstrelsy*, p. 61.
[6] See the examples in *Hebridean Folksongs* (vol. 1 edited by MacCormick, Campbell, and Collinson, vols. 2 and 3 by Campbell and Collinson), and on the record *Ireland*, from *The Columbia World Library of Folk and Primitive Music* (Columbia CSP AKL 4941).

original treatment of this pattern all over Europe. If so, this stanza type has reverted to its original form in many Negro spirituals.

In another very common pattern the refrain is confined to the end of the stanza. The length of such refrains is variable. They may be a few notes or they may be far longer than the preceding couplet or quatrain, and virtually the same verse section may have refrains of widely differing length in different variants. Since about 1700, however, a particularly popular plan has been to make the refrain just half the length of the verse, giving a twelve-bar verse form:

> VERSE: The brewer brew'd thee in his pan,
> The tapster draws thee in his can;
> Now I with thee will play my part,
> And lodge thee next unto my heart.
>
> REFRAIN: For 'tis O, good ale, thou art my darling
> And my joy both night and morning.[7]

Other, more intricate refrain patterns are possible: by far the most important is the 'Mademoiselle from Armentières' type, which originated in Elizabethan times, and has given rise to a huge family of tunes (for instance 'Froggie Went a-Courting', 'When Johnny Comes Marching Home', and the whole 'Captain Kidd' / 'Admiral Benbow' subfamily):

> My daughter, sirs, is far too young,
> Parlez-vous,
> My daughter, sirs, is far too young,
> Parlez-vous,
> My daughter, sirs, is far too young,
> She's never been kissed by anyone,
> Inky pinky parlez-vous.

Apart from refrains, there are various schemes involving repetition of words. Sometimes, as in 'Mademoiselle from Armentières', the first line is repeated; sometimes it is a middle line; but usually it is the last line:

> It's of a pretty wench that came running 'long a trench,
> And sweetheart she could not get one,
> 'When there's many a dirty sow a sweetheart has got now,
> And I, a pretty wench, can't get one, get one, get one,
> And I, a pretty wench, can't get one.' [8]

This scheme, which goes to a ten-bar tune, is also an established formula. Medial rhyme, as in this example, is a frequent feature—and one that has

---

[7] 'O, Good Ale, Thou art my Darling', Chappell, *Old English Popular Music*, vol. 2, p. 179.
[8] 'Pretty Wench', Vaughan Williams and Lloyd, *The Penguin Book of English Folk Songs*, p. 121.

persisted in popular music right up to the twentieth century. (This point is discussed further in chapter 28.)

There are idiosyncratic songs conforming to none of these patterns, and there are cumulative songs (known in the Ozarks as 'pile-up songs') like 'The Twelve Days of Christmas' and 'Green Grow the Rushes-O'. There are also the more elaborate stanza forms of the dialogue songs like 'Our Goodman', quoted in chapter 17. All these, however, are comparatively rare. The above types account for a good nine-tenths of English, Lowland Scots, and Anglo-Irish songs.

REGIONAL DIFFERENCES

To the expert on British folk music English and Irish are like chalk and cheese, and Lowland and Highland Scotland might as well be different countries; but on closer examination these distinctions lose their sharpness and dissolve into the usual mass of tendencies and preferences. In general, southern England favours straightforward, compact, heptatonic tunes with the minimum of ornament. Vocal delivery is natural, with no nasality or tension. Irish tunes are more ornate and diffuse, more likely to be pentatonic or hexatonic, and show a liking for the AABA ('come-all-ye') structure. A nasal delivery is fairly common. Scottish music is famous for its love of the pentatonic scale and wide skips, and here tunes built on the 'double tonic' scheme are common, as they are in Ireland and north-east England. (For an explanation of the 'double tonic' see chapter 23.) In general, music takes on a passionate Celtic intensity as one moves from phlegmatic England to the Celtic fringe. The music of the Gaelic-speaking parts of Scotland and Ireland, found in its purest form in the Hebridean islands, is sharply different from that of Lowland Scotland or Anglo-Ireland. It gives every evidence of preserving a very ancient tradition indeed, with its pentatonic scale, circular tunes, and call-and-response worksongs.

But all these are only broad generalizations. Alongside the intense performing styles of Scotland and Ireland we find musicians who favour a more straightforward, indeed deadpan style, especially in songs with a strong narrative element. And, conversely, the typically 'Celtic' style—ornate, diffuse, nasal, intense—can crop up in England. As a rule, important tune and text families are distributed all over the English-speaking British Isles.

Some Irish performances, both vocal and instrumental, are so Oriental in character that they could easily be mistaken for something out of the Balkans or the Near East. The exact provenance of this style is impossible to determine, but the likeliest explanation is that it is simply a survival of the Arab-influenced music that spread over Europe during the Middle Ages. In all probability the original Irish folk style was similar to the music of the Hebridean islands, and the quasi-Oriental music came, like the fiddle, flute, and bagpipe, from England.

II. AFRICA

4. THE DEBT TO AFRICA

THE African influence on the music of the United States, though profound, is extraordinarily hard to pin down to individual cultures. The half-million-odd African slaves arrived over a period of more than two centuries, beginning in 1619 and ending some time during the mid-nineteenth century. They came from a vast area, stretching from the westernmost tip of Africa to southern Angola, and reaching deep into the continent; there were also some from the south-east. Once on American soil, tribal groupings were often broken up for fear of insurrection, and in any case the internal slave trade eventually scattered the tribes far and wide. If African music were homogeneous this would not matter, but it is not. It consists of a mosaic of distinct traditions, including some which are far from the conventional African stereotype. These traditions are not neatly arranged; they are distributed over the landscape in an often baffling patchwork. Several writers have remarked on the way near-identical styles turn up at vast distances from one another, sometimes in the absence of any known contact between the groups involved.[1] In a European context, it is as though one found identical styles in Greece and Denmark, or Russia and Spain.

Even a perfect knowledge of present-day African music would be only a partial help. The heyday of the North American slave trade was the mid-eighteenth century, and what do we know of the African music of two hundred years ago?

A calculated vagueness is therefore advisable. The African origins of American idioms must remain generally West African, not specific to any particular people. It is a far cry from the survival of African musical cultures in South America, sometimes even down to language.[2] The only

---

[1] See Jones, *Studies in African Music*, vol. 1, pp. 214–15, Kubik, 'Music and Dance', p. 90, and Bebey, *African Music*, p. 53.
[2] See for instance Roberts, *Black Music of Two Worlds*, pp. 34–5.

distinction we can make with any confidence is that between the Arab-influenced savannah culture and the rest of West or Central Africa. Ever since Paul Oliver's *Savannah Syncopators: African Retentions in the Blues* (1970) it has been orthodox to take note of the Afro-Arab element in North American Music, and especially the blues. But even here we must tread carefully.

THE AFRO-ARAB CULTURE

There has been a strong Near Eastern influence in North Africa since ancient times. First the Libyans spread ancient Egyptian culture westward, then the northernmost fringes of Africa succumbed to Islam, and finally the culture of the Muslim Arabs began to work its way down into the southern portion of West Africa. By the eleventh century large sections of the West African savannah were under the sway of Islam, though conversions were patchy, frequently half-hearted, and mostly confined to the ruling classes until the nineteenth century.[3] Nevertheless, it is safe to say that by 1700 the Afro-Arab culture was firmly established in the broad belt of savannah and semi-desert running from Senegambia eastwards across the continent. In this region geographical conditions permitted and indeed often enforced a nomadic way of life, which in turn produced a relatively uniform culture, in sharp contrast to the forests of the Guinea Coast.

The Islamic influence profoundly affected attitudes to music and musicians. To the pagan African, music was an indispensable and highly honoured part of life. To the orthodox Muslim, secular music was a forbidden indulgence, akin to drunkenness or fornication. Hence the peculiar status of the musician, who became the purveyor of a sinful pleasure, a sort of musical bootlegger, at once keenly sought after and rejected, richly rewarded and despised. In the savannah culture music became largely the preserve of the professional *griot* caste, in contrast to the usual African situation where practically everyone is a musician, though (as anywhere else) the really gifted performers are a small minority.

In their attitudes to music there are fascinating resemblances between this African Islam and American Bible Belt Christianity. The stricter Protestant sects, like the Muslims, condemned secular music, and tended to look askance on musical instruments in general. In both cultures the fiddle was regarded with special abhorrence.[4] Among the present-day Hausa, fiddlers and lute players often perform in brothels and gambling

---

[3] See Trimingham, *A History of Islam in West Africa*, pp. 17–20 and 29–33.
[4] See A. Lomax, *The Folk Songs of North America*, pp. xxiii–xxiv and 467–8, and King, 'Hausa Music', *The New Grove*, vol. 8, p. 309.

dens.[5] Was this once the case in America too, with the banjo taking the place of the African lute? We have all heard about the famous whorehouse pianists of the ragtime period—did they have predecessors in the more modest establishments of earlier days? As in the savannah, the Old South relied largely on the services of wandering musicians—fiddlers who went from one isolated community to another, 'songsters', and 'musicianers'. Finally, in both areas, music was greatly relished by numerous backsliders and reprobates.

The significance of these resemblances is not, of course, that Islam in some mysterious way influenced American Christianity, but that musicians coming to America from the savannah would find themselves in a reasonably familiar environment. Whether a disproportionate number of them became professional musicians we cannot know, but it seems at least plausible.

Turning to the music itself, it is often difficult to distinguish the 'Afro' from the 'Arab' elements in the Afro-Arab style: for instance, both cultures were fond of percussion, cross-rhythms, and descending phrases. The Arab influence is at its clearest in choice of instruments and in vocal style. The Arabs introduced at least three important instruments to West Africa: the one-string fiddle, the lute, and the hourglass drum. Of these, the last eventually made its way down to the Guinea Coast, and has been thoroughly assimilated into the coastal style of music. The other two remain more firmly identified with the savannah style, while making occasional excursions southward.[6] But this does not mean that the music played on them is as Arab as the instruments themselves. Very often it is thoroughly African, with African theme-and-variation technique, African chord changes, and African rhythms. These features, being African, appear in the coastal style as well, so we should not be too hasty in assigning origins when they turn up again in America. If, for instance, certain banjo passages resemble certain African lute passages, this may be a case of direct influence—or the banjo figures may come from one of the many harps and zithers played by the forest peoples. The chord changes of Senegambian lute music have been cited as one of the influences behind blues harmony, and this may well be true.[7] But similar chord changes appear in many other places, and are, in fact, characteristic of black African music all over the continent. (This is not to say that *all* African music is built on such chord patterns, but simply that they are extremely common in Central, Southern, and East as well as West Africa.[8])

[5] See Ames, 'Igbo and Hausa Musicians', p. 257.
[6] For instance in Uganda (see Wachsmann and Cooke, 'Africa', *The New Grove*, vol. 1, p. 146) and among the Yoruba (see King, 'Nigeria', ibid., vol. 13, p. 238).
[7] See Coolen, 'The Fodet: A Senegambian Origin for the Blues?'
[8] For detailed descriptions of central and southern examples, see Kubik, 'Harp Music of the

We should never forget that African and Afro-American musicians are adept at transferring music from one medium to another. Much xylophone music, for instance, has been adapted from the harp, involving not only a different instrument, but a change from solo to ensemble playing, and purely instrumental pieces often start out as songs. A particularly telling instance of such transference is from the five-string harp to the guitar.[9] Similar things must surely have happened as the banjo ousted other African instruments in America.

For similar reasons we should not trace too direct and simple a link between the African one-string fiddle and the European violin. The African could transfer his bowing technique without much difficulty to the new instrument, but what about his left hand? The left-hand technique of European folk fiddles, with their drone strings, was a lot closer to that of the African lute or the banjo. In any case, tunes were frequently swapped between fiddle and banjo, just as, in later years, banjo technique was adapted to both the piano and the guitar.

It is in vocal music that the debt to the savannah is clearest. The Afro-Arab singing style is typically Near Eastern, with a high, tense, nasal delivery, a wavering intonation, and much use of shakes, vibrato, mordents, and turns. Another important feature is the 'passionate lengthening', as it has been called, of individual notes, particularly high ones at the beginnings of phrases. In all this it differs completely from the usual African style. Where similar things are observed in American singing, therefore, they come from Arab-influenced Africa, if they come from Africa at all.

OTHER AFRICAN STYLES

African music which has escaped Arab or European influence—what one could call mainstream African music—boasts a vast array of styles: nor does it make much difference if we narrow it down to the area from which the slaves were taken. There are scales of seven, six, five, and, sometimes, four notes; several systems of intonation; chromatic as well as purely diatonic music; monophony as well as various harmonic systems; everything from large ensembles to soloists who perform for their own amusement; music which is improvised and music in which never a note is varied; dozens of instruments; percussive and non-percussive techniques—and so on.

Stereotypes of African music, once they got beyond the jungle tom-toms stage, have tended to derive from North American practice. The

Azande', Tracey, 'The Matepe Mbira Music of Rhodesia', and Blacking, 'Problems of Pitch, Pattern and Harmony in the Ocarina Music of the Venda'.
[9] See Kubik, 'Harp Music of the Azande', p. 37.

characteristics of black American music—pentatonicism, a frequently rough vocal quality, percussiveness, and improvisation—have been imposed on Africa as a whole. While thay are all widespread in Africa, there are many equally African styles in which these features are absent. There is, in particular, a heptatonic, legato type of singing, usually in parallel thirds or triads and often without any sort of percussive accompaniment: everything, that is, which the conventional African stereotype is not. This style is found in parts of the Guinea Coast, in Angola, and in Central Africa.[10] Considerable numbers of slaves must have taken it to North America, but there it died out completely. In South America, on the other hand, it seems to have exerted considerable influence. More generally, the heptatonic scale predominates in certain parts of Africa especially associated with the North American slave trade, such as Senegambia and the Bight of Benin: in fact, it seems as though the half-million reluctant emigrants to North America took more heptatonic than pentatonic music with them. Why then did the pentatonic come to prevail in American music?

Such puzzles make it impossible to escape from generalities. Something American looks like something African, therefore it was probably derived from something of the kind in some African musical culture—that is what it comes down to; and even then we must be on the lookout for white influence. But this does not mean that the African strain in American music must remain for ever a mystery. On the contrary, I believe that it is, on the whole, as clear and certain as the European strain. Only, we must not attempt to provide our Africanisms with precise family trees. Their ancestry is far too mixed, confused, and obscure for that.

[10] See Kubik, 'Music and Dance', p. 90, and Jones, *Studies in African Music*, vol. 1, pp. 214–15.

5. SOME FUNDAMENTALS OF AFRICAN MUSIC

THIS chapter pretends to be no more than an introduction to the fundamentals of African musical practice. Details of rhythm, melody, harmony, and form find their places later on; here, I am attempting merely to sketch in some of the attitudes, assumptions, and habits that shape those details. In dealing with such generalities, it seems permissible to use the words 'Africa' or 'African' without qualification, though, as the previous chapter should make clear, it is difficult to make a really foolproof generalization about African music. All I really claim is that my generalizations are true of that part of African music that influenced American practice.

THE PURPOSE OF MUSIC

The African musician has his own answer to the fundamental question, 'What is music *for*?' The European serious musician would answer 'to be beautiful', or possibly 'to move the listener', or even 'to satisfy the mind', depending on whether his bias is Classical or Romantic. That is not how the African sees it. In Africa, music is something which generally serves a clear-cut purpose, and is judged according to its fitness for that purpose. It is not an object of beauty to be contemplated in isolation. Long lists have been made of the purposes to which music is put in Africa, some of them highly unexpected to the European mind.[1] Very often there is a clear-cut social purpose at work. This is in fact true of much highbrow European music as well, but in Africa the social purpose is far more overt. There are songs for keeping wrongdoers in line, for voicing grievances, for deriding enemies, for raising morale, and for maintaining the authority of potentates. The praise song, directed either at some local worthy or (in Islamic cultures) merely at someone who looks likely to pay for the honour, is an important African form. So is the ridicule song, which may be resorted to when payment is not forthcoming.

MUSIC AND MOTION

Although it is a well worn cliché to describe African music as 'functional', a great deal of it is functional only in the sense that it gives

[1] See for instance Chernoff, *African Rhythm and African Sensibility*, p. 34.

pleasure to participants and audience. This entertainment music is usually associated with dancing, so much so that one sometimes encounters the statement that all African music is merely an adjunct to the dance. This is certainly going too far, but it is true that there is an unusually close bond between African music and the dance, and in fact motion in general. There is usually a sort of counterpoint between African music and the motions associated with it, whether these are the motions of the musicians themselves or of others. Musicians may control the accompanying dance, choreograph it almost, carefully suiting the music to the mood of the dancers. African musicians sometimes also give verbal instructions to the dancers, like the American square dance caller, or even, through the 'talking drums', dismiss incompetent performers from the dance ring.[2]

The relation between music and motion in Africa really demands a book to itself. Here, there is just room to touch on what one might call the Upbeat (or Downbeat) Controversy. This springs from a suggestion by Hornbostel in 1928 that, to the African, the upward movement of the hand in beating out a rhythm is the real 'downbeat', while the dropping of the hand, to make the actual sound, is the upbeat;[3] or, in more general terms, that Africans associate downward motions with upbeats, and upward motions with downbeats: exactly the opposite of the European system. 'Downward' in fact includes a whole group of bodily movements: the downward motion of the drummer's hand, handclapping, lowering of feet, and bringing the shoulders forward—all actions that African and Afro-American people like to perform on the off-beat. The whole process is a collapsing downward and inward of the body. Moreover Africans, when conducting in the European style, often indicate downbeats with an upward motion, and vice versa. Ever since the theory was first proposed there has been controversy about it, some deriding and others upholding it, though usually with reservations. It is in fact fairly easy for Europeans to acquire a feeling for these motions, but even the ability to do them oneself is not enough to resolve the controversy. For whatever reason, this way of operating is extremely natural to the African: even tiny children clap on the off-beat.[4]

SPEECH, SONG, AND INSTRUMENTAL SOUNDS

To understand African music one must know how speech, song, and

---

[2] See Blum, 'Dance in Ghana', p. 21, Nzewi, 'The Rhythm of Dance in Igbo Music', and Locke, 'Principles of Offbeat Timing', p. 219.

[3] 'African Negro Music', pp. 52–3.

[4] See Chernoff, *African Rhythm and African Sensibility*, p. 48, and Hopkin, 'Jamaican Children's Songs', musical examples.

instrumental sounds impinge on one another. Most African languages have pitch accents: that is, a fixed melodic relation between syllables. Thus in a word with two syllables, for instance, either syllable may regularly have the higher pitch, or both may have the same pitch. The absolute pitches are not prescribed; the word, as a whole, may be pronounced in either a high- or a low-pitched tone. Nor is the interval between the two syllables invariable.[5] In some languages precise observance of the tones is essential to avoid ambiguity; in others they can be manhandled with little fear of misunderstanding. The complexity of the tonal system varies greatly from language to language. A famous example of a highly tonal language is Yoruba. In that language the word *oko*, for instance, may mean 'boat', 'spear', 'hoe', or 'husband', according to which of the three tonal levels is used. Tones are therefore essential to distinguish words, in rather the same way as in Chinese.[6]

Most African languages have, then, a built-in tune. Many also have a marked distinction between long and short syllables. This makes ordinary speech musical, and greatly narrows the gap between speech and song.

These African speech patterns have profound consequences for African song, which have carried over into languages constructed on quite different lines, including English. When ordinary speech is so melodious, a little stylization is enough to make it satisfyingly musical; which helps explain the common use in Africa of recitative styles of singing, and the frequent transitions between a speaking and singing delivery. Even out-and-out song is generally an enhancement of speech in West Africa. Speech tones are transformed into a melodic line, with greater or lesser freedom according to custom and language, and speech rhythm is regularized to fit the metre. (An example where the verbal pattern is strictly adhered to is 'Kuro' i nyę mo dea', Ex. 25; one where it is treated with some freedom is 'Olúrómbí, Ex. 22.) If the basic pulse is a quaver, for instance, a syllable might take on the value ♪, ♪, ♩, ♩, or ♩ . Since there is no need for stress accents to fall at the beginning of the 'bar', the song rhythm need depart little from what would be natural in speaking. For instance the text 'Dantuo muawrę ho papa. Yee m'adanse Kusi Apea menam aprǫ bǫ muoo,' could be sung to the rhythm of Ex. 1. To the European this looks like a mixture of $\frac{6}{8}$, $\frac{3}{4}$, and $\frac{2}{4}$; to the African, it is merely a regularization of the spoken rhythm.

The constraints of speaking tones on melody have some interesting consequences. In English, when a spoken text is spontaneously

---

[5] Pitch accents may also be altered according to the context of the word within the sentence: see Nketia, *The Music of Africa*, pp. 184–6.

[6] See Beier, 'The Talking Drums of the Yoruba', p. 29, and Vidal, 'Oriki in Traditional Yoruba Music', p. 58.

Ex. 1 'Dantuo mu'

Dan - tuo   mu a-wre ho pa - pa.   Yee   m'a - dan - se Ku - si A -pea me -

nam a - pro - bo mu oo.

chanted—for instance, when a railway conductor calls out a series of
stations—the result is usually literally monotonous, in the sense of being
on one note, apart from a drop at the end. Now, in a strongly tonal
language such a practice would produce gibberish. The chant would have
to be on two notes at least. Such two-note recitatives are common in
Africa and have passed into American practice, as has a partiality for
recitative in general.

Again, consider what happens when the African repeats a word or
phrase at different pitches. The natural result is a free sort of sequence,
which is preserved if the text is tranformed into song. It is possible to
discern such a process behind some of the sequential or near-sequential
passages in the early blues. (For an African example, see Ex. 25; for
American examples, Exx. 77, 78, and 83.)

Repetition of words can also have interesting rhythmic consequences,
as Ex. 2 shows. Here the intrinsic seven-pulse pattern of the words is at
odds with the basic twelve-pulse bar. It is essentially the same technique
as in Handy's 'Friendless Blues' (Ex. 3).

Ex. 2   'Erin kare'le o wa j'oba!'

E - rin   yé - yé   e - rin yè - yè
handclaps   etc.

Ex. 3   Handy, 'Friendless Blues'

When I was home the   door was nev - er closed,   door was   nev - er closed

The descending phrases that are so typical of African music also owe
their origin largely to speech habits. In Africa, as elsewhere, spoken
phrases tend to descend in pitch, and when these phrases are transformed

into song the descending line is maintained. Sometimes, particularly in Arab-influenced styles, the descending line may have an emotional origin—what Curt Sachs called 'pathogenic'—but in general it is simply a 'logogenic' enhancement of the spoken line.

There is a similar intimate exchange between instrumental and verbal patterns. Instrumental tunes are very often adaptations of songs, which may themselves be adaptations of spoken patterns, so that an instrumental figure may owe its ultimate origin to speech. And instruments, thanks to the relatively precise melodic and rhythmic patterns of African speech, are often made to 'talk'. Among the Mandinka of Senegambia, for example, a dance may begin with this announcement by the master drum: 'Good evening. The events are beginning. The visitors have arrived. We have come to play and laugh. That's what brought us here. We haven't come to fight, but only to enjoy ourselves.'[7] Drums can also send more casual messages. One account relates how a short message in the middle of a drumming lesson induced a passer-by to return a few minutes later with two bottles of beer.[8] Apart from the famous talking drums, other instruments with carrying power and some sort of melodic capacity can be made to talk—xylophones and flutes, for instance. In the Muslim culture of the Hausa the long ceremonial trumpets recite the praises of local rulers on the second and third harmonics.[9]

In a vestigial form this 'talking' has persisted in America, especially with instruments capable of glides. Bottleneck (or 'knife') guitars and trombones are made to produce vaguely speech-like sounds, and harmonicas actually say things like 'I want my mama'. It is also possible to talk with the jew's harp, making the metal tongue do duty for the vocal chords. And, in a more general way, the highest praise that a performer can be given is that he makes his instrument 'talk'.

The African is, moreover, as ready to transfer patterns from instrument to voice as the other way round. Gerhard Kubik writes of 'the training of the African from early childhood, to think of melodies as representative of words and the reverse . . .'. He goes on:

One can try going to any African village to make the experiment. Beat a short random sequence of notes in front of an assembled group of children and let them associate words and sentences with it, by saying: 'What did I play?' or 'What do you think this can mean?' One will probably be surprised at the abundance of ideas that occur to them . . . 'involuntary verbal associations from instrumental melodies' . . . is an important factor for text invention in much of Africa's accompanied vocal music. It also explains a good number of so-called 'nonsense texts'. ('Harp Music of the Azande', p. 52.)

---

[7] See Knight, 'Mandinka Drumming', p. 32.
[8] See Chernoff, *African Rhythm and African Sensibility*, p. 78.
[9] See Gourlay, 'Long Trumpets of Northern Nigeria'.

The following anecdote provides an amusing example of such a process:

We were cutting down a patch of forest to make manioc gardens when a bird nearby sang repeatedly in our hearing:

d ddd   dss dddd

After several repetitions of this phrase, it changed to:

d d sd   d d sd   d d sdd

I whistled back the first phrase each time the bird sang it. The men with me were surprised to hear the teacher and a bird exchanging calls and asked me what was happening. I told them that for me the bird was speaking Lokele and saying:

he bosongo olúwí lokonda-lo—hey white man, so you know this forest?

The whistled notes being an exact reproduction of the semantic tones of the Lokele sentence. My reply was:

he inoli ilúwí lokanda-lo—yes little bird, I know this forest,

which has the same tonal pattern as the first phrase. The bird then changed to its second tune and one of the Congolese workers himself supplied apt words:

laoláu laoláu laoláu-o—very well, very well, very well-oh!

(Carrington, 'The Musical Dimension of Perception in the Upper Congo, Zaïre', p. 50.)

This reminds one of the African love of onomatopoeia, in which it is not a matter of voices imitating instruments, but instruments imitating natural sounds—or, more recently, mechanical sounds such as trains. This, too, has been carried over to America.

Many African instruments, working on the jew's harp principle, produce the harmonic series. It is clear that this harmonic series has influenced African song. In southern Africa there are songs indisputably based on the alternation of two such series, about a tone apart.[10] In West Africa there are near-triadic vocal melodies which may ultimately have been similarly inspired. These triad-like tunes are so close to certain American worksong tunes that it is hard to escape the conclusion that they contributed to the development of the blues mode. (This point is further developed in the section 'The Triadic Mode' in chapter 16; see particularly Exx. 26(a) and (c).)

In its higher reaches the harmonic series becomes a scale, and it has been argued that this is the origin of certain African scales.

END-ORIENTATION AND END-REPETITION

The solid part of an African phrase or melody is its end. It is at the end

[10] See Kirby, 'Physical Phenomena', and *The Musical Instruments of the Native Races of South Africa*, ch. 9, 'Stringed Instruments'; and Rycroft, 'Stylistic Evidences in Nguni Song', pp. 221–3.

that cross-rhythms are most likely to coincide with the beat,[11] an effect which has been likened to a 'resolution' of the rhythmic dissonance; and when a melody is varied, the part that changes is usually the beginning, the ends of each variation being the same, or at any rate much more like each other than the beginnings. Much the same thing often occurs in call-and-response forms, with frequently varying calls against an unchanging response. If one imagines the adaptation of such a call-and-response song as an instrumental solo, it is easy to see how the two forms are related.

There is even an element of end-orientation in the African love of descending melodic lines. In European music we are accustomed to thinking of descending phrases in negative terms, as sombre, mournful, tranquil, resigned, and so on. This is no doubt because a descending phrase is thought of as a sort of diminuendo from high to low, and also usually from the melodically important to less important. The African thinks, not of high and low notes, but of small and big ones, and to him it is the end of the phrase that is melodically the more important: so that a descending phrase is a crescendo from insubstantial small notes to substantial big ones. Hence the solid, exhilarating feeling that these descending phrases so often produce.

End-repetition is not confined to Africa. In Britain it is common in Scottish, Irish, and old English dance tunes, and in certain archaic forms of Celtic song (e.g. the Irish keen, Ex. 29). Nevertheless, the frequent American examples are of a kind strongly suggesting an African rather than a European inspiration.

THE SENSE OF DIALOGUE

A conversational feeling pervades much of African music. The call-and-response form is the most famous but by no means the only example. There may, equally, be a dialogue between a singer and his accompaniment, or between one percussionist and another in a drum ensemble. 'Though a formally structured arrangement of leader and chorus may not always be present in African music,' writes John Chernoff, 'the conversational mode is usually inherent within the cross-rhythmic fabric.'[12] The horn or flute ensembles, in which each performer is responsible for a single note, are only the most extreme example of the African delight in splitting melodies between more than one performer: the very interlocking rhythms themselves conduct a conversation. And this prompts the further idea that African rhythms consist of a series of gaps for some complementary rhythm to fill,[13] an idea expressed in some

[11] See Chernoff, *African Rhythm and African Sensibility*, p. 56, and Locke, 'Principles of Offbeat Timing', p. 227.
[12] *African Rhythm and African Sensibility*, p. 57.
[13] ibid., p. 114.

of the notation systems that have recently been devised for African music. Instead of our system of long and short notes distinguished by shape, there is a row of pulses, some of them filled—indicating the start of a note—and others empty. For instance, the rhythm ♩ ♩ ♪♩ ♩ ♩ ♪ would be notated as x . x . xx . x . x . x. Here every dot represents a gap to be filled, or—it is perhaps not too fanciful to say—a question to be answered in the intricate dialogue that is African cross-rhythm.

NOTE-POSITION VERSUS NOTE-LENGTH

This type of notation also brings out another feature of African rhythm: namely, that what matters is the *position* of the note—to be more precise, of the beginning of the note—and not, as in European music, its *length*. Hence the importance attached in African music to precise articulation, and in particular to percussive effects. As has so often been remarked, most African instruments have a percussive quality, whether they are actually struck or not. Flutes, horns, plucked instruments, bowed instruments—all are made to produce that characteristically African kick at the beginning of each note. It is important to observe that this percussive delivery does not necessarily imply loudness. Indeed, African musicians often take special delight in producing percussive effects at a very low volume. But perhaps the word 'percussive' is a little misleading, especially with its European connotations of aggression. The important thing is the crisp and precise articulation of the note: and if it then rapidly dies away this does not matter, for it has served its purpose in the rhythmic scheme of things.

III. NORTH AMERICA

6. THE WHITES

> You can't make a livin'
> On sandy lan',
> I'd ruther be a nigger
> Than a po' white man.[1]

FOR over three and a half centuries black and white Americans have been living, working, and making music together, or at any rate within hollering distance of each other. It would be a miracle if there had not been profound mutual influence, and such influence there undoubtedly was. But before analysing this in detail it seems well to look at the social background against which it took place. What manner of people were the Americans, black or white, of one, two, or three centuries ago?

One generalization that can confidently be made about the whites is that they were considerably humbler folk than the stalwart pioneers or patrician grandees of popular legend. Until well on into the nineteenth century, North America was not the sort of place one went to if one was sure of a reasonably comfortable life in Europe—certainly not to the South, anyway. The rigours of the ocean crossing, which have been recorded in sickening detail, were deterrent enough. Adventurers, malcontents, religious dissidents, or people who already had some sort of connection with the place might find their way there, but generally the motive was sheer desperation.

It was as an alternative to destitution, or even starvation, that thousands entered into contracts of indentured servitude, which may be briefly defined as temporary slavery. Probably the majority of seventeenth- and eighteenth-century immigrants entered the colonies under these conditions. Servants bound themselves to serve a master for a set period—usually about four or five years—in return for board and

---

[1] A traditional couplet occuring in various forms. This particular version is from *Sharecroppers All*, by A.F. Raper and I. De A. Reid. 'Sandy land' is implicitly contrasted with the rich alluvial soil of the plantations on the river valleys. It might be along the coast, on uplands, or in pine forests.

lodging, their passage to America, and certain 'freedom dues' which were meant to set them up at the end of their term of servitude. Even at that time these conditions of servitude aroused indignation. 'My Master Atkins', wrote a Virginian servant in 1623, 'hath sold me for a £150 sterling like a damnd slave.'[2] And they continued to be sold like damned slaves till late in the next century, as this advertisement shows: 'Just arrived at Leedstown, the Ship Justitia, with about one Hundred Healthy Servants, Men Women & Boys. . . . The Sale will commence on Tuesday the 2nd of April' (from the *Virginia Gazette*, 28 March 1771).

The treatment of these white servants differed little from that associated with the black slave in later times. They could be sold to a new owner, whipped, and worked to exhaustion; and might have to put up with assault, bad food, foul living conditions, and, if female, rape. [3]

In view of this, it is not surprising that many entered servitude involuntarily. Servants were most usually adolescent boys, colloquially known as 'kids', and the business of nabbing, or 'napping' them was so widespread that it gave the word 'kidnap' to the English language.[4] Agents known as 'spirits' used similar methods to the notorious recruiting officers of the same time in 'spiriting away' their victims:

The spirits, who worked for respectable merchants, were known to lure children with sweets, to seize upon the weak or the gin-sodden and take them aboard ship, and to bedazzle the credulous or weak-minded by fabulous promises of an easy life in the New World. Often their victims were taken roughly in hand and, pending departure, held in imprisonment either on shipboard or in low-grade hostels or brothels. (Hofstadter, *America at 1750*, p. 36.)

Another involuntary group of servants was the convicts. Shipping criminals out to the colonies naturally appealed to the authorities as a means of killing two birds with one stone: on the one hand, supplying an insatiable demand for labour, and on the other removing 'the scruffe and scumme of the People' (as the indignant colonists termed it) from the mother country. This practice, occasionally resorted to in the seventeenth century, was established in 1717 by a British Act of Parliament. Some of the colonists eagerly profited from this supply of cheap labour, but others greatly resented having the dregs of the British population thrust on them, and the system was abolished when the United States attained independence—whereupon the British turned to transporting their convicts to Australia, as all the world knows.[5]

Whatever their origin, the servants who survived eventually finished

---

[2] See Morgan, *American Slavery—American Freedom*, p. 128.

[3] All these are documented in Zinn, 'Persons of Mean and Vile Condition', ch. 3 of *A People's History of the United States*, pp. 39–58.

[4] See the article 'Kidnap' in *The Oxford English Dictionary*.

[5] See Morgan, *American Slavery—American Freedom*, pp. 236 and 339, and Hofstadter, *America at 1750*, pp. 46–9.

their indentures, or else absconded to join a large population of vagrants, the prototype of the American hobo. Many of them died young—life tended to be nasty, brutish, and short in early colonial times—or returned to Europe. A few managed to make fortunes for themselves, but the great majority simply became poor whites—poor, that is, by twentieth-century standards, even if they did not meet the classical stereotype of 'poor white trash'. One should of course be wary of generalizations about the Old South, but at least two certainly hold good: that it was overwhelmingly a rural culture, and that the general standard of living was, to say the least, primitive.

The only places in the ante-bellum South that could be called big cities were St Louis, Baltimore (if one includes it in the South), and New Orleans, the capital of a former French colony. The rest consisted of small towns, villages, farms, and unsettled wastes:

Observers . . . noted the extraordinarily thin dispersal of the population through this countryside, where self-sufficiency of a sort was the goal of all good managers and where even a modest farm or plantation might occupy two hundred acres. Here . . . was a society truly and thoroughly rural. Williamsburg, the capital of Virginia, was a hamlet of some two hundred houses and about a thousand people, white and black. Richmond, a county seat, was a tiny village. (Hofstadter, *America at 1750*, pp. 156–7.)

This was in the middle of the eighteenth century. Later the Southern towns grew larger, but even in 1860 only one of the fifteen largest cities in the United States, New Orleans, was in the South;[6] and five southern states—North Carolina, Florida, Mississippi, Arkansas, and Texas—did not have a single town with a population of as much as 10,000.[7] As for literacy, even as late as 1910 one white Southerner in eight could neither read nor write; in North Carolina, the least literate of the states, it was one in five.[8]

Until well into the nineteenth century these scattered farmers lived drab, simple, and isolated lives. Housed in shacks that have since vanished, and illiterate or, if literate, scarcely given to reading or writing, they have left few or no records.[9] Even the tiny upper crust, with their slaves and their substantial wealth, were generally not much better housed. Fanny Kemble, in her *Journal of a Residence on a Georgian Plantation in 1838–1839*, harps repeatedly on the shabbiness of the planters' houses. That of her husband, the owner of a large estate, could at best be described as a rather primitive cottage:

---

[6] See Morison, Commager, and Leuchtenburg, *The Growth of the American Republic*, vol. 1, p. 476.
[7] See Stampp, *The Peculiar Institution*, p. 29.
[8] See Woodward, *Origins of the New South*, p. 400.
[9] See Land, *Bases of the Plantation Society*, pp. 2–3.

It consists of three small rooms, and three still smaller, which would be more appropriately designated as closets, a wooden recess by way of pantry, and a kitchen detached from the dwelling—a mere wooden outhouse, with no floor but the bare earth . . . Of our three apartments, one is our sitting, eating, and *living* room, and is sixteen feet by fifteen. The walls are plastered indeed, but neither painted nor papered; it is divided from our bedroom (a similarly elegant and comfortable chamber) by a dingy wooden partition . . . The doors open by wooden latches, raised by means of small bits of packthread . . . how they shut I will not pretend to describe, as the shutting of a door is a process of extremely rare occurrence throughout the whole Southern country. (pp. 26–7.)

All her descriptions of plantation residences are in this tone. One has 'a Castle Rackrent air of neglect, and dreary careless untidiness', another is 'curiously dilapidated', a third 'ruinous' and 'tumble-down', set in 'shaggy unkempt grounds'.[10]

Fanny Kemble also left some scathing descriptions of the poor white trash, including the celebrated phrase, 'the most degraded race of human beings claiming an Anglo-Saxon origin that can be found on the face of the earth'.[11] Most Southern whites, however, were neither poor white trash nor rich planters. 'If there were such a thing as a "typical" ante-bellum Southerner,' writes Kenneth M. Stampp, 'he belonged to the class of land-owning small farmers who tilled their own fields, usually without any help expect from their wives and children. He might have devoted a few acres to one of the staples for a "cash crop," but he devoted most of his land and time to food crops for the subsistence of his own family.'[12] Earlier on, the situation could have differed only by being more primitive. These independent farmers are usually resoundingly called 'yeoman', meaning that they owned their farms, but there had always been tenants as well. In any country of continental Europe they would simply have been called peasants, and it is illuminating, especially from the musical point of view, to realize how far the Old South was a peasant society.

Much can be learnt about these early Southerners from the more primitive of their twentieth-century descendants. Descriptions of the mountain dwellers of the Appalachians or Ozarks are sometimes remarkably similar to those of eighteenth-century colonists:

The Europians, or Christians of North Carolina, are a streight, tall, well-limb'd and active people . . . Both sexes are most commonly spare of body . . . (John Brickell, 1737)[13]

Physically, they are strong and of good stature, though usually spare in figure. (Cecil Sharp, 1917)[14]

[10] Kemble, *Journal*, pp. 145, 185, and 301–2.   [11] ibid., p. 184.
[12] Stampp, *The Peculiar Institution*, p. 29.
[13] *The Natural History of North Carolina*, pp. 31–2. Quoted in Land, *Bases of the Plantation Society*, pp. 198–9.
[14] *English Folk Songs from the Southern Appalachians*, p. xxiii.

They marry generally very young, some at thirteen or fourteen . . . (Ibid.)

Like all primitive peoples, or those who live under primitive conditions, they attain to physical maturity at a very early age, especially the women, with whom marriage at thirteen, or even younger, is not unknown. (Ibid., p. xxiv)

. . . by the richness of the soil, they live for the most part after an indolent and luxurious manner. . . (Ibid.)

To speak the Truth, tis a thorough Aversion to Labor that makes People file off to N. Carolina, where Plenty and a Warm Sun confirm them in their Disposition to Laziness for their whole Lives. (William Byrd, 1728)[15]

Many set the standard of bodily and material comfort perilously low, in order, presumably, that they may have the more leisure and so extract the maximum enjoyment out of life. . . . Here no one is 'on the make'; commercial competition and social rivalries are unknown. (Ibid., pp. xxii and xxiv)

The Men for their Parts, just like the Indians, impose all the Work upon the poor Women. They make their Wives rise out of their Beds early in the Morning, at the same time that they lye and Snore, till the Sun has run one third of his course, and disperst all the unwholesome Damps. (Ibid.)

. . . in the Kentucky Mountains, the womenfolk used to have to (some still do!) do all the work about the house, tending the stock, milking, raising the children, in addition to being field hands and often doing the plowing as well. (Jean Ritchie, 1965)[16]

The only Business here is raising of Hogs, which is managed with the last [least?] Trouble, and affords the Diet they are most fond of. (Ibid.)

The country abounds in little black pigs of the 'razor-back' variety which run about half wild in the forests. . . (Maud Karpeles, 1933)[17]

The only meat they ever eat—and it is very little—is pig, or hog-meat as they call it. (Cecil Sharp, 1916)[18]

. . . at their wheat-harvest. . . Some will frequently come twenty, nay thirty miles on this occasion, the entertainments are so great, and the whole scene pleasant and diverting; but if they can get musick to indulge this mirth, it greatly adds to the pleasure of the feast. (John Brickell, 1737)[19]

Many of the parties at which I have disported myself were attended by people who lived five or six miles away, and five or six miles is a long ride over the rough mountain trails. (Vance Randolph, 1950)[20]

[15] Diary, 10 March 1728. From *The Writings of Colonel William Byrd*, quoted in Land, *Bases of the Plantation Society*, pp. 52–3.
[16] *Folk Songs of the Southern Appalachians as Sung by Jean Ritchie*, p. 76.
[17] 'The Appalachians, I', in Fox Strangways, *Cecil Sharp*, p. 150.
[18] ibid., from a letter to Sharp's wife, 3 September 1916.
[19] *The Natural History of North Carolina*, pp. 31–42. Quoted in Land, *Bases of the Plantation Society*, p. 202.
[20] *Ozark Folksongs*, vol. 3, 'Humorous and Play-Party Songs', p. 286.

A particularly full and vivid picture of the archaic mountain culture can be got from the accounts of Cecil Sharp, supplemented by those of his assistant, Maud Karpeles:

They are a leisurely, cheery people in their quiet way, in whom the social instinct is very highly developed. They dispense hospitality with an open-handed generosity and are extremely interested in and friendly toward strangers, communicative and unsuspicious.[21]

They have very little money, barter in kind being the customary form of exchange.[22] They really live almost entirely upon what they make and grow. All their clothes, blankets, etc. are made by them with the wool their sheep produce. Hardly any of them wear boots.[23]

A few of those we met were able to read and write, but the majority were illiterate. They are, however, good talkers, using an abundant vocabulary racily and often picturesquely.[24]

In some homes the women did not eat at table until the men had finished; and one of our singers, a hoary-headed gentleman known as 'Frizzly Bill', informed us that he had 'owned three wives'.[25]

. . . their standard of cleanliness was not ours . . .[26]

When middle-class America first discovered these mountain folk there was a tendency to present their ways as even more primitive and archaic than they actually were. Nonsense was talked of their 'Elizabethan speech', as though they had been preserved unaltered since the sixteenth century. As an inevitable reaction, it is now fashionable to point to urban influences on this isolated rural culture, just as it is fashionable to make similar observations about British country people. Taking all such reservations into account, I still believe that the biggest danger lies in *under*estimating the strangeness of these cultures. It takes a constant effort of the imagination to realize the isolation of their lives, the lack of canned music, the scarcity of professional musicians, the grip of tradition.

THE SCOTCH-IRISH

The early settlers were predominantly English in origin, in spite of a liberal sprinkling of foreigners—incidentally, this foreign element has been disguised by the readiness with which names were Anglicized—but

[21] Sharp, *English Folk Songs from the Southern Appalachians*, p. xxii.
[22] ibid.
[23] Sharp, letter to his wife, 3 September 1916. Quoted in Karpeles, 'The Appalachians, I', in Fox Strangways, *Cecil Sharp*, pp. 149–50.
[24] Sharp, *English Folk Songs from the Southern Appalachians*, p. xxiii.
[25] Karpeles, 'The Appalachians, I', in Fox Strangways, *Cecil Sharp*, p. 151.
[26] ibid., p. 150.

with the eighteenth century non-English stocks began to flood in, the most important being African slaves, Germans, Scots, and Irish. The Germans had little influence on folk music. It was far otherwise with the Celts.

There were Irish Catholics among these eighteenth-century immigrants, and there were Scots, including some Gaelic-speaking highlanders, but by far the most important group was the rather confusingly named Scotch-Irish. Among immigrant groups they occupy a place in the history of American music exceeded in importance only by the Africans. They were originally Scottish Presbyterians who settled in north-east Ireland in the seventeenth century. Beginning around 1710, they moved on again to North America, partly because of difficulties with the ruling Anglican hierarchy, and partly because, as one observer put it, they could 'neither get victuals nor work'.[27] The Scotch-Irish seem to have been a tough, truculent, fractious people not unlike some of their present-day Ulster descendants, and those who settled in New England soon showed an inability to get on with the established colonists, who, though fellow-puritans, were not Presbyterian but Congregationalist. They then migrated yet again, gravitating towards the frontier regions of the southern states. The tide of immigration lasted until 1740, and then resumed from 1760 till the Revolution of 1775. During the latter period they were joined by Scots from Scotland, some of them Gaelic-speaking.[28]

The Scotch-Irish left a musical legacy with clear links with the Scottish Lowlands. Sometimes it is impossible to tell by the printed notes which area a tune comes from. 'Here's a Health to All True Lovers'[29] happens to be Scottish, but it could just as easily have come from the Appalachians. 'The Maid Freed from the Gallows' (Ex. 16(a)[30]) is a typically Scottish tune which happens to have been collected in North Carolina. Quite often a particular American tune can be traced to a Scottish original. A tune from a Scottish manuscript of about 1620 ('Lady Cassilles Lilt', Ex. 85) was collected in the Appalachians in a not very different form three centuries later.[31] Well-known American tunes

[27] By 1728 the English authorities were so worried by the extent of Scotch-Irish emigration that there was an enquiry into it. This phrase comes from a letter from Hugh Boulter, Lord Primate of Ireland, to the Duke of Newcastle, 13 March 1728. Boulter, *Letters*, quoted in Ridge and Billington, *America's Frontier Story*, pp. 98–101.

[28] See Hofstadter, *America at 1750*, pp. 17 and 24–30.

[29] In Bronson, *Traditional Tunes of the Child Ballads*, vol. 4, p. 20.

[30] The full version appears in Smith, *South Carolina Ballads*, p. 144; also Bronson, *Traditional Tunes of the Child Ballads*, vol. 2, p. 457, and (slightly altered) in Sandburg, *The American Songbag*, p. 72.

[31] See 'Lady Cassilles Lilt', from the Skene manuscript (c.1620), in Bronson, *Traditional Tunes of the Child Ballads*, vol. 3, p. 201, and 'Lazarus', in Sharp, *English Folk Songs from the Southern Appalachians*, vol. 2, p. 30.

of Scottish origin include 'Rye Whiskey', 'When Johnny Comes Marching Home', 'Amazing Grace' (an obvious relative of 'Loch Lomond'), 'Run Nigger Run', 'Shady Grove', and 'The Ox-Driving Song'. Some of them we shall be meeting again in this book, along with several other Scots-derived tunes.[32]

Among Scottish ballad texts which survived in the American South are 'The False Knight upon the Road', 'Earl Brand', 'The Two Sisters', 'Edward', 'The Two Brothers', 'Sir Patrick Spens', 'Young Hunting', and 'The Wife of Usher's Well'. Equally significantly, there are ballads which are *not* found in Scotland which have not survived in America, such as 'Broomfield Hill' and 'King John and the Bishop'.[33]

The Scotch-Irish, as well as being in the right place at the right time in the right numbers, brought the right sort of music with them. Scottish music at that time was among the most archaic in Europe. It was the music of a people on the fringes of urban civilization, and this helps explain why it took the fancy of Americans living in similar conditions. Besides, as we have seen from the vogue for the 'Scotch song', a taste for Scottish music was in the air.

And finally, the Scotch-Irish style had the important characteristic of closely resembling African music in many respects.

THE CATHOLIC IRISH

On the other hand, we should not think of the Scottish strain as isolated from other British folk music. A look through anthologies of American folk tunes shows English, Irish, and even Welsh tunes alongside Scottish, all blended and adapted into a distinctively American style.[34] The influence of the Catholic Irish is well known, and even possibly exaggerated in the popular mind. The colonists usually called the Scotch-Irish simply 'Irish', much to their disgust, and it is still easy to confuse the two groups. Though there had always been some Irish Catholic settlers, the heyday of predominantly Catholic Irish immigration was the mid-nineteenth century; between 1815 and 1860 two million arrived in

[32] See Exx. 6, 74, 75, 76, and 79. 'When Johnny Comes Marching Home' is derived from 'Wha's Fu'?' (Buchan and Hall, *The Scottish Folksinger*, p. 41), 'The Ox-Driving Song' (A. Lomax, *The Penguin Book of American Folk Songs*, p. 102) from 'Hishie Ba' ' (*The Scottish Folksinger*, p. 81), 'Run Nigger Run' from 'Fire on the Mountain', and 'Shady Grove' (A. Lomax, *The Folk Songs of North America*, p. 234) from 'The Keach in the Creel' (Bronson, *Traditional Tunes of the Child Ballads*, vol. 4, p. 259).

[33] See the headnotes to the Child ballads nos. 3, 7, 10, 13, 49, 58, 68, 69, 43, and 45 in Bronson, *Traditional Tunes of the Child Ballads*.

[34] American songs of Welsh origin, though rare, do occasionally crop up. Probably the best-known is 'My Good Old Man', which is derived from 'Yr Hen Wr Mwyn' ('The Gentle Old Man'). See A. Lomax, *The Penguin Book of American Folksongs*, p. 46, and Kennedy, *Folksongs of Britain and Ireland*, pp. 152 and 170.

the United States, almost half the total of five million immigrants. They were a purely Irish strain, unlike the basically Scottish Scotch-Irish, and, though of mainly peasant stock, they preferred the cities to the back country.[35]

They also had a special relationship with the blacks, with whom they shared the bottom of the social heap. The two groups were constantly being compared, with regard to laziness, dirtiness, lying, pilfering, stupidity, and so on—all the vices ascribed to subject peoples since the beginning of time. They often worked together as labourers. In 1839, when Fanny Kemble was writing her diary, gangs of black slaves and Irish were working on the same canal nearby. They were kept carefully apart for fear, as she put it, of 'tumults, and risings, and broken heads, and bloody bones, and all the natural results of Irish intercommunion with their fellow creatures'.[36] Indeed, so much is the importance of this apartheid insisted on that the reader begins to wonder whether it was working all that well. Almost forty years later, Lafcadio Hearn wrote:

One fact worth mentioning about these negro singers is, that they can mimic the Irish accent to a degree of perfection which an American, Englishman or German could not hope to acquire. . . . a very dark mulatto, named Jim Delaney, sang for us in capital style that famous Irish ditty known as 'The hat me fahther wor-re.' Yet Jim, notwithstanding his name, has little or no Irish blood in his veins. . . Jim Delaney would certainly make a reputation for Irish specialties in a minstrel troupe; his mimicry of Irish character is absolutely perfect . . . ('Levy Life', 1876; in *Selected Writings*, p. 226.)

Hearn grew up in Ireland himself, and ought to have known. Blacks even told 'thick Irish' jokes, which were noticed as late as the 1920s. There was, for instance, the one about the thick Irishmen who eat the rind of a watermelon, giving away the inside with the exclamation, 'Faith! guts is good enough for naygurs.'[37]

By the time the Irish arrived in force American music had already acquired a distinctly Celtic tinge, mainly from the Scotch-Irish, making it easy for the Irish and American folk traditions to merge. The Irish country folk brought their rustic tastes to the cities of the United States, and helped to blur the distinction between the popular music of the cities and the countryside—and between black and white music. A. L. Lloyd suggested that the influx of potato famine Irish into English cities may have influenced urban Engish folk-song, turning it in a more 'folky'

[35] See Morison, Commager, and Leuchtenburg, *The Growth of the American Republic*, pp. 451–2.
[36] *Journal*, p. 109.
[37] Five such jokes, including this one, were printed in the *Southern Workman*, May 1899, and reprinted in the *Journal of American Folk-Lore*, no. 46, September 1899, pp. 224–8. See Gutman, *The Black Family in Slavery and Freedom*, p. 301.

direction, with the revival of the old modes and the pentatonic scale.[38] Whatever the truth of this, it seems likely that such a process was at work in American cities at the same time. The 'Irish' song was already a recognized category by the mid-nineteenth century. A song collection published in 1854 was entitled 'Marsh's Selection, or, Singing for the Million, Containing the Choicest and Best Collection of Admired Patriotic, Comic, Irish, Negro, Temperance, and Sentimental Songs Ever Embodied in One Work': thereby neatly summing up the popular American taste of the time.[39]

FRENCH, SPANISH, AND OTHERS

So far we have considered only immigrants from the British Isles. What about those from continental Europe? What bearing did they have on American folk music?

Among non-British stocks, there are only three candidates for serious consideration: the Germans, the Spanish, and the French. One would expect the Germans to have considerable influence, since they arrived in great numbers from the mid-eighteenth century on, in addition to being such a notoriously musical people. Their impact, however, seems to have been minimal. For this there are two probable reasons. Firstly, they were industrious, efficient types, who early established a name as the best farmers in the colonies and quickly rose out of those levels of society in which folk music styles are created.[40] Secondly, the music they brought with them was already largely middle class in character, as we can tell from the German folk tunes that turn up in Bach, Haydn, or Beethoven. It differs little from the urban popular music of the same time:

From the 17th century the folk idiom underwent radical changes. The diatonic major came to be used almost exclusively, in certain keys, with strophic forms and rhythms. Melismatic and recitative-like singing gave way to a simple syllabic style. Harmonic structures dominated the melodies, which were often built from sequences of broken triads . . . (Wiora and Suppan, 'Germany: Folk Music', *The New Grove*, vol. 7, p. 287.)

The main German influence on American music came, not through early German settlers, but via the German (or more usually Austrian) influence on cosmopolitan popular music, the most obvious example being the waltz.

The French influence is more difficult to evaluate. A wide variety of French music, ranging all the way from folk music to opera, certainly

---

[38] See *Folk Song in England*, pp. 355–6.
[39] Quoted in White, *American Negro Folk-Songs*, p. 443.
[40] During the eighteenth century, travellers left accounts of the Germans' idyllic farming settlements. See Hofstadter, *America at 1750*, pp. 18–24.

made a profound impression on Louisiana blacks. It has been plausibly argued that the clarinet and saxophone technique of early jazz owed much to the great French woodwind tradition.[41] The question is: was this French influence significantly different from the British influence prevailing elsewhere in the United States? If Louisiana had been a British colony, would ragtime, jazz, or the blues have turned out differently? I think the answer must be no, if we are talking about fundamental points of musical language. The idiom of French concert music differed in no important respect from the cosmopolitan European style. The French *notes inégales* have been cited as the origin of the jazz or blues musician's conversion of ♫ into ♪, but a much more likely source is the jigging rhythms of Anglo-American fiddlers. In any case, *notes inégales* were far from being uniquely French. In the same way, the French folk music encountered by black Louisianans was much like the British styles of the more northerly states; if it differed, it was mainly in being more urbanized. The creole music that arose out of this encounter is mostly in the major mode and based on the three primary triads.[42] It differs little in style from the music of the English-speaking Caribbean. New Orleans played a great part in the history of American popular music, certainly, but chiefly because of its size and its links with the Caribbean—mainly the French Caribbean, but also the British and Spanish—which brought in an African culture fresher than anything on the mainland.

Much has been made of the 'Spanish tinge' said to be essential for authentic jazz. There was certainly a great deal of Spanish influence around in the late nineteenth century, and not only in the vicinity of Spanish America—one has only to think of *Carmen*. Early jazz and blues pianists were fond of the habanera or tango bass rhythm (♩ ♪ ♩ ♩), and they may have picked up other less obvious Latinisms from the many Latin American musicians active in New Orleans at the time.[43] The intricate strumming techniques of American guitar playing probably owed something to Latin America. On the other hand, the resemblance between blues singing and the Spanish *canto hondo*, remarked on ever since people began to take serious notice of the blues, is almost certainly a matter of kinship going back to Near Eastern origins, and not direct influence, unless one counts an Andalusian influence on Senegambian music.

The question whether New Orleans was indeed the 'birthplace of jazz' has long been debated. In the golden age of jazz mythology (c.1930–60) it was taken for granted that it was. Then there arose a generation of

---

[41] See Roberts, *Black Music of Two Worlds*, p. 136.
[42] An exceptional modal tune (minor third and seventh; no sixth) is 'Criole Candjo', in Cable, 'Creole Slave Songs', pp. 826–7.
[43] See Roberts, *The Latin Tinge*, pp. 34–43.

earnest and scholarly historians who pointed out that Afro-American band music was being played in many other American cities while jazz was supposedly being born in New Orleans. More recently, there has been a swing back to the former view. It is argued, for instance, by James Lincoln Collier in his massive history, *The Making of Jazz*.[44] (One of his more interesting arguments is that *white* New Orleans bands were playing better jazz around 1920 than non-New Orleans blacks.) The truth seems to be that while many other Afro-American styles were developing elsewhere, jazz proper really was a product of New Orleans, because of the influences mentioned above: the relatively fresh Afro-Caribbean influx, the Spanish tinge, the French musical heritage, particularly with regard to wind playing, the sheer size of the city, and the relatively free mixing of the races, which again was part of the French heritage. But to go into the French musical influence in detail would merely be to duplicate the remarks on European 'parlour music' in general, or, in the case of the French Afro-Caribbean, on African music; and even the Spanish tinge is mainly a matter of superficial mannerisms. In strict justice these topics should be treated at far greater length than these brief remarks, but, as I have said before, the amount of space a subject is given in this book is only a rough indication of its importance.

[44] See pp. 57–9.

7. THE BLACKS

About the last of August came in a dutch man of warre that sold us twenty Negars.

John Rolf, Virginia, 1619[1]

WHEN the first black slave set foot on North America the late Renaissance was still in full swing. King James I was on the throne of England and Scotland, and Shakespeare, had he been alive, would have been fifty-five. The last of the slaves arrived, more than two centuries later, during the smoke and grime of the Industrial Revolution. The beginning of this long forced migration was a mere trickle, coming not directly from Africa but from the West Indies, and there is controversy over whether they were officially slaves or indentured servants like the whites. Whatever their status, it seems that not much distinction was made between them and their white counterparts at first. At all events, the records show plenty of evidence of friendly relations between menials of either race.[2]

Towards the end of the century matters changed. Attitudes hardened towards blacks, now unequivocally slaves, and rich planters began to see the advantages of replacing servants with slave labour. In 1680 about one colonist in twenty was black. Gradually, over the next fifty years, this proportion rose, as ever more slaves were imported. In the 1730s the rate of importation shot up, and continued to rise until the American Revolution of 1775. With the war the slave trade slumped, but it picked up again after the Revolution and continued to flourish until it was abolished in 1807, after which it continued illegally until the Civil War of 1861. Altogether, some half a million Africans were brought to North America, rather more than half of them between 1730 and 1775.[3]

It is important to grasp just how early these slaves arrived. Admittedly there were few arrivals during the first sixty years, but those few still had the advantage of being first-comers and setting the tone for those who came later. Even the influx of the mid-eighteenth century long antedated the great waves of white immigration—the Catholic Irish, the Italians, the East Europeans. The average black American has deeper roots in his country than his white counterpart.

[1] Quoted in Foner, *America's Black Past*, p. 65.
[2] See, for example, Morgan, *American Slavery—American Freedom*, pp. 154–7.
[3] See Rawley, *The Transatlantic Slave Trade*, p. 329.

At the same time, the pattern of black settlement and assimilation was notably uneven. In the North slaves were mainly artisans or house servants. In the South most of them were herded into large plantations, the rest either working in small groups for those yeoman farmers who owned slaves—the majority did not—or finding employment in the towns. A slave might find himself a manservant to a rich New York family, a factotum on an isolated North Carolina farm along with two or three others of his race, or part of an enormous black work-force in Georgia or South Carolina. According to circumstances, he might assimilate white urban culture or white rural culture, or hardly assimilate at all. While urban slaves quickly adopted European ways, the big plantations of the lower South became little Africas, hanging on to African ways long after one might have expected them to die out. There were plantations where a white face was a rarity, and whole counties where blacks outnumbered whites by more than ten to one.[4] It was precisely on these big plantations that conditions were harshest, the mortality rate highest, and therefore the need greatest to replenish the work-force with African imports.

How many of the replenishments came after the ban of 1807 it is difficult to say. Philip D. Curtin estimates 54,000, but he himself admits that this is 'only a shot in the dark'.[5] If he is right, this is somewhat more than a tenth of the total number of slaves brought to North America. Admittedly they were a small fraction of the existing black American population, but this amounts to something more substantial than the 'trickle' one usually reads about. The exact details of this trade are, obviously, obscure: those engaged in it were not going to shout their activities from the roof-tops. Nevertheless, it seems a safe assumption that the slaves went mainly to large plantations where the owners could afford to pay contraband prices, and where new arrivals from Africa could merge inconspicuously into the work-force.

This late infusion helps explain the tenacity of African culture in such places as the Georgia Sea Islands and the Mississippi Valley. It is unlikely, however, that African traditions would have survived so well if the existing black population had not deliberately clung to them. In other words, there was an element of black consciousness at work. Throughout their three and a half centuries' history, black Americans have been torn between accepting white ways and preserving their African heritage. The dilemma has been reflected in every aspect of life, but nowhere more vividly than in music. During the twentieth century black American music has grown, not less (as one would expect) but

---

[4] See Stampp, *The Peculiar Institution*, p. 32.
[5] See *The Atlantic Slave Trade: A Census*, pp. 74–5.

more African.[6] It seems likely that similar things happened in the past: oppression helped preserve black culture, just as persecution helped preserve the Jewish religion.[7]

Superimposed on the complex pattern of racial distribution was an equally complex pattern of race relations. Southern attitudes towards blacks bewildered northern observers at the time, and they are equally bewildering to us today. Paternalism and sickening cruelty, prejudice and intimacy, affection and hatred coexisted in the strangest way. Frederick Olmsted wrote that 'when the negro is definitely a slave, it would seem that the alleged natural antipathy of the white race to associate with him is lost.'[8] At the same time as blacks were despised as an inferior species, their talents were appreciated as musicians, story-tellers, orators, nannies, and cooks.

The 'alleged antipathy' was demonstrably lacking in sexual relations. There are plentiful records on this point. As early as the seventeenth century black men were successfully competing for white women, a rare and precious commodity at that time. In these early days it was necessarily that way around, since there were still few black women in the colonies. Later, as the sex ratio evened up, one naturally hears more of the sexual exploitation of black women by white men, but it is clear that simple affection continued to play its part. There are records, for instance, of slave owners carefully providing for their children by slave women. In all its forms, miscegenation continued to flourish, in spite of furious denunciations by the authorities.[9] It soon produced a class of people who were culturally as well as racially intermediate between black and white. It was they who were most likely to become domestics or artisans, who were more likely to be hired out—above all, who were more likely to be freed. Many were a great deal closer to white than black in appearance. According to the law, the children of a slave mother were regarded as black, and themselves automatically slaves, no matter what their complexion; that at any rate was the general drift. The question of what constituted a Negro was settled differently by different states at different times. Sometimes it went purely by appearance, but usually some proportion of Negro ancestry was made the criterion. In Virginia, from 1849, the law stated that 'Every person who has one-fourth part or more of negro blood shall be deemed a mulatto, and the word

---

[6] See Evans, 'African Elements in Twentieth-Century United States Black Folk Music', p. 101.

[7] For an extensive discussion of the development of contrasting Afro-American cultures, see Berlin, 'Time, Space, and the Evolution of Afro-American Society on British Mainland North America'.

[8] Olmsted, *A Journey in the Seaboard Slave States*, p. 18.

[9] See, for instance, Stampp, *The Peculiar Institution*, pp. 350–61, Morgan, *American Slavery—American Freedom*, pp. 333–7 (for the seventeenth century), and Kemble, *Journal*, pp. 10–12, 22–3, and 246–7.

"negro" . . . shall be construed to mean mulatto as well as negro.'[10] On the other hand, there is still a law in Louisiana that makes one thirty-second part of 'coloured blood' the dividing line—or at any rate was in October 1982, when a white-looking woman, Susie Guillory Phipps, petitioned to have her racial classification changed from coloured to white.

So mothers who were already light-skinned could have yet lighter-skinned children who still remained in bondage. The result was the situation described by Olmsted in a remarkable passage:

Riding through a large gang of hoers, with two of the overseers, I observed that a large proportion of them appeared to be thorough-bred Africans. Both of them thought that the 'real black niggers' were about three fourths of the whole number, and that this would hold as an average on Mississippi and Louisiana plantations. One of them pointed out a girl—'That one is pure white; you see her hair?' (It was straight and sandy.) 'She is the only one we have got.' It was not uncommon, he said, to see slaves so white that they could not be easily distinguished from pure-blooded whites. He had never been on a plantation before, that had not more than one on it. 'Now,' said I, 'if that girl should dress herself well, and run away, would she be suspected of being a slave?'

'Oh, yes; you might not know her if she got to the North, but any of us would know her.'

'How?'

'By her language and manners.'

'But if she had been brought up as house-servant?'

'Perhaps not in that case.'

(*A Journey in the Back Country*, pp. 70–93.)

These comments are borne out by others. Fanny Kemble says of one slave: 'this young man had so light a complexion, and such regular straight features, that, had I seen him anywhere else, I should have taken him for a southern European, or, perhaps, in favour of his tatters, a gipsy'.[11] European-looking slaves were regarded as a bad risk by owners:

One former bondsman, a 'white man with blue eyes,' recalled his master's repeated attempts to sell him, always unsuccessful. A Kentucky slave, 'owing to his being almost white, and to the consequent facilities of escape,' was adjudged to be worth only 'half as much as other slaves of the ordinary color and capacities.' (Stampp, *The Peculiar Institution*, p. 196.)

Most of these white-looking 'blacks' eventually joined the white population. Not all, however—W.C. Handy remarks: 'A memorable figure . . . was our interlocutor, George L. Moxley. . . . White in appearance, Moxley was by birth and at heart a Kentucky Negro.'[12] And

---

[10] See Stampp, *The Peculiar Institution*, p. 195.
[11] *Journal*, pp. 64–5.
[12] *Father of the Blues*, p. 37.

Bruce Cook writes, of the wife of one of the bluesmen he interviewed: 'it is worth reflecting, on meeting someone like Cora Jackson, just how little these designations of race really mean. Although her hair is auburn and her face a ruddy pink, she was born and raised a Negro in rural Virginia. And is proud of it.'[13]

But not every black American was a slave. There was a free black population which first came to prominence after the American Revolution. Some were emancipated by their masters; some were freed by the British; some had fought on the American side, been promised freedom in the event of victory, and, surprisingly enough, got it. This free black community continued to grow in numbers and importance until the Civil War and general emancipation, by which time about one black in ten in the slave states was free. This, however, is only an average; the proportion was much bigger in the Upper South and in urban areas generally, particularly New Orleans, where the French had left a large population of free *gens de couleur*.

The free blacks aroused great resentment among whites, as witness the words of that egregious specimen of poor white trash, Huck Finn's pap:

There was a free nigger there, from Ohio; a mulatter, most as white as a white man . . . And what do you think? they said he was a p'fessor in a college, and could talk all kinds of languages, and knowed everything. And that ain't the wust. They said he could vote, when he was at home. . . . I says to the people, why ain't this nigger put up at auction and sold?—that's what I want to know. And what do you reckon they said? Why, they said he couldn't be sold till he'd been in the State six months, and he hadn't been there that long yet. . . . Here's a govment that calls itself a govment, and lets on to be a govment, and thinks it is a govment, and yet's got to set stock-still for six whole months before it can take ahold of a prowling, thieving, infernal, white-shirted free nigger . . . (Mark Twain, *Huckleberry Finn*, ch. 6.)

On the other hand, good relations with free blacks are recorded, usually in the form of grumblings on the part of the authorities that the proper barriers are not being observed:

Men and women who lived and worked together often ignored the stigma attached to racial mixing, and occasionally close, even intimate friendship flowered . . .

Under the pressure of common conditions, poor blacks and whites became one. They lived together, worked together, and inevitably slept together, hopelessly blurring the color line. A Florida census taker found that most of the free Negroes in his neighborhood were 'mixed blooded almost white and have intermarried with a low class of whites—have no trade, occupation or profession. They live in a Settlement or Town of their own, their personal

---

[13] *Listen to the Blues*, p. 61.

property consists of cattle and hogs. They make no produce except Corn Peas and Potatoes and very little of that. They are a lazy, indolent smooth ass race.' . . .

Fraternization between whites and free Negroes extended to all corners of working-class life. Poor whites and blacks often patronized the same tippling shops, gambling houses, and other places of entertainment. In a typical haul, Richmond police arrested 'a very interesting kettle of fish, at a Negro den . . . where white, yellow and black congregate to eat, drink and be merry,' and the Nashville guard broke into 'a cockpit on Front Street, where a large crowd of negroes and white men had congregated to fight chickens and carouse.' Some places became notorious for their racial mixing. In New Orleans, the intersection of Bourbon and Orleans Streets [in the French Quarter, later to become the legendary 'birthplace of jazz'] was 'distinguished for the equality which reigns between black and white—all was hail fellow well met, no matter what the complexion.' (Berlin, *Slaves without Masters*, pp. 260–2.)

Another area of racial harmony, of great musical importance, was crime. The pressures on the free blacks forced many of them beyond the law, and there they found willing collaborators among the white population:

In the larger cities, some white thieves encouraged black criminality by establishing depots or 'night cribs' where blacks might bring stolen merchandise, find protection, or simply spend the night. Free Negroes generally welcomed these criminal alliances with whites. Although whites cheated blacks by giving them nominal prices for valuable merchandise, white henchmen also hid them from suspicious police, wrote them passes and even forged freedom papers. (Berlin, *Slaves without Masters*, p. 262.)

Yet, in spite of everything, some free blacks did very well for themselves. The paradoxical counterpart of the white slave was the black slave owner, such as Thomas Day, who became the finest and most successful cabinet-maker in North Carolina, and, in addition to owning slaves, employed a white journeyman; or William Johnson, of Natchez, Mississippi, who, beginning as a barber, rose to become a landowner with slaves, a white overseer, and white tenant farmers.[14]

These were clearly exceptional individuals, the tiny apex of a pyramid which sloped rapidly to the struggling and harassed masses. They are, nevertheless, a significant part of ante-bellum black life, and therefore black music. If we are to remember only one fact about the American music of the past, let that fact be its sheer *variety*. White music varied from the most rustic to the most urbane, and black music varied from the near-African—itself representing several contrasting strains—to every

[14] Their stories are told in Berlin's *Slaves without Masters*. For more information on Day, see Franklin, *The Free Negro in North Carolina*. These two books and Stampp's *The Peculiar Institution* include details of other free blacks who prospered in the white man's world.

degree of approach to every kind of white music. And all of these types did not remain static and isolated: they jostled each other, intermingling and interacting from the seventeenth century to the present.

8. INSTRUMENTAL MUSIC

If they want something really native, let them consider the Ethiopian Minstrels; let them hold up as the national symbol, Jim Crow.

The American Review, 1845[1]

SOME time during the 1690s the Revd Thomas Teakle was so shocked to discover that dancing had been going on in his house—at the very hour of the Sabbath service, too—that he took the offenders to court. The revellers on this deplorable occasion were his daughter's friends. The fiddler was a slave. There is no reason to think that there was anything novel about this situation; it was only the Revd Teakle's outraged piety that happened to place the event on record.[2]

For another two hundred years the black fiddler was a prominent figure in the American musical landscape. Sometimes he performed as a soloist, but very often he was teamed with the banjo. This African instrument was noted as early as the seventeenth century, but, being exotic, took a while to win acceptance with white audiences. To eighteenth-century observers it was still very much an instrument of the blacks; nevertheless, an account of 1774 states: 'A great number of young people'—white young people, that is—'met together with a Fiddle and Banjo played by two Negroes, with Plenty of Toddy'.[3]

Whether or not accompanied by the fiddle, the banjo was often supported by percussion of one sort or another, perpetuating a common African combination.[4] In the painting 'The Old Plantation' (c.1800) there are two instrumentalists: a banjo player, and a drummer beating something that looks like a miniature kettledrum with two little drumsticks—evidently the same instrument as the Arabic *naqqara* or the medieval European naker.[5] In a similar role we encounter the triangle,

[1] A sneer at the advocates of a distinctive American culture, on the part of those favouring the European tradition. (See Morison, *The Oxford History of the American People*, p. 495.) 'Jim Crow' had appeared on the scene in the early 1830s. See Hamm, *Yesterdays*, pp. 118–23.

[2] From the Accomac County Records, vol. 1690–7, pp. 161 ff., quoted in Bruce, *Social Life of Virginia*, pp. 181–4. See Epstein, *Sinful Tunes and Spirituals*, p. 80.

[3] From the diary of Nicholas Creswell, an English visitor. See Epstein, *Sinful Tunes and Spirituals*, p. 115.

[4] Nketia lists 'bowed lute, plucked lute, a rattle and a drum *ad lib.*' as one of the commonest types of traditional ensemble in Ghana (*African Music in Ghana*, pp. 105–6). There is a picture of such an ensemble (minus percussion) in Nketia, 'Ghana', *The New Grove*, vol. 7, p. 330. Similar combinations were popular in medieval Europe.

[5] This celebrated picture has been widely reproduced, for instance in Epstein, *Sinful Tunes and Spirituals*, p. 37 (and also the cover); in Oliver, *Savannah Syncopators*, p. 22; and in Odell, 'Banjo', *The New Grove*, vol. 2, p. 121. For coloured reproductions see Spence, *Living Music*,

the bones, played castanet-fashion, and the scraper, usually in the form of a jawbone-and-key: all easily traceable to Africa.

Often, too, the fiddle and banjo would be joined by further melodic instruments. Lafcadio Hearn, in 1876, mentioned the combination of fiddle, banjo, and double-bass;[6] other additions, from about the same time, were the guitar and, sometimes, the mouth organ.

The double-bass we may perhaps see as a substitute for various African instruments, such as the larger harps or lyres, the ground bow, or even the bass xylophone or mbira. The guitar was a more radically European instrument, and is only a particularly obvious sign of a process of Europeanization which had been at work from the beginning. When only fiddle, banjo, and percussion were involved, the most likely mode of performance would be some sort of heterophony, both instruments playing the same tune but in their own highly individual styles. It is a technique typical of the Near East and those parts of Africa (and, we might add, Europe) which have fallen under Near Eastern influence. The bass and guitar in such groups make up the equivalent of the classical continuo, usually but not always supplying a chord structure on the European pattern.[7]

At the same time black musicians inevitably influenced the tastes of the white audiences they played for. We do not know how the Revd Teakle's fiddler sounded. He may have played in exactly the same style as a white fiddler of the same time and place—whatever *that* was exactly. On the other hand, it is more than possible that a little of Africa had got into his playing, and it is hard to see how the banjo-and-fiddle duet of 1774 could have avoided an African tinge.

About the time of the latter performance there are explicit accounts of whites adopting black styles of music and dancing. We learn, for instance, that no less a person than Randolph, the brother of Thomas Jefferson, 'a mighty simple man'—that is to say, unassuming or democratic in his social habits—'used to come out among black people, play the fiddle and dance half the night'.[8] Both the music and the dancing would have been called 'jigs', a term with a wide range of meanings in American folk culture. Describing a ball in Virginia around 1775, one observer writes:

Betwixt the Country dances they have what I call everlasting jigs. A couple gets

pp. 110–11, *the Larousse Encyclopaedia of Music*, facing p. 433, and *The Book of the Piano*, p. 194.

[6] 'Levee Life', in *Selected Writings*, p. 227.
[7] Even in the twentieth century, one-chord styles akin to African ostinato patterns persisted in places. See Roberts, *Black Music of Two Worlds*, pp. 197–8.
[8] The authority is Isaac, a former slave on the Jefferson estate, in Bear, *Jefferson at Monticello*, p. 22; quoted in Epstein, *Sinful Tunes and Spirituals*, p. 122.

up and begins to dance a jig (to some Negro tune) others comes and cuts them out, and these dances always last as long as the Fiddler can play. This is sociable, but I think it looks more like a Bacchanalian dance than one in a polite assembly. (Nicholas Creswell, *Journal*, pp. 52–3.)

Amplifying this description, here is another, also from Virginia:

Towards the close of an evening, when the company are pretty well tired with country-dances, it is usual to dance jigs; a practice originally borrowed, I am informed, from the Negroes.

These dances are without any method or regularity; a gentleman and lady stand up, and dance about the room, one of them retiring, the other pursuing, then perhaps meeting, in an irregular fantastical manner. After some time, another lady gets up, and then the first lady must sit down, she being, as the term is, cut out; the second lady acts the same part which the first did, till somebody cuts her out. The gentlemen perform in the same manner. (*A Concise Historical Account of All the British Colonies in North-America . . . 1776.*)

And here is a description of the original black version:

The jig was an African dance and a famous one in old times . . . For the jig the music would be changed. The fiddle would assume a low monotonous tone, the whole tune running on three or four notes only (when it could be heard,) the stick-knocker changed his time, and beat a softer and slower measure. Indeed only a few could give the 'knock' for proper effect.

It was strictly a dance for two, one man and one woman on the floor at a time. It was opened by a gentleman leading out the lady of his choice and presenting her to the musicians. She always carried a handkerchief held at arm's length over her head, which was waved in a graceful motion to and fro as she moved. The step, if it may be so called, was simply a slow shuffling gait in front of the fiddler, edging along by some unseen exertion of the feet, from one side to the other—sometimes courtseying down and remaining in that posture while the edging motion from one side to the other continued.

Whilst this was going on, the man danced behind her, shuffling his arms and legs in artistic style, and his whole soul and body thrown into the dance. The feet moved about in the most grotesque manner stamping, slamming and banging the floor, not unlike the pattering of hail on the housetop. . . . It was hard work, and at intervals of five or ten minutes, he was relieved by another jumping into the ring with a shout, and shuffling him out. (H.W. Ravenel, writing in 1876 of his youth, around 1840.)

This description accords well with the dance depicted in 'The Old Plantation', where there are however two women, both with handkerchiefs, banjo player instead of fiddler, and drummer instead of 'stick knocker'. (This use of the handerchief is reminiscent of the practice of English Morris (originally 'Moorish') dancers, who at one time performed with blackened faces.)

The mention of the male dancer's footwork, 'not unlike the pattering of hail on the housetop', recalls yet another type of jig, which differed from the above in being definitely an exhibition dance by a single performer who, far from throwing his whole body into the dance, kept its upper half as still as possible. (It was a common trick to balance a glass of water on the dancer's head.) This is obviously an Africanized variant of a type of Irish jig where, again, the upper body is held still while the feet beat out a percussive tattoo on the floor. Northern English clog dancing and modern tap dancing are members of the same family. There are reports of such jigs from the 1830s, contemporary, that is, with the near-African 'jigs' described above.[9]

Yet another form of Afro-American dancing was simply a version of the white square dance. In 1853, two Englishwomen reported seeing in Montgomery, Alabama, 'about sixty negroes, all dancing . . . to the music of two violins and a banjo . . . a negro was standing on a chair, calling out what figures were to be performed in the Virginia Reel'.[10] A similar scene of about fifty years later was recalled by W.C. Handy:'In Mississippi we played for a country dance where the baddest of the bad were in command. They danced the old square dances with one of their own calling the figures.'[11]

In the end, as inevitably seems to happen in American music, the blacks abandoned their creation to white musicians. The instrumental folk music of white America is rather a murky subject until the 1920s, when it emerged into the light of the first hillbilly records. These were the white equivalent of the black 'race' records, blacks being euphemistically known as 'the race', just as women used to be known as 'the sex'. In spite of this racial division, it is sometimes impossible to tell whether a particular performance is by black or white instrumentalists, so similar do they sound.[12] In the 1930s some white musicians developed the bluegrass style, based on the combination of fiddle, banjo, guitar, and double-bass with the possible addition of mandolin—in other words, the traditional rural black dance band, which the blacks themselves had by then almost abandoned for jazz or the blues.

Along with the black dance musician one ought to mention the black bandsman. By the mid-eighteenth century the black musician was already a well established part of the military band, not only in America but in Europe as well. Various percussion instruments were regarded as his especial province. He was elaborately dressed, and brought a good

[9] See Oliver, *Songsters and Saints*, pp. 22–4 and 29.

[10] Turnbull and Turnbull, *American Photographs*, vol. 2, pp. 60–72; quoted in Epstein, *Sinful Tunes and Spirituals*. p. 154.

[11] *Father of the Blues*, p. 85. 'Tight like That' (Ex. 80) is an example of the music that came out of this environment. It forms a fascinating link between nineteenth-century jigs and twentieth-century rock and roll.

[12] The same is true even of some vocal performances: see, for instance, 'Original Blues', recorded in 1930 (Titon, *Early Downhome Blues*, pp. 75–6). Titon concludes that the singer was white solely on the grounds of his accent.

deal of acrobatic panache to this performance; a relic of his costume and mannerisms survives in the leopard skin and stick twirling of the military bass drummer.[13] Blacks also figured as brass players: not just trumpeters, as one might expect, but also as performers on the French horn. The most eminent horn player in mid-eighteenth-century England was Cato, a black man: he was in turn in the employ of Sir Robert Walpole (the first Prime Minister), the Earl of Chesterfield, and the Prince of Wales, later George III. And Lord Barrymore, not to be outdone, kept no fewer than four black horn players.[14]

By the early nineteenth century accounts appear in the United States of purely black bands. One such band, from Philadelphia, visits Rhode Island around 1830. In 1834 it is remarked that the coloured people 'have formed many superior bands, and are much patronized for their skill in our larger cities', and in 1883 we find the statement that 'forty years ago nearly every regimental band in New York was composed of black musicians'. So there is no doubt that by the fourth decade of the nineteenth century the all-black band was a familiar feature of the northern cities. Such bands seem to have sprung into existence wherever there were cities or large towns with a fair-sized population of free blacks, whether in the North, the Upper South, or new Orleans.[15]

Some bands played for dances as well as marches, and in any case the two streams of dance and march music came together at the end of the century in ragtime. There is an unbroken tradition between 'jigs' and ragtime; in fact the words 'jig' and 'rag' were used interchangeably for a while during the mid-1890s,[16] while some of the early piano rags were actually entitled 'March'.

The employment of blacks as musicians was altogether so general as to suggest that this was widely regarded as 'nigger work', a term that needs some clarification. Nigger work was not necessarily menial or unskilled; it might in fact be both skilled and lucrative. Often, it was simply a trade which had come to be regarded as such because black workers practised it. In fact, what was regarded as nigger work in one state might be white man's work in another:

If the specific occupations varied, the character of 'nigger work' was everywhere

---

[13] See Walvin, *Black and White: The Negro and English Society, 1555–1945*, pp. 70–1, and Farmer, *Military Music*, pp. 35–7 (with a picture of a black tambourinist of the Coldstream Guards, *c.*1790, on p. 36).

[14] See Epstein, *Sinful Tunes and Spirituals*, pp. 116–17, and (for Cato *et al.*) Tuckwell, *Horn*, p. 20.

[15] See Epstein, *Sinful Tunes and Spirituals*, pp. 119–20, for the use of black musicians in American militias, and pp. 159–60 for early all-black bands. The article 'Black Musical Activities in Antebellum Wilmington, North Carolina', by Nancy R. Ping (*The Black Perspective in Music*, vol. 8, no. 2, fall 1980) is also interesting. She comes to the conclusion that 'most of the professional musicians in the area—fiddlers, fifers, drummers, and members of brass bands—appear to have been of African descent'.

[16] See Blesh and Janis, *They All Played Ragtime*, p. 23.

the same. These occupations were almost always service trades that required little capital and generally depended on white customers. . . . While some of these trades were servile in nature, they generally required considerable skill. Indeed, skill was an essential element in many of the jobs deemed 'nigger work'. (Berlin, *Slaves without Masters*, p. 236.)

To this we might add the general recognition, from as early as the eighteenth century, of the blacks' superior musical talent. 'In music they are more generally gifted than whites with accurate ears for tune and time,' as Thomas Jefferson put it.[17]

It is clear that a talent for music was a great advantage to the black American, whether slave or free; a fact attested by Solomon Northup, a well-educated free black New Yorker who was kidnapped, sold into slavery in Louisiana, and eventually rescued after twelve years:

My master often received letters, sometimes from a distance of ten miles, requesting him to send me to play at a ball or festival of the whites. . . .

Alas! had it not been for my beloved violin, I scarcely can conceive how I could have endured the long years of bondage. It introduced me to great houses—relieved me of many days' labor in the field—supplied me with conveniences for my cabin—with pipes and tobacco, and extra pairs of shoes. . . . It heralded my name round the country—made me friends, who, otherwise would not have noticed me—gave me an honored seat at the yearly feasts, and secured the loudest and heartiest welcome of them all at the Christmas dance. (*Twelve Years a Slave*, pp. 216–17.)

Northup's testimony shows both the advantages of a musical talent and the great demand there was in country areas for skilled musicians. The importance of these professional or semi-professional black musicians in the history of American popular music can hardly be exaggerated. Through them, African influences filtered into white folks' music, and British tunes made their way to the less assimilated, still relatively African blacks. They were also instrumental in the rapid spread of musical ideas over the South. Quite often a slave would escape with his fiddle, using it to earn money as he put as much distance as possible between himself and his master. This we know from advertisements for runaway slaves. After one such slave had been away for a year, his master complained: 'it is needless to mention his cloathing, as he has been out so long, and as he plays the fiddle, he has many opportunities of changing his dress.'[18] Those who had been freed often thought it prudent to migrate to another state, and were in fact sometimes forced to do so by law. The result was a constant migration of musicians, sometimes forced and sometimes voluntary, promoting the mutual influence of white and

---

[17] *Notes on the State of Virginia*; quoted in Rose, *A Documentary History of Slavery in North America*, p. 71.

[18] The advertisement appeared in the *Virginia Gazette* in 1771. It is among a series of such advertisements for runaway slaves in Epstein, *Sinful Tunes and Spirituals*, pp. 113–14.

black, folk and sophisticated, religious and secular, and in fact every conceivable musical category. These itinerant musicians (latterly known as 'songsters' and 'musicianers') continued to be important after emancipation, and in fact right up to the advent of the 'race' records of the 1920s. Paul Oliver has devoted a book, *Songsters and Saints*, to the activities of the last of the breed, whose recordings give us an invaluable picture of early twentieth-century black American music. *Mutatis mutandis*, most of his observations are equally applicable to their predecessors of a century or two earlier, and, indeed, to wandering popular musicians in many other parts of the world.

AFRICAN SURVIVALS

Among the most African music to be heard in the United States we naturally find that which blacks made for their own entertainment. George Washington Cable described dancing and music-making in Congo Square, New Orleans, which, if not African, was no more than a step away from it.[19] Among the instruments he describes are drums, of a clearly African type, a maracas-like rattle, triangle, jew's harp, jawbone-and-key, and banjo. He also mentions the mbira, but it is doubtful whether this was actually played in Louisiana. His precise words are: 'A queer thing that went with these when the affair was pretentious—full dress, as it were—at least it was so in the West Indies, whence Congo Plains drew all inspirations—was the Marimba brett, a union of reed and string principles.'[20] He then goes on to describe what is obviously a simple mbira with cane tongues.

Cable was born in 1844, and the period he was describing was just before the Civil War, a generation or so before the first recorded stirrings of early jazz. His words about Congo Square drawing its inspiration from the West Indies help to explain the strength of the African influence at this late date, since the slave population arrived, on the whole, much earlier on the mainland (particularly the upper South) than in the Caribbean. This late African influence had its affect on instrumental technique. Jazz historians have traced a line between Congo Square and early jazz drummers, and there is probably something in this, in spite of the considerable differences between African and jazz drumming technique. And John Storm Roberts has noted the resemblances between early recordings of rural black brass bands and African shawm-and-trumpet groups.[21] The jew's harp (described by Cable as producing 'an astonishing amount of sound') may well have lain behind the 'blues-

---

[19] See the famous article, 'The Dance in Place Congo', in *The Century Magazine*, February 1886.
[20] ibid., p. 519.
[21] *Black Music of Two Worlds*, p. 218.

harp' technique of harmonica playing. (One thing, at least, that the two instruments had in common was that neither was in any sense a harp.) The jawbone-and-key, which was occasionally adopted by white bands,[22] is no doubt the parent of the washboard in its role of percussion instrument, though this use was also traditional among washerwomen at their work.[23] Such examples could easily be multiplied: tracing American instruments and instrumental techniques back to Africa has become almost an industry these days.[24]

Dances and marches were the principal types of instrumental music, but by no means the only ones. There were the onomatopoeic pieces, the train or fox-hunt imitations for fiddle, harmonica, guitar, or banjo, which have relatives in both African and British traditions.[25] There was the tradition of playing to oneself to pass the time, like the herdboy with his three-note panpipes, or 'quills', in an illustration to Cable's article. He was merely carrying on a practice immemorial in Africa, to say nothing of the ancient Mediterranean. In more recent times a harmonica would probably be used for this purpose, and no doubt the 'quills' also made their contribution to the blues-harp style.[26]

The blues-harp is perhaps the most striking example in all music of a thoroughly idiomatic technique that flatly contradicts everything that the instrument was designed for. As most people know, the scale of the mouth organ is divided into 'blow' and 'suck' notes. The original idea was that the 'blow' notes should provide the main notes of the scale (principally the notes of the tonic triad) and the 'suck' notes the fillers-in. With a rare stroke of genius, the Afro-American musician reversed this scheme, making the 'suck' notes, which are easily altered in pitch, or 'bent', into the main ones. Now, on an instrument in C, these notes are d' g' b' d" f" a", etc.; so that, if we take G as the tonic, they fall easily into the triadic patterns which are basic to the blues.[27]

The same triadic bias underlies the 'knife' or 'bottleneck' guitar, which is an ordinary steel-strung guitar tuned to a major triad (usually D A d a

[22] Vance Randolph writes: 'Several country dance tunes are still known as "jawbone songs" and I myself heard the jawbone played as part of a dance orchestra at Springfield, Mo., in 1934.' (*Ozark Folksongs*, vol. 2, 'Songs of the South and West', p. 333.)

[23] 'The rhythmic possibilities of the washboard in the hands of a Negress are all but illimitable. There are many "rubbing songs," . . .' (Scarborough, *On the Trail of Negro Folk-Songs*, p. 212.)

[24] See Evans, 'African Elements in Twentieth-Century United States Black Folk Music', pp. 93–4.

[25] There are recordings of fiddle pieces imitating hunts from Niger in Africa (see Wachsmann and Cooke, 'Africa', *The New Grove*, vol. 1, p. 145), and from Ireland (on the record *Ireland* in *The Columbia World Library of Folk and Primitive Music*).

[26] David Evans suggests yet another source in the *algaita*, the African development of the Arabic shawm ('African Elements in Twentieth-Century United States Black Folk Music', p. 93).

[27] For a full explanation of these triadic patterns, see the section on the blues below.

d' f♯') and stopped with a hard, curved object like a knife blade or bottleneck. Applied to the banjo, such triadic tunings go back to the eighteenth century, if we go by Thomas Jefferson's description of the banjo being tuned like 'the four lower chords of the guitar', by which he would have meant the English guitar of the period, which was tuned to a major triad.[28] It used to be customary to trace the stopping technique to the Hawaiian guitar, but, considering that the bottleneck style was already in existence when the Hawaiian guitar was a novelty even in Hawaii, this is hardly plausible. More recently David Evans has derived it from the one-stringed 'diddly bow', a child's instrument which is stopped in a similar way;[29] this, in turn, resembles certain West African instruments, for instance a one-stringed bark zither stopped with a knife blade, found in Benin—also a child's instrument.[30]

In spite of their very different origins, the blues harp and the bottleneck guitar produce rather similar music: a pungent, wailing, undulating sound playing mainly on the notes of the major triad, which can sound very Oriental. It is a technique perfectly adapted to the blues, and it is an interesting question which came first, the blues or the technique. In other words, was the technique evolved to play the blues, or did the blues derive inspiration from patterns inherent in the instruments? When we recall the remarks in chapter 5 on the susceptibility of American musicians to implied and pre-existing patterns, and the ready exchange between vocal and instrumental music, I think there can be little doubt that both processes were at work.

To go further than these brief remarks would be beyond the scope of this chapter. In any case, a great deal has been written on the subject, especially from the black American angle. If anything, it is the *white* American instrumentalists who now need studying: in particular, what they learnt from the blacks, and the adaptations they made to black instrumental techniques. Then we shall have something like a complete picture of American instrumental music.

[28] In *Notes on the State of Virginia* (1782). See Odell, 'Banjo', *The New Grove*, vol. 2, p. 120.
[29] See 'Afro-American One-Stringed Instruments'. The sound of the diddly bow can be heard on the Library of Congress Archive of Folk Culture recording *Afro-American Folk Music from Tate and Panola Counties, Mississippi*, AFS L67, side B, track 2, with further notes by Evans.
[30] See Rouget, 'Benin', *The New Grove*, vol. 2, p. 488.

9. VOCAL MUSIC

Our best songs and dances are hybrids of hybrids, mixtures of
mixtures . . .

Alan Lomax[1]

IF anything, American vocal music is even more tangled, more maze-
like, than American instrumental music. In instrumental music one has
only the tunes to worry about; in vocal music there are the words as
well. When Newman White wrote of black American song, 'Generally
speaking, practically any stanza is at home in practically any song,' he
was hardly exaggerating.[2] In 1845 it was remarked that

The blacks themselves leave out old stanzas, and introduce new ones at pleasure.
Travelling through the South, you may, in passing from Virginia to Louisiana,
hear the same tune a hundred times, but seldom the same words accompanying
it. This necessarily results from the fact that the songs are unwritten, and also
from the habit of extemporizing, in which the performers indulge on festive
occasions. (J. Kinnard, 'Who are our National Poets?'; quoted in Epstein, *Sinful
Tunes and Spirituals*, p. 187.)

Tunes show the same protean quality. The same tunes often did
service for worksongs, spirituals, and other purposes. British folk tunes
might be transformed into blues. Instrumental and vocal tunes changed
places. Take, as an example, the tune of 'Pretty Polly' (Exx. 18 and 82). It
originated as a slightly Africanized version of a British ballad. In this
form it may be sung either completely unaccompanied, in the traditional
British way, or with a banjo accompaniment. There is also a later form
where the guitar is substituted for the banjo. It can also be heard as a
banjo or fiddle solo, in which form it becomes a piece of dance music.[3] In
a bluesy call-and-response form it serves as the worksong ballad 'Po'
Lazarus' (Ex. 83). And for good measure, it is the tune of Bob Dylan's
'Ballad of Hollis Brown' (1963). This is a fairly typical career for an
American folk tune.

It is, then, no easy thing to disentangle the subspecies of American

---

[1] *The Folk Songs of North America*, p. xvi.
[2] *American Negro Folk-Songs*, p. 26.
[3] A good guitar-accompanied variant (adapted from an earlier banjo-accompanied form) can
be heard on the Library of Congress Archive of Folk Culture recording *Anglo-American
Ballads*, AFS-L 1. There is a fine fiddle solo version, by Hobart Smith, on the record
Instrumental Music of the Southern Appalachians (Tradition Records: TLP 1007).

vocal music. Still, it will do no harm to give a brief account of the main varieties: worksongs; spirituals; the dance song; and the song pure and simple, whether lyric or narrative, black or white—a large, amorphous, and extremely important category.

WORKSONGS

> We are told of a research student who took a seat on a fence to listen to the singing of a negro work gang on a railroad. When he finally detected their words he found they were singing lines that sounded like, 'See dat white man . . . sittin' on a fence . . . sittin' on a fence . . . wastin' his time . . . wastin' his time.'
>
> Carl Sandburg[4]

Songs to accompany rhythmic, repetitive work are probably as old as the work itself. They naturally assume a call-and-response form of one kind or another, if only because this gives the workers plenty of time to catch their breath. Call-and-response singing for any purpose is very much a favourite in black Africa, so much so that it is widely believed to be peculiar to that continent. In fact, the call-and-response worksong is found pretty well all over the world, or at any rate used to be while concerted physical labour was still common. In Europe such worksongs, often quite strikingly similar to their African equivalents, have survived into modern times on the Gaelic-speaking Hebridean islands. Apart from worksongs, there are a few call-and-response songs which have remained popular in Britain to modern times, like 'The Dilly Song', otherwise known as 'Green Grow the Rushes O' ('I'll sing you one O!' 'Green grow the rushes O!' 'What is your one O?' 'One is one and all alone', etc.) and 'The Keeper' ('Jackie boy!' 'Master?' 'Sing ye well?' 'Very well', etc.). These and similar songs are, however, actual *dialogue* songs, where the conversational element is essential to the song. Whether there was a more widespread British tradition of worksong proper in former times, and whether this had any sort of influence on the American continent, is extremely difficult to tell. For practical historical purposes, the American worksong can be regarded as an African import. Not only the general practice, but the actual tunes must have initially come straight from Africa, and throughout their existence the American worksongs have retained a strongly African character, reinforced by social circumstances. Inevitably, the kind of work for which worksongs were appropriate tended to be performed by the least assimilated section of the slave, or, later, free black population, who were necessarily closest to Africa by descent and culture.

[4] *The American Songbag*, p. 139. Essentially the same story is told in Odum and Johnson, *The Negro and his Songs*, pp. 2–3.

All the same, it would be a great mistake to think of the worksongs as a relic of African culture untouched by outside influences. On the contrary. To the actual singers the worksong was not such a distinct species as it may appear to the scholar. It was a song for singing at work, and all that was necessary was a good, strong, simple tune which could be adapted to the call-and-response pattern, and words which could be either easily remembered or easily improvised.

Spirituals might fit this bill; some of the more pious workers refused to sing *any* worksongs with secular texts. For instance the 'tie-shuffling chant' (Ex. 26(*b*)) was collected from a singer who 'having refused to sing anything that had to do with "worl'ly" and thus sinful matters, objected not at all to this work song': 'If I could I surely would stand on the rock where Moses stood'.[5] Often, too, songs of white origin were adapted as worksongs. It is sometimes possible, as in the case of 'John Henry', to trace even a highly Africanized worksong tune back to British origins (see Ex. 84). In 'Stewball' or 'Go 'way f'om mah Window' (Exx. 74(*c*) and 14) it is the words that come from Britain, deriving respectively from the broadside ballad 'The Noble Skewball' (about a racehorse) and the Elizabethan lyric 'Go from my Window Go'. An early example of the latter occurs in Beaumont and Fletcher's *The Knight of the Burning Pestle* (1613):

> Go from my window, love, goe;
> Go from my window my deere,
>   The winde and the raine
>   Will drive you backe againe,
> You cannot be lodged heere.[6]

A derivative of this was popular in America during the nineteenth century:

> Oh get away from the window,
> My lover and my dove,
> Oh get away from the window,
> Don't you hear?
> Oh my love yes,
> Come some other night,
> For there's going to be a fight;
> There'll be razors a flying in the air.
>   (White, *American Negro Folk-Songs*, p. 325.)

and another derivative turns up as an old 'black mammy' lullaby.[7] There are all sorts of routes by which such a British lyric could have found its way to being adapted to a black worksong, including song-swapping by

[5] J. and A. Lomax, *American Ballads and Folk Songs*, p. 14.
[6] Act II, lines 496–500.
[7] See Scarborough, *On the Trail of Negro Folk-Songs*, p. 157. For the full story of this song, see Lloyd, *Folk Song in England*, pp. 190–3.

black and white workers engaged on the same job, for which there was
ample scope from early colonial times on. The mid-nineteenth century,
especially, was a golden age for the worksong, as a revolution in
transport generated an enormous demand for labour to construct canals,
railways, and tunnels, and to man boats and ships. During this same
period, roughly 1830–80, black labourers gradually came to predominate
on jobs of this kind.[8] In the process, there was any amount of
opportunity for them to pick up musical influences from their white
fellows.

At the same time, there is no doubt that a strongly African tradition of
worksong persisted. The British and African types can often be
distinguished by verbal patterns alone. Take the famous ballad of John
Henry:

> John Henry was a very small boy,
> Fell on his mammy's knee;
> Picked up a hammer and a little piece of steel,
> 'Lord, a hammer'll be the death of me,
> Lord, a hammer'll be the death of me.[9]
>
> John Henry went to the tunnel,
> And they put him in the lead to drive;
> The rock so tall and John Henry so small,
> That he laid down his hammer and he cried,
> Lord, Lord, that he laid down his hammer and he cried.
>
> White man told John Henry,
> 'Nigger, damn your soul,
> You might beat this steam and drill of mine,
> When the rocks in this mountain turn to gold,
> Lord, Lord, when the rocks in this mountain turn to gold.'[10]

It has been pointed out that the opening words resemble a stanza from
the Scottish ballad 'Mary Hamilton', otherwise known as 'The Four
Marys':

> Whan I was a babe, and a very little babe,
> And stood at my mither's knee;
> Nae witch nor warlock did unfauld
> The death I was to dree.[11]

In the third verse there is an example of the impossible condition, a
frequent device in British folk poetry, of which the best-known example
is probably:

> Till a' the seas gang dry, my dear,

---

[8] In 1858 a Louisiana newspaper reported that 'Negro labor is fast taking the place of white
labor in the construction of southern railroads'; see Stampp, *The Peculiar Institution*, p. 62.

[9] Cohen, *Long Steel Rail*, p. 61 (sung by Fiddlin' John Carson).

[10] J. and A. Lomax, *American Ballads and Folk Songs*, p. 6.

[11] Child, *The English and Scottish Popular Ballads*, vol. 3, p. 391. Quoted in Cohen, *Long
Steel Rail*, p. 70.

> And the rocks melt wi' the sun!
> And I will luv thee still, my dear,
> While the sands o' life shall run.[12]

But it is hardly necessary to go into minutiae to detect a British origin. The very stanza type proclaims it. Here is an example of the identical type, from another fine work ballad, only this time not American but British:

> Oh, Greenland is a barren place,
> It's a place that bears no green,
> Where there's ice and snow, and the whale-fish blow,
> And the daylight's seldom seen,
> Brave boys, and the daylight's seldom seen.[13]

It will be seen that the form is exactly the same, 'brave boys' taking the place of 'Lord, Lord', right down to the limerick-like internal rhyme in the third line, as in the second of the 'John Henry' stanzas. Now compare this with the following:

> Everywhere I, where I look this mornin',
> Everywhere I, where I look this mornin',
> Look like rain, my Lawd, look like rain.
>
> Got a rainbow, rainbow tied all around my shoulder,
> Got a rainbow, rainbow tied all around my shoulder,
> Ain' gonna rain, my Lawd, ain' gonna rain.
>
> I done walk till, walk till my feet's gone to rollin',
> I done walk till, walk till my feet's gone to rollin',
> Jes' like a wheel, my Lawd, jes' like a wheel.[14]

In their use of systematic repetition these stanzas are typically African. All sorts of repetitive patterns can be found in African song, including some that are very close to this bluesy AAB arrangement: for instance

> Enyẹ hu ṇtao mọni yaa ee ni eṣẹ lẹ etsẹ.
> Etsẹ hu ṇtao mọni yaa ee ni eṣẹ lẹ enyẹ.
> Awo Dede oo, ba ni mawo. Ṣi e nyẹ kpakpa ba ni ma wo.[15]

or

> Atsẹ mi kooloobi kooloo; mitao mangtsẹmẹi mafimọ amẹ.
> Atsẹ mi kooloobi kooloo; mitao mangtsẹmẹi magbe amẹ.
> Nyanyara ehii; okẹẹ mihii, bo hu ohii.[16]

or the words of Ex. 26(a):

---

[12] From A Red, Red Rose', by Robert Burns; derived from folk sources.
[13] From 'The Greenland Whale Fisheries', *The Penguin Book of English Folk Songs*, pp. 50–1. See also the remarks on stanza types, pp. 23–5.
[14] J. and A. Lomax, *American Ballads and Folk Songs*, pp. 84–5. For the tune, see Ex. 10(b). An example of a similar verbal pattern is the spiritual 'Way over in the New Buryin' Groun' ', Ex. 17.
[15] Nketia, *African Music in Ghana*, p. 119.
[16] Kilson, *Kpele Lala*, p. 166. The original has two lines to every one of mine. The meaning

Ọnyẹ ampa ara,
Ọnyẹ ampara
mpanyimfo e.

Yẹ atse asẹm bi o,
Yẹ atse asẹm bi o,
Yẹ atse asẹm bi o,
Ma ọnyẹ ampa.

SEA SHANTIES

A word should be said about sea shanties, which were simply shipboard
worksongs with much the same multiracial origins as their mainland
equivalents. Crews were usually racially mixed, and sometimes entirely
black; there was also an ingenious form of apartheid known as
'checkerboard crews', with black and white shifts taking alternate
watches. Stan Hugill, *the* authority on shanties, estimates that the
modern body of shanties dates from between 1820 and 1860—that is, the
forty years *before* the American Civil War and the emancipation of the
slaves.[17] This was the heyday of the trans-Atlantic cotton trade, which
brought sailors into contact with black longshoremen, and especially
those whose job it was to compress as much cotton as possible into the
hold of the ship. So the black influence entered by two routes: directly
through black American or West Indian seamen, and indirectly, through
the worksongs they heard on shore. But the complexity of the situation
does not end there. Many of the longshoremen and 'cotton screwers'
were white, usually seamen who dodged the North Atlantic winter by
working in these southern ports:

The men who yearly resort to Mobile Bay to screw cotton are, as may be imagined, a
rough set. They are mostly English and Irish sailors, who, leaving their vessels here,
remain until they have saved a hundred or more dollars, then ship for Liverpool,
London, or wherever port may be their favourite. (Nordhoff, *The Merchant Vessel:
A Sailor Boy's Voyages;* quoted in Hughill, *Shanties from the Seven Seas*, p. 17.)

With this background, it is not surprising that sea shanties and shore
worksongs have a great deal in common. Some actual songs are common
to both groups, for instance 'Hogeye Man' and 'Hanging Johnny',[18] but

is: 'I am called animal's child animal; I want chiefs in order to tie them. I am called animal's
child animal; I want chiefs in order to kill them. Nyanyara is not good; you said that I am not
good; you also are not good.' (Unfortunately no translations are available for the other two
examples.) The parallelism of these lines is reminiscent of the Hebrew psalms. It probably has
something to do with the blues singer's tendency to vary the first line of the couplet on
repetition; see for instance the one from Charley Patton quoted near the beginning of ch. 21.

[17] See *Shanties from the Seven Seas*, pp. 1–20.
[18] For the shore version of 'The Hog-Eye Man' see Sandburg, *The American Songbag*,
p. 380; for the shanty version, *Shanties from the Seven Seas*, p. 269. For the shore version of

more often it is a matter of scraps of tune, vague melodic resemblances, or couplets floating from one song to another. The sailors-cum-cotton-screwers mentioned above have more than a passing resemblance to the classical American hobo, and it is not surprising that themes and couplets from the sea shanties sometimes appear in hobo songs as well as worksongs. Hugill gives several of these floating couplets, 'to be found both in the shanties and negro and minstrel song, and in some cases in English and American folk-song and "hobo" songs':[19]

> Where there ain't no snow,
> And the winds don't blow.
>
> What d'you think we had for supper?
> Possum tails and a donkey's crupper.
>
> If whisky was a river and I could swim,
> I'd take a jump and dive right in.
>
> We dug his grave with a silver spade,
> And lowered him down with a golden chain.

(The third of these couplets appears in 'Rye Whiskey' (Ex. 74(b)) and the fourth in the 'One Kind Favour' blues (Ex. 73(e)). Hugill adds that 'there are countless others'.)

The exact *musical* relationship between the worksongs of sea and land is an interesting question. It is not just a matter of the relative importance of the African and European strains. There are sea shanties which are as African in character as any mainland worksongs ('Haul 'er Away', for instance[20]) yet even here there is a marked difference in style. In their melodic patterns the American worksongs show a kinship with the blues which, to my knowledge, is never found in the sea shanties, just as it is never found in West Indian music. The question is, just how far back does the bluesiness of these shore worksongs go? Those recorded from the 1920s onwards *sound* very archaic, but this may be deceptive. Songs which are orally transmitted, freely varied, and (so to speak) in constant use, can acquire the patina of age very quickly. Possibly these bluesy features go no further back than the development of the blues proper at the end of the nineteenth century. On the other hand, it may be that they go back to the early nineteenth century, or even before, and that they passed from the worksongs to the blues rather than the other way

'Hanging Johnny', sung by black soldiers during the Civil War, see Thomas Wentworth Higginson, 'Negro Spirituals', (quoted in Rose (ed.) *A Documentary History of Slavery in North America*, where 'Hangman Johnny' appears on p. 487). For the shanty version, see Hugill, *Shanties from the Seven Seas*, p. 284.

[19] *Shanties from the Seven Seas*, pp. 14–15.
[20] Hugill, *Shanties from the Seven Seas*, p. 316.

around. The few nineteenth-century worksong tunes known to us mostly look very much like shanty tunes. On the other hand, there is one, recorded by George Washington Cable in mid-century (Ex. 15) which already shows the triadic pattern typical of worksongs collected eighty or more year later. It is, moreover, in an African language. The reader may make of this scanty evidence what he likes. My own feeling is that we have here the isolated relic of an Afro-American tradition which gradually came to dominate the whole body of worksongs, and that it is from this tradition that what is most fundamentally bluesy in the blues derives.

SPIRITUALS

> Gimme that old time religion, it's good enough for me.
>
> Spiritual[21]

In the middle of the eighteenth century America was swept by a Great Awakening of religious feeling. That, at least, was what its supporters called it. To those who opposed the movement, it was a relapse into the most appalling barbarism, if not downright lunacy. Preachers roamed the country whipping congregations into agonies of repentance and ecstasies of religious fervour. Sometimes churches were too small to hold the multitudes they attracted, and services had to be held in open fields; or crowds followed them through the streets, singing at the tops of their voices. The more talented preachers produced fainting, convulsions, and the occasional suicide.[22]

Although this style of religion quickly lost favour among the bourgeoisie, it has persisted among some classes of Southern whites into the twentieth century. H. L. Mencken observed such a service in eastern Tennessee in 1925:

From the squirming and jabbering mass a young woman gradually detached herself—a woman not uncomely, with a pathetic homemade cap on her head. Her head jerked back, the veins of her neck swelled, and her fists went to her throat as if she were fighting for breath. She bent backward until she was like half a hoop. Then she suddenly snapped foward. We caught a flash of the whites of her eyes. Presently her whole body began to be convulsed—great throes that began at the shoulders and ended at the hips. She would leap to her feet, thrust her arms in air, and then hurl herself upon the heap. Her praying flattened out into a mere delirious caterwauling. I describe the thing discreetly, and as a strict behaviorist. The lady's subjective sensations I leave to infidel pathologists, privy to the works of Ellis, Freud and Moll. Whatever they were, they were obviously

---

[21] This is one of those spirituals that were current among both black and white. See White, *American Negro Folk-Songs*, pp. 91–2.
[22] For details of these events, see Hofstadter, *America at 1750*, pp. 217–93.

not painful, for they were accompanied by vast heavings and gurglings of a joyful and even ecstatic nature. And they seemed to be contagious, too, for soon a second penitent, also female, joined the first, and then came a third, and a fourth, and a fifth. The last one had an extraordinary violent attack. She began with mild enough jerks of the head, but in a moment she was bounding all over the place, like a chicken with its head cut off. ('The Hills of Zion'; reprinted in *The American Scene*, pp. 263–4.[23])

One might suspect Mencken of spoofing if his account did not tally so exactly with earlier observations, like this one of the camp meeting of 1803:

In some instances, persons who were not before known to be at all religious, or under any particular concern about it, would suddenly fall to the ground, and become strangely convulsed with what was called the jerks; the head and neck, and sometimes the body also, moving backwards and forwards with spasmodic violence, and so rapidly that the plaited hair of a woman's head might be heard to crack. . . . And then there was the jumping exercise, which sometimes approximated dancing; in which several persons might be seen standing perfectly erect, and springing upward without seeming to bend a joint of their bodies. (Bishop William Capers, autobiography, from the autobiographical section in Wightman, *Life of William Capers*, pp. 53–4; quoted in White, *American Negro Folk-Songs*, p. 43.)

Apart from this abandonment to extreme emotions, the Great Awakening had two characteristics. One was a fun-hating puritanism, with card playing, dancing, and secular music held in special abhorrence; and the other was a strong democratic tendency. It was not only that the Great Awakeners attacked traditional Christianity as lukewarm and hypocritical; in effect, they set themselves up against all forms of religious authority. Along with this went a social egalitarianism. Hell was hell and a sinner was a sinner, regardless of class, income—or colour.

It was natural that the Methodist and Baptist sects associated with the Great Awakening should take the lead in converting the slaves to Christianity. It was they who had the missionary zeal, and their brand of Christianity was much more to the taste of the blacks than the decorous services of the older denominations. The ecstatic behaviour popular among Awakeners had obvious parallels in African rituals, though it should be noted that the antics described above are a specifically *European* type of possession state. In Africa, as John Storm Roberts points out,[24] people in possession states tend to be much more sociable, taking part in singing and dancing and being reasonably aware of what is going on around them. When Bishop Capers mentions 'the jumping exercise, *which sometimes approximated dancing*', we may suspect an African influence.

[23] Ellis was Havelock Ellis, the pioneer sexologist, and Moll was one of his collaborators.
[24] See *Black Music of Two Worlds*, pp. 61 and 169.

Though there had been a trickle of conversions from the earliest times, it was only with the missionary efforts of the Awakeners that slaves began to be converted in large numbers. And even then it was uphill work, in the face of apathy or adherence to African traditions on the part of the slaves and frequent hostility on the part of their owners. Hymns sung by whites at that time fell broadly into three classes. There were, first, the typical staid psalm tunes of Protestant tradition, sung in the familiar slow, square, unadorned way. Then there was the style which had come to be known as 'the old way of singing', and which even in the eighteenth century was coming under fire from progressive clerics. In this, each line was 'lined out' by a precentor—it could be spoken, rhythmically chanted, or sung—before being sung by the congregation, very slowly and ornately. Thirdly, there was the fashion for making hymns out of folk tunes. 'Why', asked the Awakeners, 'should the devil have all the good tunes?'

It was the last two categories that were to be important in Afro-American religious music. 'The old way of singing' developed into the surge song, a type still used in both black and white churches today. The folk tune hymns developed into the best-known type of spiritual. Along with this use of folk tunes went a tendency to speed up the tempo of the hymn, and here one observer specifically blamed the blacks:

We have too, a growing evil, in the practice of singing in our places of public and society worship, *merry* airs, adapted from old *songs*, to hymns . . . most frequently composed and first sung by the illiterate *blacks* of the society. . . . In the *blacks'* quarter [of a camp meeting], the colored people get together, and sing for hours together, short scraps of disjointed affirmations, pledges, or prayers, lengthened out with long repetition *choruses*. These are all sung in the merry chorus-manner of the southern harvest field, or husking-frolic method of the slave blacks; and also very like the Indian dances. (John Fanning Watson, *Methodist Error*, pp. 15–16, 1819; quoted in Epstein, *Sinful Tunes and Spirituals*, p. 218.)

As this quotation indicates, influences in religious music were very much a two-way traffic. In addition to taking over European hymns, the blacks integrated many African practices into their idea of Christianity. The call-and-response pattern just referred to was one. Another was the shuffling, circular dance which came to be known as the 'ring shout'. (The word 'shout', by the way, has been conjectured to be of Afro-Arab origin.[25]) Another Africanism was the chanted sermon, which even today is strikingly similar to some African styles of praise-singing, as well as actual African sermons.[26] The line between the spiritual and the

[25] Lorenzo Turner derived it from the Arabic word *saut*, used by West African Muslims for the procession around the *Kaaba*. See Oliver, *Savannah Syncopators*, pp. 56–7.

[26] See Exx. 31 and 32. For remarks on African chanted sermons, see Roberts, *Black Music of Two Worlds*, p. 177.

chanted sermon is often vague. Fragments of spirituals, both verbal and tuneful, often make their way into sermons,[27] and it seems probable that parts of sermons could also be worked up into spirituals. 'City of Refuge' (Ex. 23) may well be a case in point judging by both its melodic structure and the following reminiscence:

... I have seen my father stop preaching suddenly and walk down to the front edge of the pulpit and breathe into a whispering song. One of his most effective ones was:

Run! Run! Run to the City of Refuge, children!
Run! Oh, Run! Or else you'll be consumed.

Whereupon the congregation working like a Greek chorus behind him, would take up the song and the mood and hold it over for a while even after he had gone back into the sermon at high altitude. (Zora Neale Hurston, *Dust Tracks on a Road*, pp. 140–1; quoted in Oliver, *Songsters and Saints*, p. 144.)

And there is no reason why some of the spirituals may not have been based on actual African tunes, simply refitted with pious English words. Numerous melodic parallels have been traced between spirituals and African tunes, but this may be a matter of extreme Africanization of European tunes.[28] At this date it is probably impossible to tell.

It is important to realize that there was a great deal of racial mingling in early religious services, especially among the Methodists and Baptists. It was only later that exclusively black churches arose, and even so the division has never been complete among some Pentecostal sects. The races were certainly singing together in 1751, when the Revd Samuel Davies described the black section of his congregation 'breaking out in a torrent of sacred harmony, enough to bear away the whole congregation to heaven',[29] and in 1816, when a traveller in Woodville, Mississippi, wrote that 'They sung in ancient style, lining the Psalm ... both white and black, frequently making discordant sounds, grating to an ear accustomed to correct music.'[30] At the great camp meetings of the early nineteenth century, as we have seen, blacks taught whites the 'merry chorus-manner of the southern harvest field'. From the black preachers, some of whom were admired even by white congregations, their white colleagues learnt the art of the chanted sermon.[31]

There have always been white as well as black spirituals; the very word

[27] See Rosenberg, *The Art of the American Folk Preacher*, pp. 16–19.
[28] See the points listed by Kolinski, cited in Roberts, *Black Music of Two Worlds*, p. 168.
[29] From a letter of 28 June 1751 to 'Mr. Bellamy of Bethlem in New England'. See Epstein, *Sinful Tunes and Spirituals*, p. 104.
[30] Pearse, *A Narrative of the Life of James Pearse*, p. 10. Pearse was a native of Massachusetts. Quoted in Epstein, *Sinful Tunes and Spirituals*, p. 202.
[31] See Rosenberg, *The Art of the American Folk Preacher*, p. 10: '... there are whites in the eastern Kentucky hills and in parts of Ohio and Pennsylvania who still preach this way. ... In Kentucky, white "old-time country preachers," as their neighbors call them, were surprised to learn that the chanted sermon was not exclusively theirs.'

'spiritual', as its book-learned air rather indicates, was used by whites before being adopted by blacks. It denoted the new, lively, popular type of hymn as distinct from the old, staid variety.[32] There is a fairly extensive common ground between black and white religious music, where there has been so much mutual influence that racial classification becomes pretty meaningless.

The spirituals were the first Afro-American songs to become popular among middle-class whites—that is, if we discount the highly dubious Nigger Minstrel productions—and this is undoubtedly in part because they were largely of European origin. Newman White, in *American Negro Folk-Songs*, devotes a page and a half to a list of black songs, sacred and secular, taken over by whites. He writes:

The well-known song of the Creation, beginning 'Lord he thought he'd make a man,' has come to me from several Negro sources, but the only times I have heard it sung were first by a lady who had learned it from students at the University of Alabama, and second, by several students of Randolph-Macon Woman's College, in Virginia, who did not seem to regard it in the least as pertaining exclusively to the Negro. (p. 28).

And in this they were probably right.

DANCE SONGS

The practice of dancing to song, with or without instruments as well, is widespread and no doubt age-old. In Africa, particularly, dance and song are intimately associated aspects of a single art. European dance music is usually purely instrumental, but there is an important exception in the mainly Celtic tradition of 'diddling' or 'mouth music'. Here, as in many forms of African song where meaning is subordinate to melody, the words consist either of traditional verses jumbled together with little regard to order, or improvisations, or nonsense syllables. This type of 'mouth music' was popular in America from early times. 'Dancing they are all fond of,' wrote one observer in 1737,[33] 'especially when they can get a fiddle, or bagpipe; at this they will continue hours together, may, [nay?] so attach'd are they to this darling amusement, that if they can't procure musick, they will sing for themselves. Musick, and musical instruments being very scarce in Carolina.' Which incidentally shows again how much appreciated slave musicians must have been in those days.

[32] 'Almost all the hymn-books of the evangelical and dissenting sects of the whites prior to 1860 were called "hymns and spiritual songs"; the spiritual songs being of a much more informal character and occupying a separate section in the back of the hymn-book.' (White, *American Negro Folk-Songs*, p. 41.)

[33] Brickell, *The Natural History of North Carolina*; quoted in Land, *Bases of the Plantation Society*, p. 202.

Like other forms of British folk-song the dance song was taken up by the blacks, who made it so much their own that before long the whites were borrowing their own songs back from them. About a hundred years after our quotation of 1737 the famous 'Zip Coon' appeared in print, to the catchy, Irish-sounding tune usually known as 'Turkey in the Straw'. I quote the first verse and chorus:

> O ole Zip Coon he is a larned skoler, (three times)
> Sings posum up a gum tree an coony in a holler.
> Posum up a gum tree, cooney on a stump, (three times)
> Den over dubble trubble, Zip coon will jump.
> O Zip a duden duden duden zip a duden day.
> O Zip a duden duden duden duden duden day.
> O Zip a duden duden duden duden duden day.
> Zip a duden duden duden zip a duden day.

Songs of this type are sometimes described as 'pseudo-Negro', but there are strong suggestions that genuine black influences are at work here. In contrast to the tune, which seems to be entirely European in style, the words have several features in common with genuine Afro-American song. There is more repetition of phrases than would be usual in British or white American folk-song. In particular, notice how the first line of a couplet is stated three times. It is a pattern most uncommon in British folk-song, but very typical of the blues.

The mention of *wild* animals is another trait with more in common with Africa than Britain. On the other hand, the chorus, one of the earliest recorded instances of scat singing, is probably closer to British diddling than similar things in Africa. Compare it, for instance, with the following example which, though actually from Newfoundland, is completely within the British tradition:

> Da dal la da da dal la dee dal la da da dal la,
> Da dal la da da dal la dal dee dal la da da dal la,
> Dal la da da dal la dee dal la da da dal la da
> Da dal la da da dal la da da dal la die ya. (etc., for four more lines.)
>
> Oh some love the girls who are pretty in the face,
> And more love the girls who are neat around the waist,
> But give me the girl with a wiggle and a twist,
> At the bottom of her belly is a cuckoo's nest.[35]

As with other Afro-American genres, it can be difficult to distinguish what is Africanized British in the dance songs from what came directly from Africa. Many African songs have melodic lines strongly remin-

---

[34] Reproduced in fascimile, complete with title-page, in *Popular Songs of Nineteenth-Century America*, pp. 258–60.
[35] 'The Cuckoo's Nest', sung by Mrs Nellie Musseau, 1960, in Peacock, *Songs of the Newfoundland Outports*, vol. 3, pp. 259–60. The tune is related to the two in Ex. 117.

iscent of certain American 'reels', like the familiar 'Shortening Bread'.
Yet 'Shortening Bread' is widely thought to be of white origin, and its
opening lines:

> Two little niggers lyin' in de bed;
> One was sick and tuther dead.
> Sent fur de docter and docter said
> Dey eat too much of dat shortnin' bread.[36]

suggest a parody of the following couplet, from the predominantly white
folk-song 'Single Girl', or 'The Married Woman's Lament':

> Two little children a-layin' in the bed,
> Both of 'em so hungry they caint raise up their head . . .[37]

   Some of the early rock and roll hits, such as 'Long Tall Sally' or 'Good
Golly Miss Molly' are very much in the style of the traditional dance
song, heavily Africanized but ultimately of British origin, with here and
there a glimmer of British folk poetry. Take the following well-known
verse from the 1955 hit, 'Tutti Frutti':

> I got a gal her name's Sue
> She knows just what to do.
> I've been to the east, I've been to the west,
> But she's the gal I love the best.[38]

The initial couplet was recorded as long ago as 1927 by a banjoist called
Papa Charlie Jackson, in almost the same words:

> Now I know a lady, name of Sue,
> She like to know just what to do . . .[39]

Even in 1927 Papa Charlie was a decidedly old-fashioned performer
(Paul Oliver describes his banjo playing as 'probably the closest to that
of the previous century that could be heard on disc'). The 'I got a gal . . .'
opening, in all its variants, is also common in Anglo-American dance
songs. It is apparently of American origin, whether white or black it is
difficult to say. The second couplet has a close relative in a play-party
song—that is, a dance song—from the Ozarks:

> Go choose to the East, go choose to the West,
> Go choose the gal that you love best . . .[40]

And here the ' . . . east . . . west' formula is clearly of British origin,

[36] White, *American Negro Folk-Songs*, p. 193. There are numerous variations.
[37] Randolph, *Ozark Folksongs*, vol. 3, 'Humorous and Play-Party Songs', p. 70.
[38] Words and music by Richard Penniman ('Little Richard'), D. La Bostrie, and J. Lubin. In
A Hundred Golden Oldies, pp. 251–3.
[39] On the record Paramount 12501, Chicago, 1927; quoted in Oliver, *Songsters and Saints*,
p. 40.
[40] Randolph, *Ozark Folksongs*, vol. 3, 'Humorous and Play-Party Songs', p. 345.

cropping up often in British ballads popular in the United States particularly 'Barbara Allen', 'The Gypsy Laddie', and 'Lord Bateman'.

In the same way, that venerable family of bawdy songs to which 'The Maid of Amsterdam' and 'Roll Me over in the Clover' belong has at least one rhythm-and-blues relative in Chuck Berry's 'Reelin' and Rockin' '; only instead of the usual 'anatomical progression' (for instance 'This is number two and I had her by the shoe . . . This is number three and I had her by the knee . . .', etc.) his progression is chronological: 'I looked at my watch and it was quarter to one . . . quarter to two . . . quarter to three . . .'.[41]

BALLADS AND BLUES

There is a large body of American song which is neither religious nor intended for work or dancing, but otherwise could be almost anything—lullabies, children's songs, street cries, or ballads, to name only a few obvious categories. The best known of these types are, on the Anglo-American side, the ballad, and on the Afro-American side, the blues: which, however, cover a multitude of complex racial interactions and intermediate types.

It seems likely that every Anglo-American song-type has been taken into the Afro-American repertory at some time or other. The old ballads have been collected from blacks often enough to suggest that they had considerable currency among them until about the mid-nineteenth century.[42] By the twentieth century they had all but dropped out of the repertory, but not before leaving a deep mark on the early blues and blues ballads. We have already seen how British stanzaic patterns were retained in the 'John Henry' ballad. In many versions of this song the following verse appears:

> Who's gonna shoe your pretty little feet?
> Who's gonna glove your hand?
> Who's gonna kiss your red ruby lips?
> Who's gonna be your man?[43]

[41] The basic theme of this family has been traced to an item in Thomas Heywood's comedy *The Rape of Lucrece* (1640): for the words and circumstances, see Hugill, *Sea Shanties*, pp. 91–2. Apart from the basic theme, certain phrases in Berry's song suggest British or Anglo-American influence, for instance the title and the phrase 'We boogied in the kitchen and we boogied in the hall': cf. 'She brought him through the kitchen, She brought him through the hall', in 'The Jolly Tinker' (Kennedy, *Folksongs of Britain and Ireland*, p. 405); 'It's whisper'd in parlour, it's whisper'd in ha' ', in 'The Broom Blooms Bonie' (Bronson, *Traditional Tunes of the Child Ballads*, vol. 1, p. 253; originally published in 1796), and 'They used me in the kitchen, they used me in the hall' in 'The Barley Corn' (O Lochlainn, *Irish Street Ballads*, pp. 176–7).
[42] See the chapter 'The Negro's Part in Transmitting the Traditional Songs and Ballads' in Scarborough, *On the Trail of Negro Folk-Songs*.
[43] A. Lomax, *The Folk Songs of North America*, p. 216.

These lines, which are completely irrelevant to the John Henry story, are to be found in various traditional ballads,[44] most notably 'The Lass of Roch Royal':

> O who will shoe my bony [bonny] foot?
> Or who will glove my hand?
> Or who will bind my midle jimp [slender]
> With the broad lilly [linen] band?[45]

Scraps of British folk poetry crop up in the strangest places. Railroad Bill, the American desperado, seems to have had a parent in the English Dirty Bill:

ENGLISH CHILDREN'S SONG	BLUES BALLAD
I'm Dirty Bill from Vinegar Hill Never had a bath and never will.[46]	Railroad Bill, Railroad Bill, He never work, an' he never will . . .[47]

And the opening lines of 'The Roving Ploughboy-O':

> Come saddle tae me my auld grey mare
> Come saddle tae me my pony-O
> And I will tak' the road and I'll go far away
> After the roving ploughboy-O[48]

are obviously the ancestor of the corresponding part of Charley Patton's 'Pony Blues':

> Hitch up my pony, saddle up my black mare. (twice)
> I'm gonna find a rider, baby, in the world somewhere.[49]

Here the initial line is retained and a new line made to rhyme with it. In other instances only the sentiment and general cast of stanza is retained:

ANGLO-AMERICAN BALLAD	EARLY BLUES
Do you remember last Saturday night Down at my father's dwelling? You passed the drink to the ladies all around And slighted Barbara Ellen.[50]	Where were you las' Saturday night, When I lay sick in my bed? You down town wid some other ole girl, Wasn't here to hold my head.[51]

or merely an effective formula:

---

[44] Coffin, in *The British Traditional Ballad in North America*, lists two dozen songs 'corrupted', as he puts it, by this interpolation (p. 81).

[45] Harvard MS Eng. 512, pp. 151–8, no. 114; quoted in Kinsley (ed.), *The Oxford Book of Ballads*, p. 147.

[46] Opie and Opie, *The Love and Language of Schoolchildren*, p. 20. The resemblance to 'Railroad Bill' is pointed out in Cohen, *Long Steel Rail*, p. 127.

[47] Odum, 'Folk-Song and Folk-Poetry as Found in the Secular Songs of the Southern Negroes', p. 289.

[48] Kennedy, *Folksongs of Britain and Ireland*, p. 571.

[49] Evans, *Big Road Blues*, pp. 146–7.

[50] Sharp, *English Folk Songs from the Southern Appalachians*, vol. 1, p. 193.

[51] Odum and Johnson, *The Negro and his Songs*, p. 185.

SCOTTISH BALLAD	BLUES BALLAD
The first shot that the foresters fired It wounded him on the knee; And the next shot that the foresters fired His heart's blood blin't his e'e.[52]	The first time she shot him, he staggered, The next time she shot him, he fell, The last time she shot him, O Lawdy, There was a new man's face in hell . . .[53]

As well as the ballads quoted above, there is a type of British lyric song that had a far more direct influence on the early blues. This is that large body of complaints about the fickleness, mendacity, unreliability, heartlessness, etc., of the opposite sex. The stanzas, or even couplets, are mostly self-contained, floating in and out of countless songs on the theme of unrequited, abandoned, or evanescent love. A comprehensive collection of these songs, British and American, would make a bulky volume. 'Meeting is pleasure and parting is grief, And a false-hearted lover is worse than a thief.' 'Love is pleasing and love is teasing, and love's a pleasure when it first is new; But love grows colder as love grows older, and fades away like the morning dew.' 'I wish, I wish—but all in vain—I wish I were a maid again. A maid again I ne'er shall be Till apples grow on a orange tree.' 'They'll hug you and kiss you and tell you more lies Than the hairs on your head or the stars in the skies'—or, in American versions, 'the cross-ties on the railroad or the stars in the skies'. Such are some of the familar lines and sentiments.

There were several reasons why this song family made a special appeal to black singers. The basic theme was one of complaint, and complaint songs were an important African tradition. The detachable, floating couplets or verses suited the method of the black musician. And the tone was personal, though the 'black: personal, white: impersonal' dichotomy has been rather overdone.[54]

If black musicians were deeply indebted to the Anglo-American song tradition, there is more than a little evidence that they left their mark on it in return. The fine variant of 'Lady Isabel and the Elf Knight' that Dorothy Scarborough got from a black woman in Waco, Texas, has little to distinguish it from a white version, apart from a trace of Negro dialect ('dat' for 'that', and so on) and the substitution of the first person for the third.[55] The tune, too, is almost identical with some that Cecil Sharp collected in the Appalachians.[56] Its one peculiarity is that the rhythm

---

[52] From 'Johnny o' Cocklesmuir', Ord, *Bothy Songs and Ballads*, p. 469.
[53] From 'Frankie and Johnny', A. Lomax, *The Penguin Book of American Folk Songs*, p. 121.
[54] For more on this song family see 'The Ladder of Thirds' in ch. 20.
[55] See Scarborough, *On the Trail of Negro Folk-Songs*, pp. 43–5.
[56] See *English Folk Songs from the Southern Appalachians*, vol. 1, pp. 5–13, especially version D on p. 8.

embodies typical Afro-American syncopations. Could it be that some of these lightly Africanized ballad tunes passed back into white use? From the frequent suggestions of a slight bluesiness in Appalachian ballad tunes, I believe that this did happen, and probably as early as the time of the Civil War.

By no means all ballads were traditional. Both in Britain and America anonymous bards celebrated newsworthy events in song form. Though the events were topical, the treatment was bound by convention. As similar events occurred over and over again—the train crash, the shipwreck, the bad man coming to a sticky end, the wronged woman disposing of her straying lover—familiar stanzas were pressed into use by changes of name, place, and detail. These changes might be of the slightest, or at the other extreme, the song might be substantially a new composition, with nothing more than a heavy reliance on traditional formulas. Both whites and blacks participated in the composition of these ballads, and some of them, like the saga of Frankie and Johnny, passed freely between the races.

Students of American folk ballads make a distinction between the 'vulgar ballad' and the 'blues ballad'. The vulgar ballad, almost exclusively a white form, consists of some newsworthy event more or less coherently related in journalistic doggerel, and often distributed on broadsides. The blues ballads were predominantly black in origin, but with a good deal of white influence. Most of the earliest versions were collected from whites—but then, we must remember that the collectors were white too. The blues ballad tells a story, but it does so in a much more fragmentary and elliptical way than the vulgar ballad. In the best examples this disjointedness is a calculated effect, not a fault. Where singers add extra verses—as they do, at great length, in the Frankie ballad—it is not so much to make the story clear as to add picturesque detail or make a humorous or ironic point. The verses, as in the blues generally, admit a great deal of rearrangement and draw heavily on tradition.[57]

As well as ballads in the strict sense, there is also an important British tradition of songs of topical complaint. For centuries such people as prisoners, vagrants, soldiers, sailors, and the poor generally have made up songs lamenting their lot and attacking authority.[58] Many of these songs passed over into North America, usually in a freely adapted form. For instance:

---

[57] For a recent discussion of the blues ballads, see Oliver, 'Natural-Born Men: Survivors of the Ballad Tradition', ch. 8 in *Songsters and Saints*. He points out that these songs are very poorly represented in the 'race' records catering for the black American market of the 1920s.

[58] For a selection of such songs, see part 4, 'Time to Remember the Poor', in Palmer, *A Touch on the Times*.

1. ENGLISH 'HARD TIMES' SONGS

(*a*)   O 'tis of an old butcher, I must bring him in
He charge two shillings a pound, and thinks it no sin
Slaps his thumb on the scale-weights and makes them go down
He swears it's good weight yet it wants half a pound[59]

(*b*)   You will see the poor tradesmen a-walking the street
From morning till night for employment to seek
And scarcely they've got any shoes on their feet
And it's, oh the hard times of old England,
In old Eng-e-land very hard times.[60]

AN AMERICAN PRISON SONG, 'HARD TIMES'

The lice and the chinches [bedbugs] are long as a rail, 'tis hard,
The lice and the chinches are long as a rail,
They raise their bristles and shake their tails, 'tis hard,
With the doors all locked and barred.
I said, 'Mister jailer, please lend me your knife,
For the bugs in your jail have threatened my life.'
'Tis hard times in the Cryderville jail,
'Tis hard times, poor boy.

And here's to the sheriff I'd like to forgot [i.e., I almost forgot], 'tis hard,
And here's to the sheriff I'd like to forgot,
He's the damndest old rascal in the whole blame lot, 'tis hard,
With the doors all locked and barred.
Your pockets he'll pick and your clothes he will sell,
Get drunk on the money, God damn him to hell.
'Tis hard times, etc.[61]

2. BRITISH PRISON SONG

At eight o'clock our skilly comes in,
Sometimes thick and sometimes thin,
But devil a word we must not say—
It's bread and water all next day.[62]

AN AMERICAN PRISON SONG, 'THE MIDNIGHT SPECIAL'

When you wake up in de mawnin',
When de ding-dong ring,
Go marchin' to de table,

[59] From 'The Rigs of the Time', in Kennedy, *Folksongs of Britain and Ireland*, p. 523.
[60] From 'The Hard Times of Old England', ibid., p. 505.
[61] A. Lomax, *The Folk Songs of North America*, pp. 438–9 (verses 3 and 5). Described by Woody Guthrie, the folk singer, as 'sung in every buggy, lousy jail from New Jersey to Portland, Oregon, from the days of the Revolution to the present' (ibid., p. 428.) For a list of other American 'hard times' songs, see Randolph, *Ozark Folksongs*, vol. 2, 'Songs of the South and West' p. 277.
[62] Collected by H. E. D. Hammond in Beaminster, Dorset, in 1906. In Vaughan Williams and Lloyd, *The Penguin Book of English Folk Songs*, p. 39.

Meet de same ol' thing.

Knife an' fork-a on de table,
Nothin' in my pan;
Ever say anything about it,
Have's trouble wid de man.[63]

3. SCOTTISH 'TINKER'S' SONG

Oh, come a' ye tramps an' hawkers an' gaitherers o' bla',
That tramps the countrie roon' an' roon', come listen ane and a'.
I'll tell tae you a rovin' tale and sights that I have seen,
Far up into the snowy North and South by Gretna Green.[64]

AMERICAN HOBO SONG, 'WANDERING'

I been a wanderin'
Early and late,
New York City
To the Golden Gate,
An' it looks like
I'm never gonna cease my wanderin'.[65]

I am not claiming that there is necessarily a direct link between these examples; it is enough that the sentiments are so similar. In the frequently multiracial climate of the American underworld, it was easy for such songs to blend with a corresponding African tradition of songs of complaint and insult. In this very widespread African form, the singer airs a grudge, insults an adversary, or scores off authority in a form which is at once ritualized and topical. The general type is familiar from the West Indian calypso and the kind of sea shanty where satirical remarks are made about the captain or first mate. An account of 1804 describes the ancestor of this sort of calypso:

The slaves [in the fields] then work in a long string, and follow each other in regular order. Some one takes the lead and breaks out with a song, to which there is always a chorus. In this they all join. . . . These songs are not without their jibes; sometimes too levelled at the master, and then they are sung with peculiar vivacity, when the negroes come under his window or near his house. They remind him of promised and ungiven holidays, additional allowance or change in the kind of their food, when long sameness has rendered variety desirable.

The facility with which the negroes dress every occurrence in rhime, and give it a metre, rude indeed, but well adapted to the purpose of raillery or sarcasm, is no slight proof of genius perhaps; as well as of vivacity. (Caines, *The History of*

---

[63] J. and A. Lomax, *Negro Folk Songs as Sung by Lead Belly*, pp. 222–3. For a full discussion of this song, see Cohen, *Long Steel Rail*, pp. 478–82.

[64] From 'Tramps an' Hawkers', Buchan and Hall, *The Scottish Folksinger*, p. 122.

[65] Sandburg, *The American Songbag*, pp. 188–9.

the General Council and General Assembly of the Leeward Islands . . ., vol. 1, pp. 110–11; quoted in Epstein, *Sinful Tunes and Spirituals*, pp. 186–7.[66])

The product of this Afro-British fusion was one of the most important elements in the development of the blues, along with the 'careless love' blues, the 'dirty mistreating woman' (or 'man') blues, and the 'far from home' blues. The bedbug stanza in 'Cryderville Jail', for instance, has its relatives in the early blues:

> Honey, babe, Honey babe, bring me de broom,
> De lices an' chinches 'bout to take my room.[67]

> My house is full of bedbugs, and chinches just crawl around (twice)
> But they bite me so hard at night I can't hardly stay on the ground.[68]

AFRICAN SURVIVALS

African call-and-response singing profoundly influenced American worksongs, spirituals, and dance songs. But not all African singing was call-and-response. There was also a strong tradition of solo singing, without the participation of a chorus. This, too, survived in America and profoundly influenced Afro-American song.

The history of these forms is necessarily murky, but there is at least enough evidence to distinguish two main types, the recitative and the melodic. African recitative styles lie behind both the chanted sermon and the talking blues. Here the words are the main thing, and the delivery is often nearer to speaking than singing. In the melodic style, by contrast, the melody is so much the more important thing that words may be reduced to a minimum, as in the one-line songs observed in the United States as early as the mid-nineteenth century.[69] Such one-line-to-a-stanza songs persisted into the twentieth century, being especially associated with the knife blues.[70] In Leadbelly's 'Blind Lemon Blues', we see how a stanza from an old Scottish ballad could be transformed:

> *from* 'THE LASS OF ROCH ROYAL':
> I dreamed a dream now since yestreen
> That I never dreamed before;
> I dream'd that the lass of the Rochroyall
> Was knocking at the door.[71]

---

[66] A world-famous modern example of this type is 'The Banana Boat Song' ('daylight come and me wan go home').

[67] Odum and Johnson, *The Negro and his Songs*, p. 203.

[68] Courlander, *Negro Folk Music, U.S.A.*, p. 135.

[69] See Kemble, *Journal*, p. 161.

[70] See Odum and Johnson, *The Negro and his Songs*, pp. 223–7.

[71] Harvard MS Eng. 512, pp. 151–8, no. 114; quoted in Kinsley (ed.), *The Oxford Book of Ballads*, p. 147.

from 'BLIND LEMON BLUES':
    'Dream las' night an' all night night befo'
    Lawd, I dream last night an' all night night befo',
    Dream las' night an' all night night befo'.'

[*Chanted:*] When she 'gin to sing, the li'l' boy jumped up; it woke him. Li'l' boy run to his mamma an' say, 'Mamma, what did you dream them las' two nights?' An' here what she tol' her son:

    [*Sung:*] I heard your papa knockin' on my do'.
        Lawd, I heard your papa knockin' on my do',
        I heard your papa knockin' on my do'.[72]

Sometimes words are dispensed with altogether, and the performer merely hums or vocalizes wordlessly, a practice recorded from ante-bellum times:

Judge W. R. Boyd, of Texas, remembers much of the slave-life in the South, and recalls vividly the songs the Negroes on the plantations used to sing, not only at their labor, but as they went to and from their work. For instance, he says that the slaves used to give a peculiar singing call, something between a yodel and a chant, as they went to their work in the early morning. My mother also has told me of this, and has spoken of its weird, uncanny effect of eerie, remote pathos.

    Hoo ah hoo! Hoo ah hoo! Hoo ah hoo!
    Hoo ah hoo! Hoo ah hoo! Hoo ah hoo!
    Hoo ah hoo! Hoo ah hoo! Hoo ah hoo!
    Hoo ah hoo! Hoo ah hoo! Hoo ah hoo!

(Scarborough, *On the Trail of Negro Folk-Songs*, p. 226.)

Or—again very characteristically—such techniques are interspersed with verbal singing, as in some African styles, for instance the Watutsi song, Ex. 27.

Such songs are known both as 'hollers' and 'field blues', the second term probably being preferable. 'Holler', though sanctioned by usage, suggests a loud cry, whereas these improvised blues were often sung softly to oneself: it would be better confined to real 'hollering', to attract attention or communicate over long distances. The 'field blues', as the name suggests, were often sung in the fields, but by no means confined to them. They were generally unaccompanied for lack of an instrument, but singers sometimes fitted their improvisation to a simple accompaniment when they could; these accompanied field blues are probably as old as the unaccompanied variety.

But whatever the form, we can do little more than speculate about these shadowy but immensely important predecessors of the blues proper. It is not surprising that we hear hardly anything of them until about 1900. As Fanny Kemble observed:

[72] J. and A. Lomax, *Negro Folk Songs as Sung by Lead Belly*, p. 165.

I have heard that many of the masters and overseers on these plantations prohibit melancholy tunes or words, and encourage nothing but cheerful music and senseless words, deprecating the effect of sadder strains upon the slaves, whose peculiar musical sensibility might be expected to make them especially excitable by any songs of a plaintive character, and having any reference to their particular hardships. (*Journal,* pp. 161–2.)

These words rather suggest that 'songs of a plaintive character' had a general underground currency, else why be at such pains to prohibit them? Such a disapproving attitude on the part of the authorities could only reinforce the folk singer's secretiveness. According to Lafcadio Hearn, 'the colored roustabouts are in the highest degree suspicious of a man who approaches them with a note-book and pencil'.[73] It is an attitude found among white singers too, but the black musician obviously had especially strong reasons for keeping his mouth shut. Even in recent years it has been noticed that blues singers have one repertory for black audiences and another for whites.[74] Small wonder that these pre-blues and proto-blues styles have sunk into almost total oblivion.

[73] '*Levee Life*', in *Selected Writing*, p. 172.
[74] See Ferris, 'Racial Repertoires among Blues Performers'.

Part Two
The Theoretical Foundation

This section is an attempt to enlarge conventional musical theory to take care of the peculiarities of popular music. The first chapter introduces the method of analysis used in this book, and the next three deal with topics somewhat neglected in classical theory: mode, the question of what constitutes a musical whole, and the beat. As in Part One, I must emphasize that this section makes no claims to comprehensiveness. It is merely an attempt to plug a few gaps, and I have tried to make it as mercifully brief as possible.

10. THE MATRIX

Artists love to be limited.

G.K. Chesterton[1]

The more art is controlled, limited, worked over, the more it is free.

Igor Stravinsky[2]

ERNEST NEWMAN wrote of Beethoven that 'a great deal of his work can easily be shown to be a series of variations upon some ten or twelve protoplasmic cell-formulae; and the same holds good of all other composers'.[3] This is true, and it is all the truer of music which is content to follow traditional lines and aims for neither novelty nor variety. In folk music, which is so much more a natural growth than composed music, the biological metaphor comes that much nearer to being a literal truth.

A notated composition is like a blueprint. It is an unaltering prescription for a performance; and even if this prescription leaves some latitude to the performer, it does not change in itself. In unnotated music there is no blueprint. Change is constant. In a single performance variations will usually be made in a repeated tune. When a single tune serves different purposes, it will take on a different form each time. In adding a new item to his repertory, the performer will probably alter it: perhaps slightly and unconsciously, perhaps radically and quite deliberately.

One might well think that this constant flux would soon change a melody out of all recognition. This does sometimes happen, but it is remarkable how often it does not. For mysterious reasons, some tune families will develop scores of highly diverse variants, while others will retain the same shape for centuries. Tunes written down during the Renaissance period have been collected from folk singers in much the same form centuries later.[4] Evidently in the latter case there is something, a kind of framework, that prevents variants from diverging too much from the basic pattern. It is as though the folk process were

---

[1] *Manalive*, part II, ch. 2, p. 258 (around the middle of the chapter).

[2] *Poetics of Music*, ch. 3, p. 63.

[3] *From the World of Music*, p. 180.

[4] Compare, for instance, 'Since Robin Hood' in Weelkes, *Ayeres or Phantasticke Spirites* (1608) with the 'Helston Furry Dance' (1802) reprinted in Palmer, *The Book of English Country Songs*, pp. 222–3.

playing countless variations on a theme, without ever forgetting it. Whether the variation is conscious or unconscious, confined to one performer or spread between many, there are details which change, and something basic to every variation which does not change. The word 'matrix' is sometimes used for that something:

The song [Camborne Hill] is a parody on *Jack Hall* . . . the ballad about the chimney-sweep burglar who was brought up Tyburn Hill on a cart to be hanged. (*Admiral Benbow* and *The Irish Famine Song* also use this as a matrix.) (Kennedy, *Folksongs of Britain and Ireland*, p. 229.)

. . . a maqām [in classical Arabic music] is marked by certain melodic patterns and is a 'matrix for composition', not merely a note-series . . . (*The History of Music in Sound*, vol. 1, p. 37.)

'Matrix' in this sense means something close to the theme of the classical set of variations, or rather those elements in the theme which are repeated in the variations. It also has something in common with the 'forms' of traditional classical theory. It is in this sense that I have decided to use the word in this book—not without misgivings, since it threatens to become part of the vocabulary of pseudo-scientific humbug, like 'paradigm' or 'parameter'.[5]

Like the textbook 'forms' these matrices suffer from the disadvantage of being too broad for analytical purposes, whether they refer to folk tune families or Asian improvisation patterns. To be truly useful, the pattern as a whole must be broken down into smaller and yet smaller patterns, like the fleas in the rhyme:

> So, Nat'ralists observe, a Flea
> Hath smaller Fleas that on him prey,
> And these have smaller Fleas to bite 'em,
> And so proceed *ad infinitum* . . .[6]

A brief analysis of a simple and familiar tune will illustrate this process (Ex. 4).

Ex. 4   'Pop Goes the Weasel'

---

[5] The use of the word 'matrix' was originally suggested to me by Arthur Koestler's *The Act of Creation*. What he meant by the term was (roughly) an established set of ideas, creativity being the linking or 'bisociation' of two of these sets. The relation between my 'matrix' and Koestler's, though real, is distant. In particular, musical matrices link up not only by twos, but by threes, fours, and dozens.

[6] Swift, 'On Poetry', lines 337–40.

The following are some of the more obvious matrices at work here:

1. the major mode
2. $\frac{6}{8}$ time
3. four-bar phrasing
4. a regular beat
5. the rhyming tune structure
6. ending both halves of the tune with the same figure
7. melodic climax
8. the perfect cadence
9. the three primary triads in the implicit harmony.

It is important to realize that the matrices are not the actual notes themselves, but well understood patterns into which they fall: not, for instance, the notes c′ d′ e′ f′ g′ a′, but the major scale; not the rhythm ♩ ♪♩ ♪| ♪♪♪♩. |, but the concept of '$\frac{6}{8}$ time'. In this case, it is easy to identify the principle matrices, because our example, in its humble way, is a typical classical tune, and therefore describable in technical terms bequeathed to us by centuries of musical scholarship. When we come to deal with music that has not received the attention of generations of theorists, it will not be so easy to identify the matrices or put into words the effects they are meant to produce.

Our list of matrices could easily be refined. The major scale, for instance, is itself a complex idea, implying, among other things, the intervals of the fifth, the fourth, and the major third; and these in turn depend on the idea of the precisely fixed melodic interval. Similarly, the perfect cadence implies the dominant and tonic chords, the concept of the keynote, and the basic feeling of returning home.

The matrix is considered here for its structural value, apart from any emotional effect it may have. The major mode is bright, the minor dark; slow tempos express repose, fast tempos animation. Deryck Cooke devoted a whole book, *The Language of Music*, to exploring the emotional values of such basic musical formulas. I make no attempt at this sort of emotional analysis. What gives shape to a tune? What makes a harmonic progression intelligible and satisfying? That is the sort of question I have tried to answer.

THE SUBJECTIVITY OF THE MATRIX

HAMLET: Do you see that Clowd? that's almost in shape like a Camell.
POLONIUS: By'th' Misse, and it's like a Camell indeed.
HAMLET: Me thinkes it is like a Weazell.
POLONIUS: It is back'd like a Weazell.

HAMLET: Or like a Whale?
POLONIUS: Verie like a Whale.

Shakespeare[7]

A matrix is a unit of musical communication. In ideal circumstances, it is intended by the composer (which can also mean the performer when there is an element of improvisation) and perceived by the listener. But circumstances are not always ideal. A matrix may be intended by the composer but remain unperceived by the listener. Or, conversely, the listener may misinterpret a matrix, or even detect one that is not there at all. The human brain will go to great lengths to make sense of the unfamiliar, and just as we read faces into clouds or the stains on walls, so strange musical idioms will be interpreted in familiar terms. A $\frac{5}{8}$ rhythm is heard as a distorted $\frac{3}{4}$; the equitetratonic scale, in which the octave is divided into four equal sections, is heard as C E G A: a European reads Western harmonic patterns into the music of Asia, and so on.

Matrices may also be deliberately ambiguous. There is probably an element of such ambiguity in all music, but it is in Africa that calculated ambiguity has been most fully developed. This feature of African music was first made known to the world at large in several papers by Gerhard Kubik in the early 1960s.[8] The gist of his discoveries is twofold: firstly, that two or more musical patterns often combine, without losing their individual identity, to form a new pattern which is what the listener is principally aware of; and secondly that a single pattern can have different meanings according to nuances of interpretation, or simply at the whim of the listener. In some East African xylophone music the same theme is repeated over and over again, without the notes being changed, and yet it seems to the listener that he is hearing a set of variations. Why? Simply because the players strike individual keys a little harder or softer, and so bring out a continually changing series of inherent tunes. In much the same way, a recurring set of twelve semiquaver pulses may suggest to the African, either consecutively or simultaneously, four groups of threes (♩.♩.♩.♩.), three groups of fours (♩ ♩ ♩), or six groups of twos (♫♫♫♫♫♫)—in other words, an effect of $\frac{2}{4}$ (to the ear, if not the eye), $\frac{3}{4}$, or $\frac{6}{8}$. It is in rhythm that such ambiguity is at its most developed, but similar things can also be found in modality and form. Is a piece consisting of two alternating tunes, A and B, to be construed as ‖:AB:‖ or ‖:BA:‖—or both? Much of the controversy about African

---

[7] *Hamlet*, III, ii., 400–5.
[8] 'The Structure of Kiganda Xylophone Music' (1960), 'Harp Music of the Azande and Related Peoples in the Central African Republic' (1964), 'Ennanga Music' (1966), and, especially, 'The Phenomenon of Inherent Rhythms in East and Central African Instrumental Music' (1962).

music, and especially African rhythm, seems to turn on attempts to give single meanings to things which are really meant to have multiple meanings. Nothing could better illustrate the truth of Tovey's remark that 'Theorists are apt to vex themselves with vain efforts to remove uncertainty just where it has a high aesthetic value.'[9]

Once a matrix is established, a composer will often expect the listener to perceive it on the slightest hint. In 'Pop goes the Weasel', for instance, the note A in the second-last bar implies the subdominant chord. This is the sort of detail a European child would feel at once, even from an unharmonized rendering, while a musician unacquainted with Western harmony would never detect it in a hundred years.

Once learnt, matrices are difficult to forget. We search instinctively for the familiar. When the conservative critic denounces an innovative work, it is usually not the novelties he objects to so much as the absence of the old familiar patterns. That is why his criticisms are mainly negative—the painter can't draw, the composer can't write a good tune, the novelist can't devise a decent story.

THE LIFE OF THE MATRIX

Except for the very simplest examples—the fixed musical note, the definite interval, the regular beat—new matrices are formed from combinations of old ones. This process of combination is not a sudden one. Typically, the new matrix will go through an extended period of gestation before being born, during which it will be vague, irregular, and sporadic. The actual birth is usually relatively quick, and is followed by the usual pattern of growth, maturity, decay, and death. As with living organisms, it is the simplest which are most durable, while the complicated and specialized are in danger of rapid extinction. Matrices on the level of the regular beat or the perfect fifth are in no danger of decay. It is the complex and delicate creations of music that have the shortest lives—the Baroque fugue, the Classical system of tonality, late Romantic chromatic harmony.

But one must be careful in drawing biological parallels. A musical form can have two lives, depending on whether one is looking at it from the point of view of the composer or the listener. To the present-day composer the fugue may be dead, but it lives on for the listener. Then again, a matrix may die in one type of music and live on in another, the obvious example being the survival in folk or popular music of matrices that have perished in 'art' music. Nor is a matrix ever irrevocably dead; revival is always possible. The history of art is, among other things, a history of revivals.

[9] *Essays in Musical Analysis*, vol. 2, p. 195.

Bearing these qualifications in mind, it is not too misleading to see something like the life of an organism in the career of a matrix. European classical music provides countless examples, ranging in complexity from individual chords or rhythmic figures to complex structures like the sonata form. Take, as a simple example, the perfect cadence. This is a combination of the matrices 'cadence' and 'contrast between tonic and dominant'. The gestation occurred during the late medieval period. The actual birth took place around 1450, followed by a rapid period of growth. This is the usual pattern. As soon as composers become conscious of a new matrix, they eagerly explore its possibilities. At first it will probably be used in a stiffly simple way, but soon it will be elaborated on and lengthened if possible. Eventually either stability is attained or the elaboration reaches its limit and decadence sets in. The perfect cadence, being a simple and fruitful formula, has had a long life. It gave rise in turn to the Renaissance and Baroque cadential formulas and the extended cadences of the Classical school. Indeed, it can almost be said that the history of harmony between Dufay and Beethoven consists of the exploration of the possibilities of the perfect and imperfect cadences. Eventually, in the early nineteenth century, the limits of these possibilities were reached, and self-consciously progressive composers turned towards other harmonic resources.

It is typical of this final phase that the matrix comes to be used less and less in its pure, direct form, and more and more in indirect, implicit ways. In the case of the perfect cadence, all manner of chromatic embellishments are introduced, dominant thirteenths and elevenths outnumber plain triads, various other chords are substituted for the tonic; and the tonic, when used, comes to be adorned with sixths, sevenths, or ninths. Eventually, by the time of Debussy and Schoenberg, even these expedients are not enough, and the perfect cadence is consigned to the scrap-heap of outworn harmonic formulas.

Similar life histories could be found for formulas in the other arts. The important points to notice are the burst of creative energy released by the discovery of the matrix, the variable length of the phase of maturity, and the relative shortness of the decadent phase.

MATRIX COMBINATIONS

The question of matrix combinations is immensely important. Here, if anywhere, lies the answer to the most baffling puzzle in music, namely, why should it interest us at all? What is it in this most abstract of arts that calls forth such sustained attention? Why should people listen raptly to nothing but a long string of noises?

The answer is that what holds our attention is the myriad of patterns, or matrices, traced out by these noises. A composition is a feat of co-ordination, and the more matrices there are to co-ordinate, the more interesting it will be. Even a simple tune is a combination of a satisfying melodic line with a satisfying rhythm and (if in the classical European tradition) a satisfying harmony. As anyone who has tried to write a tune knows, it is easy to get any one of these elements right. The difficulty is getting them all right at the same time.

Such co-ordination is mainly a matter of reconciling 'bound-upness' with 'at-oddness'[10] Bound-upness is the degree to which the matrices in a movement are connected with one another, in other words the degree to which they fit some overriding matrix. For instance, the sonata rondo form is more bound up than the plain rondo, since in addition to the basic theme-episode-theme-episode-theme pattern it must follow a sonata-like pattern of modulation.

At-oddness is the degree to which matrices go their own ways, and are therefore the more difficult to reconcile. The growth of modern harmony out of medieval organum is also the growth of at-oddness between melody and bass. The African or Indian musician savours the at-oddness of simultaneous rhythms, and finds our European coinciding beats dull.[11]

But there is little point in at-oddness which is not reconciled within some overriding matrix. In classical counterpoint it is the reconciliation of independent melodic lines within the matrix of the harmonic progression that makes the whole interesting. And the same is true, in essence, of the sonata style; only here the at-oddness is not between simultaneous, but between successive melodies.

MATRICES AND RULES

The question naturally arises of the relation of matrices to rules on the one hand and freedom on the other. It may seem as though a matrix is much the same thing as a rule, and if this is so, does it mean that the most interesting compositions are those that obey the most rules—and is it not the height of pedantry to suggest this?

The answer is that while all matrices could theoretically be stated as rules, not all rules represent true matrices. Beyond the simplest level, matrices become so subtle that rules attempting to describe them are inevitably simplifications. Moreover, while matrices are positive—that

[10] I owe the term 'at-oddness' to R. O. Morris. See *Contrapuntal Technique in the Sixteenth Century*, p. 18.

[11] Probably the greatest classical master of at-oddness was Johann Sebastian Bach. In particular, he will fit phrases of all sorts of irregular bar-lengths into his sixteen- or thirty-two-bar periods. No doubt it was the reconciliation of so much at-oddness that gave rise to the once standard saying that 'Bach is so *satisfying*'.

is, patterns calculated to produce a desired effect—rules naturally tend to be negative. The effect of a bad rule is that (1) it does not produce the desired effect, or (2) it produces an effect which is not desired, or (3) it produces no effect at all.

In the nature of things, the matrices governing a particular style tend to be codified when that style is (at best) well matured or (more probably) already going out of fashion. In the latter case, the new style which is taking its place will be still uncodified. This gives rise to the illusion that the progression is from the bad old rules to the good new lack of rules, or freedom. In fact, it is merely from the written—and probably badly written—rules to the unwritten ones.

This false distinction between the crippling old pedantry (the tyranny of the bar-line, the shackles of the major-minor system) and the glorious new freedom has never been stronger than in the twentieth century, thoroughly confused, of course, with notions of political and social freedom. In fact, the only freedom an artist can enjoy is the freedom not to produce effects which he does not want. The effects he *does* want to produce will depend on matrices if they are worthwhile; and the more matrices there are, the more interesting his work will be. Too few matrices means boring and monotonous music. If this is how a work strikes us, it may be because the unfamiliar matrices are beyond our comprehension; or, with unsuccessful innovations, because they simply are not there at all.

11. MODALITY

ONE reads a great deal about something called the major-minor system of tonality, born *c*.1600, died *c*.1900, RIP. As regards popular music, at least, this obituary seems a little suspect. On the one hand, you could say that the major-minor system is still going strong; on the other, that it never really existed at all. It all depends on what that impressive term means. Does it mean the mere use of the major and minor modes, or the use of these modes to the exclusion of any others? And is the 'minor' just the classical minor, or does it cover other minor-third modes too? And finally, does the term imply the classical system of modulation and key contrast?

This rather esoteric question of key relationships is really the crux of the matter. The peculiarity of the classical minor is that it is harmonically identical with the major. Its three primary triads have the same functions as their major equivalents; it is only the colour of the tonic and subdominant chords that is different. In effect, the classical minor is a dark major. The new minor mode was a necessary part of the classical harmonic scheme, with its three-chord basis and its systematic contrast of key. All *this* is implied in the term 'major-minor system'.

In this full sense, popular music has never accepted the major-minor system at all: major, yes; major-minor, no. I shall be going further into this question when we come to look at 'Parlour Harmony' (chapter 27), but for the moment, there is another classical characteristic to be mentioned. Classical European music is *chord-based*. Every note of the melody must conform to the prevailing chord, but otherwise it may come and go as it pleases. It has no special melodic function. In classical theory, once you have listed the notes of a mode, you have described it: C D E F G A B—major scale; D E F G A B C—dorian mode, etc. To a classical Indian or Arab musician this would seem strange, just as strange as the absence of harmony in Asian music is to the Westerner. To the Oriental, this mere list of notes is only the barest outline of the mode. To define it properly, he must describe the *functions* of the notes as well as their pitch. Thus, one can have several different modes using exactly the same notes, but using them differently.

When we examine modes outside the classical system, including those of popular music, we find some that have no tonic; some that (like the Indian) have tonics and special functions for the other notes; and some that have special functions but no tonics. The first step towards analysing these modes is to establish a set of terms to describe them. We can begin by clearing up the confusion between 'scale' and 'mode'.

It is most convenient to confine the term 'scale' to the bare set of notes, disregarding the way they are organized. We have a precedent for this in the terms pentatonic scale, diatonic scale, and chromatic scale. The pentatonic scale means the notes C, D, E, G, and A, or some transposition of the same pattern. The tonic (if any) may be any of these five notes. Similarly, the diatonic scale consists of the white notes of the piano keyboard, or one of the eleven transpositions thereof, without specifying which of these notes is the tonic.

When one or more of the notes of the scale is given a specific role—for instance, the tonic—we have a 'mode'. According to this usage, there would be five potential pentatonic modes and six diatonic modes (seven if you include the dubious locrian) including the ordinary major, and making no distinction between the 'old' ecclesiastical modes and the 'modern' major and minor scales.

The next step is to invent a term for modes that have no tonic. A familar example is the universal children's chant (Ex. 5). What is the key of this little tune? Is it in C major or A minor? The question is absurd.

Ex. 5   Children's chant

Being repetitive, it has no need to be in any key. Its miniature mode of three notes has no tonic, and can be conveniently described as atonic.[1]

Finally, a term is needed to describe the kind of mode in which notes other than the tonic have a special significance. For this, I propose the term 'modal frame' since these significant notes form a sort of frame on which the melody is constructed.

It is perfectly possible for different melodies to draw on the same set of notes and yet be in different modes. The little Indian tune 'Bigitār' (Ex. 64) and the ragtime song 'Mister Johnson' (Ex. 155) use the same notes—C E♭ F G B♭—with the same tonic—C. But a glance at these tunes will show that, while F is easily the most important note after the tonic in 'Biglitār', in 'Mister Johnson' it appears only as an insignificant passing note. 'Biglitār' is built on the fourth between tonic and subdominant, 'Mister Johnson' on a series of thirds: C E♭ G B♭. Though

---

[1] This word, though used in certain other senses, has never to my knowledge been applied to music before. After some hesitation, I chose it rather than the awkward 'tonicless', in spite of possible confusion with 'atonal'.

the *mode* is the same, the *modal frames* are different—and, one might add, typical of their respective musical cultures.

SHIFTING TONICS AND NOTE FRAMES

It can happen that the modal frame becomes more important than the position of the tonic, and variants of the same tune end sometimes on one note and sometimes on another (see Ex. 6).[2] Apart from the refrains, these two tunes are obviously nearly identical, except that one is in C and the other in A minor. In this case, whether the final is C or A is less important to the singer than the framework of notes on which the tune is built: a c′ e′ g′ a′—or some transposition thereof.

Ex. 6

(a) 'She was a Rum One', (b) 'Had I Wings'

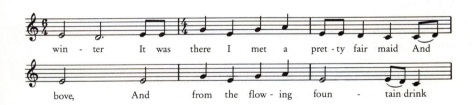

---

[2] The tune-type of these two examples was very popular in America: see also the four examples in Ex. 76. The well known spiritual 'Didn't my Lord Deliver Daniel' is derived from the refrain of 'Had I Wings': see Jackson, *White and Negro Spirituals*, pp. 212–13.

day   But a bon -ny one Fol-the-did-dle - di - do

fly   a - way and   be   at   rest,

And I'd   praise   God   in his bright a - bode.

FLOOR NOTES AND CEILING NOTES

Note frames usually have a well-defined upper and lower limit; in Ex. 6 top and bottom A. But we often find that the melody may dip below the bottom limit, as when those in Ex. 6 descend to G, or rise above the top limit. It is therefore inaccurate to talk of these limits as top or bottom notes. Let us call them, instead, 'floor' and 'ceiling' notes. In these two examples, the floor notes are A, but the bottom notes are G.

DEGREES OF EMPHASIS

The idea that modes are sharply distinguished, clear-cut things is a heritage from the Classical tradition. In fact, the sharp and unmistakable contrast between the two modes of Classical music is something rather exceptional. It is very much a Classical trait, the product of an age that liked sharp distinctions in everything. Elsewhere, it is much more usual for the modes to shade into one another subtly and ambiguously, whether from piece to piece or from section to section in an individual piece.

The same vagueness affects individual features of the mode. The tonic, for instance, is not always the fixed thing described by the textbooks. There are tunes with perfectly unambiguous tonics, there are tunes with no tonics at all, and there is a wide spectrum between these two extremes. Many African, American, and British tunes fall into this ambiguous category.

The same variations in emphasis can be found in floor notes and ceiling notes, and other melodically sensitive notes. They may be quite unmistakable or the merest hint, or even both within the same composition. A comparison of the three tunes in Ex. 7 will make this clear. There is a world of difference, for instance, between the way the first and last of these examples end. The African paddle song and the Afro-American axe song are both circular, atonic. (At any rate, this is true for the European ear. The singers of these tunes may, just possibly, have found more finality in these endings.) The Scottish ballad tune does

Ex. 7

(*a*) 'Great God-amighty'*

He's a-chop-pin' in de new groun', He's a-chop-pin' in de new groun',

He's a-chop-pin' in de new groun', Great God a' - migh - ty.

* From John A. and Alan Lomax, *American Ballads and Folk Songs*, p. 80 (Macmillan, 1934).

(*b*) African paddle song

Ye-vu-donen-ye nu ma-du, So- gã, kpa kpa, nen-ye a-vo ma-ta, So - gã, kpa kpa,

paddle
strokes

(*c*) 'The Beggar Man'

A beg - gar man cam' owre yon lea, An' mo-ny a fine tale he tauld me,

Seek-ing out for cha - ri - ty, Will ye lodge a beg-gar man? La lal-tee too roo a ree.

have a tonic, though of a subtle kind, so that it too may sound unfinished to the classically trained ear.

But this is only the most obvious of the differences. In the paddle song there is a quite unmistakable floor note, easily the most prominent note of the mode. It seems to draw the higher notes of the melody down like a magnet, yet somehow the effect is not that of a tonic. In 'Great God-amighty' the floor note is almost as unmistakable, but far less important. Here the most important note is C, which acts as a pivot around which the melody circles. This we can call a 'central note'. It is a common occurrence in many folk styles. (The D in the Irish Keen, Ex. 29, is an excellent example.) In 'The Beggar Man' the feeling of a floor note is weak. One could make the final note C instead of G as the final note without greatly changing the character of this tune, as we have just seen in the comparison between 'She was a Rum One' and 'Had I Wings'.

Another striking difference lies in the middle notes of the mode. Both the first two pieces emphasize C, E, and G, giving a strong suggestion of C major. 'The Beggar Man', on the other hand, gives a slight emphasis to the notes A, C, and E that vaguely hints at A minor

A series of kindred tunes might illustrate further subtleties; in fact, it would be easy to fill a book with the modal subtleties of purely melodic music, to which this chapter is only the sketchiest of introductions.

Possibly the hardest thing to grasp is the atonic mode. The classically trained musicologist feels a bewildering sense of disorientation when the terra firma of precisely defined key is pulled from under him. No longer can he talk of the third, fifth, or any other degree of the mode—and he must keep on reminding himself of this fact. This is more confusing than any new modal refinements: another instance of the law that it is far easier to learn new matrices than to forget those we know already.

12. WHOLENESS

ONCE we get away from the familiar terrain of the major-minor system the question of what constitutes a musical whole arises. If it seems a simple question, this is because European classical traditions have simplified it for us. In European classical music from the Middle Ages to the twentieth century there is almost invariably a pre-ordained end. The movement executes a design, and once the design is finished the piece comes to an end.

Outside the European classical tradition this pattern is distinctly exceptional. The matrix of the pre-ordained end seems to be a fairly recent and sophisticated development. The natural musical form is the repeated cycle. Repetition is built into the human body, into the breath and the heartbeat. Many of our actions—walking, swimming, the simpler forms of manual labour—are repetitive. The short, endlessly repeated phrase, at first probably no more than a rhythmic cry, must have been one of the earliest forms of musical expression.

Ethnomusicologists use the term 'cycle' for the repeated element in such repetitive forms. A cycle may be a single melody, or, in the case of a song with a chorus, it may be the verse plus the chorus. As long as there is not much variation, there is no problem in identifying the cycle; but as soon as variation becomes important, the cycle changes from a definite theme to a matrix serving as the basis of the variation. It may be, among other possibilities, the outline of a tune, a mode, or even a set of chords.

The Western classical tradition rather looks down on mere repetition, but this is not a view shared by all musical cultures. According to A.M. Jones, the African 'would think our broad changes of melody coarse and inartistic. His is a much more refined art. He knows the artistic value of a good repetitive pattern.'[1] And according to John Chernoff, an African drummer 'uses repetition to reveal the *depth* of the musical structure'.[2] The same respect for repetition can be felt in European folk music. With practice one learns to appreciate these repetitions, and, in the vulgarity of excessively varied commercial arrangements, one begins to see what the African finds 'coarse and inartistic' in 'broad changes of melody'.

African repetition is, in fact, virtually always subtle variation. As in folk music from other parts of the world, the variations of the expert folk

[1] 'African Music', p. 293.
[2] *African Rhythm and African Sensibility*, p. 112.

performer *can* sometimes be as enterprising as those of the European classical tradition, but, in general, they consist only of a slightly changed rhythm, an altered note, a discreet ornament, and so on. It is not the boldness of the variations that is admired, but their *rightness.*

Like other matrices, the repeated cycle developed in different ways. Variation was one of them. The cycle came to be lengthened and elaborated on, and contrasting episodes were introduced, producing a rondo-like effect. Then there came a radical innovation. The cycle was made to come to a stop. It no longer repeated itself. The independent movement had been born.

This development was almost confined to sophisticated composed music. In European folk music, as in African music, the repeated cycle remained the standard form. It might be closed, that is, come to an end in the familiar way, or open (or, as it is sometimes put, circular), where instead of coming to a close, the tune simply repeated itself indefinitely. In British popular music this scheme was common till the early eighteenth century. There are, for instance, eight examples in *The Beggar's Opera*.[3] During the eighteenth century the classical idea of the self-contained whole gradually prevailed, even in urban popular music. By the twentieth century all urban popular tunes were closed, and then, from the 1950s on, we find open tunes coming into their own again.

The problem of how to finish an indefinitely repeated cycle is solved in several different ways. In Africa, where matters are complicated by overlapping cross-rhythms, musicians sometimes break off without ceremony, sometimes add a short coda, often involving a new rhythmic twist (as in 'Mkwaze mmodzi', Ex. 33), and sometimes prolong the final notes into a held chord.[4] Pop songs have the fade-out; British and British-American folk music often breaks off with a dismissive, to-hell-with-it gesture; singers often drop into a speaking tone at the end of a song, and so on.

There is an unbroken gradation between the completely open-ended and the completely self-contained. In this gradation three stages of what one could call 'followability' can be discerned. At one extreme we have a section which is so open-ended that it *must* be followed by something else, whether it be a repetition, a variation, a continuation, or an episode. Then we have a category where the section—or perhaps it had better be called the movement—may or may not be followed at will. Here we have, at the one end, simple but self-contained folk tunes, and at the

---

[3] 'Oh London is a Fine Town', 'Over the Hills and Far Away', 'Gin Thou wert mine Own Thing', 'O the Broom', 'All in a Misty Morning', 'The Sun Had Loos'd his Weary Teams', 'Irish Howl', and 'O Bessy Bell'.

[4] See Akpabot, 'Functional Music of the Ibibio', p. 91, and Blacking, 'Problems of Pitch, Pattern and Harmony', p. 23.

other, the first movements of symphonies. In the last category anything further is unthinkable. Long works like symphonies and tone poems obviously belong in this category, but length is not compulsory. Some short pieces are equally unfollowable, as for instance some of Chopin's preludes, or certain bugle calls like 'The Last Post'.[5]

Followability is easy. It is the unfollowable movement that is difficult—not necessarily higher art, but certainly more tightly organized art. In Western music the development of forms has usually been in the direction of the less followable, because more organized; a movement towards more bound-upness, and the reconciliation of greater at-oddness: plus, of course, sheer length. The infinitely extendible fugues and fantasies of the early Baroque evolve into the tightly knit structures of the later Bach. The serenades and cassations of the early eighteenth century, with their long processions of movements, become the mature Classical symphony. Folk or popular music is generally eminently followable until it acquires artistic pretensions. Then, if it conforms to the European pattern, it becomes more organized and so less followable.

Even with the most pretentious popular music of the present day, however, there is little sign of this happening. Will the popular style betray its European tradition so far as to develop into subtle but loose and improvisatory styles, like those of Asia? Or shall we again see the growth of large, closed, unfollowable forms? Only time will tell.

---

[5] This famous call ends the day in the British army. (The American equivalent is 'Taps'.) It appears in Hurd, *The Oxford Junior Companion to Music*, p. 206.

13. THE BEAT

WESTERN musical notation forces on us a view of rhythm which is predominantly mathematical. It tells us the ratios between the note lengths, and, if the music is of the conventional, measured type, it gives some idea of a recurring pattern. Beats are something imposed on this pattern. There is a beat, presumably, at the beginning of the bar, and possibly elsewhere—we aren't too sure. Does a piece in brisk $\frac{3}{4}$ time have three beats to the bar or only one? We are a little vague on this point, possibly because the composer wants us to be a little vague.

Quite the reverse is true of the popular dance music of the world. There, the proper place to start analysing the rhythm is with the beat. But what is this beat? It is not a regularly recurring accent, though such an accent may be used to mark it. The beat, in essence, is the musical reflection of a regular, physical, human motion. The precise nature of the motion varies. It may be a walking or dancing step, a swaying of the upper part of the body, a rhythmical contraction of the shoulders. Whatever it is, it will be regular and natural. Whenever we spontaneously move in time to the music, we are marking the beat. In an obvious and superficial way, the music produces the motion; but it can only do so because, in a deeper sense, the motion has produced the music.

The spaces between the beats may be divided into halves, thirds, or smaller rhythmic values. It is unnecessary to go into such details here, except to remark that such filling-in is often much less mathematical than conventional notation would suggest. 'Dotted' rhythms, for instance, might be anything between a slight leaning on the first note of a duplet at one extreme and a ♩.♪ effect at the other, passing through ♩♪ and ♫ on the way. When the beats themselves are grouped together, there is no doubt that the fundamental unit is the pair, reflecting the left-right, left-right of simple bodily movements. Triple groupings can develop by two methods: either another beat can simply be tacked on to a left-right grouping (left-right-left, or left-right-right)— this is the method, for instance, of the minuet rhythm, which can easily be felt as a three-legged march time—or else a duple rhythm, after being divided into two lots of threes (*one*-two-three *one*-two-three) can be regrouped into three lots of twos (*one*-two *one*-two *one*-two). The latter is the hemiola method. Though apparently more complicated, it appears to have preceded the first: in European music, at least, the straightforward triple time of the minuet and the waltz seems to have developed as a simplification of the hemiola time of dances like the courante and the galliard.

The neglect of the beat in European theory comes partly from the development of an advanced system of musical notation, which had the effect of cutting off composition from performance, and partly from the hostile European attitude to the dance. The latter, varying from furious condemnation to a mere snobbish disdain, has generally ensured that the less music was connected with motion, the greater was its prestige. The notion of 'the sanctity of immobility' is deeply ingrained in the European psyche. So we find that, though most of the great music in the classical tradition had its origins in the dance, these origins were quickly put aside when artistic pretension took over. As a general rule, especially since 1800, the higher the art (in pretension, anyway) the less evident is the beat.

In other cultures, including the European and American popular culture, no such scruples have prevailed. There the beat has been refined, complicated, subtly differentiated. Like the classical 'andante' ('walking'), the tempo directions of popular music frequently describe a gait—'shuffle', 'bounce', and so on, reflected in the notes by means which are often very subtle. Just as folk singers put their spoken accents into their singing voices, so popular or folk dance musicians put dance movements into the notes they play. It is largely a question of whether music springs from basic human impulses, or from a vision of little marks on paper.

Part Three
The Blues

'Bluesy music' might be a better title for this section. Throughout this book styles are defined primarily by their musical peculiarities, and so it is with the blues. The range of American music touched with bluesiness is very wide: hence, partly, the length of this section. But there are other reasons. The sheer peculiarity of the blues style, its opposition to the norms of European classical music, takes a lot of explaining. So does its tangled, complex, and frequently obscure history.

A word of warning about the musical family trees that figure so prominently from here on. They are not to be taken too literally. When Tune (*a*) is described as the origin, or parent, or ancestor of Tune (*b*), this is actually a shorthand way of saying that Tune (*a*) belongs to a family which, by a complex and perhaps indirect route, gave rise to the family of which Tune (*b*) is a member. The relation is far more likely to be collateral than linear.

I. THE UNIQUENESS OF THE BLUES

14. THE PLACE OF THE BLUES IN AMERICAN MUSIC

There are moments when anyone setting out to discuss the blues must wish devoutly that the term had never been coined.

Humphrey Lyttleton[1]

TO bring out the full confusion surrounding 'the blues', let us consider the progress of a hypothetical blues fan. To start with, he has read the dictionary definitions and the introductions to the subject in the jazz histories. From these he knows that the blues is melancholy, dejected, a song of lamentation, in a slow tempo; that it follows a certain harmonic pattern and a twelve-bar form, with plenty of 'blue notes'; that it was invented by black Americans. It is true that, when he looks up the term 'blue note', he finds that some definitions describe it as a minor interval where a major one would be expected, and others as an interval between major and minor in pitch. Could it be that the subject is not as clear-cut as it seems to be?

Along with these technical matters, our blues fan has absorbed some of the atmosphere of the subject. He knows the pictures of the old bluesmen, their black faces engraved with the sorrows of ages. He knows the bizarre names: Howling Wolf, Blind Lemon, Muddy Waters. He knows about the atmosphere of loneliness, suffering, squalor, violence, oppression, and discrimination out of which the blues came. All this is highly congenial to him, since, like most present-day blues fans, he himself is of comfortable middle-class white origin.

Let us suppose that he is of an observant and scholarly turn of mind. Presently he begins to notice that what he is hearing does not always square with what he has read in books. Not every blues he hears follows the usual twelve-bar form. In spite of most definitions, there are instrumental blues with no voice parts at all. He discovers that the

[1] *The Best of Jazz: Basin Street to Harlem*, p. 61.

joyous, exhuberant boogie-woogie and rock and roll styles are also, technically, blues—so what becomes of all the melancholy, dejection, and lamentation? Next he begins to explore other forms of black American music: spirituals, worksongs, play songs—and behold, they all sound bluesy too. It begins to look as if 'the blues' is simply another name for black American music.

And then he discovers an even more disconcerting fact. Branching out into white American folk music, he finds the blues there as well. He finds banjo pieces full of blue notes, and songs like 'Every Night when the Sun Goes in':

> Every night when the sun goes in
> I hang down my head and mournful cry.

—songs which are undeniably of British folk origin, and equally undeniably a sort of blues. At this point, our hypothetical fan may be forgiven for wondering whether the blues has any definable meaning at all. No wonder everyone is always falling back on the statement that 'the blues is, you know, a *feeling*'.

It would be bad enough if the confusion were only musical; but, to make it worse, the blues is an object of ethnic politics. To the dutiful white liberal, wallowing in the pain and oppression of the blues is an expiation for the monstrous wrongs done by the white race to the blacks, a sort of vicarious masochism. Among the blacks themselves there is a certain ambivalence. On the one hand, the blues is a handy stick to beat the whites with. On the other, middle-class blacks can hardly be expected to relish a picture of their race which is so saturated with crime and squalor. In many quarters, the blues has become a sacred monument to black suffering at the hands of whites. To such people it is a sort of blasphemy to suggest that whites as well as blacks may have had a hand in the development of the style, or even that some of the whites may themselves occasionally have had something to feel blue about. Even just viewing such an emotionally charged subject in an objective way is somehow shocking to certain temperaments.

The greatest source of misunderstanding is the word 'blues' itself. It is so easy to forget that many blues are not blue. By friend and foe alike, the purely musical features of the style are inextricably muddled with the idea of melancholia. The conservative European critic is as likely to fall into this trap as the jazz historian:

Music of poverty can be neither gay in the proper sense nor beautiful. It is savagely hilarious or melancholy. Jazz and the Blues came with heavy syncopation, 'breaks', 'swings', 'smears' and 'dirty notes', like swarms of birds of prey or locusts, to devour all the charming European tunes. (Ernst Roth, *The Business of Music*, p. 246.)

There is little to choose between this and the attitude of many friendly critics, except that the tone is regretful and not triumphant.[2]

If the blues is to be discussed rationally, the first thing to do is to clear up this confusion. We must distinguish between the blues in general and the blues in this narrow sense, the 'blues of oppression', we might term it, with its haunting lines: 'Sometimes I wonder, would a matchbox hold my clothes', 'It's hard to stumble when you got no place to fall', 'If the blues was whiskey I'd stay drunk all the time'. By the beginning of the twentieth century most black American folk music was more or less bluesy, with the blues, in this narrow sense, only one style among many. By that time the blues influence had begun to spread to white folk music as well, and this process has continued ever since. As Alan Lomax truly said, the special features of the blues 'have become national musical trade-marks with which Americans stamp any music they are really fond of'.[3] By the middle of the century this influence was not even confined to the United States. Apart from its well-known impact on British popular music, one might mention its welcome in France, where some singers have created a distinctively Gallic blues style, midway between the American blues and the traditional *chanson* in character. The world-wide influence of the blues in the twentieth century is comparable with the influence of the Italian popular style in the seventeenth and eighteenth centuries.

The ancestors of the blues are as diverse as its progeny. Concentration on the blues of oppression has obscured its link with other styles. Its genealogy includes clear connections with both British and African folk music, as well as the jigs, dance songs, minstrel tunes, and even parlour music of the nineteenth century. The processes by which these very different traditions have combined into a single style are among the most fascinating in musical history.

Some may wonder whether the term 'blues' does not become meaningless when used so broadly. Is anything really left of the blues style, apart from that proverbial, ineffable 'feeling'? The answer is yes: apart from being a feeling, bluesiness is a set of musical features, which can be analysed like any others. They obey laws which are very different from anything in orthodox classical theory, but these laws can be explained, and turn on the same few ultimate principles that govern all music. We begin with the most fundamental of these features—the blues mode.

[2] Paul Oliver gives an amusing and interesting history of scholarly attitudes to the blues in *Songsters and Saints*, pp. 3–7.
[3] *The Folk Songs of North America*, p. 573.

15. THE BLUES MODE AND THE TWELVE-BAR FORM

MANY of the typical features of the blues can be removed without destroying the basic, unmistakable quality of bluesiness. We can take away the twelve-bar structure, the typical chords, the bent notes, the shuffling triplet rhythms, the half-speaking vocal quality—in fact we can remove the voice part altogether—and still be left with blues. And when we have eliminated the unessential features, what remains? What is the essence of the blues? All blues tunes have two things in common: one is syncopation, and the other is a mode, which is in fact not merely a mode, but a particular kind of modality, dominating and controlling the whole style in much the same way as a particular kind of tonality dominates the Classical style.

If the invariable features of the blues are a certain type of rhythm and mode, this suggests that these two features are in some way connected with each other. Anyone familar with the blues style will somehow feel this connection. If one tries the experiment of singing a blues tune in perfectly 'straight' rhythm, a certain discomfort is apparent at once. Evidently, the blues mode depends on a background of syncopated rhythm for its full effect. (On the other hand, blues-like syncopations can happily be used apart from the blues mode, as for instance in early ragtime.) Ultimately, both mode and rhythm are part of the overriding system of organization which constitutes the blues form.

The familiar twelve-bar scheme, when it is used, is another part of that form. Just as the blues mode will not work without syncopation, so the twelve-bar scheme will not work without the blues mode.[1] The indefinable but unmistakable blues effect is the product of a subtle interaction between these three features. In trying to explain this interaction, it is easiest to deal with the mode and the twelve-bar scheme together, both because they are intimately linked and because they evolved together. Rhythm can conveniently be left till later.

The first and most fundamental thing to explain is the mode. The blues mode is actually a modal frame: that is, a framework of melodically sensitive notes interspersed with less important notes. Among the notes constituting the framework are the famous blue notes, and any explanation of the blues mode must start by defining them.

[1] Bob Dylan's 'Rainy Day Women' is an apparent exception: harmonically a twelve-bar blues, it is in a march-like $\frac{6}{8}$ with no syncopations except a solitary Scotch snap. Yet there is something indefinably bluesy about its beat.

THE BLUE NOTES

Like the blues in general, the blue notes can mean many things. One quality that they all have in common, however, is that they are flatter than one would expect, classically speaking.[2] But this flatness may take several forms. On the one hand, it may be a microtonal affair of a quarter-tone or so. Here one may speak of *neutral* intervals, neither major nor minor. On the other hand, the flattening may be by a full semitone—as it must be, of course, on keyboard instruments. It may involve a glide, either upward or downward. Again, this may be a microtonal, almost imperceptible affair, or it may be a slur between notes a semitone apart, so that there is actually not one blue note but two. A blue note may even be marked by a microtonal shake of a kind common in Oriental music.

The degrees of the mode treated in this way are, in order of frequency, the third, seventh, fifth, and sixth. Ex. 8(*a*) sums up the basic possible blue notes against the tonic C, and Exx. 8(*b*) and (*c*) give two blue note shakes from actual performances. One also occasionally finds an ultra-flat minor third (see Ex. 21(*a*)) sometimes masquerading as the supertonic in transcriptions.

Ex. 8

(*a*) Blue notes

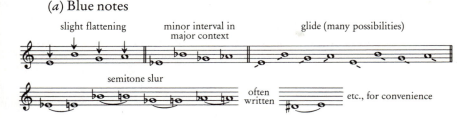

(*b*) Shake on third: Charley Patton, 'Tom Rushen Blues'

(*c*) Shake on fifth: Bessie Smith, 'Poor Man's Blues'

[2] The slightly sharpened fourth sometimes occurs in blues performances, but this is not usually accounted a 'blue note'.

Any selection of these blue notes may be found mixed up with ordinary major (or, in the case of the fifth, perfect) intervals. For instance a blues tune may have major thirds right through to the end, where one or two minor thirds appear. Or major and minor or neutral thirds may be juxtaposed throughout. Sometimes the minor intervals will predominate, and sometimes they will be rare: the more minor intervals, the bluesier the effect. But, while we may say that one tune is more bluesy than another, if they are both genuine blues tunes there will be no question of a clear-cut contrast such as we find between the classical major and minor. The blues mode depends on other principles altogether.

MELODIC DISSONANCE

The reason why these notes change their pitch in this apparently haphazard way is that their function within the mode is also changing. It is a matter of a kind of instability rather analogous to harmonic dissonance. So close is the parallel that it is not misleading to use the term 'melodic dissonance'. Just as a discord resolves on a concord, so a melodically dissonant note resolves on a melodically consonant note. And just as a seventh or ninth is the mark of a discord, so the various forms of flattening that make a blue note are the mark of a melodic dissonance.

It should be emphasized that melodic dissonance is completely independent of harmonic dissonance. Melodic dissonances may occur against a background of pure triads, or in a single melodic line with no accompanying harmony at all; while conversely melodic consonance may go with a dissonant harmony.

The best way to illustrate melodic dissonance in the blues is to build the blues mode up from its basic components; a process which incidentally illuminates the historical development of the form

THE LADDER OF THIRDS

One of the great puzzles of music is the mysteriously satisfying quality of the minor third. It is easy to see why acoustically simple intervals like the octave, fourth, and fifth are among the great building blocks of music. But why should an awkward interval like the minor third—really a dissonance, from the acoustical point of view—come so readily to the human voice? Why should it have that air of what can only be called solidity? I can see no answer to these questions, but there is no doubt that it does. The primeval chant consisting in essence of nothing but a falling minor third appears in places as different as the Catholic liturgy and the school playground (Ex. 9).[3] What we have here is a two-note,

Ex. 9

(*a*) Gregorian tone   (*b*) Schoolboy chant

atonic mode. It is not, as it may appear at first glance, a skeletal version
of A minor. Both the Gregorian and schoolboy versions of this chant,
different as they are, agree in dwelling on but not accenting the last note:
it is the higher note that carries the accent. The result is a finely balanced
ambiguity. The top note cannot be the tonic, because it is not final; while
the bottom note cannot be the tonic either, because it is not accented.

By a shift of emphasis the bottom note can be turned into a true tonic,
giving us the basis of some African and Afro-American chants and
worksongs as in Ex. 10.[4] Usually there are one or two outlying notes
elaborating on the two-note structure. Here we have the blues mode in
its barest form, simply the tonic with the blue third dropping down to it.
Here, too, we have the simplest possible illustration of melodic
dissonance. The tonic is the consonant note, and the third is the
dissonance, resolving onto it exactly as a dominant seventh might resolve
onto the tonic triad.

Ex. 10

(*a*) Mossi song

---

[3] Another example of this ubiquitous chant is the street cry 'Any old iron?' quoted in *The
New Grove* (see Maniates, 'Street Cries').
[4] Ex. 10(*b*) is a pick song; according to a note, 'The "hanhs" represent the violent exhalations
of breath that occur when the point of the pick sinks into the earth.'

(*b*) 'Goin' Home'*

Ev'-ry-where   I ___ hanh ___ Where I look this morn-in' ___ hanh

Look like   rain ___ hanh ___   My Lord, looks like   rain ___ hanh.

* From John A. and Alan Lomax, *American Ballads and Folk Songs*, pp. 84–5 (Macmillan, 1934).

We could call this the 'dropping' form of this two-note mode. There is also a 'hanging' form, in which the upper note is the tonic (see Ex. 11).

Ex. 11   'Show Pity, Lord!'

Show   pi-ty, Lord!   Oh   Lord, for-give!   Let   a   re-pen-tant   sin-ner   live!

Ex. 12 is a summary of the possibilities of this two-note minor-third mode (actually, the third can vary between a true minor third and a neutral third).

Ex. 12   The two-note mode

atonic type   dropping third   hanging third

By putting together the dropping-third and hanging-third form of this mode, we get a three-note mode consisting of two minor or neutral thirds. Once again, pure examples are hard to find. Ex. 13 is an almost

Ex. 13   'Gwineter Harness in de Mornin' Soon'*

CHORUS   *Fine*

Gwine to   har-ness in the morn-ing   soon, soon, Gwine to har-ness in the morn-ing   soon.

D.C.

STANZA

Cap - 'n, Cap - 'n, what time o' day?   Bil-ly done hol-ler for his   oats and hay.

* From John A. and Alan Lomax, *American Ballads and Folk Songs*, p. 47 (Macmillan, 1934).

pure one, complicated only by the appearance of a couple of dominants. In actual performance the top third would be neutral, not major as transcribed here.

In another version of this mode the tonic is at the bottom, the three notes being grouped like a tonic triad with a minor or neutral third. Here there is no shortage of pure examples (see Ex. 14), particularly among the simpler black American worksongs. A triadic worksong of this type was quoted by Cable in his famous description of the dancing in Congo Square, New Orleans:

With what particular musical movements the occasion began does not now appear. May be with very slow and measured ones; they had such that were strange and typical. I have heard the negroes sing one—though it was not of the dance-ground but of the cane-field—that showed the emphatic barbarism of five bars to the line, and was confined to four notes of the open horn. ('The Dance in Place Congo', p. 523.)

Ex. 14   'Go 'way f'om mah Window'

Ex. 15   Cable's worksong

The two forms of this triadic mode, one with the tonic in the middle and the other with it at the bottom, may look very different, but we must not let the appearance of the notes on the page deceive us. Instead of the major and minor thirds of the printed page, most of the thirds will be neutral in actual performance. In such cases the fifth formed by the outer notes will be a perfect fifth, and the two forms of the mode will be identical except for the position of the tonic. The effect is so similar that it is sometimes possible to find both forms in variants of the same song (see Ex. 16). The tonic is C in both cases.

Ex. 16

(*a*) 'The Maid Freed from the Gallows' (beginning)

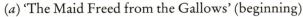

(*b*) 'Hangman'

The process of piling up thirds need not stop at this point. It is possible to add another third below the triad, as in the spiritual 'Way over in the New Buryin' Groun' ' (Ex. 17). It is also possible to put a

Ex. 17   'Way over in the New Buryin' Groun' '

minor third on top of the triad, so producing the blue seventh (Ex. 18).[5] These examples show the blues mode in skeletal form. In all but the

---

[5] Another example of this mode is 'Blin' Man Stood on de Way an' Cried', Ex. 73(*d*).

Ex. 18   'Pretty Polly', variant M

simplest forms, the basis of the mode is the tonic triad, but we must be careful to distinguish this *melodic* triad from the familiar harmonic variety. This melodic triad we can adorn with a third above (as in 'Pretty Polly') or a third below (as in 'Way over in the New Buryin' Groun' '). We can also add passing-notes, like the supertonic in 'Pretty Polly', or the subdominant, usually falling to the third.

In short, the blues mode takes the form of a ladder of thirds, but it is a flexible ladder that can be extended up or down at will. Sometimes it goes a third above the dominant, and sometimes a third below the tonic. There is nothing to stop it doing both in the same tune (as for instance in 'Get along Home, Cindy', Ex. 66(*b*)). There is also nothing to stop the sixth or seventh of the mode from behaving in two ways during the same tune, now as a passing-note and now as a part of the ladder. Passing-notes in the blues behave much the same as passing-notes in the classical style. It is non-passing-notes which must explain themselves to the ear. In the classical style, they do so by their relationship to the chord prevailing at the moment. In the blues, they do so by their relationship to the mode, which consists essentially of the ladder of thirds and the tensions within it. That is the basic difference; though, to be absolutely precise, the blues mode *does* sometimes take account of prevailing harmonies—a point we shall be returning to in later chapters.

THE BLUE FIFTH

So far we have assumed that the blue third is associated with a fixed tonic. But this is an assumption that cannot always be made. In British and American folk music, the contrast between relative major and minor is sometimes so slight that the two modes almost fuse into one, as proved by the variants of 'She was a Rum One' / 'Had I Wings' (Ex. 6) and 'The

Maid Freed from the Gallows' / 'Hangman' (Ex. 16). Ultimately, all such cases spring from the ambiguity of the minor third seen in the two-note chants of Ex. 9.

Now, what if there are two such versions of a blues tune? In Version A there is no problem: the blue third is simply a third above the tonic. But what about Version B? Take the lullaby 'Go to Sleep' (Ex. 19(*a*)) for

Ex. 19

(*a*) 'Go to Sleep'*

* From Alan Lomax, *The Penguin Book of American Folk Songs*, p. 59 (Penguin, 1964). From the singing of Lomax's Texan mother. (©1934, renewed 1962 by Ludlow Music, Inc., New York. Used by permission of TRO and Essex Music of Australia Pty Ltd.)

(*b*) 'Hush-You-Bye' (end)*

* Sung by Harriet McClintock at Livingston, Alabama, in 1940. Recorded by John A. and Ruby T. Lomax and Ruby Pickens Tartt. On the Library of Congress Archive of Folk Culture recording *Afro-American Blues and Game Songs*, AFS L4, side B, track 11.

instance. What if it ended on A instead of C, as some variants in fact do (Ex. 19(*b*))? In such a 'relative minor' version the blue third would become a blue fifth. This is perhaps the easiest way to understand the blue fifth—as, in effect, the relative minor equivalent of the blue third. But we should remember that there is no sharp contrast between major and minor in the blues. There are blues tunes which are entirely in the major,[6] others where every third is minor, and an infinite range of gradations in between. Instead of the clear contrast between major and

[6] For instance 'Corinna' (Ex. 118), though anyone who sings it will feel an overwhelming temptation to flatten the thirds at the end slightly.

minor of the classical style, there is a spectrum between the two, minor in this case being synonymous with 'bluesy'. It is at this minor or bluesy end of the spectrum that blue fifths appear, assuming something of the function of the blue third at the major end.

In spite of the popular notion to the contrary, the blue fifth is probably just as old as the blue third. It can be heard in the earliest recorded blues and the most archaic of worksongs and spirituals, and can also be found in the most conservative style of white hymn singing.[7]

BLUE SEVENTHS AND SIXTHS

Folk music is often vague about the distinction between the major sixth and the minor seventh, especially when the mode is pentatonic. In African and Afro-American music it is often a puzzle how to notate notes that fall midway between the two.[8] Even when a clear distinction is made, these two degrees of mode may have the same function. A minor seventh may appear in one variant of a tune where another has a sixth. It is therefore not surprising to find the comparatively rare blue sixth behaving in much the same way as the blue seventh, the most typical function of which is to 'resolve' onto the dominant, in the same way as the blue third 'resolves' onto the tonic (Ex. 20). But sometimes the sixth has a more pronounced individuality. In its blue form, it may resolve

Ex. 20

(a) Blue seventh: 'Freight Train Blues' (end)

Ev-ery time   I hear it blow-in'   I feel like rid - in' too.

(b) Blue sixth: 'M. and O. Blues'

I start' to   kill my wom-an   till she   lay down 'cross   the bed____

[7] See, for instance, 'The Day is Past and Done' in Ritchie, *Folk Songs of the Southern Appalachians as Sung by Jean Ritchie*, p. 52.
[8] See Evans, *Big Road Blues*, p. 24.

either upwards or downwards to the tonic (Ex. 21(*a*)). The downward-resolving sixth is not peculiar to American music: it can also be found in Scotland, as in Ex. 21(*b*).[9]

Ex. 21

(*a*) 'Got the Blues, Can't be Satisfied'

(*b*) 'The Banks of Fordie' (end)

Yet another type of blue sixth resolves onto the subdominant, when that is the root of the prevailing chord. More than any other degree of the blues mode, the sixth changes its character according to the context. It may behave in any of the following ways:

1. like the sixth of the ordinary pentatonic major mode;
2. as a species of leading note *up* to the tonic, like the 'Landini sixth' of medieval European music; this often goes with the suggestion of an A C E melodic triad;
3. as the same, only resolving *down* a sixth to the tonic below;
4. as a blue note resolving onto the dominant a tone below;
5. as the 'blue third' of the subdominant chord.

The other notes of the blues mode show a similar versatility, but none of them bring out so strikingly that subtle, shifting modal ambiguity which is part of the essence of the blues.

THE BLUES MINI-MODES

There is a tendency for the principal notes in the blues mode to cluster into two groups, one around the tonic and the other around the dominant. The blue third corresponds, as we have already seen, to the blue seventh, while the sixth below the tonic corresponds to the major third below the dominant. The worksong 'Po' Lazarus' (Ex. 83)

[9] For a good example of the downward-resolving blue sixth, see the end of 'Frankie and Albert', Ex. 77.

beautifully illustrates these correspondences. The question of the origin of these blues 'mini-modes' is dealt with in the section 'Focus Contrast' in the next chapter.

THE TWELVE-BAR FORM

The term 'twelve-bar blues' is, as usual, a misnomer. The twelve bars can grow to twenty-four if each bar is cut in half, or shrink to six if each pair of bars is joined together. (An example of a six-bar 'twelve-bar blues' is 'Hangman', Ex. 16(*b*).) Both these schemes are fairly common, but they are of course merely a matter of notation. More important are those variations, involving additions or subtractions of bars or fractions of bars, which may swell the twelve bars into thirteen, fourteen, or any number of other lengths, or shrink it to nine, ten, or eleven. In fact, the essence of the twelve-bar blues lies not in its length but in its three-part structure. In its commonest form it consists of three parts of four bars each, but these four bars can be extended, or, more rarely, contracted, without destroying the essential nature of the form. The first of the three sections is the one most likely to be extended. Often it is doubled from four bars to eight, giving one type of the sixteen-bar blues. Modern examples of this form are Leiber and Stoller's 'Jailhouse Rock' and John Lennon's 'The Ballad of John and Yoko'. Further extension is also possible. In Richard Farina's 'Hard Loving Loser', the first section is no less than sixteen bars long, giving a total of twenty-four bars, but it is still basically a twelve-bar blues (16+4+4).

In view of this variability it would be more logical to talk about the 'three-part blues', 'three-section blues', or something of the kind. In spite of this temptation, however, the term 'twelve-bar blues', like so many misnomers, is so well established that it seems best to retain it. Even popular music has its traditions.

Most definitions of the twelve-bar blues include the harmonic formula that usually goes with it: tonic (four bars), subdominant (two bars), tonic (two bars), dominant (two bars), tonic (two bars). (Sometimes the last four bars are given as one bar dominant, one bar subdominant, two bars tonic.) The whole question of blues harmony will be dealt with in its due place, but it should be pointed out here that this harmonic formula is strictly optional. The basic logic of the twelve-bar blues is independent of harmony. Not only are there twelve-bar blues tunes with no harmony at all; there are also many with harmonic schemes different from this standard one.[10]

In any case this harmonic formula is a comparatively late development, and seems to have played no part in the early history of the blues.

[10] Ex. 86 gives a few of these alternative harmonizations.

The essential features of that history are the blues mode and the three-part form, evolving separately in Africa and Britain, and finally coming together in the United States in the nineteenth century. It is to the story of this complex, subtle, and fascinating evolution that the following chapters are devoted.

II. AFRICAN ORIGINS OF THE BLUES

16. THE BLUES MODE IN AFRICA

THE African antecedents of the blues are just as mixed as common sense would suggest them to be. There are many parallels to individual features, but nowhere—to the best of my knowledge, but who knows what research may turn up tomorrow?—is there anything like the blues mode in its complete form. The notes may sometimes look the same, but when one examines them carefully the unique logic of blues modality is lacking. All the components of the blues mode are to be found somewhere in West Africa, but separately, awaiting assembly on American soil.

PENDULAR THIRDS

The most basic of these components was the interval of the third. The blues mode is constructed out of thirds, and in Africa, too, the third is an important interval, though we never find it used in quite the same way. As we have seen, long phrases built on the alternation of two notes a minor or neutral third apart arise naturally out of African speech habits.[1] Such 'pendular thirds', to use J.H. Nketia's term,[2] frequently appear at the end of a descending phrase (as in Exx. 24 and 26(a)) and also sometimes at the beginning (Ex. 22). Here the singer is declaiming these

Ex. 22   'Olúrómbí' (beginning)

[1] See 'Speech, Song, and Instrumental Sounds' in ch. 5.
[2] *African Music in Ghana*, p. 45.

words to the natural speech-tones of the Yoruba language, slightly
adjusted to fit the mode. (Since an acute accent indicates a high tone, a
grave accent a low tone, and the absence of either a medium tone, the
reader can here compare sung tones with their rendering in song.)
Exactly the same thing is sometimes found in American songs, with
English treated as though it had a pitch accent like an African language
(Ex. 23). Similar passages, though not usually following the accent so

Ex. 23   'City of Refuge'

neatly, are common in the blues. The notes involved are not always the
tonic and third. They may be third and fifth, fifth and seventh, or sixth
and tonic. Examples are:

1. tonic and third: Chanted sermon, Ex. 31, and also 'Tight like
   That', Ex. 80, and 'Long Tall Sally', Ex. 81, though here the
   element of pitch accent is minimal; in 'John Henry' (II), Ex. 84(c),
   we have an example of how a European tune could be adapted to
   this pattern;
2. third and fifth: 'Josie', Ex. 76(c);
3. fifth and seventh: 'Captain Holler Hurry', Ex. 35;
4. sixth and tonic: 'Way over in the New Buryin' Groun' ', Ex. 17.

Similar alternations of notes a third apart are equally common in Afro-
American instrumental music.[3]

FOCUS CONTRAST

'A structure consisting of two halves, the first one resting on the upper
fifth (dominant), and the second one built analogously on the tonic is
typical of it'—that is, African melody, wrote Erich von Hornbostel in

[3] See, for instance, 'Tom Brigg's Jig', Ex. 55, 'Mississippi Rag', Ex. 153(c) 'One o' them
Things!', Ex. 159, and Ben Harney's raggy version of 'Annie Laurie', Ex. 156.

1928.[4] Ex. 24 is an example of what he meant.[5] This melodic type is one example of the African love of setting phrases at contrasting pitches against one another. In this example the first phrase is a fifth higher than

Ex. 24 'Maḍe yi vódú yǫ́wé'

the second, but the distance can also be a second, third, or fourth, and the movement up as well as down. Where the words of both phrases are the same, the opposition generally has a strong touch of the sequence about it, again arising naturally out of African speech habits, as for instance in Ex. 25. Similar things are to be found in many Afro-

Ex. 25 'Kuro'i nye mo dea' (beginning)

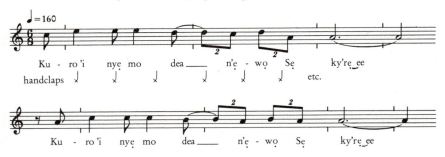

American styles: examples in this book are 'Frankie and Albert' (Ex. 77), 'I Went to the Hop-Joint' (Ex. 78), 'Way over in the New Buryin''

---

[4] 'African Negro Music', p. 45. More recently Lazarus Ekwueme has written a long article expanding on this and similar African melodic patterns, 'Analysis and Analytic Techniques in African Music'.

[5] Note how the melodic line follows the rhythm of the bell. The words mean '[Solo:] Anyone who goes to call a god [vódú, hence the English 'voodoo'] [Chorus:] must bow down his head,' etc.

Groun' ' (Ex. 17), 'Po' Lazarus' (Ex. 83), and the boogie-woogie bass, Ex. 96.[6] In all of these the melody turns on the contrast between an upper and lower focus, to borrow a phrase from Lazarus Ekwueme.[7]

THE TRIADIC MODE

Many of the most archaic Afro-American styles, such as the early blues, spirituals, and, most of all, worksongs, are built on the bare tonic triad, unadorned except perhaps for the occasional passing-note.[8] Similar tunes occur in African song, though usually not with the same starkly triadic quality. A comparison of Exx. 26(a) and (b) will show how close this African type could be to its American counterpart.[9]

ARABIC INFLUENCES

This resemblance is close enough to suggest direct influence, especially in view of the importance of the Gold Coast in the North American slave trade. Before we can fully account for the blues, however, we must look further north, to the Arab-influenced savannah. The famous hollers, those rhapsodic forerunners of the early blues, seem to have derived as much from the savannah as from the coastal style. At the end of the nineteenth century Jeannette Robinson Murphy gave an account of the black American singing style which leaves no doubt about its Near Eastern character:

We find many of the genuine negro melodies in Jubilee and Hampton Song Books, but for the uninitiated student of the future there is little or no instruction given, and the white singer in attempting to learn them will make poor work at their mastery; for how is he, poor fellow, to know that it is bad form not to break every law of musical phrasing and notation? What is there to show him that he must make his voice exceedingly nasal and undulating; that around every prominent note he must place a variety of small notes, called 'trimmings,' and he must sing tones not found in our scale; that he must on no account leave one note until he has the next one well under control? He might be

---

[6] See also the ante-bellum spiritual 'Religion so Sweet' (Allen *et al.*, *Slave Songs of the United States*, p. 13), apparently the same tune as the early blues, 'Another Man Done Gone' or 'Now your Man Done Gone' (Courlander, *Negro Songs from Alabama*, p. 83). The Afro-American 'double tonic' tunes discussed in ch. 23 also fall into this category.

[7] 'Analysis and Analytic Techniques in African Music', p. 94; though he uses the terms in a slightly different sense, to refer to individual notes rather than melodic groups.

[8] As well as Ex. 26(b), examples are 'Go 'way f'om mah Window', Ex. 14, Cable's worksong, Ex. 15, 'City of Refuge', Ex. 23, 'One Kind Favour', Ex. 73(e), and 'John Henry' (knife blues), Ex. 84(d).

[9] Ex. 26(b) is an example of a worksong with spiritual-like words. 'Tie-shuffling' is the process of levering the railway track into position, and the purpose of this song was to ensure that everyone doing the levering heaved at the same time.

Ex. 26

(a) 'Ọnyẹ ampa ara' (beginning)

(b) Tie-shuffling chant*

* From John A. and Alan Lomax, *American Ballads and Folk Songs*, p. 15 (Macmillan, 1934).

(c) 'Ọl'ọ́kọ́ d'ẹhìn' (beginning)

tempted, in the *ignorance* of his twentieth-century education, to take breath
whenever he came to the end of a line or verse! But this he should never do. By
some mysterious power, to be learned only from the negro, he should carry over

his breath from line to line and from verse to verse, even at the risk of bursting a blood-vessel. He must often drop from a high note to a very low one; he must be very careful to divide many of his monosyllabic words in two syllables, placing a forcible accent on the last one, so that 'dead' will be 'da—*ade*,' 'back' becomes 'ba—*ack*,' 'chain' becomes 'cha—*ain*.'

He must also intersperse his singing with peculiar humming sounds— 'hum-m-m-m'. ('The Survival of African Music in America', pp. 664–5.)

Ex 27,[10] an example of the Afro-Arab style, shares most of these features. It has the 'trimmings', the long phrase on one breath, the

Ex. 27   Watutsi song

* explosive pulses

humming, and the undulating vocal style, as well as certain other features common to the holler: the 'passionate lengthening' of the first note, the breaking up of the same note by explosive pulsations, and the gradual descent of the melody, first to the dominant and then to the tonic; all of which appear in Ex. 28.

Ex. 28   Cornfield holler

* The notes marked 'x' are sung with a catch in the voice like a descending yodel.

[10] A historical song glorying past military exploits. Compare the initial grace-note a third below the tonic with the beginning of 'Cripple Creek' (Ex. 54).

Both these last two examples belong to an extremely widespread melodic type, to be found over large areas of Asia, Europe, and North Africa. Its characteristics are the following:

1. The melody is a set of free variations on a basic pattern.
2. Each variation begins at a high point (possibly led up to by a brief introductory phrase) and gradually sinks, through a florid and rather meandering melody, to a floor note which we may call the tonic, though it has neither the solidity nor the finality of a true tonic.
3. The rhythm is free, with long notes on the strong degrees of the mode and melismatic graces on the weak ones.
4. In the course of its descent the melody tends to linger around the note a fourth or fifth above the floor note.
5. The compass is about an octave.
6. The ends of the variations will resemble each other more than the beginnings. This is an 'end-repeating' form.
7. Variations may differ greatly in rhythm, melody, ornamental detail, and length.

One variety of this general type is the *doina* ('lament') or *hora lunga* ('long song') discovered by Béla Bartók in Romania in 1913, and subsequently found to extend from Morocco to China.[11] Bartók himself came to the conclusion that the place of origin was Persia. It is interesting, by the way, that similar names have been given to kindred forms: the Irish 'caoin' ('keen' in English) means 'lament', and the cornfield hollers like Ex. 28 were sometimes known as 'long metre songs'.[12] Ex. 29 is an example of what could be called an Irish 'holler'. I

Ex. 29   Keen for a dead child

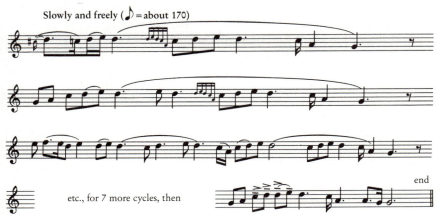

---

[11] See A. L. Lloyd's article 'Hora Lunga', *The New Grove*, vol. 8, p. 694.
[12] They were so described by the blues singer Son House. See Evans, *Big Road Blues*, p. 43.

quote it partly to show how those typically African features, the descending line and the end-repeating phrase, appear in Celtic music too, and partly to illustrate the difficulty of disentangling the Celtic and Afro-Arab strains in American music. The florid Near Eastern style entered black American song by two routes: directly, from the savannah culture, and indirectly, from British (and predominantly Celtic) sources. The most important of the latter was the florid hymn style that black church-goers began learning in the mid-eighteenth century, and which came to be known as the 'old way of singing'.[13] (Another name was 'Long metre songs': hence the application of this term to the florid field hollers.) This 'old way of singing' must have been all the more congenial to the African ear in that it embodied a call-and-response structure. In the English form, each line was recited by the preacher, or some other functionary, before being sung by the congregation. Originally, this was a concession to illiteracy; but in Scotland, where the line was sometimes sung instead of spoken, it is probable that the call-and-response form was liked for its own sake.

It is interesting that the resemblance between antiphonal psalm singing and African song has been noticed by the Africans themselves:

MAPOBOLO.
This is a very sweet kind of singing, sung slowly and gently. . . . One woman at a time will stand in the middle of the gathering to start her *Ipobolo*, then all the people, men and woman will answer, the women of course singing an octave higher than the men. This kind of singing is similar to Psalm-chants. . . . There is no clapping or beating of any kind, but all the people must pay great attention to the song so that they may join in at exactly the right moment. (Robert Kabombo, 'Some Types of African Song', in Jones, *African Music in Northern Rhodesia and Some Other Places*, p. 17.)

In the Afro-American 'surge songs' the response of the congregation is very slow and very florid, with no two people singing quite the same thing.[14] A similar florid singing style may also appear in solo, extempore prayers like Ex. 30. The mode here is reminiscent of 'Amazing Grace', a favourite surge song tune, and a close relative of the Scottish tune associated with the songs 'Loch Lomond' and 'The Bonny House o' Airlie'.[15] There is also a marked resemblance to the Irish keen already quoted (Ex. 29). On the other hand, melodies with a very similar structure can be found in the Afro-Arab tradition.[16] Does 'Run Sinner'

---

[13] This style has lingered on to the present day in certain white churches in the American backwoods (see Temperley, 'The Old Way of Singing: Its Origins and Development'), as well as the remoter parts of Scotland (for a transcription of the Hebridean style, see Cooke, 'Heterophony', *The New Grove*, vol. 8, pp. 537–8).

[14] See Bailey, 'The Lined-Hymn Tradition in Black Mississippi Churches'.

[15] For 'The Bonny House o' Airlie' see Bronson, *Traditional Tunes of the Child Ballads*, vol. 3, pp. 194–5.

[16] See, for instance, Födermayr, 'The Arabian Influence in the Tuareg Music', p. 28.

owe more to Britain or to Africa? Even if we had a minute knowledge of its history, this would most likely prove so mixed and complex as to render the question meaningless.

Ex. 30   'Run Sinner'[*]

* Sung by Huddie Ledbetter ('Leadbelly') and recorded for the Library of Congress by John A. and Alan Lomax. On *Leadbelly: The Library of Congress Recordings* (Elektra EKL-301/2), side 4, track 2.

PRAISE SONGS AND SERMONS

The African links to black American music are strongest where function, as well as style, was preserved in America. Examples are utilitarian music like the worksong and personal music like the holler. Sometimes the process is a little less direct, as when African ceremonial dances become the ring shout of Christian worship. Another instance is the transformation of the praise song into the chanted sermon. Stylistic resemblances are strong enough to leave little doubt of the links between the two forms, and, in any case, what is a sermon but a praise song directed to God? The typical chanted sermon begins in a speaking tone, works up into a chant, and culminates in the singing of the whole congregation. Similar processes are common in Africa.[17] Ex. 31 gives a sample of the preacher's technique when in full flight. It will be seen that the narrative portions are in a recitative on two notes a third apart; but every so often,

[17] For an account of how an entertainment song can be developed in this way, see Akpabot, 'Functional Music of the Ibibio', pp. 88–9.

Ex. 31   Chanted sermon[*]

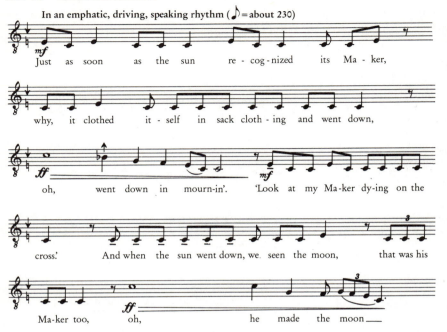

In an emphatic, driving, speaking rhythm (♪ = about 230)

mf
Just as soon as the sun re-cog-nized its Ma-ker,

why, it clothed it-self in sack cloth-ing and went down,

ff _____ *mf*
oh, went down in mourn-in'. 'Look at my Ma-ker dy-ing on the

cross.' And when the sun went down, we seen the moon, that was his

Ma-ker too, *ff* oh, he made the moon___

[*] Delivered by 'Sin-Killer' Griffin at Darrington State Farm, Sandy Point, Texas, on Easter Day, 1934. Recorded by John A. Lomax. On the Library of Congress Archive of Folk Culture recording *Negro Religious Songs and Services*, AFS L10, side A, track 9.

for an especially emotive phrase, the voice leaps up an octave to a powerful, bluesy, descending strain. It is these descending strains that most strikingly recall the technique of the praise singer—that, and the generally tense and urgent vocal delivery that has given to this style the description of 'straining' preaching.[18] Ex. 32 shows how close the melodic resemblance can be.

Ex. 32

(*a*) Hausa praise song

SOLO   CHORUS   SOLO

CHORUS

[18] Paul Oliver comments on this in *Savannah Syncopators*, p. 65.

(*b*) Sermon extract

Oh ___   I want you to know   when you get rea-dy to leave the hall breth-rens

THE TAPERING PATTERN AND THE TWELVE-BAR BLUES

In the classical European style the centre of gravity of a melody typically comes towards the end. In the melodies we have been considering here it comes at the beginning, with a tapering off in both loudness and emotional intensity towards the end, which is often no more than a whispy pianissimo, a grunt, or a sigh. In Africa this same tapering pattern is often applied to larger melodic aggregates, with cycles of descending phrases, all sinking to the same note (and often the same melodic figure), but with a gradual flattening of the melodic line; until eventually, when the process has exhausted itself, the cycle is resumed from the beginning. Ex. 33[19] is a specimen of this form.

Ex. 33

(*a*) 'Mkwaze mmodzi'

[19] The words mean 'Can I give cattle to my wife? When I am dead I shall go together with her to the grave'. (Note their blues-like character.) The alternative notation shows how the notes are probably distributed between the thumbs. (I owe this reconstruction of the playing technique, which, if not absolutely certain, is extremely likely, to Andrew Tracey.) It also illustrates the 'pulse-lines' commonly used in transcriptions of African music.

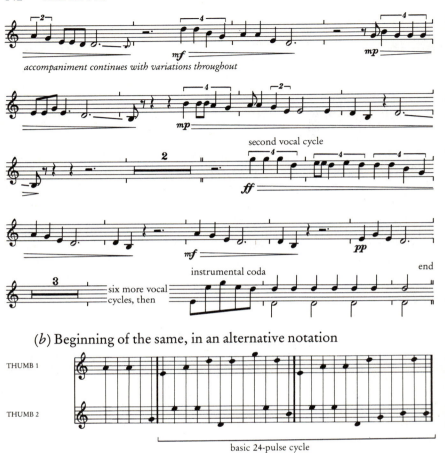

accompaniment continues with variations throughout

second vocal cycle

instrumental coda   end

six more vocal
cycles, then

(*b*) Beginning of the same, in an alternative notation

THUMB 1

THUMB 2

basic 24-pulse cycle

The same pattern is frequent in American hollers like Ex. 34.[20] In the more song-like hollers there is a tendency to construct these long, loose paragraphs out of groups of three strains. In Ex. 35 the first paragraph consists of four strains and the second of three, as does the third,

Ex. 34   'I've Got a Boy Child'*

Freely, half-speaking (♩ = about 128)

Mmmm. _____   Boys,   I've got a boychild in Tex-as,

[20] This piece is actually in the equiheptatonic scale (minus the second and sixth degrees, and with slight variations in pitch) and should really be notated on a special equiheptatonic stave, such as that used by Gerhard Kubik in the article 'Angola', *The New Grove*, vol. 1, p. 433.

he ought to be 'bout grown. ____ Oh, go march-in' to the

ta - ble oh Lord, find the same old thing. ____

Ummm. ____ Boys, I'll be so ____

glad when pay-day comes. Oh ____ cap - tain, cap - tain, ____

when pay - day comes. I'm gon' catch that Il - li - nois

Cen - tral, oh ____ Lord, goin' to Kan - ka - kee.

new cycle begins

Mmmm. ____ etc.

* Sung by Jim Henry at the State Penitentiary, Parchman, Mississippi, in 1937. Recorded by John A. Lomax. On the Library of Congress Archive of Folk Culture recording *Afro-American Blues and Game Songs*, AFS L4, side A, track 1, under the title 'I Don't Mind the Weather'.

Ex. 35 'Captain Holler Hurry'

The Cap-tain hol-ler hur-ry, ____ goin' to take my time. ____

Say the Cap-tain hol-ler hurry, ____ goin' to take my time. __

Say he mak-in' mo-ney   and I'm tryin' to make time.

Say he can lose his   job____   but I can't lose   mine.

I ain't got long   to   tar - ry,____   just   stop by   here.____

I ain't got long   to   tar -   ry,____   just   stop by   here.

Boys if you got   long____   you bet-ter move along.____

unquoted paragraph.[21] In Ex. 36 this loose grouping of three strains has turned into a regular twelve-bar blues. This, the famous 'Joe Turner

Ex. 36   'Joe Turner'

Dey   tell me   Joe   Tur-ner   he done   come, ____   Dey   tell me   Joe

Tur-ner   he done   come,____   Got my   man an'   gone.____

Blues', has been cited by old-timers like W.C. Handy, Bill Broonzy, and Lucius Smith as one of the first of the blues.[22] Joe Turner has been identified with Joe Turney, a Tennessee prison officer of the 1890s in charge of transporting convicts.[23] But certain aspects of the song—the

---

[21] Exx. 34 and 35 both contain traditional phrases mixed with improvised words. In Ex. 34 the words 'go marchin' to the table . . . find the same old thing' are from 'The Midnight Special' (quoted in ch. 9, 'Ballads and Blues'). As for Ex. 35, the line 'Cap'n says, hurry, I say take my time' was reported in Alabama as long ago as 1916 (see White, *American Negro Folk-Songs*, p. 255). The process of mingling improvised and traditional words in the blues and other American folk-song was much discussed in the 1970s.

[22] See Scarborough, *On the Trail of Negro Folk-Songs*, pp. 265–6, Broonzy, *Big Bill Blues*, pp. 27–8, and Evans, *Big Road Blues*, p. 47.

[23] See Green, *Only a Miner*, pp. 195–6.

words, the tune, the muddle about who Joe Turner was, and what he did exactly—suggest an even older tradition. Could it be that Joe Turner was only the last of a series of similar officials commemorated in similar songs, going back even to slavery days? With its descending line and final 'pendular' thirds, 'Joe Turner' is obviously akin to some of the African tunes quoted in this chapter; and the resemblance would be even more marked if it were sung in a rapid tempo, as, according to Lucius Smith, it originally was: 'See, when "Joe Turner" first come in, it wasn't in the blues way. And they changed it to the blues, all, you see.'[24]

CONCLUSION

The transformation of African idioms into the blues was very much a matter of *limitation*. The raw materials of the blues already existed in Africa, but mixed with an enormous wealth of other material. Gradually and unconsciously this other material was winnowed away, and what was left was the blues. Modes were simplified until they were stripped down to the bare tonic triad, a process that can be followed in detail in the case of British-derived tunes like 'John Henry' (Ex. 84) and no doubt happened to African ones too. The wealth of African cadences was almost restricted to the characteristic dropping third. In rather the same way as the richness of Renaissance harmony was eventually whittled down to little more than the three primary triads, that of African modality was reduced to the powerful simplicity of the blues mode. One can only guess what forces lay behind this tendency; but it seems reasonable to suppose that one of them was the catalytic influence of British folk styles.

[24] Evans, *Big Road Blues*, p. 47. The context makes it clear that the 'blues way' involved a slower tempo, among other things.

17. THE TALKING BLUES

PARTLY because African speech is itself so songlike, the boundaries between speech and song are often vague in Africa. A singer may drop into a speaking tone for a few notes, or work up from speech to song, or regularly alternate between a speaking and singing delivery. Or there may be long stretches of something intermediate between the two, variously called 'sing song', 'recitative', 'sprechstimme', and 'melodic speech'. There are two aspects to this 'sing song', the rhythmic and melodic. If both are slightly regularized, the result is merely a stylized speech; if both are made completely songlike, the result is song. If one is regular and the other free, the result is a delivery which is either rhythmically strict but melodically free, or melodically strict but rhythmically free.[1] Both these types are found in Africa, and both have passed into black American usage. The introductory words of the tie-shuffling chant (Ex. 26(b)) are one example of the melodically strict but rhythmically free type; so, in a different way, is the chanted sermon (Ex. 31). It is, however, the other type, rhythmic speech or near-speech, which is the more important in both Africa and America, and in both places it often goes with an instrumental accompaniment. In its American form, it most typically appears in the guise of the 'talking blues'.

Though Africa is the obvious place to look for the origins of the talking blues, there were certain British influences at work too. British folk singers often like to oppose the speaking and singing voice in an almost African way. Sometimes the singer will begin a song in a speaking tone, and after a few words glide into song.[2] Often a parlando verse will be contrasted with a cantabile refrain.[3] And there are songs systematically incorporating spoken lines. This seems to occur especially where there is dialogue, as in the following (spoken lines in italics):

OUR GOODMAN

Hame cam oor goodman, an' hame cam he,
An' he got a horse in a stall where nae horse should be.
'An' how cam this horse here, an' how can it be?

---

[1] For examples of various kinds of rhythmic speech and sing song, see Jones, *Studies in African Music*, vol. 2, play songs 3, 6, 7, and 8 (pp. 2 and 4–7).
[2] For instance 'The Cunning Cobbler' in Kennedy, *Folksongs of Britain and Ireland*, p. 453.
[3] An American example of this style is 'Sorghum Syrup', Ex. 79(b).

An how cam this horse here withoot the leave o' me?'
'*A horse?' quo' she; 'Ay, a horse' quo' he.*
'Ye aul' blin' dottered carle, blinner mat ye be,
It' s but a little milk coo my minnie sent to me.'
'*A milk coo'? quo' he; 'Ay, a milk coo,' quo' she.*
'Far hae I ridden an' muckle hae I seen,
But a saddle on a milk coo saw I never neen.'[4]

Another potent influence was the music-hall stage. In the mid-nineteenth century it was customary on both sides of the Atlantic to deliver comic songs with spoken interpolations. These interpolations helped to flesh out the character being portrayed—usually a bombastic half-wit with a taste for long words, generally misused. The only difference was that in London this comic proletarian was a Cockney, or perhaps a country bumpkin, while in the United States he was most likely to be black. As an English politician on a visit to the United States put it, 'Sambo is a natural-born cockney'.[5] The closeness of the stereotypes can be seen in the following examples:

ENGLISH MUSIC-HALL SONG, 'VILLIKINS AND HIS DINAH'

Spoken: Now this is the most melancholy part of it, and shows what the progeny was druv to in conskivence of the mangled obstropolosness and ferocity of the inconsiderable parient . . .
Sung: Now as Villikins was a-walking the garding all around . . .
Spoken: It was the back garding this time
Sung: He spied his dear Dinah lying dead on the ground,
With a cup of cold pizen all down by her side
And a billey-dow which said as 'ow 'twas by pizen she died.
Spoken: The label was marked 'British Brandy'
Sung: Singin' Too-ra-li, too-ra-li, too-ra-li-da.[6]

MINSTREL SONG, 'GINGER BLUE'

Spoken: Says I, look here Pete, I doesn't like to be cutting round that daughter of yours when Clum Grum is throwing his affections at her, besides he's such a mighty consequential nigga, you can smell him half a mile off, because he carries musk, cologne water, and all the perfumications, round him. Well, says Pete, Ginger, I don't care nothing for that; but if de nigga comes cutting round my daughter I be dam if I don't make him. [The chorus then follows.][7]

In due course this pseudo-Negro patter was taken up by genuine

[4] Sung by Mrs Gillespie, Glasgow, 1905. In Bronson, *Traditional Tunes of the Child Ballads*, vol. 4, p. 99.
[5] See Gutman, *The Black Family in Slavery and Freedom, 1750–1925*, pp. 300–1. The politician's name was Robert Somers.
[6] Garrett, *Sixty Years of British Music Hall*, pp. [9]–[10].
[7] Marsh's *Selection*, 1854, part 2, p. 157. Quoted in White, *American Negro Folk-Songs*, p. 448.

blacks, who turned it into an African-style chanted recitative with instrumental accompaniment. The following early twentieth-century example shows a distinct kinship with the kind of routine still used by British and American stand-up comics ('My mother-in-law's mouth is so big, when she . . .'):

CROSS-EYED SALLY

The Negro's tendency to put everything into song is well illustrated by the following monotone song. The singer appeared to be making it as he sang, all the while picking his guitar in the regular way; but he repeated it in the exact words except for the usual variations in dialect. This he could do as often as required. . . .

> Had ole gal one time, name was Cross-eyed Sally.
> She was the blackest gal in Paradise Alley.
> She had liver lips an' kidney feet.
> Didn't know she was so black
> Till I took a fire-coal one morning
> An' make a white mark on her face.
> An' I didn't know she was so cross-eyed
> Till one morning she come up to me an' say:
> 'Look here, boy, I want to eat!
> I tole her if she had anything
> She had better go to eatin' it,
> I never had nuthin'.
> It hurt my gal so bad when I tole her this
> That she cried; an' cryin she so cross-eyed
> Till the tears run down her back!
> [etc., for three more pages.][8]

This is also very much in the style of the talking blues associated especially with white folk singers like Woodie Guthrie.[9] It is this type of talking blues which has since become one of the trademarks of the country and western style. If anything, the talking blues technique is now more characteristic of white American music than its black counterpart—where the two can still be distinguished, that is.

---

[8] Odum and Johnson, *The Negro and his Songs*, pp. 241–2. It is hardly necessary to remark on the tragic self-contempt expressed in the first six lines.

[9] See A. Lomax, *The Folk Songs of North America*, pp. 432–4, for some Guthrie talking blues.

18. BLUES ACCOMPANIMENT

THERE are two African accompaniment techniques of special importance to Afro-American music. One is the familiar ostinato, in which a
short phrase is repeated over and over again, with or without slight
variation. The other, though less well known, seems to have been even
more important in the development of the early blues. This is the
'dialogue' form of accompaniment, in which voice and instrument
alternate, as in the African lament 'Tukhong'ine tulauya' (Ex. 37).[1] This

Ex. 37 'Tukhong'ine tulauya'

is the technique of the accompanied 'holler', as collected by David Evans
from Othar Turner, a Mississippi farmer. Turner described his song as
'just the old cornfield blues':

[1] The words mean 'Though we all gather here together yet one day shall we die and meet no
more.'

Turner's text is highly repetitive, and in both an unaccompanied version of the song and one accompanied by the guitar he sings the same kind of long, strident, highly ornamented, descending lines. The only important musical difference between the two versions is that when he accompanies himself he leaves spaces between the sung lines for his simple, highly percussive, guitar playing. His song must be close to the sound of the first accompanied blues. (*Big Road Blues*, p. 43.)

This is basically the same technique as in Leadbelly's 'Alberta' (Ex. 38).

Ex. 38   Leadbelly, 'Alberta'[*]

[*] On *Leadbelly* (Columbia C 30035), side 1, track 7. Recorded in 1935, probably under the supervision of John A. and Alan Lomax (according to the sleeve note).

(Quite apart from the accompaniment technique, these songs have several features in common: the long instrumental introduction (in 'Alberta' taking the form of a twelve-bar blues); the descending phrases ending with the fall of a third; the way both singers later drop into a speaking delivery; and the percussive backing throughout both pieces, provided in Ex. 37 by the singer's son, on the sound-box of the zither, and in Ex. 38 by Leadbelly's foot.)

Sometimes the dialogue form is combined with a drone effect, the instrument backing the voice with the drone and launching into more melodic passages when the voice falls silent, as in Ex. 39.[2] Here again,

Ex. 39   Arap Kapero's song

similar things can be found in the primitive blues (see John Lee Hooker's, 'Late Last Night', Ex. 40[3]), including the extremely blues-like fourth chords which constitute the drone.

Ex. 40   John Lee Hooker, 'Late Last Night'

----

[2] The harmonic basis of this piece is the alternation of two fifth chords a tone apart (A–E and G–D), like the Scottish 'double tonic'. 'Mkwaze mmodzi', Ex. 33, has a similar construction. I am told by a Ugandan acquaintance, Mike Kizito, that Ex. 39 is a ribald commentary on the shortcomings of various types of women—an eminently blues-like theme.

[3] Another example of the tapering holler form, like Exx. 33, 34, and 35.

THE DESCENDING STRAIN AS ACCOMPANIMENT FIGURE

Though no doubt vocal in origin, the African descending strain is far
from being confined to the voice. In Ex. 41 we have an example of an

Ex. 41   'Chemirocha'

ostinato figure built along these lines. This figure, too, has its Afro-American relatives. Something very like it appears in a mid-nineteenth-century banjo tune significantly entitled 'Genuine Negro Jig' (Ex. 42).

Ex. 42   'Genuine Negro Jig'

And an obviously related accompaniment figure appears in a rhythm and blues hit of the 1950s, 'Susie Q' (Ex. 43).

Ex. 43   'Susie Q'

It should be noted that the banjo was used to accompany the voice from early times—in all probability from the beginning, in fact. In 1774 it was mentioned that 'Some of them'—that is, the blacks—'sing to it, which is very droll music indeed.'[4] Bill Broonzy recorded that his father sang the 'Joe Turner Blues' (Ex. 36) to a banjo accompaniment in the 1890s.[5] The banjo may seem an unlikely blues instrument, but the early

[4] From the diary of Nicholas Creswell, 29 May 1774. Quoted in Epstein, 'The Folk Banjo', p. 353.
[5] *Big Bill Blues*, p. 28.

blues ballads were often sung to a fast tempo perfectly suited to the typical breakneck banjo style. We should realize, too, that the primitive banjo, with its relatively slack strings, absence of frets, and gourd sound-box, would produce a far gentler tone than the modern instrument. Not that the banjo was the only possible accompanying instrument before the days of the guitar: there were also various musical bows, of obviously African origin.[6]

All in all, the strong similarity between African and American accompaniment styles casts great doubt on the theory that the blues began when somebody had the idea of accompanying the holler. It seems far more likely that accompanied and unaccompanied hollers (or simply melodies) existed side by side from the start. Somewhere along the line African accompanied song turned into blues. By a gradual and complex process African melodies took on the contours of the blues mode, and the African instrumental styles turned into the one-chord accompaniments of pieces like 'Alberta' and 'Late Last Night'. The merest push in the direction of European triadic harmony was enough to turn African accompaniment figures into elaborations of the tonic chord—but elaborations, with their added sixths and sevenths, simultaneous major and minor thirds, and pentatonic figurations, of a completely un-European kind.

Why the one-chord blues should have developed at all is another of those puzzles of which the blues offers such a plentiful supply. Outside the United States, Afro-European accompaniment styles are normally based on the three primary triads. This includes the Europeanized styles of Africa itself, some of them very little removed from their African origins. It is true even of the Creole music of Louisiana. One-chord accompaniment, like the blues mode, seems to have developed only where African music came into contact with British folk music. One could argue that the blues mode, with its triadic framework, arose under the influence of a triadic accompaniment. Or, turning the argument around, it may be that the accompaniment developed to fit the voice part. Most likely both processes were at work.

Another interesting question is whether European folk instruments had anything to do with this process. The fiddle and Appalachian dulcimer, with their drone strings, had fairly close relatives in West Africa, and the Afro-American fiddling style makes great use of these drones. When a blues-like tune is accompanied by a tonic-and-dominant drone the result is already close to a one-chord blues. All that is

---

[6] There is an account of a mouth bow dating from 1858 (see Venable, 'Down South Before the War', p. 498; quoted in Epstein, *Sinful Tunes and Spirituals*, p. 128) and various types of musical bows have been encountered in the United States in recent years (see Evans, 'Afro-American One-Stringed Instruments').

necessary to complete the effect is the third of the chord. In other words, British folk music may have served as a bridge between African instrumental styles and urban triadic harmony, so that when triadic harmony did come to the blues in the late nineteenth century, it took a form completely new to music.

19. AFRO-AMERICAN RHYTHM

I tell you rhythm is the thing, rhythm is the thing, rhythm is the thing of today.

Popular song of the 1920s[1]

THE WEST AFRICAN BACKGROUND

EVER since the pioneering work of Ward and Hornbostel in the 1920s[2] the Great African Rhythm Controversy has rumbled on in learned books and journals. Two peculiarities have marked the discussion: firstly, the quite disproportionate amount of space devoted to what others have already said on the subject, and secondly the equally disproportionate concentration on one small part of the African continent. More has probably been written on the rhythms of the southern Gold Coast (now known as Ghana) than the rest of Africa put together. This at least means that these rhythms are by now fairly well understood. How good a guide, we must ask, are they to West Africa as a whole? The answer seems to be that in their basic principles they are entirely characteristic of the whole area from Senegambia to Angola. Further east and further south we find other rhythmic styles, but even these are not very different, from the non-African point of view.[3]

Such real controversy as remains centres mainly on the nature of the beat. Is there a single regulative beat in African music? If so, all the other rhythms are measured against it, consciously or unconsciously. If not, every regular pulse in the fabric of cross-rhythms has an equal and independent status. It is a relief to know that the general view nowadays is that there *is* a beat, though some still argue that this is a European idea falsely imposed on African music, or at any rate certain important West African styles.[4] Not only is there a beat, but a feeling for it is essential if African cross-rhythms are to be appreciated to the full.

This feeling, however, is no easy matter for the outsider. The African loves to emphasize the cross-rhythms at the expense of the main beat. It

---

[1] Quoted in Lambert, 'The Spirit of Jazz', *Music Ho!*, p. 210.
[2] Ward, 'Music in the Gold Coast' (1927) and Hornbostel, 'African Negro Music' (1928).
[3] See, for instance, A.M. Jones's study of the East African Luo, 'Luo Music and its Rhythm', and David Rycroft, 'Stylistic Evidence in Nguni Song', especially pp. 238–41.
[4] See Pantaleoni, 'Three Principles of Timing in Anlo Dance Drumming', p. 60, and Ladzekpo and Pantaleoni, 'Takada Drumming', p. 13. For a short bibliography of the beat controversy, see Locke, 'Principles of Offbeat Timing', p. 245, n. 7.

is not always necessary that the beat should be audibly represented at all. One of the characteristic tricks of African and Afro-American rhythm is the 'false trail' introduction, in which the listener is presented with a rhythm which turns out, once the main beat is brought in, to be something quite different from what it seemed at first. Another device is to stop the beat for a bar or two, so as to induce a moment of delightful rhythmic disorientation. Even when the beat is present as a regular, audible pulse, it is usually relatively soft. In the West African drum ensembles, it is generally also high-pitched, low pitches being left to the solo, or 'master' drum. Like West Indian reggae musicians, but unlike Europeans, these African drummers like to put the melodic interest in the bass and the backing in the treble.

The beats are usually arranged in a straightforward duple pattern, like the European common time, and since this is the arrangement that has passed into American music there seems no point in labouring the exceptions. But, for the sake of accuracy, it should be noted that odd-numbered time signatures (or the African equivalent thereof) are fairly common. Probably the most frequent is the nine-pulse bar;[5] there are also quintuple and septuple groupings, among other irregularities.[6] They seem to have had no lasting influence in North America. Simple triple time of the waltz type is foreign to African music, though African musicians are perfectly capable of performing triplet groups *against* the beat. In the United States and Caribbean such triple-time tunes do appear where European influence is strong, but not where African traditions predominate. In the long run, they tend either to be converted to common time or drop out of the repertory.

What concerns us, then, is the African equivalent of the familiar 'simple' and 'compound' common time. For convenience we may as well call them $\frac{8}{8}$ and $\frac{12}{8}$, as long as we are careful to avoid confusion with European time signatures.

CROSS-RHYTHMS

The way African cross-rhythms arise out of basic patterns can be understood from a few simple experiments. Let us start with the following.[7]

[5] See for instance Stone, 'Liberia', *The New Grove*, vol. 10, p. 718, Besmer, 'Hausa Court Music', pp. 239 and 240, and Nketia, *The Music of Africa*, p. 173.

[6] For $\frac{5}{8}$ time (notated as $\frac{5}{16}$) see King, 'Hausa Music', *The New Grove*, vol. 8, p. 311; for $\frac{10}{8}$ times, see Coolen, 'The Wolof Xalam Tradition', p. 491; for $\frac{7}{8}$ time (notated as $\frac{7}{16}$) see Rycroft, 'The Zulu Bow Songs of Princess Magogo', pp. 82, 86, and 89.

[7] For convenience I mark these rhythms as played by Drum 1, Drum 2, etc., starting with the bass and working up to the treble. The reader is welcome to substitute table tops, tin cans, rubbish bins, or anything else capable of contrasted timbres. It should be remarked, too, that the same patterns can be produced from melodic instruments like harps, xylophones, or marimbas.

Ex. 44   Drum pattern 1

Drum 2
Drum 1

This is a little dull. To make it more interesting, let us think in threes instead of twos:

Ex. 45   Drum pattern 2

Drum 2
Drum 1

Immediately there are, from the African point of view, three rhythms at work, all at odds with one another. There is, firstly, the overriding three-pulse unit: ♫♫ ♫♫. Then there is the rhythm of Drum 1: ♩ ♩ ♩; and finally, there is the rhythm of Drum 2: ♪ ♩ ♩ ♪. The basic rhythm and the Drum 1 pattern are in a hemiola relationship, while Drum 2 echoes the rhythm of Drum 1 at the distance of one pulse.

The hemiola, and more generally 'two against three' is of almost proverbial importance in African music. From infancy African are trained to hear the six-pulse unit as interchangeably 3+3 and 2+2+2, beginning with the lullabies they hear from their mothers.[8] In some styles there are long stretches of two-against-three rhythm, performed with such a balance of emphasis that it is difficult for the outsider to know which of these patterns qualifies as the beat, as for instance in Ex. 46.[9]

Ex. 46   African harp accompaniment pattern

But let us continue with our experiments. What happens if ♩♫♩ is changed to ♩ ♫♫ ?

Ex. 47   Drum pattern 3

Drum 2
Drum 1

The overriding pattern is now ♩ ♩ ♩ ♩. Against this if we listen to the combined rhythm of the two drums, we hear ♩ ♫♩ ♫; if we listen to

    [8] For two examples, see Turkson, 'Effutu Asafo Music', pp. 97–9.
    [9] Kubik, 'Harp Music of the Azande', pp. 48–50. He goes on to consider the question of whether the main beat occurs every two or three pulses, finally deciding for the latter. The oscillating bass of this example is widespread in African music, in various forms, and is probably related to the familiar boogie-woogie or rock and roll accompaniment figure exemplified in 'Long Tall Sally' (Ex. 81).

Drum 1, we hear ♩. ♩. ♩, and if we listen to Drum 2, we hear ♩ ♩ ♩. ♪.[10] The Drum 1 pattern, in its many variants (♩ ♪♩ ♪♩, ♩. ♩ ♪♪♫, ♩ ♪♩. ♩, ♩. ♪♩, ♩♫. ♩. ♩ etc.) is one of the favourite African and Afro-American rhythms. For convenience, we can call it the 'rumba rhythm'. [11] (It should be remarked that when the rhythm ♩. ♪♩ ♩ occurs in African music, as in Chemirocha' (Ex. 41) it is likely to be yet another variant of this rhythm: ♩. ♪♩ ♩, not ♩. ♪♩ ♩. The slurring of the middle two notes of this same rhythm in the tango or habenera is a vestige of this feeling.)

This is not the end of the complexities this simple exercise can produce. Suppose, now that we 'swing' the ♩ ♫ rhythm, like a jazz player, turning it into ♩. ♩ ♪ (Ex. 48). We are now back in $\frac{12}{8}$

Ex. 48   Drum pattern 4

Drum 2   ♩ ♩. ♪

Drum 1   ♩. ♪ ♩

time, and the rumba rhythm has turned into ♩ ♩ ♩ ♩.. (It may be noticed that these rhythmic values are in the mathematically pleasing ratio of 5 : 4 : 3 .) This is one variant of the rhythm that has been called 'the African signature tune'[12] or the 'standard pattern' of African rhythm. The essence of the standard pattern is that it divides the $\frac{12}{8}$ bar into 5+7 (or sometimes 7+5) while the rumba rhythm divides the $\frac{8}{8}$ bar into 3+5. It occurs in many forms all over black Africa, and has been the subject of a great deal of discussion.[13] Its kinship with the rumba rhythm comes out in the West African 'highlife' style, where $\frac{8}{8}$ ♫ ♩ ♪♩ is interchangeable with $\frac{12}{8}$ ♩ ♩ ♩. ♩ ♩♩,[14] and in the early blues, where one rhythm can turn into the other in the course of a single movement (as in Leadbelly's Alberta', Exx. 57(c) and (d)).

In this simple series of exercises we have already made the acquaintance of the essentials of African rhythm: the eight- and twelve-pulse patterns; the division of the twelve-pulse pattern into both four lots of three and three lots of four; the irregular division of 8 into 3+5, or 5+

---

[10]   For a detailed discussion of an actual African use of the drum pattern in Ex. 47, and much other interesting information, see Knight, 'Mandinka Drumming'.

[11]   In the actual rumba a distinction is made between the tresillo (triplet) rhythm, ♩. ♩. ♩, and the cinquillo (quintuplet) rhythm, ♩ ♪♩ ♪♩.

[12]   See Jones, *Studies in African Music*, vol. 1, pp. 210–13.

[13]   For a small selection, see Jones, ibid., King, 'Employments of the "Standard Pattern" in Yoruba Music', Pantaleoni, 'Three Principles of Timing in Anlo Dance Drumming', pp. 58–9, Locke, 'Principles of Offbeat Timing', pp. 218–19 and 230, and Akpabot, 'Theories on African Music', p. 62.

[14]   See Chernoff, *African Rhythm and African Sensibility*, p. 145.

3,[15] and of 12 into 5+7 or 7+5; and the staggering of whole rhythmic groups between the beats. When several such devices are employed simultaneously, as they frequently are, the result can be highly complex. Suppose, for instance, that we combine the patterns of Exx. 45 and 48 (see Ex. 49). The combination is fairly typical of West African practice,

Ex. 49   Drum pattern 5

in a simplified way. One refinement not shown is the frequent use of duplet rhythms across a triplet beat, ♫ against ♩. Notice that, if this ♫♫ rhythm were superimposed over the above combination, it would involve not only twos against the threes of the basic pulse, but also fours against the threes of Drum 2. All this is typically African.

The rhythms of Ex. 49 could be produced by two performers, one doing Ex. 45 and the other Ex. 48 (and remember that, as well as drums, the instruments could be xylophones, mbiras, stringed instruments, or any of many other possibilities). On the other hand, each individual rhythm could be allocated to a single performer, according to a favourite African practice, typified by the well-known flute, horn, and of course drum ensembles.

In this one-man-one-rhythm situation, the question at once arises: how, in such a tumult of cross-rhythms, does the individual performer keep his place? Mainly, it seems, by listening to the 'time line'. This is a repetitive pattern, usually asymmetrical in build, struck on some high-pitched instrument. The simplest form of time line consists of mere handclaps on the beat (as in 'Erin kare'le o wa j'ọba!', Ex. 2, 'Olúrómbí', Ex. 22, and the Mossi song, Ex. 10(a)) but in the big drum ensembles some form of the standard pattern is generally used, at any rate among the Ewe and the Yoruba.[16] In various forms, the device of the time line has been carried across the Atlantic. In some Afro-Brazilian music, for instance, the Yoruba (and also Ewe) pattern ♩ ♩ ♪♩ ♩ ♩ ♪ has survived intact. In North America the survival of the time line has

---

[15] In Afro-American music the 3+5 division is by far the commoner, but 5+3 does occur: see the tie-shuffling chant, Ex. 26(b) (to the words 'Stan' on de rock where'), and the knife guitar version of 'John Henry', Ex. 84(d).

[16] See 'Madé yi vódú yówé', Ex. 24. Nketia, in The Music of Africa, p. 132, gives a large selection of time lines.

not been so vigorous, but there, too, relics of it have been recorded in the practices of 'patting juba' and 'stick knocking'.[17]

Utterly independent though they may sound, cross-rhythms are usually consciously related to the beat, or the time line, or both. Consider, for instance, this simple pattern, which I present in the non-committal sort of notation now favoured by Africanists:

> Drum: . . xx . . xx . . xx
> Basic beat: x . . x . . x . . x . .

Ought the drum pattern to be regarded as ♩ ♫♩ ♫♩ ♫ or ♩ ♪♩. ♪♩ ♪♫ ? David Locke, who poses this question, comes up with a somewhat surprising answer:

. . . in my opinion the second transcription more faithfully adheres to the basic principles of performance in southern Eʋe drumming, namely that each instrument relates its pattern both to the bell [a ♩ ♩ ♪♩ ♩ ♩ ♪ time line] and the primary metric accents, that is, beats . . . ('Principles of Offbeat Timing', p. 222.)

Here is another of those cases, so common in African music, where a single pattern can be simultaneously regarded in different ways. As Gerhard Kubik would put it, it has various 'images'. In one image it is related to the beat, and in the other it stands alone. Each transcription reflects a different image, and each is equally valid.

Whatever the interpretation, these African cross-rhythms have no special, 'syncopated' accent attached to them. In this they differ radically from the syncopations of the European classical tradition. To take a famous example, the much repeated | ♩ ♩ ♩ | figures of Beethoven's *Leonore* overtures could never be mistaken for | ♩ ♩ ♩ | retarded by a crotchet. But this seems to be a relatively recent practice, at least as the invariable rule. In earlier European music, when cross-rhythms were so much more a normal part of the music fabric, they were often performed in the African way, just like on-beat phrases. Traces of this practice survived as late as J. S. Bach. The Courante in his Partita in E minor, for instance, is notated as in Ex. 50(*a*). Played as this notation suggests, this passage is rather stiff and jerky. But suppose that the right-hand part is interpreted simply as a cantabile melody that happens to have been brought forward by half a beat, as in Ex. 50(*b*). This interpretation is surely far more beautiful and incomparably more natural. It may look strange to a classical pianist, but it would be commonplace to a jazz player.

[17] See Epstein, *Sinful Tunes and Spirituals*, pp. 141–4 for 'patting juba' and pp. 140, 144, and 158 for 'stick knocking'.

Ex. 50

(*a*) Bach, Partita in E minor, Courante

(*b*) The same, in an alternative notation

THE UNITED STATES

Commentators on African rhythm like to emphasize how un-European it is. The most complex of African rhythmic combinations are selected for analysis, and contrasted with European rhythms apparently derived from *Hymns Ancient and Modern*. Such comparisons give a misleading impression of African rhythm in general, and in particular those rhythmic styles that had most influence in North America, where African percussion ensembles quickly died out (except in New Orleans) to be replaced by smaller and rhythmically less complex groups. The most important instruments to survive were the banjo, the string bass, various small percussion instruments like the bones and the washboard, the panpipes, and the musical bow. It is to the West African antecedents of these instruments that we should look for the origins of American rhythm, not to the big drum ensembles of southern Ghana.

In the simpler African rhythmic styles the distinction between beats divided into threes and twos is clear even to the non-African ear, and not radically unlike the parallel distinction between simple and compound time in British folk dance music. The African and European versions of $\frac{12}{8}$ time merge in many American styles, from country fiddling to the blues, approximating now to one and now to the other tradition. A special American development is the blurring of the distinction between simple and compound metres, whereby the same dance tune may be performed to a lilting $\frac{12}{8}$ when 'allegretto' and a straight $\frac{4}{4}$ when 'presto'.

It is even possible for the transition from one to the other to take place in the course of a single movement, as in 'Alberta' (Exx. 57(c) and (d)). The 'swinging' of straight pairs of notes (♪♪) can be anything from a slight leaning on the first note of the pairs to a full-blown ♩³♪. In the blues, especially, the distinction between simple and compound time breaks down, with duplets and triplets freely interspersed, in the African style. In the blues the distinction is not so much between simple and compound divisions of the beat as between simple and compound-plus-simple divisions. The blues $\frac{12}{8}$ can be viewed as really having 24 very rapid pulses, capable of being split up in several ways, each of them equally normal: two twelves, three eights, four sixes, six fours, eight threes, or twelve twos; or, in musical notation, ♩. ♩., ♩ ♩ ♩, ♩. ♩. ♩. ♩., ♩ ♩ ♩ ♩ ♩ ♩, ♫♫♫.♫♫♫. (or ♫♫♫ ♫♫♫), and ♫♫♫♫♫♫♫♫.[18]

A fairly important point is that there are certain styles, like the early blues and hillbilly, where it is unusual for a common-time beat to go on for long without being disrupted by some irregular rhythm. Particularly at the ends of phrases, the four-in-a-bar rhythm will often be broken by a two-beat or even three-beat bar.

The syncopations erected on these metrical frameworks are mainly but by no means entirely of African origin. The European influence was not limited to simplifying African rhythmic complexities; it also had a few twists of its own to contribute, all connected in one way or another with perversion of the accent. Either an accent was created where it would not normally exist (as in the Scotch snap type of figure); or an ordinary accented note was replaced with a rest; or an accented note was made to arrive before its due time.

It is hardly necessary to expatiate on the Scotch snap type of syncopation, which includes such forms as ♪♩ ♪, ♪♩ ♫, ♫♫♫, etc., as well as the familiar ♪♩.. Is is common to many musical cultures, presents no difficulties, and was recognised from the first as one of the features of ragtime rhythm.[19]

The second type of syncopation, where an accented note is replaced by a rest, is a more complex matter. For convenience, we can call it the 'missed beat' type of syncopation, though it should be understood that this is short for 'missed accented beat'. (A more accurate but pedantic-sounding term would be 'missed pulse'.) As Ex. 51 shows, a fairly jazzy form of missed-beat syncopation already existed in mid-eighteenth-century British dance music, similar rhythms appearing in banjo tunes

[18] In this it resembles its African antecedents. See for instance Kubik, 'Music and Dance', pp. 92–3.
[19] For an example of Scotch snap in an actual Scottish tune, see Ex. 76(a).

Ex. 51 'The Reel of Tulloch'

from about a century later (see Ex. 52).[20] Although there is an obvious African influence at work here, it seems as though these banjo rhythms owe more to music like 'The Reel of Tulloch' than to anything African.

Ex. 52 'Marty Inglehart Jig'

The third type of syncopation, where an accented note is slightly advanced, appears in two quite distinct forms, depending on whether the note in question is initial or final. Anticipation of the last note of a phrase is fairly common in British folk-songs, as in Ex. 53.[21] It is one of a

Ex. 53 'Soldier, Soldier' (end of tune)

Here my small man put them on.

battery of devices for reconciling a near-speaking rhythm with a regular beat—what one might call rubato-within-the-beat. Anticipation of the first note of the phrase, on the other hand, seems to be mainly a dance musician's mannerism. In $\frac{6}{8}$ time, where for instance we might have ♪♩ ♪♩♩ ♪♩♩ ♪♩♩ instead of ♩ ♪♩♩ ♩ ♪♩♩ ♪♩♩ ♩, or ♪♩♩. ♩ ♪♩♩. ♩ ♪♩ instead of |♩. ♩ ♪♩ ♩. ♩ ♪♩|, it produces a very Irish effect. In common

---

[20] The turns on the Gs probably indicated the preceding grace-notes FGA: see Nathan, 'Early Banjo Tunes and American Syncopation', pp. 462–3.

[21] See also 'Rue the Day', Ex. 79(*a*).

time, it is part of the idiom of American country fiddlers (see Ex. 54). All these forms of syncopation were subject to various processes of

Ex. 54   'Cripple Creek'

Africanization at the hands of black musicians, the most important being the following:

1. European rhythms were assimilated to familiar African forms. Thus the Scotch snap figure usually appears in early ragtime as | ♫♩♪ | (for instance in 'Mississippi Rag', Ex. 153(c))—like its close relatives | ♫♩♪ | and | ♫♪♪ | a favourite African pattern.
2. Without changing radically in form, syncopation became far more frequent and insistent, as one can see by comparing certain American banjo tunes with the British fiddle tunes from which they are derived.[22]
3. The British rubato-within-the-beat was fitted to strict pulses: in other words, from being a free rubato, derived from speech rhythms, it became true syncopation.
4. Rhythms arising from missed beats or displacement of the accent were reinterpreted as African-style cross-rhythms. In particular, the 'Reel of Tulloch' type of missed-beat rhythm, | ♪♫♫ ♫♫♪ | ♪♫♫ ♫♫♪ |, could be heard as | ♪♫♫ ♫♫ | ♪♫♫ ♫♫♪ | .

Overt examples of African cross-rhythms do not occur in the earliest banjo tunes that have come down to us, but some interesting disguised examples do. Ex. 55(a), for instance, presents us with the typically jaunty ragtime rhythm | ♫♩♫ |. But if we regard it as a polyrhythmic exchange between two voices, we get Ex. 55(b); as so often is African music, there are multiple rhythmic images at work.

Ex. 55   (a) 'Tom Brigg's Jig'

(b) The same, in an alternative notation

[22] See Nathan, 'Early Banjo Tunes and American Syncopation', pp. 458–9.

One of the main purposes of the short drone string on the banjo, which in this example produces the reiterated E, is precisely to produce such ambiguous rhythmic effects. It has parallels in many African instruments. Ben Harney, one of the pioneers of ragtime, derived the piano rag style precisely from this drone string:

On the banjo there is a short string that is not fretted and that consequently is played open with the thumb. It is frequently referred to as the thumb string. The colored performer, strumming in his own cajoling way, likes to throw in a note at random, and his thumb ranges over for this effect. When he takes up the piano, the desire for the same effect dominates him, being almost second nature, and he reaches for the open banjo-string note with his little finger. Meanwhile he is keeping mechanically perfect time with his left hand. The hurdle with the right-hand little finger throws the tune off its stride, resulting in syncopation. He is playing two different times at once. (From a newspaper interview, quoted in Blesh and Janis, *They All Played Ragtime*, pp. 226–7.)

We can see what Harney meant by his raggy version of 'Annie Laurie' (Ex. 156).

This mid-nineteenth-century banjo music was also one of the many sources of the early blues. 'Dr. Hekok Jig' (Ex. 56(*a*)) is equally remarkable for looking back to the theme-and-variation forms of Africa, such as the Senegambian *fodet*,[23] and forward to the blues. In a slower tempo and slightly different rhythm its main theme is one of the standard blues accompaniment figures (Ex. 56(*b*)).

Ex. 56

(*a*) 'Dr. Hekok Jig' (beginning) with (*b*) a blues transformation of the same

[23] See Coolen, 'The Wolof Xalam Tradition' and 'The Fodet: A Senegambiam Origin for the Blues?'.

It seems as though much of the early blues was taken directly from banjo music, by simply slowing the tempo and swinging the rhythm. As to the slowing of the tempo, we have the testimony of two contemporary witnesses, Lucius Smith and Mance Lipscomb.[24] Both viewed the blues as a new, slow kind of dance music which became fashionable in the early years of the twentieth century. In view of Henry Ravenel's description of the moderate-paced, shuffling 'jigs' of his youth[25]—that is, around 1840—we may wonder whether these new 'slow drags' were really so new. Apart from this, there is a well-known general tendency for dance tempos to slow down, famous examples being the saraband and the waltz.

Since banjo music was an antecedent of early ragtime too, it follows that early blues must have been closely related to early ragtime; and this was in fact the case. Leadbelly's 'Alberta' (Ex. 57(c)) begins at a typical blues tempo. In the course of the movement, as with many early blues (and also African) performances, the beat accelerates, eventually attaining a lively ragtime tempo (Ex. 57(d)). In the process the accompaniment figure, which is reminiscent of another of these early banjo pieces (Exx. 57(a) and (b)), changes from the African 'standard pattern' to a straightforward rumba rhythm.

Ex. 57

(a) 'Pea Patch Jig' with (b) a blues transformation

(c) 'Alberta' (beginning) and (d) (near end)

By 1900 American popular rhythm had assumed its modern form in all essentials. Apart from those already discussed, there are two features that

---

[24] For Smith's view, see Evans, *Big Road Blues*, pp. 47–8; for Lipscomb's, see Roberts, *Black Music of Two Worlds*, pp. 184–5.
[25] See ch. 8.

deserve mention. One is the long series of three-quaver groupings against a four-quaver background as in Ex. 58. This clearly derives from

Ex. 58 'Hilarity Rag'

African practice, as in the harp accompaniment quoted in Ex. 46, though similar things are sometimes found in earlier European music.[26]

The other is the bringing forward of entire phrases by half a beat. The advancement of individual notes which is so typical of American syncopation can take various forms. The advanced note can be accented, as we have seen, but it may also be unaccented. A 'jazzed up' version of 'Who's Gonna Shoe your Pretty Little Feet?', for instance, might take the form illustrated in Ex. 59. But this is a fairly arbitrary selection of

Ex. 59

(a) 'Who's Gonna Shoe your Pretty Little Feet?', straight, and (b) the same, jazzed up

notes, chosen to fit the words as much as anything. Literally any combination of the notes of this tune could be treated in this way. The words 'pretty little feet', for instance, might be sung to the rhythm ♪♩ ♪♪♩ ♪|♩ ₒ, or even ♪|♩ ♪♩ ♪♪♩ ♪|₍ₒ. In the former case the last four notes, and in the latter the whole phrase, has simply been shifted forward by half a beat. Such wholesale rhythmic shifts are very much a part of many American styles, particularly the blues (see Ex. 60). It should be remarked that the phrases so treated may already contain cross-rhythms before being shifted, as in Ex. 61.[17]

---

[26] e.g. William Byrd's Fantasia, no. lii in *The Fitzwilliam Virginal Book* (vol. 1, p. 192) section 2, bars 22–32.

[27] This can happen in African rhythm too. See Locke, 'Principles of Offbeat Timing', pp. 236–7.

Ex. 60   Charley Patton, 'Pony Blues'

Ex. 61

(*a*) 'Honky Tonk Women'

(*b*) 'It's Always You'

American rhythm, like African rhythm, is full of ambiguities. The pattern | ♩♩♩♩ ⁊ ♩♩♩ | (missed beat) might be interpreted as ♩♩♩ ♩♩ (rumba rhythm). The pattern | ♩. ♩. ♩ | might again be an instance of the rumba pattern, or it could be considered as | ♩ ♩ ♩ | with the middle note advanced by half a beat. The same doubts arise between | ♩ ♩♩. | (anticipated beat) and | ♩ ♩ | (hemiola). Suppose we advance the main beats of a simple jig-time rhythm thus: ♩♩ ♩♩ ♩♩ ♩ ♩♩ ♩|, etc. This could be seen as simple anticipation of the beat, but it could also be seen (and heard) as a | ♩. ♩♩ | rhythm set against a ⁶⁄₈ back-ground and advanced by a third of a beat. The more African the rhythmic style is, the more intractable such conundrums become, but they occur even in early ragtime. The rhythm of 'Mississippi Rag' Ex. 153(c)—‖: 𝅘𝅥𝅮 ♪♪| 𝅘𝅥𝅮𝅘𝅥𝅮𝅘𝅥𝅮 :‖—can be interpreted in at least three ways:

1. as | 𝅘𝅥𝅮 ♪ | , etc.;
2. as | 𝅘𝅥𝅮 𝅘𝅥𝅮 | , etc., with a retarded beat in the middle;
3. as ‖: 𝅘𝅥𝅮 ♪ | 𝅘𝅥𝅮 𝅘𝅥𝅮 ♪ :‖

Similarly, the extracts from 'Maple Leaf Rag', Ex. 158(a) notated as ♪| 𝅘𝅥𝅮 𝅘𝅥𝅮| 𝅘𝅥𝅮𝅘𝅥𝅮𝅘𝅥𝅮| 𝅘𝅥𝅮𝅘𝅥𝅮𝅘𝅥𝅮| 𝅘𝅥𝅮 ♪‖ in the original, can be interpreted as:

1. 𝅘𝅥𝅮𝅘𝅥𝅮| 𝅘𝅥𝅮𝅘𝅥𝅮| 𝅘𝅥𝅮𝅘𝅥𝅮| 𝅘𝅥𝅮 ♪‖ with the notes marked with asterisks advanced by a semiquaver; or
2. 𝅘𝅥𝅮 𝅘𝅥𝅮𝅘𝅥𝅮| 𝅘𝅥𝅮𝅘𝅥𝅮 , etc.

To summarize, then, here are the main features of Afro-American rhythm:

1. It is in common time. Waltz time does occur sometimes, but only where the European influence is particularly strong.
2. This common time shades imperceptibly from a straight $\frac{4}{4}$ into $\frac{12}{8}$. This $\frac{12}{8}$, however, is typically mixed with duplet figures, and is really a combination of $\frac{4}{4}$ and $\frac{12}{8}$ time.
3. In some styles the four-beat bar is frequently interrupted by two- or three-beat bars.
4. Apart from the usual classical European syncopation, American rhythm has the following devices:
   (a) the hemiola;
   (b) asymmetrical division of the bar as either 3+5 or 5+7;
   (c) advancement of notes by half a beat in $\frac{4}{4}$ time or a third of a beat in $\frac{12}{8}$ time: almost any combination of notes can be treated in this way, including whole phrases;
   (d) the missed beat, particularly at the beginning of the bar.
5. The distinction between these various forms of syncopation is not always clear-cut: many rhythmic patterns can be construed in various ways.

These brief principles do not of course account for the whole of Afro-American rhythm, but they may serve as an introduction. It has often been rather condescendingly compared with African rhythm. Certainly it does not have the same *sort* of complexity as African rhythm, but it has complexities of its own. Complexity is, in any case, a very doubtful gauge of artistic merit. It is also far from easy to evaluate objectively. In fact, it is generally far from being as simple a matter as is often thought.

III. BRITISH ORIGINS OF
THE BLUES

20. THE BLUES MODE IN BRITAIN

THE BLUE THIRD

ONE thing that greatly struck early collectors of English folk-song was the variable nature of the folk modes. Cecil Sharp wrote:

It must be understood that the third is not a fixed note in the folk-scale, as it is in both of the modern scales. The English folk-singer varies the intonation of this particular note very considerably. His major third is never as sharp as the corresponding interval in the tempered scale, to which modern ears are attuned. On the other hand, it is often so flat that it is hardly to be distinguished from the minor third. Frequently, too, it is a 'neutral' third, *i.e.*, neither major nor minor, like the interval between the two notes of the Cuckoo's song, when the Spring is waning. Apparently, the folk-singer, not having any settled notions with regard to the pitch of the third note of the scale, varies it according to the character of the phrase in which it happens to occur. The third of the scale may, therefore, be sung with two or even three different shades of intonation in the same tune, not arbitrarily but systematically, *i.e.*, consistently in every verse. (*English Folk Song: Some Conclusions*, p. 71.)

while his contemporary Percy Grainger came to the conclusion that

. . . the singers from whom I have recorded do not seem to me to have sung three different and distinct modes (Mixolydian, Dorian, Aeolian), but to have rendered their modal songs in *one single loosely-knit modal folk-song scale* . . . consisting of:
    Firstly—the *tonic, second, major and minor (or unstable) third, fourth, fifth, and flat seventh* . . .
    Secondly—the *sixth*, which is generally major, though sometimes minor . . . and the *sharp, or mutable seventh*; which intervals do not, as a rule, form part of the bed-rock of tunes, but act chiefly as passing and auxiliary notes. ('Collecting with the Phonograph', p. 147; quoted in *The New Grove*, vol. 12, p. 419.)

In Ex. 62 we can see precisely what Sharp and Grainger meant. The B♮ in bar 1 is Grainger's 'sharp, or mutable seventh', the B♭ in bar 4 his stable flat seventh. In some ways this omnibus British folk scale is strikingly like the blues mode, but if we look carefully at the fluctuations in pitch it becomes evident that they are governed by very different principles. In

Ex. 62   'Fanny Blair'

the blues, unstable or 'blue' notes resolve onto stabler ones. The pitch of these fluctuating notes is thus governed by the notes that *come after them*. In the British tunes there is no feeling of melodic dissonance, and the fluctuating notes are generally governed by the *preceding* notes, assuming the form that brings the two notes closest together. When approached from below, these variable notes are lower; when approached from above they are higher.

This tendency for passing-notes to cling to the previous note is probably the main principle governing fluctuating pitches in British folk music. There are others. Melodically important thirds and sevenths will usually take the minor form, like the minor seventh in the fourth bar of 'Fanny Blair'. There is also a tendency for minor intervals to come towards the ends of tunes, as in Ex. 63, and here the effect can sometimes

Ex. 63   'Dives and Lazarus'

be strikingly blues-like. There are also, it must be admitted, cases where no rule at all can be discovered.

THE BLUE SEVENTH

This is the only feature of British folk music which can be said to be unmistakably bluesey. Unlike the rather vague and unsatisfactory 'blue third' of Britain, the seventh is a well-defined matrix with a venerable history. Its origins go beyond northern Europe to the Near Eastern Cradle of Musical Civilization, and it can be found in Asian tunes like Ex. 64. Though this tune comes from northern India, it could as easily

Ex. 64   'Biglitār'

have come from the Scottish Highlands or the Appalachian mountains.

What distinguishes such blue sevenths from ordinary minor sevenths is the melodic contour. Typically these blue sevenths come at the top of the phrase and fall to the dominant, resolving onto the dominant in much the same way as the blue third resolves onto the tonic. This type of melodic contour has even been quoted as one of the characteristics of English folk music: 'Sir Hubert Parry (*Art of Music*, p. 79)', wrote Sharp, 'points out "that a pathetic rise up to the minor seventh of the scale through the fifth" is characteristic of old German folk-tunes. It is, however, equally characteristic of English folk-airs.'[1]

Though this 'pathetic rise' and the equally pathetic descent to the dominant are standard, it can happen that the seventh is the first note of the phrase, or the descent is to some note other than the dominant. An Irish example of the typical idiom has already appeared in the keen quoted as Ex. 29. Ex. 65 gives further examples from England and

Ex. 65

(*a*) 'Hangèd I shall be' (English, beginning)

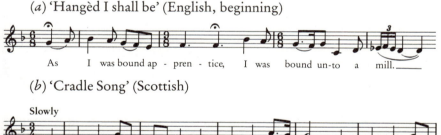

As   I was bound ap - pren - tice,   I was   bound un-to   a   mill._____

(*b*) 'Cradle Song' (Scottish)

Slowly

Ba - la   loo,   lam - my, now   ba - loo,   my   dear;   Now,   ba - la   loo,

lam - my, ain   min - nie   is   here: What   ails   my   wee   bair - nie?   what

ails   it   this night? What   ails   my wee   lam - my?   is   bair - nie   no   right?

[1] *English Folk Song: Some Conclusions*, p. 84.

Scotland. (Note also the end of 'Dives and Lazarus', Ex. 63.) Ex. 66, for comparison, gives two American examples. It will be seen that the verse part of Ex. 66(*b*) derives from the second half of the 'Cradle Song', and the chorus part from 'Here We Go round the Mulberry Bush'.

Ex. 66

(*a*) 'Got dem Blues' (beginning)

Got   dem blues, but I'm   too mean,   lor - dy,   I'm   too damn'd mean to   cry. __

(*b*) 'Get along Home, Cindy'

I   went   to   see   my   blue - eyed   gal,   She   met   me   at   the

door, ___   Her   shoes an'   stock - in's   in   her   hand   An' her   feet   all

CHORUS

ov - er the   floor. ___   Get   a - long   home,   Cin - dy,   Cin - dy,
Get   a - long   home,   Cin - dy,   Cin - dy, I'll

1.
Get   a - long   home,   Cin - dy,   Cin - dy,

2.
mar - ry   you   some   day. ___

As Ex. 67 shows, varieties of the same idiom appear also in European 'art' music. One type, where the 'blue' minor seventh clashes with a

Ex. 67

(*a*) Praeludium no. xxv from *The Fitzwilliam Virginal Book* (end)

(*b*) Purcell, Fantasia no. 7 (beginning)

(*c*) Dvořák, String Quartet Op. 34 (beginning)

major leading note in another part (as in bar 4 of Ex. 67(*b*)), was so common in English music of the sixteenth and seventeenth centuries that it has been designated 'the English cadence'. It greatly perplexed those Victorian scholars who were rediscovering the 'Tudor' composers; Ernest Walker, in *A History of Music in England* (1924) devotes several pages to it.[2] In a related formula, which can be found as late as Ravel's *Bolero*, the whole process of ascent and descent takes place within the tonic chord. Ex. 68[3] gives a few examples. The suggestion of folk influence is especially strong in this one-chord formula. When it appears in the 'art' music of the nineteenth century and later the influence will usually be East European (as in Ex. 68(*d*)—compare also Ex. 67(*c*)) or

Ex. 68

(*a*) Byrd, 'John Come Kiss Me Now' Variations (end of var. 6)

---

[2] p. 342 ff.
[3] The double strokes through the stems of some of the notes of Ex. 68(*a*) and other examples from *The Fitzwilliam Virginal Book* indicate some sort of ornament—it is not known precisely what. See Donington, 'Ornaments', section VI: 'English Virginalists' Strokes', *The New Grove*, vol. 13, pp. 857–9.

(*b*) Bach, English Suite in A minor, Bourrée II (beginning)

(*c*) Handel, Dead March from *Saul* (beginning)

(*d*) Chopin, Mazurka in G♯ minor/C♯ minor, Op. 6, no. 2 (beginning)

else, as in the case of Ravel's *Bolero*, Spanish. Just how close 'folk' and 'art' formulas could be in the seventeenth century is shown in Ex. 69. Most probably this formula originated when tunes like 'The Bonny Bunch of Roses' were accompanied by drones. Of all these examples, the one from Byrd (Ex. 68(*a*)) is the most strikingly blues-like. It would look quite at home in a twentieth-century piano blues. A

Ex. 69

(*a*) 'The Bonny Bunch of Roses'

Near by the swell-ing o - ce - an, One morn-ing in the month of June,

(*b*) Purcell, 'A Pastoral Elegy on the Death of Mr. John Playford'

Mu - ses, bring your ro - ses hith-er, Strew them gent-ly on his hearse

rock and roll classic of the 1950s (Ex. 70) provides examples of both this and the 'English cadence' formula.

Ex. 70   Chuck Berry, 'Sweet Little Sixteen'

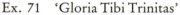

THE LADDER OF THIRDS

This is an old feature of European music.[4] There are numerous examples in Gregorian chant, for instance 'Gloria Tibi Trinitas' (Ex. 71).[5] It is also

Ex. 71   'Gloria Tibi Trinitas'

common in British folk-song, especially, for some mysterious reason, members of the 'Forsaken Maiden' family, which has been described as follows:

A young woman loses her virginity, becomes pregnant, and is then deserted. Filled with sorrow and despair, she longs for death. This gloomy theme was

[4] See Sachs, 'The Road to Major'.
[5] 'Glory to thee equal Trinity, single Godhead, at once before all ages, now, and for ever.' Famous as the basis of the 'In Nomines' of English sixteenth- and seventeenth-century composers. See Scholes, *The Oxford Companion to Music*, article on 'In Nomine'.

popular among country singers, especially men, and it gave rise to a huge family of songs, usually with very fine tunes. Among the many titles are 'Apron Strings' ('Oh, when my apron strings were low, / My love followed me through frost and snow; / But now my apron strings are high, / My love passes by and never looks nigh'); 'I wish, I wish'; 'A bold (or Brisk) Young Farmer (or Sailor, or Lover, or Man)'; and, reflecting later adaptations, 'There is a Tavern (or Alehouse) in the Town'. (Palmer, *The Book of English Country Songs*, p. 143.)

The 'very fine tunes' of this family are mostly based on the same melodic pattern, and this pattern can be traced back through more than five centuries. The first known instance is a Burgundian dance tune of about 1470, entitled 'Le Petit Roysin' (Ex. 72).[6] ('Roysin' is an earlier form of the modern French 'raisin', meaning grape. The title therefore means 'The Little Grape', the implications evidently being vinous.) The

Ex. 72   'Le Petit Roysin'

wonderfully strong and flexible pattern of this tune gave rise to hundreds of variants. They can be found all over Europe, but they seem to have been particularly popular in Britain and, especially, the United States. It is hard to find any category of American folk-song, white or black, without examples. Here is a small selection:

love lament: 'A Fair Beauty Bride';
murder ballad: 'Pretty Polly' (Ex. 18);
white blues: 'I Wish I were a Mole in the Ground';
prison blues: 'It Makes a Long Time Man Feel Bad';
Negro spirituals: 'This Train is Bound for Glory', 'When I'm Gone', 'I Been 'Buked and I Been Scorned';
children's song: 'Froggy Went a-Courtin' ' (See Ex. 154(*b*), where it is called 'Mister Frog');
worksong: 'Po' Lazarus' (Ex. 83, third phrase omitted).

Perhaps because the ladder of thirds is an African as well as European matrix, this tune pattern seems to have appealed especially to black musicians. It is therefore not surprising that many 'Petit Roysin' tunes show some degree of Africanization, or perhaps we should say 'bluesification': Ex. 73 gives an idea of how this happened. Though the words going with these tunes are diverse, they all have two things in common: a blues-like quality, and white origin. 'One Kind Favour', like 'Every Night', is derived from floating scraps of British folk poetry; while

---

[6] The European derivatives of this song are discussed in Salmen, 'Towards the Exploration of National Idiosyncrasies in Wandering Song-Tunes', and Lloyd, *Folk Song in England*, pp. 81–3.

in Sandburg's *American Songbag* there is an earlier version of the 'Blin'
Man' words: 'Blind man lay beside the way. He could not see the light of
day. The Lord passed by and heard him say: "O Lord, won't you help
me!"', the elaborate rhyme scheme and neat construction of which clearly
betray the hand of a white versifier. Turning to the tunes, we find them
marking in the clearest possible way the steps by which British folk-song

Ex. 73

(*a*) 'Barbara Allen' (Newfoundland version)

(*b*) 'Barbara Allen' (Appalachian version)

(*c*) 'Every Night when the Sun Goes in' (white blues)

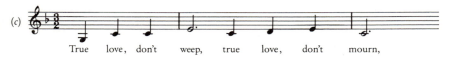

(*d*) 'Blin' Man Stood on de Way an' Cried' (spiritual)*

* From John A. and Alan Lomax, *American Ballads and Folk Songs*, p. 596 (Macmillan,
1934).

(*e*) 'One Kind Favour' (folk blues)†

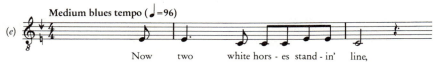

† Sung by Smith Casey at Clemens State Farm, Brazoria, Texas, in 1939. Recorded by John
A. and Ruby T. Lomax. On the Library of Congress Archive of Folk Culture recording *Afro-
American Blues and Game Songs*, AFS L4, side A, track 6, under the title 'Two White Horses'.

When the green fields they were spring - ing,

The flo - wers all ___ were bloom - in'; ___

True love, don't weep, true love, don't mourn,

Blin' man stood on de way an' cried,

Now two white hors - es stand - in'

When a young man on ___ his death bed lay

Sweet Wil - liam on his death - bed lay

True love, don't weep nor mourn for me,

Cry - in', 'O Lawd, ___ show me de way.'

Now two white hors - es standin' in a

For the   love   of   Bar - ba - ry   El - len.

For the   love   of   Barb - ry   Al - len._____

I'm   going   a - way   to   Mar - ble   town.

Blin'   man   stood on   de   way   an'   cried.

Gon'   take   me   to my bury - in'   groun'.

turned into the blues. Greatly as the first two resemble each other, they
differ in this respect: the second is touched with a blues feeling, and the
first is not. The subtle bluesiness affects many aspects of tune (b),
including the rhythm, but its most obviously bluesy feature is the blue
third at the end of the third phrase, which, however, is only one part of a
general transformation of the mode. where tune (a) was heptatonic, this
is pentatonic; it is as though the flesh of the melody were being stripped
away to reveal the modal bones beneath. In tune (c) the stripping process
is carried further, and by Tune (d) we are down to a four-note mode:
only the tonic, third, fifth, and minor seventh remain. (This is of course
disregarding the fluctuations in the pitch of the third.) And in tune (e)
there is nothing but a bare triad left.[7]

As the ladder of thirds is stripped down to its essentials, the forces
between the notes become correspondingly greater. This is particularly
true of the magnetic pull of the tonic. With every new step this feeling
that the tonic is dragging the other notes down to it becomes stronger. In
other words, it becomes a 'floor note', just as in the African paddle song,
Ex. 7(b); while the approximation of the third phrase to 'Ọnyẹ ampa ara'
(Ex. 26(a)) is even more striking. As a result, the drop from the third to
the tonic becomes more and more prominent. In the first tune it does not
appear at all, while in the last it appears no less than six times.

The triadic mode of 'One Kind Favour', which we have already
encountered in chapters 15 and 16, seems to have exerted a considerable
influence quite apart from the ladder of thirds, and on white as well as
black folk music. Ex. 74 shows how the Scottish tune best known in the

[7] The B♮ at the end of bar 3 is unobtrusive enough to be discounted. The bracketed notes in
this example are supplied by the guitar, 'talking' in dialogue with the singer.

Ex. 74

(a) 'Fareweel tae Tarwathie'

Fare - weel tae Tar - wath - ie, a - dieu Mor-mond Hill, And the dear land o'

Cri-mond I bid ye fare - well. I'm bound out for Green-land and

rea-dy to sail, In hopes to find rich - es in hunt-ing the whale.

(b) 'Rye Whiskey'

Rye whisk-ey, rye whisk-ey, rye whisk-ey I cry, If whisk-ey don't kill me, I'll live till I die.

(c) 'The Noble Skewball'

When the   day was ap - point - ed for Skew - ball to run,   The
            hors - es was   rea - dy, the   peo - ple did

come,   Some   from old   Vir - gin - ny, and   from Ten - nes -

see   Some   from Al - a - ba - ma, and   from   ev - 'ry - where.

United States as 'Rye Whiskey' could be 'triadized', as it were.[8] The strong suggestion of a triadic framework is common in Southern white folk music.[9] It is hard to see where it could have come from, if not from

---

[8] These tunes belong to the 'Todlen Hame' tune family, so called after the Scotts drinking song of that name (see Foster, *The Songs of Scotland*, vol. 2, p. 193).

[9] Examples are 'Lord Thomas and Fair Ellinor', variant C (Sharp, *English Folk Songs from the Southern Appalachians*, vol. 1, p. 118), 'Sir Hugh', variants A, B, C, and J (ibid., pp. 222, 223, and 229), 'The Nightingale', variant D (Belden, *Ballads and Folk Songs*, p. 241), 'A Married Woman's Lament' (Randolph, *Ozark Folksongs*, vol. 3, 'Humorous and Play-Party Songs', p. 70—a variant of 'Single Girl', Ex. 76(*b*)), and 'Tylus and Talus' (ibid., p. 344). Another example of 'triadization' is the remodelling of 'The Maid Freed from the Gallows', Ex. 16(*a*), as 'Hangman', Ex. 16(*b*).

black influence. A similar triadic emphasis does sometimes occur in British folk music, but not often, and never to the same degree.[10] The mark of this particular idiom is not only that the notes of the tonic triad are very prominent, but that this prominence persists throughout the tune. This happens very often in black American music, and fairly often in Southern white music, but not, so far as I know, in British music.

Ex. 75 is another specimen of this type. It is yet another version of the Barbara Allen tune, very close to the Appalachian rendering already quoted (Ex. 73(*b*)), but even more blues-like in outline. The interesting

Ex. 75 'Barbro Allen'

One Mon-day morn, in the month of May, When all gay flowers was swel-lin',____ Sweet

Wil-liam he   was   ta-ken sick For the love of Bar - bro   Al - len.____

thing about it is that it was collected in 1893. This means that a bluesy strain was already seeping into white American folk music as early as the late nineteenth century; and, if we allow for the often considerable time-lag between the development of folk styles and their discovery by middle-class collectors, perhaps long before.

[10] e.g. 'Trooper and Maid' (Bronson, *Traditional Tunes of the Child Ballads*, vol. 4, p. 433) and 'Lord Thomas and Linda' (ibid., vol. 2, p. 107, no. 27).

21. THE TWELVE-BAR BLUES: FRANKIE AND OTHERS

> If America has a classical gutter song, it is the one that tells of Frankie and her man.
>
> Carl Sandburg[1]

THE FRANKIE-BOLL WEEVIL FAMILY

IF one examines the twelve-bar blues songs of the early twentieth century, it is hard not to be struck by the importance of one particular tune family. This is the one to which the ballads 'Frankie and Johnny' and 'The Boll Weevil' belong. The Frankie family alone exists in literally hundreds of variants. In 1927 Carl Sandburg could write:

Prof. H.M. Belden of the University of Missouri showed me sixteen Frankie songs, all having the same story though a few are located in the back country and in bayous instead of the big city. Then I met up with R.W. Gordon; he has 110 Frankie songs, and is still picking up new ones. The Frankie and Albert song, as partly given here, was common along the Mississippi river and among railroad men of the middle west as early as 1888. (*The American Songbag*, p. 75.)

By the time John and Alan Lomax's *American Ballads and Folk Songs* was published in 1934, Gordon's collection had swollen to 300, according to a footnote on page 103.

'The Ballad of the Boll Weevil', thought not quite in the Frankie class, is also important in its own right; and the same tune family is found linked to yet other words, for instance 'Got dem Blues', 'De Blues ain' Nothin' ',[2] and 'I Went to the Hop-Joint'.[3]

All these songs differ from the standard blues pattern in several important respects, the most obvious being the different fit of the words. Where the standard pattern has a couplet with the first line repeated, the Frankie-Boll Weevil family has a couplet followed by a refrain:

STANDARD PATTERN
Took my baby, to meet the morning train.
Took my baby, meet that morning train.
And the blues come down, Baby, like showers of rain.[4]

---

[1] *The American Songbag*, p. 75.
[2] ibid., pp. 232–3 and 234–5.
[3] Scarborough, *On the Trail of Negro Folk-Songs*, p. 90. See Ex. 78.
[4] Charley Patton, 'Pony Blues' (Fahey, *Charley Patton*, p. 75).

FRANKIE-BOLL WEEVIL PATTERN

Frankie and Johnny were lovers, lordy how they could love,
Swore to be true to each other, true as the stars above.
(Refrain) He was her man, but he done her wrong.

A second departure from the usual blues pattern is that these songs are built around a well-defined melodic arch. And a third is the chord-based nature of the melody. Where the typical blues is purely melodic in structure, with no suggestions of the harmony in the tune, most members of the Frankie family, though not quite all, spell out the harmony as plainly as a Bach unaccompanied violin sonata (see Ex. 78).

All these peculiarities—the couplet-plus-refrain, the melodic arch, and the harmonic implications—point towards a European origin; as, indeed, does the sheer popularity of this song family with white singers, audiences, and collectors.[5] It is therefore no surprise to find that the Frankie tune can be traced to a Scottish folk-song by a series of easy transitions (see Ex. 76). Tune (a) represents the British ancestor of this

Ex. 76

(a) 'Tattie Jock'

(a) When we ar-rive in Bot-any Bay Some let-ters we will send,

(b) 'Single Girl'

(b) Six lit-tle chil-dren all for to re-tain,

(c) 'Josie'

(c) Jo-sie she's a good girl, as ev-'ry-bo-dy knows,

(d) 'Frankie' (Mississippi John Hurt version)

(d) Fran-kie was a good girl, _____ ev'ry-bo-dy know.

----

[5] See also the comparison between a stanza from 'Frankie and Johnny' ('The first time she shot him . . .') and a Scottish ballad on p. 84.

Tae tell oor friends the hard-ships we En - dure in a fo-reign land. Sing -

Na-ry a one is large e-nough to help — me one grain.

She gave one hun-dred dol - lars for an i - vo - ry suit of clothes;

She paid a hun-dred dol - lars for Al - bert's one suit of clothes.

in' ah rid-dle aye roo dum di do, Ah riddle aye roo dum day. —

Boo - hoo, I wish I was a sin-gle girl a - gain.

'He is my man, — but he won't come home.' —

He's her man, And he done her wrong. —

family, most probably brought to America in the eighteenth century by Scotch-Irish settlers. In Tune (*b*) we find it slightly Americanized. The difference between these two tunes is much the same as the difference between the two versions of 'Barbara Allen' in Ex. 73. Here, as there, it is probably a question of a slight black influence. In Tune (*c*) the Appalachian folk tune has turned into a hillbilly blues, and in Tune (*d*) we have the song in its full-blown Afro-American form.

This metamorphosis of a Scottish folk tune into an Afro-American blues is even more interesting than the transformation of 'Barbara Allen' into 'One Kind Favour', for that was only a matter of the mode, while here phrasing and harmony are involved as well: in fact, the entire form of the tune in the most all-embracing sense of the word 'form'.

It will be noticed that the family likenesses in this series are mainly confined to the first eight bars, in other words the verse part. In all such verse-and-refrain tunes the two sections tend to lead separate lives. When we come to compare Tunes (*a*) and (*b*) two things are noticeable: firstly, the fall of a third to the tonic becomes more prominent, just as it did in the 'Barbara Allen'–'One Kind Favour' series; and secondly, a triadic figure appears in bars 6–7 and 9–10 of the second tune. It is by such subtle touches that the Scottish pentatonic is given a bluesy flavour.

The obvious difference between Tune (*c*) and Tune (*b*) is that in the former the second phrase has been shifted up an octave; but the really important difference is that the relation between the three phrases has been radically altered. Where 'Single Girl' is still eight bars of verse plus four bars of refrain, 'Josie' is a fully integrated twelve-bar blues. Instead of 8+4 we have 4+4+4. The difference between these two songs can be summed up by the statement that while 'Single Girl' is a bluesy folk-song, 'Josie' is a folky blues.

Mississippi John Hurt's version of 'Frankie' was recorded in 1928, and, as David Evans says,[6] would probably have sounded much the same in 1910 or earlier. It is an example of the old, fast blues ballad, which could be accompanied as happily by the banjo as by the guitar. Here the 'Josie' tune has been assimilated to the typical African pattern, with each of the three phrases descending to the tonic, now conceived as a floor note.

But this is by no means the end of the Frankie tune family. Dorothy Scarborough wrote: 'There are two tunes for the song. The more common air . . . is the one I have always heard in Texas.' The example she gave of it was a rather less bluesy variant of the Mississippi John Hurt version. She then went on: 'Another variant of the ballad has a different tune, somewhat more sophisticated. The words and the air are less frequently heard than the others, yet they are fairly popular in the south.'[7] Her second tune is given in Ex. 77.[8] The peculiarity of this branch of the Frankie tune family lies in the second phrase, which more or less reproduces the first a fourth higher. The probable origin of this type can be seen in 'I Went to the Hop-Joint' (Ex. 78)[9], which is virtually the 'Josie' tune with the first two phrases treated in this way. This feature recalls two things, one being the move to the subdominant in the standard blues harmonic scheme, and the other the quasi-sequences of African song, arising out of the repetition of words at a different pitch (as

---

[6] *Big Road Blues*, p. 45.

[7] *On the Trail of Negro Folk-Songs*, pp. 83–4.

[8] It seems probable that the last two bars of this song have been notated at half their actual speed.

[9] The words of this song are obviously related to the famous ragtime song, 'Bill Bailey, Won't You Please Come Home?' (Ex. 144), but what the connection was I cannot say. 'Hop' was cocaine.

Ex. 77 'Frankie and Albert'

Fran-kie and Al - bert were   lo-vers.   O, lor - dy, how they did   love!

Said they'd be true   to each   o - ther,___ True as   the bright stars   a -

bove.   He   was   her   man,   but he done her   wrong.

Ex. 78 'I Went to the Hop-Joint'

I went to   the   hop-joint And thought I'd have some   fun.   In walked Bill

Bai - ley__ With his   for - ty - one!(Oh, ba - by   dar - lin', why don't you come home?)__

in 'Kuro'i nyẹ mo dea', Ex. 25) which, as we have seen, made their way into Afro-American music. In a spiritual like 'Way over in the New Buryin' Groun' ' (Ex. 17), or a worksong like 'Po' Lazarus' (Ex. 83) we see the idiom in almost its original African form. The odd thing about its appearance in 'Frankie and Albert' is that it appears where the words are not repeated; whereas in the standard pattern of the blues, where the words *are* repeated, this feature is hardly ever found.

Apart from this general African partiality for sequences, there are specific instances of transposition in African music (as in 'Ọl'ọ́kọ́ d'ẹhìn, Ex. 26(c)) and even canons at the fourth or fifth.[10] This branch of the Frankie tune family seems to have arisen through a fusion of such African patterns with the subdominant of European folk harmony.

Just when and how the two Frankie tune families evolved is a fascinating but unanswerable question. How long did it take for the 'Josie' tune to turn into Mississippi John Hurt's variant? If we date the latter at about 1910, how much earlier is 'Josie'? One decade? Two decades? Fifty years? Much has been written on the origins of the Frankie ballad, but as far as I know no exhaustive and scholarly study has been made. Putting all the evidence together, it seems that something like 'Josie' began as a mountain song, touched by black influence,

[10] Such canons are mentioned by Akpabot, 'Functional Music of the Ibibio', p. 89.

somewhere around the time of the Civil War.[11] However far back its origins, there is no denying the wildfire rapidity with which it spread; and this, I believe, has as much to do with the strength of its musical structure as the squalid glamour of its theme.

PROTO-ROCK AND ROLL

The Frankie family was by no means the only American offshoot of the twelve-bar, verse-and-refrain form. Around the turn of the century there were also the musically akin 'Boll Weevil' family already mentioned, and the Casey Jones', 'Railroad Bill', and 'President McKinley' ballads, to name only some of the better-known examples. To examine them in detail would not add much to what has already been said about the Frankie family. But there was another class of song with a history separate enough to deserve special mention. This was the dance song, with its humorous (and often bawdy) verses jumbled up in any order occurring to the singer. These dance songs are mainly a Celtic tradition, and, like so many Celtic musical traditions, were taken over to the United States. Ex. 79 shows how a Scottish song could be transformed

Ex. 79

(a) 'Rue the Day'   (b) 'Sorghum Syrup'*

* Sung by Alec More, a cowboy, of Austin, Texas. From Alan Lomax, *The Folk Songs of North America*, p. 255 (Cassell, 1963).

[11] There is a story that the song was sung by troops engaged in the war itself. See Belden, *Ballads and Folk Songs*, pp. 330–1, for a concise but detailed account of the history of the song.

Rue all the day Rid-dle all the day Ah rue the day A - riddle - a-the-da - lie___

By and by, be-fore I die, I'll mar-ry me a girl with a right blue eye.

into an American dance tune.[12] An Africanized version of the same type was popular around the turn of the century (see Ex. 80).[13] Musically, it resembles Mississippi John Hurt's 'Frankie', with the same breakneck tempo and a similar three-chord, twelve-bar blues harmonic structure.

Ex. 80   'Tight like That'*

Very fast (♩ = 300)

Had a li'l dog whose name was Bald   [?   ] It's tight like that,

woo,   tight like that,   woo,   [?   ]   it's tight like that.

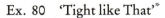

* Sung by Huddie Ledbetter ('Leadbelly') and recorded for the Library of Congress by John A. and Alan Lomax. On *Leadbelly: The Library of Congress Recordings* (Elektra EKL-301/2), side 2, track 2.

The differences lie in the words and the melodic line, which are enough to identify it as the grandparent of rock and roll classics like 'Good Golly Miss Molly' and 'Long Tall Sally' (Ex. 81). These songs have a very characteristic form, springing from the assimilation of songs like 'Sorghum Syrup' (Ex. 79(b)) to the African call-and-response pattern. The whole verse is squeezed into the first four bars to make the call, the

Ex. 81   'Long Tall Sally'

Bright rock tempo

VOICE PIANO

mf

Gon-na   tell Aunt   Ma - ry   'bout Un-cle John,   He says he has the blues, But he

[12] 'Courage' in Ex. 79(a) means sexual potency.
[13] Performed by Huddie Ledbetter ('Leadbelly') in response to the invitation to 'give us a little sketch of "Tight like That" the way they used to play it at the square dances with really square dance time'. 'It's Tight like That' enjoyed a great vogue after being performed by Hudson Whittaker ('Tampa Red') in 1928, but everything about both the words and the music suggests a much earlier folk origin.

has a lot of fun, Oh,   ba - by,   yes _____   ba - by   woo _____

ba - by,   Hav-in' me some fun   to - night.   Yeah!

response being spread out over the remaining eight bars. In the most typical form the verse is delivered at a rattling pace in a semi-monotone, and, to emphasize its call-like quality, is usually accompanied only by staccato chords on the main beats; after which the refrain crashes in with a full accompaniment on the subdominant chord. The effect is highly exhilarating.

Among other resemblances between 'Tight like That' and 'Long Tall Sally' are the bawdy nature of the words, which goes back to songs like 'The Cuckoo's Nest'[14] as well as to African traditions;[15] falsetto yelps; and short, abrupt phrases separated by pauses. Clearly, there is a direct trail leading from one to the other, via a series of obscure musicians in rustic backwaters, custodians of a tradition looking backward to the 'jigs' of the nineteenth and even eighteenth centuries, and forward to the triumphs of Little Richard, Chuck Berry, and Elvis Presley.

PRETTY POLLY AND PO' LAZARUS

Among the more than 1,500 tunes that Cecil Sharp collected in the Appalachians from 1916 to 1918, there are no fewer than twenty-one versions of a ballad called 'The Cruel Ship's Carpenter'. It concerns a young man who lures a woman away with a promise of marriage, seduces her, and then kills her. He then goes to sea as a ship's carpenter, where the ghost of the murdered woman appears to him and he comes to a bad end. At least, that is the original, full version of the story. In the condensed version common in America, usually called 'Pretty Polly' after the name of the victim, the seagoing episode is dropped.

Of Sharp's twenty-one versions, nine are in the usual British form of the four-line stanza. The others have only two lines to a stanza, sometimes in the form of an eight-bar tune, but sometimes—and this is

[14] Quoted on p. 80.
[15] It is said that Long Tall Sally is a phallic symbol, but there were songs about a certain Sally Long in the 1920s, who, in turn, has been traced back to a minstrel song of the 1830s (see Oliver, *Songsters and Saints*, p. 45). Of course, the two explanations are not mutually exclusive.

what interests us—in the form of a threefold repetition of the first line
followed by the second:

> Pretty Polly, pretty Polly, you're guessing just right, (4 bars)
> Pretty Polly, pretty Polly, you're guessing just right, (4 bars)
> Pretty Polly, pretty Polly, you're guessing just right, (4 bars)
> I was digging your grave the bigger part of the night. (4 bars)

In yet another form, represented by no fewer than six variants out of the
total of twenty-one, one of the repetitions is dropped:

> Pretty Polly, pretty Polly, come go along with me (4 bars)
> Pretty Polly, pretty Polly, come go along with me (4 bars)
> Before we get married some pleasure to see. (4 bars)

This is, of course, simply the classic form of the twelve-bar blues. It
seems that the three-line form was derived from the four-line form by
the simple process of dropping one of the middle lines, as can be seen by
comparing Ex. 82 with the version already quoted as Ex. 18.

Ex. 82   'Pretty Polly', variant T

She threw her arms round him, she suf-fered no fear, She threw her arms round him, she

suf-fered no fear. How can you kill the girl that has loved you so dear?

As well as being a popular folk-song, 'Pretty Polly' is well known as
an instrumental piece. It also has a close relative in the worksong 'Po'
Lazarus' (Ex. 83). Melodic and rhythmic details may differ, but the basic
plan is the same: the first phrase, circling around and ending on the
tonic; the second phrase, doing much the same around the dominant,
rather like a fugal answer; and the third phrase, finishing on the tonic.

Ex. 83   'Po' Lazarus'*

With great drive (♩ =92)

High Sher-iff,___ he tol' the dep-u-ty,   (Hunh-unh!)   he says,

'Go out an' bring me   Laz'-us.' (Hunh-unh!) High Sher-iff,__ he tol' the dep-u-ty,

* From Alan Lomax, *The Folk Songs of North America*, p. 567 (Cassell, 1963). Collected in
the Mississippi Valley.

(Hunh unh!)   he says   'Go out an' bring me   Laz'-us,   (Hunh unh!)   Bring him

dead or a-live,   Wo,   Law-dy, bring him dead or a-live.'   (Hunh unh!)

We have seen a similar process in 'Blin' Man Stood on de Way an' Cried' (Ex. 73(*d*)). All three are instances of the typically African procedure of 'focus contrast' at the distance of a fifth, as explained in chapter 16, with repeated words sung to similar melodic contours.

This 'Pretty Polly'–'Po' Lazarus' family once again shows the intimate connection between black and white American folk music. It also shows the futility of trying to trace the twelve-bar blues to a single source. By the early twentieth century the twelve-bar or three-part form had obviously become a favourite with American folk musicians, white as well as black. 'Pretty Polly' was not the only sixteen-bar tune to be reduced to twelve bars by dropping one phrase. The same thing happened to 'Nottamun Town', an especially interesting case; for here we see the transition taking place before our eyes, as it were, with the singer vacillating between the three-line and four-line pattern:

> In Nottamun Town not a soul would look up,
> Not a soul would look up, not a soul would look down
> To tell me the way to Nottamun Town.
>
> I rode a big horse that was called a grey mare,
> Grey mane and tail and grey stripes down his back,
> There weren't a hair on him but what was called black.
>
> She stood so still, she threw me to the dirt,
> She tore my hide and bruised my shirt.
> From stirrup to saddle I mounted again,
> And on my ten toes I rode over the plain.[16]

(Musically, the difference between the two patterns is simply that the middle phrase is sometimes repeated and sometimes not.) Some of these early twelve-bar songs are reshapings of well known tunes—'Yankee Doodle', for instance, or 'The Campbells are Coming', the obvious parent of the following:

> I love little Willie, I do, I do,
> I love little Willie, but don't you tell Paw!
> For I caint help it. How can I now, Maw?[17]

[16] Sharp, *English Folk Songs from the Southern Appalachians*, vol. 2, p. 270, variant A. The town is spelt 'Notamun' in the text, but 'Nottamun' elsewhere.

[17] Randolph, *Ozark Folksongs*, vol. 3, 'Humorous and Play-Party Songs', p. 98. In the original the words 'but don't you tell Paw!' are on a new line.

Yet another example is 'The Frog Would a-Wooing Ride', which was transformed from its Jacobean English origins, as 'The Marriage of the Frogge and the Mouse':

> The Frogge would a wooing ride,
>   humble dum, humble dum.
> Sword and buckler by his side,
>   tweedle, tweedle twino.[18]

into the blues-like 'Mister Frog':[19]

> Mister Frog went a-courtin', he did ride, uh-hum.
> Mister Frog went a-courtin', he did ride,
> A sword and pistol by his side uh-hum.

JOHN HENRY AND THE TEN-BAR BLUES

The main stanza-types in British folk-song—four- or eight-line, six-line, and five-line—have all given rise to blues patterns. The four- or eight-line type became the eight- or sixteen-bar blues like 'One Kind Favour' (Ex. 73(e)). The six-line pattern became the twelve-bar blues. And the five-line pattern, likewise, had its progeny among the blues; but whereas the other patterns are found among songs of all kinds, the ten-bar form is overwhelmingly dominated by a single song, though this appears in countless variants. It is the ballad of John Henry, the Steel-Driving Man.

John Henry's story is sung to several tunes, of which the ten-bar one is the commonest. It is one of those tunes where there seem to be almost as many variants as there are singers to sing them. Ex. 84 shows its genealogy. 'The Birmingham Boys' (Ex. 84(a)) conforms to an old melodic pattern, basically $A_1A_2A_3B$, where each 'A' consists of a

Ex. 84

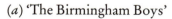

(a) 'The Birmingham Boys'

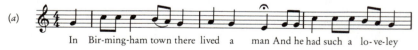

In Bir-ming-ham town there lived a   man And he had such a lo-ve-ley

(b) 'John Henry' (I)

Smoothly and fast

John Hen - ry tol' his cap' - n Dat a man wuz a na - tu-ral

---

[18] From Ravenscroft's *Melismata*, 1611. Quoted in Opie, *The Oxford Dictionary of Nursery Rhymes*, pp. 179–80; facsimile of the original tune on p. 181.
[19] See Ex. 154(b) for the tune and history of this song.

(c) 'John Henry' (II)*

John Hen - ry was a li-'l ba - by, uh-huh, Set-tin' on his ma - ma's

* From John A. and Alan Lomax, *American Ballads and Folk Songs*, p. 5 (Macmillan, 1934).

(d) 'John Henry' (knife blues)

accompaniment continues on one chord with variations

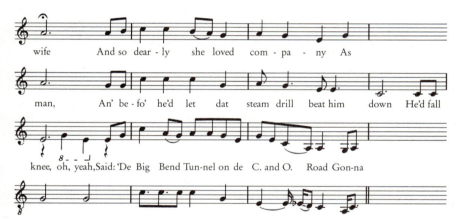

wife And so dear - ly she loved com - pa - ny As

man, An' be-fo' he'd let dat steam drill beat him down He'd fall

knee, oh, yeah, Said: 'De Big Bend Tun-nel on de C. and O. Road Gon-na

dear-ly as she loved her life, boys, life As dear-ly as she loved her life

dead wid a ham-mer in his han', He'd fall dead wid a ham-mer in his han'.

cause de death of me, Lawd, Lawd, Gon-na cause de death of me.'

repeat with variations

miniature arch formation lying in the upper part of the octave, after which 'B' dips to the tonic. Another example of this pattern is the second half of the Scottish cradle song, Ex. 65(*b*). One subgroup of this family has been traced back to 'Lady Cassilles Lilt' (Ex. 85), which appears in a Scottish manuscript of about 1620.[20] Though a surprisingly close relative

Ex. 85   'Lady Cassilles Lilt'

of the whole tune has been preserved in the Appalachians,[21] most of the progeny of 'Lady Cassilles Lilt' derive from the second half only, just as 'Get along Home, Cindy' derived from the second half of the cradle song (Exx. 66(*b*) and 65(*b*)). They are extremely common in American folk music of the Appalachian type. To this basic type the 'Birmingham Boys' type simply adds the feature of repeating the final phrase, producing the pattern $A_1A_2A_3B_1B_2$.[22]

In the 'Birmingham Boys' pattern the British folk muse produced something closely akin to the descending strains of Africa. It is no wonder that black musicians seized on it so avidly. Exx. 84(*c*) and (*d*) show two ways in which it could be Africanized, respectively as a call-and-response worksong and a one-chord blues. 'The Birmingham Boys' is African not only in its descending lines, but also in the way it repeats first one and then another short phrase with variations. In Africa the repetitions are taken to far greater lengths. It is interesting to see 'John Henry' approaching this pattern in some variants, where the tune is broken up and repeated to an extent that would make it impossible to guess its British origin, were it not a member of a great song family.[23]

CONCLUSION

What can we learn from Frankie, Barbara Allen, Pretty Polly, Po' Lazarus, John Henry, and all the other interesting folk who people this chapter? I think several lessons stand out.

[20] See Bronson, *Traditional Tunes of the Child Ballads*, vol. 3, p. 198, for the relation of this tune to some common American tune-types.

[21] 'Lazarus', ibid., vol. 2, pp. 20–1.

[22] Another British example of the same type, also very close to 'John Henry', is 'The Keach i' the Creel', Bruce and Stokoe, *Northumbrian Minstrelsy*, p. 82.

[23] An example is the treatment of 'John Henry' in Courlander, *Negro Folk Music, U.S.A.*, pp. 280–1.

First, there is the surprising directness of the links between black American and British folk-song, if only you know where to look. Second, the history of these songs bears out again the extraordinarily mixed up character of American folk music. Black and white, instrumental and vocal, religious and secular—all were busily reacting, and the deeper one digs, the further back in history these reactions seem to go. The development of American popular styles around the turn of the century was certainly spectacular, but not quite as spectacular as it might seem at first glance. Like any other worthwhile art form, the blues had a long, gradual process of evolution behind it.

Probably the most striking lesson these songs have to teach us, however, is the astonishing importance of a handful of tune forms. Why were the 'Petit Roysin', 'Frankie', and 'John Henry' patterns so fruitful and important? Part of the answer lies in their great strength and flexibility. They not only *permit* extensive variation, they positively *demand* it. With most classical tunes, if you get a note wrong you spoil the whole. This is not true of these great folk tune patterns. With them it is always possible to substitute something new with perfectly good effect. The stability of the general framework is balanced by the instability of the details, and the natural result is an unending succession of variants.

No wonder that the blacks, with their love of improvisation, were attracted to these tune patterns. There were other attractions as well. These tunes were purely melodic, with a strong modal character. Unlike so many British tunes, they did not rely on the un-African matrix of recapitulation. In short, they presented nothing puzzling to the African point of view.

The 'Birmingham Boys' pattern went even further than this. It was thoroughly African. Sensing its kinship to their ancestral music, the blacks seized on its African features and exaggerated them. The whole process can be seen in Ex. 84. It is the Africanization of British folk music in a nutshell.

IV. BLUES HARMONY

22. THE HISTORY OF GREGORY WALKER

THE twelve-bar blues has been associated with many harmonic schemes, of which the simplest is the one-chord form mentioned in chapter 18. To this one-chord scheme either a subdominant or, at the final cadence, a dominant chord can be added. In Charley Patton's 'Pony Blues' (Ex. 60), for instance, the only chord other than the tonic is the subdominant at the beginning of the second phrase. Or both subdominant and dominant may be used in a I IV I V I pattern, the exact fit of harmony to tune being variable, especially in the early blues. The standard pattern consists of four bars of the first tonic chord and then two bars each of the remaining chords, but a common variant is to replace the two bars of dominant with one of dominant followed by one of subdominant, as in Ex. 86(*b*).

A list of some of the more important of these variations is given in Ex. 86. It is by no means exhaustive. For instance, any one of the tonic chords can be adorned with an interpolated subdominant. The cadence in Type (*b*) could be used in Types (*d*) or (*e*). Any of the chords can have sevenths or sixths added to them, in the usual blues way, and so on, through endless possibilities.

There is no question, however, about the primacy of Types (*a*) and (*b*). To many people, including the framers of dictionary definitions, this is what 'the blues' means. The interesting thing about these chord strings is

Ex. 86 Blues patterns

(*a*) Standard blues pattern

(*b*) Common variant, e.g. 'Long Tall Sally', Ex. 81

(c) The one-chord type, e.g. 'Pretty Polly', Ex. 82

(d) One chord, except for the perfect cadence, e.g. 'Josie', Ex. 76(c)

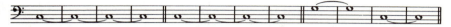

(e) The 'Frankie' pattern

(f) The 'Railroad Bill' pattern

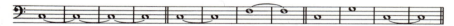

that they avoid the usual three-chord pattern of I IV V I, fundamental not only to the European classics but also to most Europeanized African music. Why did black Americans prefer to put a tonic chord between subdominant and dominant? Part of the answer, at least, lies in the interesting career of Gregory Walker.

THE BIRTH OF GREGORY WALKER

'Nay' says one of the characters in Thomas Morley's *Plaine and Easie Introduction to Practicall Musicke*, ' . . . you sing you knowe not what, it should seeme you came latelie from a Barbers shop, where you had *Gregory Walker*, or a *Curranta* plaide in the newe proportions by them lately found out . . .', to which Morley appends a footnote, explaining that 'That name in derision they have given this quadrant pavan, because it walketh amongst the Barbars and Fidlers, more common than any other.'[1]

Gregory Walker, alias the Quadran, Quadrant, or Quadro Pavan, alias the *Passamezzo Moderno*, was the chord scheme I IV I V : I IV I–V I. He was born around 1500, and has continued to walk through musical history ever since. He appears here because, of all the three-chord tune patterns that influenced the early blues, he was easily the most influential. Here is an outline of his story.

As far as we know, Gregory Walker first appeared in Italian and French collections of dance music during the first half of the sixteenth century, soon acquiring the name of *passamezzo moderno*. As such, this pattern became one of the favourite harmonic formulas of sixteenth-century dance music, though usually with a second strain, or episodes

---

[1] p. 120. 'Quadrant' referred to the 'square' natural sign that distinguished the major mode.

known as *ripresi*. In Morley's time it was at the height of its popularity, not only among 'Barbars and Fidlers' and similar despised pop musicians, but also in the cultivated music of the time. As 'The Quadran Pavan' there are several examples in *The Fitzwilliam Virginal Book*, in which it is interesting to see how the original pattern has been drawn out and elaborated in the course of a century or so. It remained popular through the seventeenth century, principally in the form of simple dance tunes, but after 1700 it began to go out of favour, ousted by more up-to-date harmonic fashions. It does not appear in *The Beggar's Opera* (1728) for instance. But as Ex. 87 shows, dance tunes of this type did however linger on, in both Britain and America.[2] What kept these tunes popular

Ex. 87

(*a*) 'Up and Ware Them A Willie' (*b*) 'Jimmie Rose'

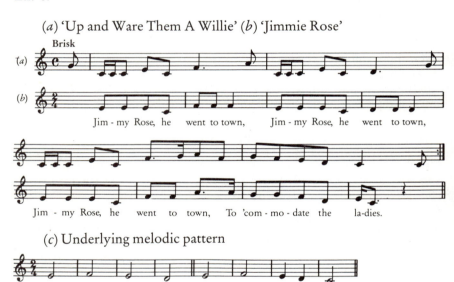

(*c*) Underlying melodic pattern

was probably not so much the harmony as the catchy, to-and-fro pattern underlying the melody (Ex. 87(*c*)), familiar to the twentieth century from 'The Lullaby of Broadway'.

For a while the career of Gregory Walker becomes obscure. We can only guess that harmonic formulas like this were kept alive by musicians, whether professional or amateur, who were neither sophisticated nor 'folk', but something in between: accustomed to thinking in harmonic terms, but probably unable to read music. Then, in the middle of the nineteenth century, Gregory Walker enjoyed a great revival. Tunes like 'Darling Nelly Gray' (Ex. 88) became immensely popular. By mid-

[2] 'Bile them Cabbage down' (A. Lomax, *The Folk Songs of North America*, p. 506) is practically the same tune as Ex. 87(*b*), 'Jimmy Rose'.

Ex. 88   'Darling Nelly Gray'

There's a low green val-ley on the old Ken-tuck-y shore, There I've whiled ma-ny hap-py hours a - way,   A sit-ting and a sing-ing by the lit-tle cot-tage door   Where lived my dar-ling Nel-ly Gray.

Victorian times such American Gregory Walker tunes had become familiar in Britain, and in 1885 Bernard Shaw was attributing the unpopularity of Bach's B minor Mass partly to the lack of them:

The work disappointed some people, precisely as the Atlantic Ocean disappointed Mr Wilde [on his recent trip to America]. Others, fond of a good tune, missed in it those compact little airs that can be learnt by ear and accompanied by tonic, sub-dominant, tonic, dominant, and tonic harmonies in the order stated; or, pedantry apart, by the three useful chords with which professors of the banjo teach their pupils, in one lesson, to accompany songs (usually in the key of G), without any previous knowledge of thoroughbass. ('The Bach Bicentenary', in *The Dramatic Review*, 28 March 1885, p. 133; reprinted in *Shaw's Music*, vol. 1, p. 219.)

The Gregory Walker pattern has remained popular ever since. It is found in old hillbilly favourites like 'The Old 97', and Woody Guthrie's 'There is a House in this Old Town' (another of the 'Forsaken Maiden' family; see chapter 20, 'The Ladder of Thirds'), in ragtime (Irving Berlin's 'Alexander's Ragtime Band'), and in more recent popular styles (the Beatles' 'I Saw Her Standing There' (1963), the Rolling Stones' 'Honky

Ex. 89

(*a*) Gregory Walker   (*b*) The American Gregory Walker

Tonk Women' (1969), Carole King's 'You've Got a Friend' (1971)).

But Gregory Walker is important not only in himself, but also for his progeny. One of these was the pattern which we could call the American Gregory Walker (Ex. 89). In this, the subdominant chords are split into the progression IV–I. Examples are 'Jesse James' (Ex. 90),[3] 'The Titanic', 'My Little Old Sod Shanty', 'Cottonfields', and, in the blues line, Gus Cannon's 'Walk Right in' (1929). This I IV–I chord pattern had long

Ex. 90   'Jesse James'[*]

* From Alan Lomax, *The Penguin Book of American Folk Songs*, p. 103 (Penguin, 1964). (©1934, renewed 1962 by Ludlow Music, Inc., New York. Used by permission of TRO and Essex Music of Australia Pty Ltd.)

been popular in what I call 'parlour' music. It appears in the Chopin Mazurka, Ex. 108(*a*); in the 'Battle Hymn of the Republic', otherwise known as 'John Brown's Body', Ex. 108(*b*); and in Stephen Foster's 'My Old Kentucky Home', Ex. 135(*a*). The American Gregory Walker is simply the old Gregory Walker merged with this newer progression.

GREGORY WALKER AND THE TWELVE-BAR BLUES

The basic harmonic pattern of the twelve-bar blues, I IV I V I, underlies the Gregory Walker pattern in both its standard and American forms. At the turn of the century, when blues tunes were often performed to a bright tempo (see, for instance, Exx. 76(*d*) and 80) it was quite possible to use the self-same accompaniment for a Gregory Walker tune like 'Darling Nelly Gray' (Ex. 88) and a twelve-bar blues, merely by omitting a quarter of the Gregory Walker pattern, as in Ex. 91(*a*). Another way in which Gregory Walker could be adapted to the twelve-bar blues was simply to use the second half for the last eight bars of the blues, the first four being on the tonic as usual (Ex. 91(*b*)). This is the pattern of the blues ballads 'Railroad Bill' and 'Mister McKinley', both dating from the turn of the century.[4]

---

[3] 'Mister Howard' was the alias James was using when he was shot for a $10,000 reward by a member of his own gang.
[4] 'Mister McKinley' tells of the assassination of President McKinley, which took place in 1901. For much interesting information on these ballads, see Cohen, *Long Steel Rail*, pp. 122–31 and 413–25.

Ex. 91

(*a*) Gregory Walker accompaniment adapted to the twelve-bar blues

Twelve-bar blues (standard pattern)

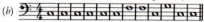

(*b*) The same, adapted to the 'Railroad Bill' pattern

Twelve-bar blues ('Railroad Bill' pattern)

SOME EIGHT-BAR PATTERNS

One of the great forces in American music, both white and black, but especially black, is what one could call creative fragmentation. A tune is broken down into simpler and simpler elements, while, in compensation, these elements may develop a new complexity of their own.[5] The process was helped along by the African fondness for the extensive repetition of short scraps of melody. Already in 1867 it was observed that 'In repeating . . . The custom at Port Royal [in the Georgia Sea Islands] is to repeat the first part of the tune over and over, it may be a dozen times, before passing to the "turn," and then do the same with that.'[6] With such treatment it is easy for a section to come completely adrift from the parent tune. If, in addition, this detached section is slowed down—as we have seen, a common process in the early blues—it becomes easy for the second half of the American Gregory Walker pattern to be transformed into an eight-bar blues. (There are several Gregory Walker tunes in *Slave Songs of the United States*.) Long ago it was noticed that the rousing spiritual 'Before I'd be a Slave' was derived from the chorus of 'Lilly Dale' (a 'Nelly Gray'-like tune) by such a process of fragmentation.[7] Slow down the tempo of 'Before I'd be a Slave', change the melody somewhat but retain the implicit I IV–I I–V I chord scheme, and you have the eight-bar blues 'Hattie Belle'.[8] The same chord scheme appears

---

[5] For examples elsewhere in this book, compare 'Lady Cassilles Lilt' (Ex. 85) with 'John Henry' (Ex. 84), and the Scottish 'Cradle Song' (Ex. 65(*b*)) with 'Get along Home, Cindy' (Ex. 66(*b*)). See also Sutton, 'Shape-Note Tune Books and Primitive Hymns', pp. 21–4.

[6] Allen *et al.*, *Slave Songs of the United States*, p.xxii.

[7] The resemblance was first remarked on by H.E. Krehbiel. See Jackson, *White and Negro Spirituals*, pp. 146–7, for the tunes of 'Lily Dale' (set to the words 'Land of Rest') and 'Before I'd be a Slave'.

[8] See A. Lomax, *The Folk Songs of North America*, pp. 584–5.

in 'How Long Blues',[9] which was wildly popular during the 1920s and 30s. In a similar way, the well-known 'Troubled in Mind' is probably derived from the second half of the late nineteenth-century reel 'Becky Dean'.[10] And 'Show Pity, Lord' (Ex. 11) derives from the beginning of the hymn tune 'Devotion'; in the process of being shortened it has also been assimilated to the end-repeating form.[11]

This slowing down of blues ballads, jigs, reels, and spirituals involved far more than just tempo. At the slower pace the whole musical structure alters. The relation between both phrases and chords is different. The old, classical principles governing harmonic progressions are replaced by principles peculiar to the blues. The next few chapters will try to explain what these are.

[9] See Titon, *Early Downhome Blues*, pp. 89–90, and A. Lomax, ibid., pp. 589–92.
[10] For 'Troubled in Mind' see A. Lomax, ibid., p. 589, and for 'Becky Dean', J. and A. Lomax, *Negro Folk Songs as Sung by Lead Belly*, pp. 214–16, and *Leadbelly: The Library of Congress Recordings* (Elektra EKL-301/2), side 2, track 4.
[11] For 'Devotion' see Sutton, 'Shape-Note Tune Books and Primitive Hymns', p. 24.

23. MORE ABOUT PRIMITIVE HARMONY

Football Chants and the 'Double Tonic'

A REGULAR back-and-forth motion like the swinging of a pendulum is one of the fundamental matrices of music. It is found at its most basic in simple chants like Ex. 92, to be heard at sports stadiums. This is a

Ex. 92   Football crowd chant

Chel - sea,   Chel - sea

melodic example. Harmonic forms are equally possible, as in the regular swing between tonic and dominant so familiar in the Classical style, or the alternating discords of Debussy or Stravinsky. In fact it is such a simple idea that it can take almost any form, melodic or harmonic, diatonic or chromatic, consonant or dissonant. Some of the oldest harmonic progressions take this form, and here the most ancient and fundamental interval seems to be, not the fourth or even the minor third, but the tone. One unit—it may be a chord or a purely melodic figure— alternates with another a tone higher or lower. In its simplest form this pattern can be seen in the little Arab tune, Ex. 93. In Europe it is best

Ex. 93   Arab tune

known in the Scottish form sometimes described as the 'double tonic': 'Donald MacGillavry' (Ex. 94) is an example. Various theories have been advanced to account for this favourite Scottish pattern. One holds that it grew out of the alternation of stopped and open fifths in fiddle music; another, that it developed from the inability of bagpipers to play leading notes. The great popularity of the pattern in Scotland—and also in Ireland—may well owe something to these factors; but as explanations of origin they are unconvincing, since the basic idea of the double tonic is far from being confined to the Celtic fringe. It is to be found in medieval English music ('Sumer is Icumen in', *c*.1250), in the popular music of the Elizabethan period ('The Woods so Wild' (Ex. 95), 'Dargason', etc.), and in Oriental music (Ex. 93 above). It also underlies the beginnings of the *passamezzo antico* pattern of the Italian Renaissance (Am G Am E : C G Am–E Am). In all probability the Scottish double tonic is merely a survival of a common medieval pattern.

The 'double tonic' is also extremely common in African music,[1] and it is strange that a pattern so popular in both Africa and Scotland should have virtually died out in the United States. Probably the only example that is still widely known is the spiritual 'Rock my Soul'. But it is interesting that one of the first worksongs to be notated, 'Roun' de Corn, Sally' (from a novel published in 1859, but set in 1832) is in this form.[2] 'Roun' de Corn, Sally' again illustrates the close links between worksongs and sea shanties. It is introduced as a 'corn song' adapted as a boat song, but the reverse is surely true. The words 'round the corn, Sally' can only be a corruption of 'round the *corner* Sally' (or 'Sallies'), which, according to Hugill, 'is often found in nigger minstrelsy and means anything from a female species of "corner boy" to a fully-fledged prostitute'. Later, in the mouths of sailors, the words 'round the corner' came to mean 'around Cape Horn'.[3] The further corruption to 'round the corn' no doubt came about through the association of the song with corn-huskings. In any case, 'Roun' de Corn, Sally' sounds much more like a sea shanty than a shore worksong. The interesting thing about this and another open-ended, double-tonic shanty, 'Shallow Brown',[4] is the completeness with which the Celtic and African elements have merged. With 'Shallow Brown', in particular, it is hard to tell whether we are dealing with an Africanized British tune or an actual African tune slightly Europeanized. I incline to believe the latter.[5] In recent decades double-tonic patterns have again become common in American popular

---

[1] See 'Mkwaze mmodzi' (Ex. 33), and, for elaborations on this pattern, Arap Kapero's song (Ex. 39) and 'Alfa Yaya' (Ex. 97). There is an extensive discussion of how such patterns arise out of the technique of some musical bows in Kirby, *The Musical Instruments of the Native Races of South Africa*, ch. 9, 'Stringed Instruments'. Compare also the harp accompaniment figure, Ex. 46.

[2] In Hungerford, *The Old Plantation*, p. 191. The song is reproduced in facsimile in Epstein, *Sinful Tunes and Spirituals*, p. 169.

[3] See Hugill, *Shanties from the Seven Seas*, pp. 389–90, and Lloyd, *Folk Songs in England*, pp. 283–4.

[4] See Sharp, *English Folk-Chanteys*, p. 35 (also quoted in Lloyd, *Folk Song in England*, p. 284).

[5] There have been many conjectures as to the origin of the name 'Shallow Brown'. One possibility is that the words, which are used merely as an apparently meaningless refrain, are not a name at all but the corruption of an African phrase.

music, but if they have any origins in earlier Afro-American music, these are extremely obscure.

Double-tonic tunes can be divided into two broad categories, according to whether they start on the upper or lower unit. Most Scottish tunes, the *passamezzo antico*, 'Roun' de Corn, Sally', 'Shallow Brown', 'Mkwaze mmodzi', and our little Arab tune all start on the upper unit. 'Sumer is Icumen in', 'The Woods so Wild', and 'The Irish Washerwoman' start on the lower one. There are other differences too. Sometimes the interval is not quite a tone: in the Arab tune it is about three quarters of a tone, and in African examples it can vary from something like a minor third to a semitone, in the latter case producing a chromatic effect. But, whatever their differences, all these types are united in the challenge they pose to orthodox ideas of harmony and tonality, especially when, as in 'Donald MacGillavry', the Arab tune, 'Roun' de Corn, Sally', or 'Shallow Brown', the two units are merely repeated indefinitely. Here there is no tonic—or is it two tonics, as the phrase 'double tonic' suggests? And here there need be no harmony, or if there is harmony, it is often of a decidedly quirky and unfamiliar kind.

Passamezzi Ancient and Modern

A tune like 'Donald MacGillavry' can be given a much more conventional appearance by endowing it with a tonic close: Am G Am–G A, instead of merely Am G Am G Am G . . . *ad infinitum*. Most Scottish double-tonic tunes do in fact conform to some variant of this 'closed' form. Matters can be further complicated by developing it into a binary pattern, ending first on the dominant and then on the tonic: Am G Am E: Am G Am–G Am, or, changing the final cadence, Am G Am E : Am G Am–E Am. The latter is a favourite pattern of the Italian Renaissance; as we have seen, with C substituted for the A minor beginning the second half, it is the basis of the classic *passamezzo antico*. This pattern, beginning around 1500, proceeded to captivate Europe for more than a century, and is still not quite dead as a force in popular music, since the immortal 'Greensleeves' is one of the countless tunes based on it.

The major-mode counterpart of the *passamezzo antico* was none other than our friend Gregory Walker, the *passamezzo moderno*. (In those days the major mode was associated with a B natural, or 'squared' B, hence its alternative name of the 'quadrant', etc., pavan.) In both *passamezzi* the one-way swing of the pendulum in tunes like 'Donald MacGillavry' has been converted into a two-way swing. First the harmony swings to the subdominant side—either to the subdominant (*moderno*) itself or to the minor seventh (*antico*)—then to the dominant. Then the whole double swing is repeated, only this time ending on the tonic. This gives us a matrix combination—'binary form' plus pendular harmony—the power of which made these formulas so popular during the Renaissance period.

With the triumph of the Baroque and Classical styles, it was inevitable that the *passamezzi* should fall from favour. In these styles the basis of harmony became the cadence; though non-cadential passages do occur, they will almost always be founded on the presence of a scale, diatonic or chromatic, somewhere in the harmony; and these passages always give the feeling that the normal processes have been temporarily suspended. This domination by the cadence sealed the fate of both *passamezzi*, with their fundamentally uncadential chords: not only the 'modal' chords of the *antico* but equally the subdominant of the *moderno*.

In developing the twelve-bar blues chord scheme, the American folk musicians were retaining the pendular aspect of these patterns, but abandoning the binary one—a considerable sacrifice. I shall later explore the question of how they made up for it. For the moment, let us consider what it was about what they kept—the pendular movement—that they found so powerful and so attractive.

LEVELS AND SHIFTS

Levels versus Chords

In the Celtic double-tonic tunes there is obviously something different, something non-classical, about the feel of the harmony. The chords are not quite the same as classical chords, and the movement from one chord to another is not the same as a classical progression.

In fact, the very word 'chord'—or for that matter 'harmony'—seems a little inappropriate. As we can see from the little Arab tune (Ex. 93) a very similar formula can occur in purely melodic music. Whether a particular example is harmonic or melodic, we are usually dealing with straightforward-looking triads, but what of 'Donald MacGillavry' (Ex. 94): what are we to call the unit from bars 9 to 11? If it is the chord

Ex. 94 'Donald MacGillavry'

of A minor, how do we account for the very prominent Gs? Evidently this is a triad surmounted by a seventh. The triad can be viewed as purely melodic, or as the spelling out of a chord. The seventh, on the other hand, can only be melodic. (In practice, Scottish tunes of this kind are usually performed without harmony, except perhaps for an unvarying drone.)

What we need is a broader term than merely 'chord'. Ethnomusic-ologists describing similar things in African music have used the terms 'shifting tonality levels', 'tonal steps',[6] and 'root progressions'.[7] I propose the simple word 'level', precisely because it is so vague and non-committal. Every level is firmly based on a single note, which we can call the 'foundation note'. In 'Donald MacGillavry', for instance, the foundation notes are A and G. On the foundation note it is possible to erect a third (as in the Arab tune), a triad (as in 'Shallow Brown'), or a seventh (as in 'Donald MacGillavry'). And this third, fifth, or seventh can be heard as either purely melodic or melodic-plus-harmonic.

Shifts versus Changes

Just as a level is more than a mere chord, so the movement from one level to another is more than a mere harmonic progression. The traditional term 'double tonic' suggests an actual modulation to a new key, as though the first three bars of 'Donald MacGillavry' were in A minor and the next one in G major. This is going too far, but it does give some idea of the abrupt and emphatic nature of the change. To distinguish this change of level, we can talk of 'shifts' as opposed to the familar chord 'changes' of the classics.

In general, the *shift of level* is a more basic and primitive matrix than the *change of chord*. As we have seen, it is found in Celtic, African, and Asian folk music. In the realm of 'art' music we find it in the dance music of the Renaissance. Here, as the style gradually shades into the early Baroque, shifts of level give way to changes of chord of the familiar classical kind. With the development of the blues in the twentieth century, we find the opposite process. Here, chord changes gradually become shifts of level.

Wherever we find it, the shift of level shows some characteristic features. There is always great emphasis on the foundation note, so that, when there are chords, they are almost always in root position. (The only important exceptions to this rule occur in sets of variations.) Next to the root, the fifth of the chord is the most important note; consecutive fifths, far from being banned, are strongly emphasized. This is probably the answer to the famous riddle of why consecutive fifths are prohibited

[6] See Kubik, 'Harp Music of the Azande', p. 53.
[7] See Blacking, 'Problems of Pitch, Pattern and Harmony', p. 23.

in the classical style: if they were allowed, they would make chord changes sound like shifts. As Tovey says in his analysis of Haydn's Symphony no. 88:

The trio is one of Haydn's finest pieces of rustic dance music, with hurdy-gurdy drones which shift in disregard of the rule forbidding consecutive fifths. The disregard is justified by the fact that the essential objection to consecutive fifths is that they produce the effect of shifting hurdy-gurdy drones. (*Essays in Musical Analysis*, vol. 1, p. 142.)

If the root and fifth of the chord are the important notes, the third is correspondingly weak. A sign of this weakness is that it tends to waver between major and minor. The blue notes are the most famous example of this feature, but we find it in other styles as well. The English virginalists, for instance, are full of it. Some of their harmony, puzzling from the orthodox viewpoint, makes excellent sense when analysed in terms of shifts rather than classical chord changes. 'The Woods so Wild' (Ex. 95), for instance, probably began life as a simple double-tonic tune.

Ex. 95   Byrd, 'The Woods so Wild' Variations (theme and end)

If so, several things have happened to it: the end of the tune has been provided with a cadence; the tune has been elaborated, and diverged from the accompaniment; and subsidiary chords have been introduced into the harmony. The last of these developments is particularly interesting. The 'level' ceases to be a single chord, blossoming, on occasion, into a complete little cadential phrase. To the modern eye it seems as if the music is abruptly jumping between the keys of F and G. In fact these are not keys, but extreme elaborations on the foundation notes F and G. Apart from these points, this example admirably illustrates the mixture of major and minor thirds and the tendency towards consecutive fifths.

We should never encounter such blatant fifths in Byrd's vocal music, whether sacred or secular. In these variations he is composing in a sophisticated version of the current popular style, a style which was soon to disappear from 'art' music, though it retained its hold on popular musicians. No doubt the 'shifting hurdy-gurdy drones' continued to be used between Byrd's time and Haydn's allusion to them two hundred years later. But as far as cultivated music was concerned they had ceased to exist.

The Boogie-Woogie Bass

With the coming of the blues all this changed. Though the first three-chord blues tunes seem to have been in a compact style with conventional chord changes, like 'Tight like That' (Ex. 80), 'Frankie' (Ex. 76(*d*)), or 'Railroad Bill', these changes gave way to shifts as the style developed. Then, like other features of the blues, these shifts gradually spread to popular music in general. The whole process is an almost precise reversal of what happened in the Renaissance period.

There are, however, some important differences between the blues shifts and those we have been considering up to now:

1. The blues shifts are between the three primary triads instead of levels a tone apart.
2. As a rule, the melody does not follow the outline of the bass. This is in keeping with that general independence of melody and accompaniment which is one of the strongest features of the blues style.
3. As in 'The Woods so Wild', a level can be considerably elaborated, but the form of the elaboration is quite different. There is not much of the interpolation of chords used by Renaissance composers; instead, the elaboration takes place *within* the chord.

The most familiar example of shifting levels in the blues is the celebrated boogie-woogie bass (Ex. 96).[8] Like 'The Woods So Wild', this

Ex. 96   Boogie-woogie bass

[8] This is actually only one of many boogie-woogie basses. They all show the same sort of shift.

passage seems a little puzzling when viewed with classical eyes. It contains B♭ as well as B♮, and E♭ as well as E♮. From the classical point of view, this suggests either a change of key or a change of mode, while the dominant seventh-like appearance of the chords suggests that they 'ought' to resolve onto the appropriate tonic. In fact, there is no change of key or mode, the position being much the same as in 'The Woods so Wild'. The difference is that instead of being elaborated into a little cadential progression, the level is treated rather like a miniature one-chord blues.

Like the one-chord blues, the boogie-woogie bass is close enough to African instrumental technique to suggest direct influence. The music of the banjo-like West African lutes, such as Ex. 97, uses a shifting-level harmonic technique which may well lie behind the boogie-woogie piano style.

Ex. 97   'Alfa Yaya' (theme)

As in the one-chord blues, the question of the resolution of discord does not arise in the boogie-woogie style. The logic of the boogie-woogie sevenths lies in their relation to the current chord, not the following one; and this raises the interesting question of the status of the dominant itself in the blues. When all the primary triads are provided with sevenths, the dominant seventh naturally ceases to be unique. How do we then mark the V7–I progression as something special? One solution is to insert a subdominant between the two chords, as in 'Long Tall Sally' (Ex. 81).[9] It is difficult to say what it is about this progression that makes it so natural and satisfying, though we may guess that African formulas like Ex. 97 had something to do with its genesis. From the classical viewpoint, it is a sort of cross between a perfect and plagal cadence. One thing is clear about it, however, and that is that all suggestion of chord changes or resolving dominants is gone. Here, the evolution from change to shift is complete.

---

[9] See also the introduction to 'Hard Headed Woman', Ex. 143(b).

V. THE RIDDLE OF THE TWELVE-BAR BLUES

24. THE STRANGE TRIUMPH OF THE BLUES

> He played nothing but blues and all that stink music and he played it
> very loud.
>
> George 'Pops' Foster, of Buddy
> Bolden, the early jazz trumpeter[1]

IMAGINE that you are a cultivated, well informed European musician.
The year is 1900. Like so many of your friends, you spend a great deal of
time wondering about the future of music. What will the new century
hold? Your views on this point depend on your individual inclinations.
You may be one of the growing band of brave young revolutionaries, or
on the other hand you may be a member of the old guard. Possibly, if
you are an Englishman or a Hungarian, say, you may be an enthusiast
for the folk music of your country. Your prophesies, coloured as always
by wishful thinking, will vary accordingly.

It would certainly not occur to you that anything interesting could
come from the United States of America: and not merely from that
notoriously uncultured country, but from the very dregs of its lowest
classes. If anyone had told you that the most potent musical force of the
twentieth century was to be American gutter music, you would have
doubted his sanity.

The triumph of the blues is one of musical history's best jokes. It is
also a mystery which has attracted many attempts at explanation, most of
them turning on social, economic, or political factors—racial conflict,
class conflict, urbanization, the rise to economic and political power of
the black Americans, or of the working class in general, middle-class
guilt, white guilt, the newly discovered adolescent market—that sort of
thing. Now, factors of this kind are obviously important, not only in
popular music, but in the arts generally. But they are extraordinarily
difficult to relate to stylistic developments. There is a theory—and I cite

---

[1] From *Pops Foster: The Autobiography of a New Orleans Jazzman*; quoted in Bruce Cook,
Listen to the Blues, p. 88.

it merely as an example—that the blues triumphed because of the general dislocation and alienation of twentieth-century life. After the Civil War, this theory runs, the freed slaves were dispersed all over the American South (and later the North too), cut off from their friends and families, often unemployed, hounded by laws that sought to preserve the conditions of slavery without the institution itself. And so they created the blues. Later the whites, too, came to know the pains of an itinerant life: they, too, learnt the harshness and loneliness of the big city, and found a response to their emotions in the blues.

The first objection to this theory is that it assumes that all blues styles are melancholy. If we grant this assumption, it is true that nothing better expresses the strange, poetic bleakness of the modern city than the blues, and one feels instinctively that this is an important reason for its popularity. But if one examines the circumstances of middle-class white blues-lovers, one finds, disconcertingly, that the better off they are the more they like the blues. It was during the prosperous 20s that middle-class America discovered the blues, and it was during the slump of the 30s that the vogue for the blues waned. The most poignant song of the Great Depression, 'Brother Can You Spare a Dime?', derived its melancholy not from Afro-America but from eastern Europe. And it was during the post-war boom of the 50s and 60s that the blues really came into its own among white, middle-class audiences.

I mention this theory, not for the pleasure of picking holes in it, but because it strikes me as exceptionally plausible. *Any* such attempts to explain the processes of history seem to me futile. The issues involved are just too complex. It is always possible to provide a pat explanation for such-and-such an event; but, if the opposite had occurred, who can doubt that an equally pat explanation would be forthcoming for that?

And, even if one could convincingly explain the triumph of the blues in social terms, this would still leave the musical questions unanswered. The teenage rock and roll fans of the 50s may have been exerting their newly acquired spending power. They may have been expressing rebellious attitudes towards their parents' bourgeois cultural values. But they were also expressing a liking for twelve-bar tunes, for blue notes, for certain types of syncopation, for certain melodic contours. It is easy to imagine how anti-bourgeois music (or whatever fits your theories) might have taken a completely different musical shape. Why did it have to be the blues?

Having just said that such a question is unanswerable, I have no intention of answering it. But this I will say, that purely musical trends often show a remarkable vigour and persistence; and that the forces that produced the blues towards the end of the nineteenth century are a case in point. The most diverse styles, including even the 'parlour music' of middle-class European tradition, conspired to develop that musical product which we lightly dismiss as 'the twelve-bar blues'. Part of the process can be explained by 'twin culture reinforcement', a handy phrase which I borrow from John Storm Roberts.[2] By this is meant that when two cultures meet, the elements common to both tend to reinforce each other and therefore persist. In Afro-American music we find this twin culture reinforcement wherever we look. The preceding chapters are full of examples. The working out of the process depends as much on the differences between the twin influences as on their similarities. For instance, African and European fiddles have much in common, both in themselves and in playing technique, making it easy for an Afro-American fiddle style to develop. But they also have many differences which continually present the fiddler with the choice: European or African? The same is true of modal systems, rhythms, melodic contours, form, and harmony. Conveniently for the growth of the popular style, the peculiar history of the American South has ensured that the sum of such moments of choice has been unusually great.

Very often, of course, the choice was not between 'Europe' and 'Africa', but between one European or African strain and another. And as time went on, it became more and more a choice between one Afro-European cross and another. Whatever the complications, it was a matter of choices, mostly spontaneous and even unconscious, which had the cumulative effect of nudging Afro-American music in the direction of the blues. Before the term 'blues' was even invented, American musicians, both black and white, were showing a preference for bluesy patterns. In the long run, if it was a choice between ending a tune with the notes G D C or G E C, or between casting it in a sixteen- or twelve-bar form, or between accompanying it with a I IV V I or a I IV I V I chord pattern, it was the bluesy alternative that would prevail. On the purely musical level there was something that was, quite simply, highly satisfying about the blues. Before we leave the subject, let us see if we can work out what it was.

[2] See *Black Music of Two Worlds*, p. 186. Whether the phrase originated there I cannot say. It has rather the air of a bit of anthropological jargon.

25. WHY TWELVE BARS? WHY BLUES?

W<small>HEN</small> W. C. Handy showed the publishers his 'Memphis Blues' back in 1912, he found that they were bewildered by the twelve-bar form. It struck them as lop-sided. We can hardly blame them, because this form was something completely new in music. Never before had there been a three-part tune-type, which derived its strength precisely from being in three parts. There had been twelve-bar tunes, but these were consciously asymmetrical. They were satisfying *in spite of* being in twelve bars; the phrasing lent a certain piquant irregularity to the effect. In any case, like the British twelve-bar tunes we have examined, they were probably essentially two-part rather than three-part structures.

The twelve-bar blues was quite different. Firstly, it was most definitely a three-part structure; and secondly, there was something about this structure that was not irregular, but on the contrary satisfyingly regular. The humblest rock and roll fan of today can feel what Handy's publishers could not feel, this mysterious slotting together of the three sections of the twelve-bar blues into a satisfactory whole.

Although there is a hint of it in some earlier British tunes, it was only in the United States of the late nineteenth century that the three-part form became really popular. And then it became very popular indeed. By all sorts of adaptations, old tunes were made to fit this new pattern. The verse-and-refrain type was refashioned as the twelve-bar blues. Sixteen-bar tunes had four bars chopped out of them. The endless descending strains of the 'hollers' were marked off into sections of three. There was obviously something very satisfactory about the three-part form to the American folk musician, black or white, of 1900. It is one part of the mystery to explain what this was. The other part is to explain why it had never been discovered before.

WHY BLUES?

The twelve-bar blues combines a certain phrasing—the three-part structure—with a certain harmonic scheme. In the same way, the *passamezzo antico* (chapter 23) or the Gregory Walker pattern (chapter 22) combine two-part phrasing with their own harmonic schemes. So far the kinship is obvious, but there is an important difference. Matrices of the *passamezzo* sort work equally well in any rhythm or mode. Examples could be found in all sorts of time—simple or compound, duple or triple, syncopated or unsyncopated—and all sorts of mode— major, minor, dorian, mixolydian, and (in the case of Gregory Walker) even the blues modes. The twelve-bar blues, on the other hand, must be a blues. That satisfying slotting together of the three sections depends in some way on the blues mode and the syncopated rhythm. It is an interesting experiment to undermine the modal structure of a blues—by, for instance, substituting a supertonic for a mediant, or a leading note for a penultimate submediant—or to straighten out the rhythm. The result is always that the coherence of the tune falls to pieces. Where the older tune-types are a combination of phrasing and harmony, the twelve-bar blues is a combination of phrasing, harmony, mode, and rhythm, all playing their part in the total effect and interacting in a way new to music.

THE PROBLEM OF COMPLETENESS

The whole problem turns on the question of completeness, a quality so taken for granted in classical music that little effort has been made to explain how it is achieved. If we confine ourselves to small forms (and remember that it is more difficult to make a short piece sound complete than a long one) classical theory can offer little more than the theory of binary and ternary forms.

As explained in textbooks on musical theory, binary form consists of two sections, the first ending away from home and the second returning to it. In a long movement 'home' will mean the tonic key. In a short movement, the departure at the end of the first section may mean nothing more than a half close. Ternary form, on the other hand, consists of three sections making the pattern 'theme: new theme: return of first theme'. All this is merely the commonplaces of 'the rudiments of musical form', but how much does it really explain? Some have maintained that the real distinction is not between two-part and three-part forms, but between forms with complete and incomplete first sections. The confusion is due to the inadequacy of the concept of 'forms'. As soon as we analyse these patterns into matrix combinations, all becomes simple. The chief matrices involved are:

1. *The binary matrix.* This is something more basic than the 'binary form' of the textbooks. It is found whenever two sections combine to make a whole, not only in music but in poetry as well; for instance, the parallel statements of Hebrew poetry are a binary structure.
2. *The matrix of return.* In 'ternary' form there is a return to a

previously heard theme. In 'binary' form there is a return to the tonic key or chord. Both involve the feeling of coming back to more solid ground after a period of instability. When it is a question of key, the same matrix is found in such themeless movements as Bach's arpeggio preludes.

3. *The broadening matrix.* This is found when an initial passage is followed by another that is either longer, or, if the same length, somehow more elaborate. The process need not be confined to two sections. Sometimes we find several in a row, each longer than the one before.

4. *The matrix of key.*

5. *The matrix of theme contrast.*

These short forms can now easily be explained: textbook binary is a combination of the binary, key, and return matrices; textbook ternary is a combination of the binary, theme contrast, broadening, and return matrices, often with key as well, and so on.

The most powerful means of achieving completeness is by a combination of matrices: the more that are combined, the stronger the impression of completeness will be. This technique is not confined to music. Something very similar can be found in verse:

> Some praise at Morning what they blame at Night;
> But always think the *last* Opinion right.[1]

What gives this couplet (another binary form, of course) its satisfying, epigrammatic completeness? It is not the simple prose meaning, 'some people are always dogmatically cocksure in spite of constantly changing their opinions', which, while true enough, is not particularly striking. Nor is it the iambic pentameter rhythm or the rhyme. The sense of completeness depends on the combination of all these things.

Now let us return to the twelve-bar blues. Here the surprising thing is that none of the familiar matrices apply. The structure is not binary but ternary: ternary in a far more fundamental sense than the 'ternary' of the textbooks. There is no sense of return, no broadening, nor any systematic contrast of key or theme. Instead, we have the matrices examined in the preceding chapters: the blues mode, the two-way pendulum swing of the harmonic scheme, and the syncopated rhythm.

The blues type of ternary matrix is intrinsically more complex, and therefore weaker, than a binary one. The binary matrix was a starting-point. It arose instinctively very early in the development of music, and was then elaborated and strengthened by being combined with other matrices. The ternary matrix, on the other hand, gradually emerged from patterns which were originally quite different.

---

[1] Pope, *An Essay on Criticism*, lines 430–1.

The nature of this emergence tells us something about how musical form works. All the earliest forms of the twelve-bar blues are strongly modal, whether they belong to the Frankie or Joe Turner families. Even the British ancestors of the Frankie family, like 'Tattie Jock' (Ex. 76(a)), tend to be pentatonic if the ternary structure is at all emphasized. It is no accident that 'Pretty Polly' (Ex. 82) and 'Nottamun town'[2] both have a strong ladder-of-thirds structure. Once one grasps the concept of matrix combination the reason is simple. It was only when the ternary matrix was combined with a modal matrix that the result was strong enough to produce a sense of completeness. In the earliest examples, like 'Tattie Jock', this ternary-plus-mode combination is, as it were, superimposed on the familiar verse-and-refrain form. Later, as the pentatonic mode passes into the blues mode, the ternary-plus-mode combination becomes correspondingly stronger, and the verse-and-refrain feeling fades out and finally disappears. This is because the blues mode is a stricter and more elaborate matrix than the simple pentatonic. It therefore introduces more at-oddness into the combination, and it is the reconciliation of this at-oddness that makes for completeness.

When the familiar blues harmonic pattern is added to the form the same at-oddness plays its part. The satisfying quality of this scheme springs from two things. One is the strength and simplicity of the harmonies considered in themselves: first the swing to the subdominant, then the swing to the dominant, then back to the tonic. The other is that this harmonic scheme is at odds with the ternary phrasing, the first swing, to the subdominant, ending in the middle of the second section.

At-oddness is also behind the preference for a syncopated rhythm. Even the simplest blues syncopation contains a hint of cross-rhythm, that is, of rhythm that strikes out on its own rather than tamely conforming to the main beat. ('Corinna', Ex. 118, is an example of a blues tune without blues syncopation, at least as it is notated here: but even this cries out to be 'swung' a little.) The contribution of this at-oddness to the strength of the blues form is very considerable, and it is hard to imagine how the twelve-bar blues could have developed without it.

In its artful use of at-oddness the blues owes much to African traditions, particularly in the conflict between rhythmic phrasing and harmony. In describing the mbira-accompanied singing of Zimbabwe (or perhaps one should say the vocally-accompanied mbira playing) Andrew Tracey writes:

How does one know where to 'start' one of these chord sequences? The music rolls round and round and in most songs there is no place where the words

[2] For the words see p. 193; for the whole song, sharp, *English Folk Songs from the Southern Appalachians*, vol. 2, p. 270, variant A.

enter—different phrase, different entry point. . . . However, it is only the demands of paper writing that make it necessary to choose *one* starting point. In a very real sense this music has *no* start nor end. To achieve maximum freedom while playing it, if one is tied down to any one scheme, be it harmonic, metrical or rhythmic, one is missing half the point, which is to appreciate several different conflicting schemes at the same time. ('The Matepe Mbira Music of Rhodesia', p. 42.)

'To appreciate several different conflicting schemes at the same time'—that comes close to describing the essence of the blues form.

EPILOGUE TO THE BLUES

So the riddle of the twelve-bar blues is answered—or is this being a little too optimistic? I believe that the foregoing pages do, at least, explain the coherence of the twelve-bar blues pattern. They explain how it has managed to bear the burden of so many tunes, not to mention innumerable thousands of improvisations. They also explain, at least partially, how it developed in the nineteenth century and why it did not develop earlier.

But there are still mysteries. The importance of mode should be evident by now, but why did it have to be the triadic mode? Could one construct a twelve-bar blues using one of the modes of India, for instance? Then again, though it is possible to explain more or less *how* the twelve-bar blues developed, we are still far from answering the question *why*. In the end the most thoughtful and intelligent explanation runs up against the inexplicable where taste is concerned. In the words of a once-popular song:

> Why they changed it I can't say—
> Maybe they liked it better that way.[3]

---

[3] From 'Istambul, Not Constantinople', words by Jimmy Kennedy, music by Nat Simon, 1953.

Part Four
Parlour Music and Ragtime

It may seem strange to include ragtime in a section devoted mainly to parlour music, but 'classical' ragtime *was* parlour music, with Afro-American syncopations and a touch of the blues thrown in. Non-classical ragtime, in so far as it differed from the parlour style, belongs with the nineteenth-century 'jigs', or with the early blues. In any case, a full account of ragtime would belong with the story of early twentieth-century jazz. My chapter 29 is merely an attempt to disentangle the main strands in its development.

26. THE PARLOUR MODES

ANYONE who thinks that the intellectual's scorn for popular music is something recent should read Sir Hubert Parry's denunciation of the music-hall in *Style in Musical Art* (1911). After comparing music-hall songs with Cockney speech ('the result of sheer perverse delight in ugly and offensive sound') and, worse, women's fashions, he embarks on a lengthy analysis of their disregard for musical grammar, in particular unresolved leading notes, the tritone between leading note and subdominant, and consecutive fifths. His words on the first of these crimes are worth quoting at length:

The note in the scale which is called the 'leading note' was so called because it obviously led to the tonic and was dependent on it. . . . To wrench it away from the tonic and endow it with a special and marked independence would, therefore, be an obvious severance with the traditions of the history of its existence, and essentially the kind of thing which the mischievous and perverse mind would fasten on. It is a curious fact that, among the special traits which distinguish even good second-rate music in the latter part of the nineteenth century, an insistence on the independence of the 'leading note' from the note to which it has been supposed to lead is most conspicuous. The taste for going from it to anywhere in the scale except its tonic was probably first diffused by the composer Grieg, who, among many delightful and lovable qualities, had just a touch of impishness in his nature. . . . For the purposes of argument it will be advisable to cull several illustrations from various low-class tunes which were very popular a few years ago. (pp. 115–16.)

After quoting his low-class tunes, each one of which now strikes us as a gem of nostalgic Edwardiana, Sir Hubert goes on to say:

. . . the idea of a new treatment of such a feature having taken hold of beings who are not nurtured in things of beauty as Grieg was, could only be satisfied by increasing the excess of offensiveness. That is, by finding more objectionable notes to move to instead of the natural destination. One of the most objectionable is the drop from the leading note to the third of the scale, especially when the leading note is not part of a chord but merely a reckless intrusion. (p. 117)

Ex. 98   Music-hall tune

Notice those words: 'when the leading note is not part of a chord but merely a reckless intrusion'. It is easy to laugh at Sir Hubert's remarks, now that the object of his fury has safely receded into the past. But the really interesting thing about them, the thing that makes them worth quoting, is that fundamentally he is right. His denunciations, like those of many conservative critics, are more informative than the bland enthusiasms of the followers of fashion.

What he objected to was the insubordinate behaviour of the melodic line. Hitherto the melody had been the obedient servant of the harmony. Here the melody begins to show a will of its own, regardless of what the harmony may be doing. Of all the degrees of the scale, the leading note is the one which is most subservient to the harmony in the classical scheme of things, and therefore the one in which this subordinate behaviour is most obvious. Hence Parry's strictures. He is wrong, however, in describing the leading notes in Ex. 98 as reckless intrusions. Even in low-class tunes reckless intrusions are not tolerated. Everything must explain itself to the listener as part of a pattern, which is just what these intrusive notes do; only the pattern is not harmonic, but melodic—that is to say, modal.

THE BEGINNINGS OF THE PARLOUR MODES

The same sort of independent behaviour can be found on the part of the third and sixth of the mode as well. These two notes, together with the leading note, form the framework on which the parlour modes are built, the most important of the three being the third. It is an interesting exercise to go through the familiar tunes of the nineteenth century and count how often this is either the first note or the first accented note. Very often the whole tune, or at any rate the opening phrase, is more or less built around it. Examples, which range from Beethoven's 'Hymn to Joy' to the 'Radetsky March' and from 'Abide with Me' to the Grand March from *Aida*, can be found as far back as the late eighteenth century. (See, for example, the end of Mozart's 'Ronda alla Turca', from the Piano Sonata in A, K331.)

Now the third is, after all, the most emotionally sensitive note in the major mode; it is the note which gives it its major quality—in fact, its very name. It is also a part of the tonic triad. So it is not surprising that it should receive such melodic prominence. The sixth, on the other hand, is probably the most nondescript degree of the mode, from the orthodox point of view; yet this note, too, began to receive an unusual emphasis from the late eighteenth century on, as we can see from Ex. 99. The

Ex. 99 Mozart, 'Sechs deutsche Tänze', K600, no. 3

repeated submediants of this little tune are filled with historical significance. We shall find them ringing more and more clearly through the waltzes of the following century.

THE ESTRANGEMENT OF MELODY AND HARMONY

By about 1820 the third and sixth already had a special place in the lighter Viennese style. Schubert, expecially, had a great fondness for the former. Ex. 100 shows two characteristic ways of using it, either as a floor or ceiling note. The second, incidentally, shows the beginnings of

Ex. 100
 (a) Schubert, 'Pause'

(*b*) Schubert, 'Des Baches Wiegenlied'

Ruh', gu - te Ruh', thu' die Au - gen zu, gu - te Au - gen zu!
accompaniment repeats first four bars

Wand' - rer, du mü - der, du bist zu Haus.

Sir Hubert Parry's delinquent leading note. It is strange that he should have blamed this particular feature on Grieg when it is so much a part of the Viennese dance style.[1] In these two examples we see melodic patterns beginning to assert their independence over harmonic ones. Instead of the melody simply following the prevailing chords, independent melodic patterns begin to appear which live a life of their own regardless of what the harmony happens to be doing. The floor and ceiling notes are examples of such patterns. Another is the central note. The classical example of the mediant as central note must surely be the Trio from the third movement of Schubert's Great C Major Symphony, from the beginning to the double bar-line. It brings out in the strongest possible way something also evident in Ex. 100, namely, the way a melodic note can persist through changing harmonies. The C♯ around which this long passage is built appears first as the third of the tonic chord; then as the fifth of the submediant; and finally as the root of the mediant, in which key the passage ends.

A similar device, on an even grander scale, can be seen in the second of Chopin's four Scherzos. This is one of a significant number of Romantic movements that begin in one key and end in another; in this case, the intitial key is B♭ minor and the closing key D♭ major. Ex. 101 shows how this long movement is bound together by an insistence on the single note F, or, if we transposed it into 'white note' notation, E. In the Trio section Chopin abandons this note, but plays equally obsessively on C, the

[1] It was only long after writing this paragraph that I discovered that one subspecies of the parlour or Parrian seventh is known as the 'Viennese note', defined in *The New Grove* as 'the unflattened seventh degree of the major mode when it resolves by step downwards in a "subdominant context" . . .'. See the short article ' "Viennese" Note', by William Drabkin, vol. 19, p. 741. For examples in this book, see Strauss's 'Morgenblätter' (Ex. 122(*c*)), bars 3–6, and 'Artist's Life' (Ex. 122(*d*)), bars 3–4.

keynote of the work as a whole and the *third* of the new key of A♭ major. The whole movement is an excellent example both of Chopin's uncanny sense of modality and of his close links with the parlour style. It is no accident that so many of the examples in these chapters on parlour music are drawn from his works. They are as remarkable for their anticipations of the popular style as for their oft-quoted prophecies of 'serious' modernists from Wagner on. Considering their great popularity, there is also more than a possibility of direct influence. It is usually rash to assume that the development of an art, especially a popular art, would be different if any particular individual had not existed; but it may well be that Chopin is an exception to this rule.

The emotional effect of these persistent major thirds varies interestingly from composer to composer. Verdi is as fond of them as Schubert ('Libiamo' from *La Traviata*, the Grand March from *Aida*, the 'Anvil Chorus' from *Il Trovatore*) and they contribute greatly to the wonderful surging, dynamic spirit of his music. Yet in Schubert's hands they create a feeling of sadness, or at least wistfulness. Why the difference? The most likely reason seems to be that Verdi contrasts the third with the tonic, or possibly (as in 'Libiamo') with the dominant below, whereas Schubert contrasts it with the dominant a minor third above. In effect, it becomes

Ex. 101   Chopin, Scherzo no. 2 in B♭ minor/D♭

(*a*) beginning

(*b*) a later theme

(c) beginning of the Trio

(d) end

a sort of secondary tonic, to which the dominant plays the part of the
minor third and the leading note that of the fifth. This comes out quite
explicitly in the introductions to both Exx. 100(*a*) and (*b*), and I believe
it is often implied even when the dominant is not sounded.

The idea of a secondary or even co-tonic is strange to the theory of
European classical music, but it is commonplace in Asia. Chopin,
obviously under Oriental influence, gives us an example in the Mazurka
in B♭ minor, Op. 24, no. 4 (Ex. 102). I quote the beginning to show how

Ex. 102   Chopin, Mazurka in B♭ minor, Op. 24, no. 4

(*a*) beginning   (*b*) end

there, too, the dominant note is emphasized. In the concluding passage
the melody has a dual personality: if we regard C as the tonic, it is in the
East European mode which is like the mixolydian with a minor sixth, as
in Ex. 68(*d*); but if we regard G as the tonic, it is in an Oriental variety of
the phrygian, with a *major* sixth. Similar instances of a melodic tonic a
fifth above a drone can be found in Celtic and American music, for
instance the union pipe solo 'Were You at the Rock',[2] also very Oriental
in effect, and the Appalachian dulcimer solo 'Shady Grove',[3] a tune of
Scottish origin.[4]

[2] Played by Seamus Ennis on *Ireland*, from *The Columbia World Library of Folk and
Primitive Music* (Columbia CSP AKL 4941).
[3] Played by Mrs Edd Prescell on *Instrumental Music of the Southern Appalachians* (Tradition
Records: TLP 1007).
[4] See 'The Keach in the Creel' in Greig, *Last Leaves of Traditional Ballads and Ballad Airs*,
p. 233, and Bronson, *Traditional Tunes of the Child Ballads*, vol. 4, p. 259, where the
resemblance is pointed out.

The third, too, can be a co-tonic. A familiar classical example is the so-called 'Passion Chorale' of which Bach made eleven harmonizations, five of them in the *St Matthew Passion*. (Most versions are set to the words 'Herzlich tut mich Verlangen' or 'O Haupt voll Blut und Wunden'.) It first appeared, in 1601, as a far livelier and and distinctly folk-like secular song by Hans Hassler, 'Mein G'müt ist mir verwirret'.[5] The melody, viewed by itself, is clearly in a kind of phrygian mode, very much like the plantation song 'Pains in my Fingers' (Ex. 114); and indeed in some of his arrangements Bach harmonized it as such. But in Hassler's original, and in most of Bach's harmonizations, the key of the harmony is a third below that implied by the tune.

Yet another possibility is the co-tonic on the sixth, which we shall be meeting in Weill's 'Mack the Knife' (Ex. 106).

To return to the early nineteenth century: in spite of the considerable independence shown by the melody in the examples quoted above, it still harmonizes with the bass in the conventional way. This was soon to change. More and more, melody notes would be completely at odds with the accompanying chord. Mediants would appear accompanied by dominant or subdominant chords, or submediants by the tonic. The theorists of the nineteenth century were greatly perplexed by this development, and invented a lot of nonsense about dominant thirteenths and the like to account for it. The truth was that the relation between melody and harmony had received a new twist. Up to that time the classical style had been thoroughly chord-based. Melody notes either belonged to the accompanying chord, or were transitional between notes that were, or staged a token rebellion against the prevailing harmony in the form of some sort of appoggiatura or suspension. In any event the melody was explained away, directly or indirectly, by reference to the harmony. This explaining away is preserved in these early examples, but in the course of the nineteenth century it is gradually abandoned. In the later examples, the melody is no longer required to harmonize with the accompaniment, in the classical sense; all that is necessary is that it should form some sort of euphonious combination.

The progress of this gradual emancipation can best be followed in the Viennese waltz. The first stage has been illustrated by Ex. 99. There the sixth of the mode already had the prominence typical of the style, but was duly explained away as an appoggiatura to the dominant or tonic chord. In Ex. 103 melodic independence is carried a step further. The important melody notes here are the third, sixth, and seventh, but of these only one, the seventh, actually belongs to the accompanying chord, and even that does not resolve in the orthodox way. But even these notes, though they contain the essence of parlour modality, can be

[5] Quoted in Westrup and Harrison, *Collins's Encyclopaedia of Music*, pp. 117–18.

Ex. 103   Lanner, 'Terpsichore Waltz'

explained according to the rules of classical harmony. This ceases to be
true of the familiar strains of 'The Blue Danube' (Ex. 104), and with
Sousa's 'Washington Post' (Ex. 105) the emancipation is complete. The
next and final step is to treat the submediant as a tonal centre in its own

Ex. 104   Strauss, 'The Blue Danube'

Ex. 105   Sousa, 'The Washington Post'

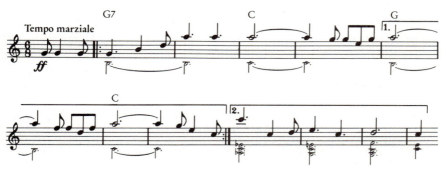

right, and this is actually carried out in one of the best-known tunes of the early twentieth century, Kurt Weill's 'Mack the Knife', or 'Morität vom Mackie Messer', to give it its original title (Ex. 106). The result is a sort of bitonality: A minor in the melody, C major in the harmony. Although the piece is headed 'Blues-Tempo' there is no reason to put this remarkable development down to any exotic influence. It is the end

Ex. 106   Weill, 'Mack the Knife'

of a purely European process of evolution, already implicit in Mozart's little waltz of more than a century before.

In Ex. 100 we saw how the third came to be used as a floor or ceiling note. One of the most popular melodic patterns of the nineteenth century combines both these methods; in other words, it encloses the melody between two mediants an octave apart, except possibly for a few outlying notes. Like the other parlour modes, this 'mediant-octave' mode, as we can conveniently call it, already appears in the last quarter of the eighteenth century (see Ex. 107). From the early nineteenth century till well into the twentieth, this feature appears in countless tunes,[6] many

---

[6] Other examples of more or less the same type as those quoted in Ex. 108 are Beethoven's 'Turkish March' from the 'Ruins of Athens' music, Chopin's waltz theme, Ex. 141 (*a*), Alford's 'Colonel Bogey' march, Sousa's 'The Thunderer', 'The Yellow Rose of Texas', 'Silent Night', and Tannhäuser's song from Wagner's opera. This is early, 'vulgar' Wagner; in his later works similar melodic lines, though still found, are disguised by a less square-cut harmonic and rhythmic treatment.

Ex. 107   Mozart, *Die Zauberflöte*, Papageno's glockenspiel tune

of them still familiar today (Ex. 108).[7] As well as emphasizing the third of the mode, all these tunes give special prominence to the sixth. This, combined with the inevitable prominence of the tonic and dominant,

Ex. 108

(*a*) Chopin, Mazurka in D♭, Op. 30, no. 3.

(*b*) 'Battle Hymn of the Republic'

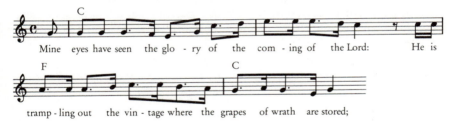

(*c*) 'Rock-a-bye Baby'

[7] The earliest known form of Ex. 108(*b*) dates from the 1850s. The history of the tune, with its various lyrics, is extremely complex and murky: see Scholes, 'John Brown's Body', in *The Oxford Companion of Music*, and Jackson, *Popular Songs of Nineteenth-Century America*, note on 'Battle Hymn of the Republic', pp. 263–4.

(d) 'I'm Henery the Eighth, I am'

produces a suggestion of the pentatonic, which is especially clear in the descent from the mediant or supertonic to the dominant which occurs in most of these tunes ((e″) d″ c″ a′ g′). There was a tendency for this implied pentatonicism to become more explicit with time, until in the late nineteenth century we find passages like Ex. 109, from the first movement of Tchaikovsky's Sixth Symphony. How much this tendency

Ex. 109   Tchaikovsky, Sixth Symphony, first movement

had to do with folk influences it is difficult to say. In any case, the more one examines the borders between 'folk', 'parlour', and 'classical' styles, the more insubstantial they become. Probably the folk influence simply accelerated existing trends.

There is also a similar but rather rarer mode stretching between sixth and sixth, with an equally evident pentatonic framework. Ex. 110 gives

Ex. 110

(a) 'Oh! Mr. Porter'

(*b*) Tchaikovsky, Second Symphony, last movement

two examples, one a music-hall classic made famous by Marie Lloyd, the other again a theme from Tchaikovsky, which incidentally is in the rumba rhythm.

THE PSEUDO-PHRYGIAN MODE AND THE WHITE PATERNOSTER

In an important subspecies of the mediant-octave mode the seventh acts as a sort of dominant to the third, with a lesser emphasis on the sixth. This is the mode of the little passage that Sir Hubert Parry was so hard on (Ex. 98) and of Lanner's waltz theme (Ex. 103). Ex. 111 is another example, dating from 1867. It illustrates another frequent feature of this mode: the emphasis on the subdominant, and the way that note is contrasted with the leading note, even to the extent of leaping an augmented fourth. (Sir Hubert was very indignant about this too.) This mode has remained popular ever since the days of 'Champagne Charlie', among the best known examples being the Second World War song 'Lili Marlen' and 'Lara's Theme' from the film *Doctor Zhivago*. It bears an odd resemblance to the phrygian mode: a resemblance which is illuminated by the example of 'The White Paternoster'.

This beautiful song, found in 1890 by the Reverend Sabine Baring-Gould in the west of England, was published in his collection *Songs of the West*. It appears in Frank Howes's book *Folk Music of Britain—and Beyond* (he calls it the 'pearl' of Baring-Gould's collection) quoted in the same form as that given here (Ex. 112). The reason why it is quoted in

Ex. 111   'Champagne Charlie'

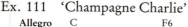

Ex. 112 'The White Paternoster'

Howes's book—and why it appears here—is that he regards it as 'one of the few English tunes in the Phrygian mode'. But if we look at the original in *Songs of the West*, we find that it has been tampered with. The final note was not G, but E♭ (E and C respectively in my transposition). What Baring-Gould himself has to say is:

> The tune, as it stands, is in the Major mode, and is so harmonised.[8] But if the last note were G instead of E♭—as, indeed, it is in the two previous repetitions of the same phrase—the melody would then be in the Phrygian mode. The termination in E♭ is probably a modern corruption. (p. 32.)

So much for the phrygian mode. In fact, the effect is not in the least exotic or antique, as we should expect from this mode, but intensely Victorian. It is none the less beautiful for that; indeed, to us of the late twentieth century the Victorian quality is an added charm, imparting to the melody an achingly nostalgic feeling, as of brass band music filtering through the trees on a sunny autumn afternoon.

There are tunes that genuinely end on the third; good Scottish examples are 'The Jolly Beggar'[9] and 'The White Cockade',[10] though these are built around the notes e' g' c'' e'', not e' g' b' e'' or e' f' a' b' e''. Examples are, however, far commoner in the United States. Ex. 113, 'Andrew Bardeen', is a haunting tune in the same mode as 'The White Paternoster'. Examples from the blues include 'Peg an' Awl' (a bluesy

Ex. 113 'Andrew Bardeen'

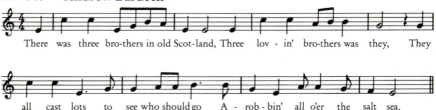

---

[8] He is referring to his own harmonization. The original was of course purely melodic.
[9] See Bronson, *Traditional Tunes of the Child Ballads*, vol. 4, p. 216, no. 6.
[10] See 'My Love was Born in Aberdeen' in Foster, *The Songs of Scotland*, vol. 2, p. 106.

hillbilly song),[11] 'Yonder Come a Yaller Gal' (a tuneful specimen of the holler),[12] 'One Time Blues' (a twelve-bar country blues),[13] 'One o' them Things!' (the first published twelve-bar blues: see Ex. 159), Chuck Berry's 'Reelin' and Rockin' ', and Bob Dylan's 'Rainy Day Women'.

Occasionally one comes on an example of what looks like the genuine phrygian mode. The ante-bellum 'Pains in my Fingers' (Ex. 114) is a case

Ex. 114   'Pains in my Fingers'

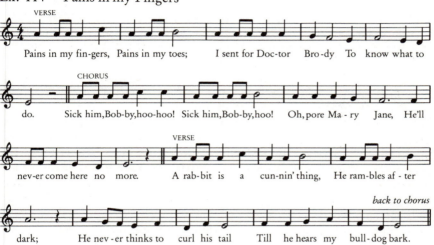

in point. It has such a pronounced Near Eastern flavour that it is hard not to suspect Afro-Arab influence. The banjo song 'Old Joe Clark' has a similar character, at least in some versions.[14]

Finally, to conclude this note on the American phrygian, there is a curious cowboy song from Missouri (Ex. 115).[15] Something about this snatch of tune suggests that, like so many other cowboy things, it came from Mexico. In Mexico (as in other parts of Latin America) the parlour

Ex. 115   'Cowboy's Challenge'

[11] See A. Lomax, *The Folk Songs of North America*, p. 283.
[12] See White, *American Negro Folk-Songs*, p. 411.
[13] See Titon, *Early Downhome Blues*, p. 79.
[14] See, for instance, J. and A. Lomax, *American Ballads and Folk Songs*, p. 277.
[15] The words are as given, though they seem to fit the tune badly. According to the headnote, 'It was a challenge to combat, and continued with a clog-like dance and clank of spurs till the singer found a man brave enough to accept his challenge.'

modes met the old Spanish phrygian, and there are examples where the two seem to merge, such as the ballad 'Heraclio Bernal',[16] which, like the previous examples, ends on the third.

THE PARLOUR MODES AND FOLK MUSIC

As the history of 'The White Paternoster' shows, it did not take long for parlour idioms to penetrate folk music. Early researchers, imagining that they were uncovering a folk culture untainted by urban civilization, systematically edited out such influences. Even so they appear quite clearly here and there, particularly in more recent collections. Examples of folk-songs in the parlour modes are 'If I was a Blackbird',[17] the sailors' song 'Rolling Home' (the same tune is used for the Irish nationalist song 'Kevin Barry'),[18] 'The Babes in the Wood', 'Fare Thee Well, Cold Winter', and 'Raking the Hay'.[19] Some of these may be parlour tunes that have passed into the folk repertory, or possibly folk tunes that originated under parlour influence. Generally , however, such tunes are 'parlourized' variants of widespread tune families. Sometimes, by comparing close variants, we can actually observe the process of parlourization at work. Ex. 116 shows how a few touches to a melodic line can shift the emphasis to the 'parlour' notes: in particular, notice the 'Lili Marlen'-like cadence at the end of Ex. 116(b) (which, by the way, is easily the more beautiful of the two variants). In another type of

Ex. 116

(a) 'The Golden Victory' (I)   (b) 'The Golden Victory' (II)

(a) There was the gal-lant ship on yon wes-tern coun-ter - ee, And the name of that ship was the 'Gol - den Vic - to - ry',

(b) There lies a ship in the North Coun - tree, An the name o that ship is the 'Gol-den Vic - to - ree',

---

[16] See J. and A. Lomax, *American Ballads and Folk Songs*, p. 369.

[17] See O Lochlainn, *Irish Street Ballads*, p. 92.

[18] See Hugill, *Shanties from the Seven Seas*, pp. 181–92; note the 'pseudo-phrygian' version on p. 188.

[19] See Palmer, *The Book of English Country Songs*, pp. 106, 142, and 157 respectively.

parlourization illustrated in Ex. 117,[20] the minor seventh of the folk modes was assimilated to the parlour seventh.

Ex. 117

(a) 'Come Ashore Jolly Tar and your Trousers on' (b) 'The Cuckoo's Nest'

If the distinction between folk and popular music is nebulous in Britain, in the United States it all but vanishes. American democracy extended to aesthetic as well as political, economic, and social matters. Far more than in Europe, we find folk-like idioms appearing in commercial popular music and parlour idioms making their way into folk music. When it is remembered that 'folk', in this context, could mean either British or African traditions, we get some inkling of the complexity of the influences that went into the early blues. In addition to African modal patterns and British modal patterns, we must reckon with parlour modal patterns; and in the earliest blues that have come down to us, like 'One o' them Things!' (Ex. 159), Handy's 'Memphis Blues', and other ragtime-blues, it is the parlour modes that are uppermost. In the outline of its first eight bars 'Corinna' (Ex. 118), a hillbilly blues collected in the 30s, clearly resembles 'John Brown's Body' (Ex. 108(b)). Only the slightest twist is needed to turn those parlour thirds into unmistakable blue thirds.

The chromatically decorated blue third can easily be traced from the late eighteenth century, when it first became popular (Ex. 119(a)), to

---

[20] This tune, in its many variants, is more usually associated with the 'cuckoo's nest' words (for the words to 'Come Ashore Jolly Tar', see Palmer, *The Oxford Book of Sea Songs*, pp. 148–50). Apart from Ex. 117(b), see the Scottish version in Buchan and Hall, *The Scottish Folksinger*, p. 69, and the Newfoundland diddling version quoted on p. 80.

Ex. 118 'Corinna'*

* From Alan Lomax, *The Folk Songs of North America*, p. 588 (Cassell, 1963). According to a note, 'Collected and arranged by Alan Lomax from oral Negro sources in the 30's. A bluesy piece widely popular among blues and hillbilly singers.'

Ex. 119

(*a*) Mozart, String Trio in E♭, first movement

(*b*) Joplin, 'A Breeze from Alabama'

early ragtime (Ex. 119(*b*)). Again, only the slightest twist is needed to turn this ragtime idiom into the type of blue third found in 'One o' them Things!' and other early blues.

No doubt this parlour idiom appealed to folk musicians because it resembled chromatic glides already familiar from both African and British traditions, just as the parlour modes appealed to them because they were already used to modal patterns. In other words, parlour music was reinterpreted by folk musicians in folk terms. And, at the same time, folk music was being reinterpreted by parlour musicians in parlour terms. In particular, the professional musicians who toured country districts with the 'medicine shows' (so named because one of their functions was the touting of patent medicines) must often have felt the need to present their audiences with something rather more 'down-home' than what they were accustomed to performing. Their attempts to reproduce the rustic manner, or to adopt rustic items into their repertory, were probably as important in the development of American popular music as the opposite process on the part of country musicians.[21]

THE PARLOUR MODES AND THE CLASSICS

It was the light, melodious, Italianate music of the third quarter of the eighteenth century that carried the seeds of the parlour modes. The characteristically 'parlour' treatment of the third and the seventh developed initially out of a purely expressive emphasis on these notes. Following a common tendency, the expressive gradually gave way to the structural. This process had hardly begun, however, when this Italian influence was joined by that of southern German or Austrian folk music, typified by the waltz. The relation between this folk strain and the international, basically Italian style was similar to that between Afro-American folk music and the parlour style a century later. In both cases popular musicians seized on and carried further certain tentative melodic developments in 'bourgeois' music. It is to the waltz that the special treatment of the sixth, illustrated in Exx. 99 and 104, is due. On the other hand, the 'parlour' seventh is not found in the early, folk-like waltzes. From about 1820 the two styles began to mingle. The waltz became an international craze and a permanent feature of French and Italian opera, while in its turn absorbing much of the Italian-based lingua franca of the time. This Austro-Italian hybrid is the basis of the parlour style. For a while it seemed as though it would carry all before it; but its natural development was thwarted, or at least diverted, by the nineteenth-century divorce between intellectual and popular music.

In the time of Mozart (born 1756) or even Beethoven (born 1770) it was natural for the same composer to write both serious and popular compositions: symphonies, masses, and operas on the one hand, dance music on the other. By the time of the great Romantic generation born between 1800 and 1815 things were changing. The distinction between the 'serious' and 'popular' composer was already evident. Chopin could

---

[21] See Oliver, *Songsters and Saints*, particularly pp. 260–4.

write his great piano waltzes and Berlioz could put a waltz into the *Symphonie fantastique*, but these were 'serious' waltzes: they were not meant for dancing. The real dance music was now being written by specialists like Lanner and the elder Johann Strauss. Even so, though something like a professional caste distinction was developing, there was still no marked difference in musical language. The rhythmic, harmonic, and modal patterns of Chopin's waltzes, for instance, are basically the same as those of the Strausses. More and more, from about mid-century on, this ceases to be true. Composers became aware that there were certain features that stamped popular music, and either cultivated these features if they were writing for the general public, or avoided them if they were writing for the elect. Brahms admired the waltzes of Johann Strauss the younger, but he took care to keep his own waltzes free of Strauss-like melodic turns. This feeling was perhaps most advanced in the German-speaking countries. In France, Italy, and the Slavonic east the Schism was longer in coming; and as late as 1893 Tchaikovsky could put an unmistakable parlour tune like Ex. 109 into his last symphony. No doubt Teutonophile critics thought it served him right when it was made into a sugary popular song.

Such was the power of the parlour taint that it acted retrospectively, debarring composers from imitating parlour mannerisms in Schubert, Chopin, or Liszt—though not, oddly enough, from admiring the compositions in which they occurred. If they did imitate them, it could only be under the cover of an ironic or satirical manner: as for instance in the compositions of Mahler, where many a touch of parlour modality can be found. (Perhaps it was this feature that prompted Colin Wilson to write that 'Mahler is full of these tunes'—like the main theme from the finale of the Third Symphony—'that might well be adapted for popular songs . . .'.[22]

It should be realized that 'parlour modality', in the preceding remarks, is part of something much more general. From the start it upset the classical relationship between melody and harmony, so that the 'parlour revolution', if I may be allowed the term, can only be understood if we take harmony as well as melody into account. Now that we have dealt with the one, let us look at the other.

[22] See *Colin Wilson on Music*, p. 47.

27. PARLOUR HARMONY

The strawberry jam of music.

Description of the harmonic style
of *Hymns Ancient and Modern*[1]

THE old libel about popular composers using the outworn cast-offs of their musical betters comes closest to the truth with harmony. In the nineteenth and early twentieth centuries, at any rate, popular harmony is usually an echo of what serious composers had been doing several decades before. The lush Romantic chromaticism of the years between 1830 and 1850 took half a century to reappear in the parlour ballads of the 80s and 90s, just as, in the next century, Impressionist harmonies turn up a few decades later in jazz. From early times serious composers had sought the striking progression, the telling, unusual chord. The popular composer had no such ambitions, sharing the 'courage in using without hesitation the obvious commonplace phrase, of words or music' that Cecil Sharp admired in the folk musician.

Late nineteenth-century parlour harmony therefore tends to run very much to hard-worked clichés. But it would be a great mistake to dismiss this cliché-ridden stuff as devoid of interest. Some of its formulas lead on into the twentieth century, and others look back to, and often illuminate, the Romantic harmony from which they were derived. In a way, parlour harmony is a purer and more innocent version of Romantic harmony. From the start certain tendencies had conspired to obscure the natural bent of the Romantic movement: the pull of the past, whether the recent past of the Viennese School, the less recent past of the Baroque, or the still remoter past of the sixteenth and seventeenth centuries; nationalism and its obsession with folk styles; and a desire to be original and progressive. All these tendencies grew mightily as the century progressed, and continued to grow after 1900, so that one finds more and more passages that owe their existence to archaizing or nationalistic leanings, or to the striving to be modern. Popular composers were too unselfconscious and too much bound by the necessities of the marketplace to indulge in this sort of thing, except where a folk idiom appears by way of a little local colour, or in the occasional pretentiousness of salon music—the salon being a sort of half-way house between the parlour and the concert-hall.

[1] Quoted in Scholes, *The Oxford Companion to Music*, p. 504.

The basic harmonic style of the Romantics—that is, minus the archaizing, folk, and modernistic tendencies—is in many ways radically different from the Classical style of the late eighteenth century. On the whole, the most conspicuous differences, such as the lusher chromaticism and the bolder use of dissonance, are the less important. The really profound changes turn on fundamental questions of tonality and the relation between melody and harmony. The eighteenth century loved contrasts, not necessarily strong but clear-cut. It was the Age of Antithesis. In music we find such contrasts between orchestra and soloist, fast and slow, soft and loud, learned and popular, bright and sombre, woodwind and strings; and, in the particular case of harmony, between consonance and dissonance, major and minor, tonic and dominant—this last being probably the most fundamental feature of the Classical harmonic style, pervading it at every level from the cadence to the key contrasts of big sonata-form works.

Another characteristic of the Classical style is its love of balance and unity. Its movements are poised and symmetrical like Georgian country houses, so that the addition or subtraction of a unit would spoil the whole. It would be unthinkable, for instance, for such a movement to end in a different key from the one it started in; and in the finer details of the harmony, one usually finds that chords and keys on the dominant side balance those on the subdominant side. Such balance calls for a clear-cut harmonic structure, so chromaticism is not allowed to blur the firm outlines of the tonality. Excursions into chromaticism, where they occur, merely throw the return to diatonic clarity into yet stronger relief.

Finally, the eighteenth-century style is chord-based. Its formal strength lies very much in its harmonic schemes, and a musician experienced in the style can usually understand pretty well what is going on by a reading of the chords alone. The melody, no matter how tuneful or interesting, is firmly based on the harmony. There are no purely melodic modal patterns like the 'parlour modes' of the last chapter.

Such are the essentials of the pre-Romantic harmonic style. Now let us see what happened to them in the nineteenth century, beginning with tonality.

TONALITY

One of the most characteristic sensations in eighteenth-century music is that of striking out from the home key to the dominant (or, if the movement is in the minor, to the relative major) knowing that we shall eventually come back home again with a feeling of balance and completeness. It is probably this outward-going feeling that most distinguishes the Classical style. It appears on a grand scale in the big sonata-form expositions of the Viennese School, and on a small scale in the ordinary imperfect cadence, or half close. It pervades the style.

With the romantics, though it does not vanish entirely, it is suddenly very much diminished. The typical Romantic movement is no longer centrifugal, like these Classical movements; it is centripetal. A good index of the change is the decline in the fortunes of the half close. In some composers, such as Schumann and Brahms, this decline is masked by the influences of German folk music and pre-Romantic styles; but in the waltz, always in the vanguard of the parlour style, it can be clearly seen. A look through Chopin's waltzes, written from about 1830 on, will show just how rare half closes are, particularly when followed by answering full closes. (The two most prominent exceptions, Op. 34, no. 2 and Op. 64, no. 2, are both in the minor and not typically waltz-like.) The same is true of the famous Strauss waltzes of the 1860s, except where the cadence—in reality not very cadential—is the first half of a I–V V–I pattern.[2]

On the other hand, themes that *begin* with the dominant are commonplace in the waltzes of Chopin, Strauss, and their contemporaries. The first examples appear towards the end of the eighteenth century: for instance the Trio of the Minuet from Haydn's 'Military' Symphony, no. 100 in G (1794), or the little waltz tune by Mozart, quoted in Ex. 120. It is significant that these are both trios. From Bach to

Ex. 120   Mozart, 'Sechs deutsche Tänze', K600, no. 1, Trio (1791)

Beethoven, the trios of dance movements are a good place to look for popular influence. And, because they come in the middle of the movement, it is possible to start them in ways that would seem abrupt at the actual beginning. The Lanner waltz tune (Ex. 103, dating from before 1825) is likewise from the middle of the movement, though not a trio. It was therefore a real innovation when the twenty-one-year-old Chopin began his *Grande valse brillante* in E♭, Op. 18, with a ringing theme starting on the dominant. It is an interesting instance of the historical

[2] See for instance 'The Blue Danube', Ex. 104.

process whereby features are allowed to become more conspicuous as they grow more familiar. Tunes beginning on the dominant later became very common, and not only in waltzes.[3]

Extended moves to the dominant key are also foreign to the Romantic style:

In almost any work of Haydn and Mozart, the twin poles of tonic and dominant are firmly maintained . . . This polarity has a much less fundamental role in the work of the first generation of romantic composers, and sometimes disappears completely: the A flat Ballade of Chopin never employs E flat major, and the F minor Ballade has little to do with either C major (or minor) or A flat major; only an already reactionary and high-principled view of sonata form imprisoned Schumann at times within a tonic-dominant relationship which was evidently largely uncongenial to him, if one is to judge by the more imaginative works: *Davidsbündlertänze*, the *Carnaval*, the C major Fantasy, and the great song cycles. . . . When the Romantic composer is not following an academic theory of form—that is, when he is not writing what he felt should be called a 'sonata'—his secondary tonalities are not dominants at all, but subdominants . . . Each of the three movements of Schumann's C major Fantasy goes clearly to the subdominant, and all its material is directed towards this modulation. For much of the F minor Ballade, Chopin avoids establishing a secondary key with any degree of clarity: when one arrives, it is astonishingly B flat major. These are two of the most remarkable works of the period, and they are only two instances out of many. (Rosen, *The Classical Style*, pp. 382–3.)

This predilection for subdominant relationships is equally marked in dance and lyric forms. In the above-mentioned *Grande valse brillante* the young Chopin is so taken by the exhilarating effect of plunging into a new theme in the subdominant that he repeats it again and again, passing first to the subdominant, then to the flat seventh (the subdominant of the subdominant), and then to the flat mediant (the subdominant of the subdominant of the subdominant) before abruptly jerking us back to the tonic and the main theme. Altogether, the effect of a move to the subdominant occurs no fewer than six times in the movement.

Suppose Chopin had not bothered to return to the tonic—would any listener have noticed the difference? Probably not. Several of his works do end in different keys from the ones they started out in, for instance:

	begins	ends
Mazurka, Op. 6, no. 2	G♯	C♯ minor
Mazurka, Op. 30, no. 2	B minor	F♯ minor
Fantaisie, Op. 49	F minor	A♭
Second Scherzo, Op. 31[4]	B♭ minor	D♭

[3] See the themes from 'The Washington Post', Ex. 105, and the *Poet and Peasant* Overture, Ex. 151. Another Chopin waltz example is the theme from Op. 34, no. 1, Ex. 141(*a*).
[4] See Ex. 101 in the previous chapter.

But the most radical case of all is the Mazurka Op. 7, no. 5, which, marked 'Dal Segno Senza Fine', oscillates indefinitely between C and G major. No doubt, if the facility had been available, Chopin would have ended it with a fade-out like a modern pop song.

Later on in the Romantic period it became almost commonplace for movements to begin in a minor key and end in its relative major, like Chopin's Fantaisie and Scherzo: and, as we shall see, this procedure was far from unknown in popular music too. Towards the end of the century popular composers also took to ending their compositions with a strain in the subdominant, or rather, the key a fifth below the opening key— for why should the beginning of a movement have a greater claim than the end to determining the tonic? This second key always comes in with an exhilarating impression of solidity, just as in Chopin's *Grande valse brillante*, and it is worth noting that the whole scheme is like the V–I chord progression of the waltz theme, Ex. 141(*a*), or the 'Poet and Peasant' theme, Ex. 151, writ large. As far as written compositions were concerned the fashion seems to have been started by John Philip Sousa, but, as he himself admitted, he was merely following an established performance practice:

In the accepted form of compositions of march order it was always customary to make the third part go to the subdominant, the most usual, and the dominant, the most unusual form. In my childhood in Washington I noticed that the band parading with the regiments in nearly every instance, although the composition called for a da capo, would finish playing on the last strain of the march; therefore, if it was done practically in the use of the march I could not understand why it should not be done theoretically in the writing of the march. Accordingly, in composing my marches, I ignored the old established rule and wrote with the idea of making the last strain of the march the musical climax, regardless of the tonality. ('A Letter from Sousa', *Etude*, August 1898, p. 231; quoted in Berlin, *Ragtime*, pp. 100–1.)

Sousa's example was followed by many composers of both marches and rags. Among marches constructed on these lines one might cite his 'Washington Post', 'Semper Fidelis', and 'The Thunderer'; and among rags Joplin's 'Easy Winners', 'Elite Syncopations', and 'The Favorite', Morton's 'Kansas City', 'King Porter', and 'Black Bottom' Stomps, James Scott's 'Hilarity Rag', and Lewis Muir's 'Waiting for the Robert E. Lee'. But these, I should emphasize, are only a small selection.

MODALITY AND MODULATION

With the development of the parlour modes the melody ceased to be merely 'the skin on the harmony' and became, at times, something more akin to the bone holding the musical tissues together. As a consequence, not only melody but harmony too attained a new independence. We have already seen how an insistence on a simple modal pattern, or even a single note, could bind together long movements like the Trio from Schubert's Great C Major Symphony or Chopin's Second Scherzo. Another example is the first scene from Act II of Verdi's *Il Trovatore*, comprising the 'Anvil Chorus' and Azucena's song 'Stride la vampa!' The whole scene, which goes through several contrasted themes in the keys of E minor, G, and C, is held together by the notes E and B. Fortunately the passage is so well known and Verdi's methods so crystal-clear that it is unnecessary to quote it here.

Even without modulation or chromatic chords the harmonically-independent melody produces non-classical added sixths, added ninths, subdominant sevenths, and so on, as shown in Ex. 121.

Ex. 121   Parlour chords, produced by the divergence of melody and
harmony

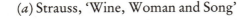

There is, also, a very common nineteenth-century pattern which, without being modal, behaves in rather the same way. This is the elaborated descending scale, the descent being usually from tonic to dominant. Ex. 122 gives a few examples. Among other favourite Victorian and Edwardian tunes of this type are 'The Highland Laddie', 'Wait till the Clouds Roll by', 'The Holy City' (Ex. 127), 'Soldiers of the Queen', Elgar's 'Land of Hope and Glory' tune, and Mendelssohn's Wedding March.[5] It was also much favoured in the Viennese waltz style.

Ex. 122

(*a*) Strauss, 'Wine, Woman and Song'

Tempo di Valse

(*b*) 'The Band Played on'

Valse

Ca - sey would waltz with a straw - ber - ry blonde

[5] Scholes, *The Oxford Companion to Music*, p. 628.

(*c*) Strauss, 'Morgenblätter'

(*d*) Strauss, 'Artist's Life'

The strength of the descending line is such that the clash with the underlying harmony may sometimes be intensified by doubling the melody in thirds, as in Ex. 122(*d*). 'Clash', however, is a misleading word for these carefully calculated, luscious sonorities.

Similar things can be done with the actual parlour modes. But it is in connection with chromatic harmony that the overriding effect of the parlour modes is most striking. Parlour chromaticism takes three forms: decorative, cadential, and structural. Decorative chromaticism, which we shall be returning to later, consists merely of embellishment of diatonic chords or progressions. Cadential chromaticism consists of transient modulations treated like cadences: for instance, a modulation to the dominant serving as a half close. It is not always very distinct from the last category, structural chromaticism, which is chromaticism on a large scale that may or may not include modulation.

In its familiar Classical or Baroque form of a smooth and sustained transition to a foreign key, modulation is seldom encountered in the parlour style. Apart from the brief cadential modulations just mentioned, a parlour modulation is almost always a jump into the new key with no transition at all. On a large scale this takes the form typical of those marches and rags already described, where a theme in the tonic is followed by a theme in the subdominant or some other key. The different sections are completely self-contained, and, as we have seen, it is not even always thought necessary to return to the tonic at the end of the movement. On a smaller scale such modulations as do occur generally lead *back* to the tonic after a jump into the new key which usually occurs, in the turn-of-the-century style, half-way through the verse part of a verse-and-refrain song. Once again, the movement is centripetal.

Whether modulatory or not, structural chromaticism is almost
invariably accompanied by some sort of unifying modal element in the
melody. In Ex. 123, for instance, the melody clearly revolves around the
notes A, C, and E, the last being the most prominent. The bold stroke

Ex. 123   Chopin, Waltz in D♭, Op. 70, no. 3

comes after the double bar-line, where the emphasis on the E in the
melody persists against the $\text{II}_{\sharp}^{7}$ chord in the harmony. In beginning with
this chord Chopin was taking the process of starting a tune on the
dominant a step further. But, once again, this bold step could at first only
be taken in the middle of a movement. Later, as it became more familiar,
it made its way to the beginning, as in Ex. 124. Here the melody traces a
suggestion of the tonic triad over the chromatic harmonies. The

Ex. 124   'Ain't You Coming Back to Old New Hampshire, Molly?'
          (beginning)

tendency to extend the cadence backwards, so to speak, did not end at
this point. By the middle of the nineteenth century we find, in Liszt's
'Liebestraum', not merely the dominant of the dominant, but the
dominant of the dominant of the dominant of the dominant (Ex. 125).

Ex. 125   Liszt, 'Liebestraum', no. III (beginning)

Modally, this theme is close to Chopin's Waltz in D♭ (Ex. 123). Its III$^7_\sharp$–VI$^7_\sharp$–II$^7_\sharp$–V7–I harmonic pattern (often without the first chord) was to become a great favourite in the popular music of about half a century later, not only in the parlour style but in ragtime as well. It has even been called the 'ragtime progression'.[6] Following the usual pattern, the initial tonic chord often drops out in these later examples: as for instance in 'Sweet Georgia Brown' (Ex. 126), composed just three-quarters of a century after 'Liebestraum'. To support the harmonic boldness the

Ex. 126 'Sweet Georgia Brown'

modal element is here emphasized to the point of suggesting bitonality (A major or minor against C major).

Parlour modulation comes nearest to classical norms when it proceeds to the key of the dominant. Often these dominant passages will be fairly extended; but instead of ending with a cadence marking off the first half of a binary structure, they lead straight into the refrain, as in the notorious sacred solo, 'The Holy City' (Ex. 127). There is a basic kinship here with the jumps into the subdominant already discussed, so that, in spite of the emphasis on the dominant, the main thrust of the harmony is still centripetal, not centrifugal.

[6] See Fahey, *Charley Patton*, p. 45.

Ex. 127   'The Holy City'

I heard the chil-dren sing-ing, And   ev-er as they sang, Me-thought the voice of An-gels From

Heav'n in an-swer rang;   Me-thought the   voice   of   An - gels   From

Heav'n   in an-swer   rang.   Je - ru - sa-lem! Je - ru - sa-lem!

When modulations are to keys other than the dominant, the new key will be integrated into the musical fabric by some overriding modal pattern, just as in the ragtime progression. A passage in A minor, for instance, can be integrated into a C major context by emphasizing the A C E melodic triad that we have already seen in Exx. 123, 125, and 126. As Ex. 128 illustrates, this sort of modulation was a favourite of the period for 'registering' pathos.[7]

Ex. 128   'Daisy Bell'

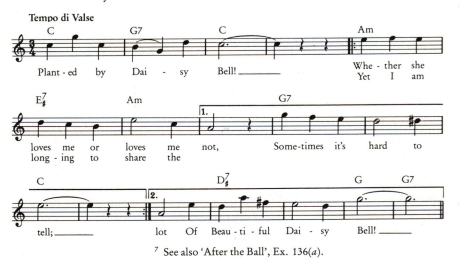

Plant-ed   by   Dai - sy   Bell! _____   Whe - ther she
                                          Yet   I   am

loves   me   or   loves   me   not,   Some-times it's   hard   to
long - ing   to   share   the

tell; _____   lot   Of   Beau-ti-ful   Dai - sy   Bell! _____

[7] See also 'After the Ball', Ex. 136(a).

Dai - sy, Dai - sy,

The same treatment can be applied to more distant keys, and if necessary the notes of the modal frame can be inflected, so that a melodic triad like A C E or E G B, for instance, could change to A C♯ E or E G♯ B. Ex. 129 illustrates the second of these possibilities. The first sixteen bars

Ex. 129 'Day by Day'

A Sai - lor was bid-ding his sweet-heart good-bye, One sun - ny sum - mer's day, _____ While out in the har-bor and rea - dy to sail, his proud ship lay. _____ And soon he was sail - ing to lands far a - way, Ov - er the bound - ing main, ___

emphasize the notes E, G, and B—not very strongly, but enough to establish them in the listener's mind. Then this triad changes from minor to major, and becomes, for a few bars, the tonic chord of the key of the mediant. Our next example (Ex. 130) is essentially similar, but far more elaborate. Here again, the mode is built around the triad E G B. Again, there is a passing modulation to the mediant, though this time it is the diatonic, minor mediant. Then we are back in the tonic, there is a

Ex. 130 'My Cosey Corner Girl'

pro - per place for love__ By sil - v'ry stream, some say love's dream Takes
cheek to cheek on moun - tain peak Some

cadence on the dominant, and we are plunged straight into the flat
mediant key. The melodic mode remains the same, except that the E
and B are now flat. As a further tie to the main key there is also an
insistence on the note C, at odds with the accompanying harmonies. On
a casual hearing the effect of the modulations in these last two examples
is rather like the transient changes of mode that Schubert was fond of
putting into his songs; and it is quite astonishing that the mechanics of
these apparently simple effects should turn out to be so complex,
especially in music which most people would regard—and I think
rightly—as the height of banality. The conclusion we should draw is not
that there are hidden depths to these trivial works, but that musical
structure in general is far more subtle and complex than we think.[8]

The sort of major-minor contrast seen in 'Daisy Bell' (Ex. 128) was
often applied, from the late nineteenth century on, to whole sections.
Thus, in some music-hall and ragtime songs, the verse is in the minor and
the refrain in the relative major, both sections being on the same note
frame. Examples are 'What Cheer Ria!',[9] 'Knocked 'em in the Old Kent
Road'[10] (an interesting example in which verse and refrain begin with the
same melodic figure), 'Bill Bailey' (Ex. 144), and 'Sweet Georgia Brown'
(Ex. 126). The same principle can also be seen in marches with the main

[8] Chopin's Scherzo no. 2 (Ex. 101) is a similar case, beginning with the note frame A C E,
which is inflected to Ab C Eb in the middle section.
[9] Words by William Herbert, music by Bessie Bellwood, 1885; no. 20 in Garrett, *Sixty Years
of British Music Hall*. Bessie Bellwood was also the original singer of this song. The attribution
of the music to her is a little suspect, since such attributions were often part of a deal between
the real composer and the performer. If she *did* write the tune, this helps explain the aeolian-
mode character of the verse, since she was born Kathleen Mahoney and began her career as a
singer of Irish ballads.
[10] Also known as 'Wot cher!' (i.e. 'What cheer?'). Words by Albert Chevalier, music by his
brother 'Charles Ingle', 1891. In Gammond, *Music Hall Song Book*, pp. 27–9.

section in the major and the trio in the relative minor, like 'High Society', of which some fine jazzed-up recordings exist, or 'Colonel Bogey'.[11] In such cases, whether of the verse-and-refrain or march-and-trio type, there is often a touch of modal harmony, with a hint that the distinction between relative major and minor is breaking down. 'Cheyenne' (Ex. 131) is an instance of this, and is worth quoting as possibly the very first example of the species of harmony which might be called 'horse opera modal'. The cover is adorned with a picture of the

Ex. 131

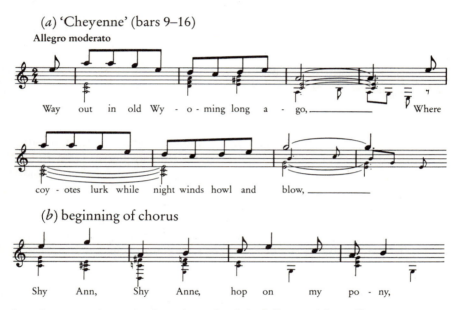

(a) 'Cheyenne' (bars 9–16)

Allegro moderato

Way out in old Wy - o - ming long a - go, _____ Where

coy - otes lurk while night winds howl and blow, _____

(b) beginning of chorus

Shy Ann, Shy Anne, hop on my po - ny,

heroine, escaping pursuit on horseback in full cowgirl regalia.

To the parlour composer the major mode was the normal one, and the minor usually implies a tension to be resolved by passing to the major: usually relative, but sometimes tonic. As the principal mode the minor is decidely rare, and usually implies a strong folk influence, if not (like 'When Johnny Comes Marching Home') an actual folk tune, or a splash of Oriental or East European colour.

The breakdown of the major-minor distinction appears also when the two modes are on the same tonic. It is, admittedly, no more than a hint, but interesting in the light of later developments. The tendency is actually most marked among 'serious' composers like Beethoven,

[11] 'High Society' was composed by Porter Steele in 1901, 'Colonel Bogey' by Kenneth J. Alford (real name Frederick Joseph Ricketts) in 1914.

Schubert,[12] and Brahms, but it appears also in certain lighter compositions like Ex. 132. The wavering major and minor sixths of this

Ex. 132 Auber, *Fra Diavolo*, Romanza

Allegretto non troppo

thoroughly French passage are interestingly reminiscent of Chopin's Mazurka in D♭ (Ex. 108(*a*)), where they obviously derive from Polish influence. The East European mode with a major third and a minor sixth was fairly popular in the nineteenth century,[13] but here, as always, the folk influence served only to reinforce already existing tendencies.

By the late nineteenth century a certain ambiguity about the third and sixth of the mode had crept into popular pieces like Ex. 133. Just a hint, as I have said, but oddly prophetic of the next century.

Ex. 133 'Oh! That Gorgonzola Cheese' (second half of introduction)

Allegro moderato

con 8 -

SEQUENCES

In its treatment of sequences the parlour style remains true to its principles. Melody and harmony seldom go in harness, as they usually do in the classical style. If the harmony is sequential, the melody is not, as in Schubert's 'Des Baches Wiegenlied' (Ex. 100(*b*), final bars of extract); and if the melody is sequential, the harmony is not, as in

[12] For instance the opening of the String Quintet, Ex. 140(*a*).
[13] See also Chopin's Mazurkas Op. 6, no. 2 (Ex. 68(*d*)) and Op. 24, no. 4 (Ex. 102), and Suppé's *Poet and Peasant* Overture (Ex. 151).

Strauss's 'Artist's Life' (Ex. 122(*d*)). On the comparatively rare occasions when true sequences occur, as in Ex. 134, they are likely to be something other than the circle-of-fifths type usual in the classical style.[14]

Ex. 134

(*a*) 'I'd Leave ma Happy Home for You'

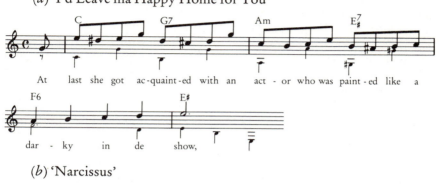

At last she got ac-quaint-ed with an act - or who was paint-ed like a dar - ky in de show,

(*b*) 'Narcissus'

Andante con moto

(*c*) 'Because'

Poco adagio

Be - cause you speak to me in ac-cents sweet, I

find the ro-ses wak-ing round my feet, And I am led through tears and joy to

thee, _____ Be - cause _____ you speak to me. _____

[14] In the circle-of-fifths sequence the roots of the chords drop by fifths, usually beginning with the tonic. There is a good example in Bach's Courante in E minor, Ex. 50, bars 4–8.

ARPEGGIOS

Eighteenth- and nineteenth-century tunes make frequent use of arpeggios built on the notes of the accompanying chord, particularly when it is the tonic. Familiar examples quoted in this book are Papageno's tune from *Die Zauberflöte* (Ex. 107), 'The Blue Danube' (Ex. 104), and 'Daisy Bell' (Ex. 128, beginning of chorus). From about 1900 on a new type of arpeggio begins to appear, in which the notes do *not* fit the harmony. An early intimation of this type is the c″ e″ c″ a′ figure in 'Cheyenne' (Ex. 131(*b*), bars 3–4), and a far more striking example from a quarter of a century later is the D minor triad in 'Mack the Knife' (Ex. 106, bars 4–7). In the course of the twentieth century this second type of arpeggio has gradually almost ousted the first in popular music. The melodic tonic triad of the blues, capable of being harmonized by chords other than the tonic, is a special case of the 'non-harmonic arpeggio', as one might call it; but the parlour idiom developed quite apart from any blues influence. As popular music developed a distaste for too facile a fit between melody and harmony the old-style arpeggio gradually dropped out of use, particularly if it was on the tonic. 'Sweet Georgia Brown' (Ex. 126), composed in 1925, has ordinary arpeggios, as well as the non-harmonic one on c″ a′ e″ c′ in bars 5–6; but notice that they are not on the tonic chord.

CADENCES

Parlour music uses the familiar classical cadences—perfect, imperfect, plagal, and interrupted—but in its own way. The subdominant, as a chord of approach to the dominant, became increasingly rare in the course of the nineteenth century. Where Bach or Beethoven would have used it, the parlour composer is likely to have $II_\sharp^7$; indeed, this chord is such a parlour favourite generally that it almost qualifies as an honorary diatonic triad. The subdominant, when it does appear, is far more likely to precede the tonic than the dominant, often with an emphasis that creates more than the suggestion of a plagal cadence. Mozart's *volkstümlich* little waltz tune (Ex. 120) already shows this feature. It was

Ex. 135

(*a*) Foster, 'My Old Kentucky Home' (chorus)

sing one song for the   old Ken-tuck-y Home, For the old Ken-tuck-y Home far   a - way.

(b) 'The Sidewalks of New York' (beginning of verse)

Down   in   front   of   Ca - sey's, ____   Old brown   wood - en   stoop, ____

On   a   sum - mer's   eve - ning, ____   We formed   a   mer - ry   group; ___

only in the mid-nineteenth century, however, that it attained real popularity.[15] Ex. 135 gives two examples.[16]

Meanwhile, the distinction between cadences and transient modulations was becoming blurred. Ordinary imperfect and interrupted cadences tended to be superseded by modulations to the dominant and submediant, and the classical range of cadences came to be supplemented by cadences, or near-cadences, on the supertonic and mediant. Here is a table of parlour cadences, with a few illustrations in Ex. 136:

PARLOUR CADENCE	EQUIVALENT DIATONIC CADENCE, IF ANY
1. Full close in dominant: $II_\sharp^7$–V. See 'Daisy Bell' (Ex. 128) and 'The Sidewalks of New York' (Ex. 135(b)).	Imperfect (usually IV or I-V)
2. Full close in relative minor: $III_\sharp^7$–VI. See Ex. 136(a) below.	Interrupted (V-VI)
3. Full close in supertonic: $VI_\sharp^7$–II. See Ex. 137(a).	
4. Half close in dominant: $VI_\sharp^7$, VI, I, etc. –$II_\sharp^7$. See Ex. 136(b) below, bars 1–4.	
5. Full close in mediant: $VII_\sharp^7$–III(♯). See Exx. 136(c) and (d) below.	
6. Half close in submediant: IV, II, etc.–$III_\sharp^7$7. See Ex. 136(b) below, bars 5–8.	

[15] Compare the history of Gregory Walker in ch. 22.
[16] Ex. 135(b) is also known as 'East Side, West Side', from the words of the chorus.

Ex. 136

(a) Cadence 2: 'After the Ball'

Why   are   you   sing - le;   why   live   a - lone?____

Have   you   no   ba - bies;   have   you   no   home?____

(b) Cadences 4 and 6: 'In the City of Sighs and Tears'

Wand'-ring   a - long where each   smi - ling   face   hides its   sto - ry   of

lost   ca - reers,____   And per - haps   she   is   dream - ing   of

you   to - night,   In the   Ci - ty   of   Sighs   and   Tears.____

(c) Cadence 5: 'The Dream'

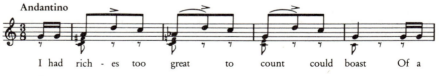

I had   rich - es   too   great   to   count   could   boast   Of a

high   an - ces - tral   name.____   But   I   al - so

(*d*) Cadence 5: 'Love Me, and the World is Mine'

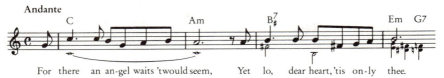

For there an an-gel waits 'twould seem, Yet lo, dear heart, 'tis on-ly thee.

In the interesting and favourite formulas of Exx. 136(*c*) and (*d*)—note that more than sixty years separate these two examples—the voice pauses on the leading note, while the harmony changes from mediant (whether major or minor) to dominant seventh. The result is a cross between a modulation to the mediant and a half close in the main key. Once again, melody is becoming the dominant partner in relation to harmony.[17]

DECORATIVE CHROMATICISM

There was nothing the *fin de siècle* parlour composer loved more than to bury a basically simple chord scheme under a wealth of harmonic ornament. If a chord was dwelt on for any reason, it was likely to enclose another one, often standing in a subdominant relation to it, like those in Ex. 137. Apart from such straightforward cases, there were all sorts of

Ex. 137 'I Love a Lassie'

(*a*) decorated supertonic: bars 11–14

saw her you would fan - cy her as well;

(*b*) decorated dominant and tonic: bars 19–24

So I'll soon be hav - in' her a' to ma - sel'. Her

fai - ther has con - sen - ted, so I'm

---

[17] For a further example in a contrasting style, see Bizet's *Carmen*, Prelude, bars 7–8. Here the progression is IV VII III♯ V7, so the modulation is a matter of a half close in the submediant, rather than a full close in the mediant.

chromatic possibilities involving passing-notes which sometimes combined to form triads or sevenths, and sometimes did not. Ex. 138 gives
some of the possibilities for chromatic decoration *within* a single chord,
while Ex. 139 deals with decoration *between* chords. Some of these
progressions are illustrated elsewhere in this book, and those that are not
can easily be found in any collection of popular music from the late

Ex. 138   Chromatic decoration within a chord
(*a*) tonic   (*b*) dominant

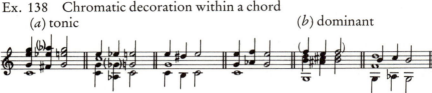

Ex. 139   Chromatic decoration between chords
(*a*) I–V

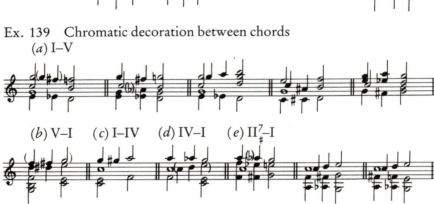

(*b*) V–I   (*c*) I–IV   (*d*) IV–I   (*e*) II$^7_\sharp$–I

nineteenth or early twentieth centuries. Sometimes the chromatic chords
are grouped into clusters around a chromatic scale somewhere in the
harmony, as in Exx. 137(*b*) (bars 1–2 and 5–6), 141(*c*), and 143(*a*). This
'chromatic creep', as it might be called, became even commoner in the
twentieth century, and is one of the hallmarks of the style of the 1930s.
Most of these formulas go back to the early nineteenth century, if not the
late eighteenth century, but parlour composers certainly used them with
a new abandon. In the classical tradition chromatic chords or passages
were viewed as splashes of colour against a sober diatonic background:
hence the term 'chromatic', or 'coloured'. Hack composers of the later
nineteenth century—and, one might add, serious purveyors of late
Romantic schmaltz—grievously misused this easy resource, with the
inevitable effect of cheap sentimentality. This development has rather
obscured another tendency of the parlour style, namely, the *normaliz-
ation* of chromaticism. More and more, chromatic chords lose their aura
of sentiment, drama or lushness, and become everyday items in the
harmonic vocabulary. Ex. 140 illustrates three stages in the development

Ex. 140

(*a*) Schubert, String Quintet (beginning)

(*b*) Barnby, 'Sweet and Low' (beginning)

(*c*) 'Buy Me Some Almond Rock'

of nineteenth-century chromaticism. First we have the High Romantic, exemplified here by the opening of Schubert's String Quintet. Then there is what might be termed the Low Romantic, or schmaltz. And finally, we have a usage which is not romantic at all—anything but. This particular example is from one of those gloriously vulgar music-hall songs that seem to have the winks and nudges built into the melodic line.[18] On the other hand, it cannot really be accused of bad taste, since there is none of

[18] Like Ex. 110(*a*), Ex. 140(*c*) is a Marie Lloyd song. It is a political skit, 'Randy Pandy' being the nickname of Randolph Churchill, father of the famous Winston.

the sense of aspiration on which bad taste depends. Bad taste, in the arts, is always a sort of failed good taste, the result of the Barnbys of the world trying to be Schuberts. Composers of the lighter styles of parlour music—marches, music-hall ditties, and the like—were not trying to be like Schubert, or, to be more specific, to produce the emotional effects of his progressions. In their hands the clichés of Romantic harmony—and this particular progression is nothing if not a cliché—become something quite different.

TONIC SEVENTHS

The Romantics invented various ways of decorating the final tonic chords of phrases with sevenths, sometimes major and sometimes minor. Ex. 141 illustrates the major-seventh type. As Ex. 141(a) suggests, it probably originated as a leading note appoggiatura to the sixth, which itself resolved on the dominant. Ex. 141(c) illustrates a turn-of-the-century cliché which developed out of these formulas.

Ex. 141

(a) Chopin, Waltz in A♭, Op. 34, no. 1

(b) Liszt, 'Liebestraum' no. III (end)

(c) 'An Old Man's Darling'

The related idiom with a chromatic slide from minor seventh to dominant, so evocative of the barbershop,[19] also had its origin in the High Romantic period (see Ex. 142). Like its major-seventh relative, it is akin to the blue seventh in resolving *within* the chord on the dominant, thereby challenging the basic principles of classical harmony.

Ex. 142   Chopin, Nocturne in C minor (end of first section and beginning of second section)

As with modality, there are many teasing parallels between parlour harmony and American folk harmony: parallels which greatly facilitated the fusion of the two styles around 1900. Some features of parlour harmony certainly passed directly into blues and ragtime, most notably the 'ragtime progression'. The harmonic pattern which I call 'the American Gregory Walker' is in all probability a fusion of the old Gregory Walker pattern with the parlour I IV–I progression: and this, in its turn, evolved into certain blues chord patterns. Sometimes it is a puzzle whether to ascribe a particular blues idiom to parlour influence. Does the bluesman's habit of ending his guitar accompaniment with a tonic seventh chord have anything to do with the 'barbershop' progression of Ex. 142? It is difficult to tell.

In its essence, blues harmony is based on the three primary triads, though these may be decked with sevenths, sixths, and even more outlandish additions. Any chromaticisms outside these will usually be of parlour origin, as for instance the rock and roll cliché of Ex. 143 (*b*).[20] This is, incidentally, a good example of the sort of change a formula undergoes by being adapted to a different instrument. The parlour style

Ex. 143

(*a*) 'Sweet Adeline' (introduction)

---

[19] See 'Ain't You Coming Back to Old New Hampshire, Molly?', Ex. 124.
[20] An Elvis Presley song.

(*b*) 'Hard Headed Woman' (introduction)

is eminently pianistic, but by the beginning of the twentieth century it had been taken up by guitarists, who inevitably adapted it to their own habits. The pair of chords of Ex. 143(*b*) is a guitarist's idiom: he simply stops the first chord and then slides his whole left hand up one fret.

But the most important parallel between the two styles lies in the relationship between harmony and melody. In both styles we find an uncoupling of the harness that had held the two together in the European classical tradition. In its harmonico-modal relationship (if the reader will forgive such a barbarous phrase) the early blues certainly learnt something from parlour music, as we can see from the earliest published blues, which are much closer to the parlour style than to the folk blues. Altogether, the parlour style is the most neglected influence on the Afro-American style. Without it, twentieth-century popular music would have been a very different thing.

28. PARLOUR RHYTHM

PARLOUR music, like most types of popular music, tended to divide rather sharply into the slow and emotional on the one hand and the brisk and rhythmic on the other. Popular songs in a slow tempo, known then, as now, as 'ballads', might be in common time ('My Old Kentucky Home' (Ex. 135(*a*)), 'The Holy City' (Ex. 127), 'Sweet Adeline' (Ex. 143(*a*), etc.), or, more rarely, in triple time ('Sweet Genevieve'). In either event the tempo was a flowing andante. At a quicker tempo one might find marches, polka-like rhythms, or jigs, generally of a real or pseudo-Irish origin. Straddling both types was the waltz, which might be slow, medium-paced or quick.

At a first glance this catalogue of rhythms seems remarkably dull, and it is true that not even the most enthusiastic admirer of parlour music could claim rhythmic interest as its strong point. But look a little closer, and certain intriguing oddities and even subtleties come to light. One is the partiality for triple rhythms, which increased as the century went on. This is most marked at quicker tempos, but even the ballad writers were fond of accompaniments in throbbing triplets. Another is the subtle distinctions made between the various forms of triplet. A great many tunes were written in $\frac{6}{8}$ time, or in a $\frac{6}{8}$ rhythm disguised by a conventional dotted common-time notation. And yet the effect of these triplets is not always the same. A march like 'The Washington Post' (Exx. 105 and 157(*b*)) has a quite different rhythmic effect from a jig like 'When Johnny Comes Marching Home', even though the latter, too, may be used as a march, and at the same tempo. And a music-hall tune like 'Oh! Mr. Porter' (Ex. 110(*a*)) or 'Buy Me Some Almond Rock' (Ex. 140(*c*)) is different from either.

Many of the best-known music-hall songs of the 1890–1910 period are in this last rhythm. As well as those just named one could mention 'Wot Cher! (Knocked 'em in the Old Kent Road)', 'The Man who Broke the Bank at Monte Carlo', 'I Do Like to be beside the Seaside', 'A Little of what You Fancy Does You Good', 'Hello! Hello! Who's your Lady Friend?', and 'I'm Henery the Eighth, I am', (Ex. 108(*d*)).[1] This 'music-hall $\frac{6}{8}$' generates a strong body rhythm: not a dance rhythm like the jig, and not a march step, but rather a swaggering walk. It is as much a matter

[1] All these songs are in Gammond, *Music Hall Song Book*.

of the interaction between melody and rhythm as of tempo, accent, accompaniment, and the like. Serious composers of the time no doubt thought these rhythms unspeakably vulgar, too strongly suggesting movements of a less than dignified type, and also—it is worth noting— the rhythms of colloquial English. In the best of these songs the tune fits the words with a naturalness far beyond the reach of the serious composer. When Constant Lambert wrote that 'certain jazz songs show a more apt feeling for the cadence of English speech than any music since the seventeenth century'[2] he was apparently forgetting the indigenous music-hall.

When one comes to examine the formal organization of parlour rhythms, the striking things are the squareness of layout and the repetitiveness of detail. There was, of course, nothing new about either of these features; but in the early nineteenth century they combined in a manner unmistakably stamping the parlour composer. One of the earliest tunes in which we catch this new parlour note is 'Home! Sweet Home!' (1823) which consists, rhythmically, of little more than the repetition of ♪| ♫♫| ♩ ♪♪| ♫♫| ♩ , and later parlour ballads were even more monotonously repetitive. 'Just before the Battle, Mother' (1863), 'Silver Threads among the Gold' (1873), and 'I'll Take You Home Again, Kathleen' (1875) all use close variants on the same rhythm, respectively | ♩. ♪♫♫| ♩. – | ♩. ♪♫♫| ♩. ♪| , ♪| ♩. ♪♫♫| ♩. ♪|, and ♪| ♩. ♪♫♫| ♩. ♪| ♩. ♪♫♫| ♩ ♩, repeated through verse and chorus with minimal variation and no relief at all. The result is an unctuous lugubriousness greatly esteemed by Victorian audiences.

Many of the livelier tunes were almost equally repetitive in their way. 'Bill Bailey' (Ex. 144), a familiar turn-of-the-century example, is typical. This is not the whole song. It is merely the refrain, and is preceded by the

Ex. 144   'Bill Bailey, Won't You Please Come Home?'

2 *Music Ho!*, p. 220.

'Mem-ber dat rain-y eve dat I drove you out, Wid noth-ing but a

fine tooth comb? I knows I'se to blame; well, ain't dat a

shame? Bill Bai-ley, won't you please come home?

verse section, itself preceded by a short instrumental introduction. In earlier songs, for instance the fine old music-hall song 'Polly Perkins', the refrain was too short and too closely connected with the verse to make musical sense by itself: in other words, it was a true refrain of the traditional type. Later we find refrains getting longer and longer and more and more independent of the verse. Where in 'Polly Perkins' the verse was twice the length of the refrain, by the end of the nineteenth century verse and refrain were often of equal length, and from about 1920 on the refrain was usually twice the length of the verse. In the course of this process the two sections became more and more detached from each other and the 'verse' more and more preludial in character, until in the mid-twentieth century the final step was taken and it began to be dispensed with altogether. But even in the time of 'Bill Bailey' the refrain was no doubt the only part that was whistled in the streets, and it is certainly the only part that is remembered now.

In their rhythm and phrasing these turn-of-the-century songs have several noteworthy features that are typical not only of the popular songs of their time, but of those of the following fifty years. Firstly, as already mentioned, the squareness of the phrasing. They are symmetric-ally constructed thirty-two-bar tunes, built up in the clearest possible way out of four-, eight-, and sixteen-bar sections. Secondly, we often find, as in 'Bill Bailey', a sort of limerick effect towards the end, whereby the final cadence is preceded by a short repeated rhythm. Often, as in the limerick itself, it is reinforced by an actual verbal rhyme. This rhyme scheme goes back at least to sixteenth-century songs like 'Go from my Window Go', and has remained popular in British and American folk-song,[3] as well as urban popular music. In addition to 'Daisy' and 'Bill

---

[3] See ch. 9, 'Worksongs' for 'Go from my Window Go', and also 'John Henry' and 'The Greenland Whale fisheries. Another example is 'Pretty Wench', p. 24.

Bailey', we find it in Cockney music-hall song like 'If It wasn't for the 'Ouses in between' (1894):

> Wiv a ladder and some glasses,
> You could see to Ackney Marshes,
> If it wasn't for the 'ouses in between.[4]

and 'Buy Me Some Almond Rock' (1893), Ex. 140(*c*):

> Randy pandy
> sugardy candy
> Buy me some Almond Rock.

and it appears in ragtime songs much later than 'Bill Bailey', for instance 'The Darktown Strutters' Ball' (1917):

> Goin' to dance out both my shoes
> When they play the 'Jelly Roll Blues'
> Tomorrow night, at the Darktown Strutters' Ball.[5]

and 'Sweet Georgia Brown' (1925), Ex. 126:

> Georgia claimed her,
> Georgia named her
> Sweet Georgia Brown.

as well as being a frequent feature of later, non-ragtime popular songs.

Thirdly, in some of these songs (a good example is 'Daisy Bell') there is a tendency to group rhythms in pairs of diminishing length: in the chorus of 'Daisy Bell' the sequence is [musical notation], then [musical notation], then [musical notation].

Fourthly, the rhythmic repetition is typically *non*-sequential.

In all these respects 'Bill Bailey' and its contemporaries are the ancestors of the thirty-two-bar song, which held mainstream popular music in a tyrannical grip from about 1920 to 1950. As with these turn-of-the-century examples, the term 'thirty-two-bar song' applies only to the refrain section; and, just as a twelve-bar blues may actually be six or twenty-four bars long, so the thirty-two-bar song may actually be sixteen or sixty-four bars long.[6] It is merely a matter of notation. In any case, the vast majority of thirty-two-bar songs really *are* thirty-two bars long, so we may conventionally suppose that all are.

The thirty-two-bar songs of the second quarter of the twentieth century are like their nineteenth-century forerunners, only more so. The form, like most musical forms, tended to get longer as time went on, and

---

[4] Words by Edgar Bateman, music by George Le Brunn. Reprinted in Walsh, *There Goes that Song Again*, pp. 18–20.
[5] Words and music by Shelton Brooks. Reprinted in ibid., 66–8.
[6] For instance 'Barney Google', by Billy Rose and Con Conrad, is sixteen bars long, and Cole Porter's 'Just One of those Things' is sixty-four bars long.

also squarer, more rhythmically repetitive, more mechanical, more predictable. There were two varieties, the earlier and the later. The earlier followed the 'Bill Bailey' pattern: a binary structure in which each sixteen-bar section began the same (and, by and large, continued the same too). 'Sweet Georgia Brown' (Ex. 126) is an example of this: call it the binary type. Around 1925 this form yielded in popularity to the later form, which distributed its themes in an AABA pattern, thus:

first 8 bars: main theme, ending on dominant chord;
second 8 bars: main theme, ending on tonic;
third 8 bars: new theme in a more fragmented rhythm, known in the trade as the 'middle eight';
fourth 8 bars: main theme again, ending on tonic.

It is hard to account for the prolonged popularity of this form. In a way, it is the exaggerated outcome of trends already evident in the nineteenth and even late eighteenth centuries. Many of the most popular classical tunes are marked by emphatically repeated rhythms: Mozart's 'Non più andrai', Schumann's 'Träumerei', and Verdi's 'La donna è mobile' are examples chosen almost at random. But what is characteristic of the thirty-two-bar song is not so much the rhythmic repetition itself as its combination with a squareness of layout that produces a deadly predictability hardly equalled in music. In the feebler examples, once one has heard the first eight bars one seems to know already how the remaining twenty-four will go. Perhaps the truth is simply that this is a decadent form, designed to be turned out by the least inspired hack and understood by the meanest musical intelligence. Listening to the bulk of these tunes inclines one to this uncharitable verdict. On the other hand there are some, notably the best work of Gershwin and Cole Porter, that are undoubtedly classics of a kind. They tend to be a little more rhythmically enterprising and less predictable than the average, and there is often a witty interplay between words and music.[7]

At all events, the thirty-two-bar song, like all popular music, is intensely evocative of its time, partly perhaps for the very reason that it is so mechanical. After all, was this not a period that revered the machine as it has never been revered before or since?

SYNCOPATIONS IN THE CLASSICS

Coming down to the finer details of parlour rhythm, it is difficult to lay one's finger on anything distinctive. When one encounters a striking

---

[7] For the sake of fairness and precision, it should be mentioned that a few 'thirty-two-bar songs' break out of the thirty-two-bar straitjacket. 'Jeepers Creepers' (words by Johnny Mercer, music by Harry Warren) and Gershwin's 'I Got Rhythm', for instance, both have two

rhythm, it is usually of some sort of folk origin, whether Irish, Scottish, Spanish, or American. But it must be admitted that, generally speaking, the nineteenth-century popular composer was far outdone in rhythmic resource by his more serious brethren. Those were still the days when it was customary to precede the word 'syncopation' with 'learned'. Though it is something of a digression from our main theme, the question of sycopation in the classical tradition is worth having a look at. It is a mistake to draw too sharp a distinction between the 'popular' and 'classical' styles of the nineteenth century. The first middle-class audiences to hear ragtime syncopations were familiar not only with the 'parlour' music I have been describing, but also with a rich variety of what would now be described as 'light classical'. What sort of rhythms are found in this light classical tradition?

Syncopation in general was highly fashionable during the late medieval period, partly, no doubt, as a result of the general Near Eastern influence. The rumba rhythm appeared in the fourteenth century, and remained popular through the late medieval and Renaissance periods. With the later Baroque its popularity waned, though vestiges can be found in Bach: for instance, the subject of the fugue in D minor from *The Well Tempered Clavier*, Book II, or the musette from *The Little Music Book of Anna Magdalena Bach* (Ex. 145)—significantly, an imitation of a folk style. Thereafter it went thoroughly out of fashion for

Ex. 145   Bach, *The Little Music Book of Anna Magdalena Bach*, Musette

more than a century. Though a diligent search will reveal rhythms of the | ♩ ♩ ♩ ♩ | ♩ ♩ ♩ ♩ | or | ♫♫♫♫ | type among the Classical and earlier Romantic composers, they obviously meant nothing special to them. Haydn, Mozart, and Beethoven were all fond of syncopation, but they much preferred to divide the common-time bar into 3+2+3, rather than 3+3+2: | ♩♪ ♩ ♩ ♩♪ |, not | ♩ ♩♪ ♩♪ | .

From about the middle of the nineteenth century unmistakably rumba-like effects begin to appear (see Ex. 146), usually under East European influence.

The history of the hemiola roughly parallels that of the rumba rhythm. It, too, appeared in the Middle Ages, probably from Near Eastern origins, remained popular until the early Baroque, and faded out with

extra bars at the end; 'Hard Hearted Hanna' (words and music by Yellen, Ager, Bigelow, and Bates) is twenty bars long—though this may have something to do with blues influence—and 'Ten Cents a Dance' (by Rodgers and Hart) is twenty-four bars long.

Ex. 146

(*a*) Liszt, Piano Concerto no. 1, second movement

Allegro maestoso

(*b*) Mussorgsky, *Boris Godunov*, Act III

Allegretto con grazia

(*c*) Franck, Symphony in D minor, last movement

Allegro non troppo

dolce cantabile

the general incline in interest in cross-rhythms during the eighteenth century. A vestige of the medieval type of hemiola can be found in the operas of the late eighteenth and nineteenth centuries, where it serves as the

Ex. 147   Mozart, *Don Giovanni*, 'Batti, batti'

not - te é   di ___ vo - gliam   pas - sar, _____ vo -

gliam, vo|- gliam   pas - sar, _____ vo - gliam,   vo - gliam   pas - sar!

distinguishing mark of peasants (Ex. 147) or, after they became fashionable, of gypsies. From about 1790 this 'folk' hemiola had a popular parallel in the waltz style. This new formula was the *valse à deux temps*. Spike Hughes has pointed out an early example in *Cosi fan tutte* (Ex. 148).[8] In its strict

Ex. 148   Mozart, *Cosi fan tutte*, 'Terzetto'

form (♩ ♩♩♩♩. ♪ or a close variant) the *valse à deux temps* rhythm appears in several favourite Romantic compositions: the Finale of Schumann's Piano Concerto, the waltz from Act III of Gounod's *Faust*, and so on. In a more general way, lapses into some sort of $\frac{3}{2}$ rhythm are extremely common in the concert waltz; there are, perhaps, more famous waltzes with them than without them.[9] Even apart from the hemiola, some of the most familiar concert waltzes show ingenious cross-rhythms. The apparently banal strains of Tchaikovsky's *Swan Lake* waltz (Ex. 149(*a*)–(*c*)) reveal the hemiola, displacement of the beat, the combination of both these, and what has been called 'secondary ragtime': that is, the repetition of a short figure against the beat, as in Ex. 149(*d*).[10] Such cross-rhythms, however, remained a feature of light classical rather than popular music. The music-hall song in *deux temps*

Ex. 149

(*a*) Tchaikovsky, *Swan Lake* waltz (*c.* 1875), bars 19–50

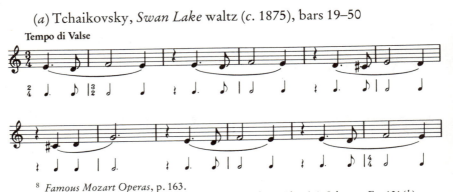

---

[8] *Famous Mozart Operas*, p. 163.
[9] For a typical example, see the waltz-like theme from Chopin's Scherzo, Ex. 101(*b*).
[10] See Berlin, *Ragtime*, pp. 130–4.

(b) bars 83–90

(c) bars 229–33

(d) Handy, 'Memphis Blues' (1909)

Tempo di Blues

rhythm about the man who wanted to sing in op-pop-pop-popera turns out to be a parody of a salon piece, Arditi's 'Il Bacio'.

Returning to syncopation in general and the classical style in general, we find examples of most types familiar in popular music: the missed beat, anticipation of the beat,[11] and delaying of the beat. In the Classical period, moving a theme on by half a beat, as in Ex. 150, was a standard way of varying it, just as it was in mid-nineteenth-century banjo music.

Ex. 150

(a) Beethoven, Piano Sonata in G, Op. 14, no. 2, second movement, beginning of theme, with (b) beginning of second variation

(a) Andante   (b)

When ragtime and jazz erupted on the world of 'serious music' much was made of these classical syncopations. What, asked the guardians of tradition, is there in ragtime that you cannot find in Beethoven's *Leonore*

---

[11] e.g. the first movement of Beethoven's Piano Sonata Op. 31, no. 1.

Overture? (That was the stock example.[12]) They had a point, with regard at least to early ragtime, which boasted little that, *on paper*, could not be paralleled in the classics. The ragtime and jazz fans replied that, whatever it might look like when written down, their music *sounded* totally different from the classics—and this was undoubtedly true. No matter how much they may resemble each other in theory or on paper, learned and popular syncopations have a quite different effect in performance. When we encounter an apparent exception, like the distinctly raggy theme from Suppé's *Poet and Peasant* Overture (Ex. 151), this turns out to be another case of popular influence, in this instance East European.

Ex. 151   Suppé, *Poet and Peasant* Overture

If nothing else, the syncopations in light classical and salon music prepared the public for ragtime and jazz. The latter brought a new naturalness, a new liveliness, a new catchiness to these rhythms, but there was nothing in them to baffle the ear accustomed to the Finale of Franck's D Minor Symphony. As proved by the success of other rhythmic novelties, chiefly Spanish and East European, the world was not only ready but eager for exhilarating syncopations. Like all successful fashions, ragtime was the right thing at the right time.

[12] Bernard Shaw's view was typical: 'Greenhorns write of syncopation now as if it were a new way of giving the utmost impetus to a musical measure; but the rowdiest jazz sounds like The Maiden's Prayer after Beethoven's third Leonore overture . . .'. ('Beethoven', *The Radio Times*, 18 March 1927, pp. 573–84; reprinted in *Shaw's Music*, vol. 3, p. 743.)

29. RAGTIME

Got more trouble than I can stand,
Ever since ragtime has struck the land.

Gene Jefferson, 1900[1]

HOW JIGS BECAME RAGS

A FEW years before the end of the nineteenth century, genuine black American music became a lucrative commercial property. For generations it had gradually been making its way up in the world; now, suddenly, it managed to attract the attention of big business. Like all apparently sudden historical developments, however, this was really a more gradual affair than appears in retrospect. Comic black characters, speaking a pseudo-Negro dialect, were a feature of English ballad operas, which were also popular in America.[2] What was later to be called the 'coon song' was familiar to late eighteenth-century English audiences; one, of 1790, actually mentions the banjo.[3] There is no evidence that the popularity of these characters had anything to do with genuine Afro-American music. They were simply another species of funny foreigner, and their songs were set to tunes distinguished, if at all, only by a totally un-African simplicity of rhythm.

At the same time a genuine interest in the Afro-American 'jigs' described in chapter 8 was developing in America. One such 'Negro Jig' (Ex. 152) was published in Scotland in 1782. In its concentration around

Ex. 152 'Pompey Ran Away'

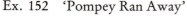

[1] Opening words of the song 'I'm Certainly Living a Ragtime Life' (words by Gene Jefferson, music by Robert S. Roberts).
[2] See Hamm, ' "Jim Crow"; or, The Music of the Early American Minstrel Show' in *Yesterdays*, pp. 109 ff.
[3] 'The Negro and his Banja' by Charles Dibdin. See ibid., p. 110.

a central note, its repetitiveness, and its end-repeating phrasing, this little tune is typically African, and provides convincing evidence of the influence of black American music at the time.

Clearly, it was only a matter of time before show business had the inspiration of combining those two winning formulas, the capering darkie and his irresistible rhythms. This happened with the start of the Nigger Minstrel movement around 1830. It must be admitted that little of the minstrel music that has come down to us shows much real Afro-American influence, and there was a great deal that was simply bogus, the Negro flavour being imparted by turning 'evening' into 'ebening', 'love' into 'lub' and 'is' into 'am' in songs otherwise as negroid as Mendelssohn's Wedding March. The genuine folk element in minstrel music was mainly Celtic—Irish, Scottish, or Scotch-Irish—though there is every evidence that performance techniques, with virtuoso fiddling, banjo picking, and percussion, really did owe much to Africa. There is also, in some of the mid-century tunes,[4] a hint of a substratum of real Afro-American music.

It was not until near the end of the century that the more commercial form of minstrel music began to change its nature. As so often with popular music, the continuity of the tradition was masked by a misleading profusion of names. Jigs, coon songs, cakewalks, rags, ragtime, and later jazz—all marked successive stages in the same slowly changing tradition. What happened in the mid-1890s was typical of the history of American popular music. A new kind of music suddenly caught the fancy of the white, middle-class audience—new, that is, to them, though well established in folk tradition. The impresarios and music publishers then responded like typical American businessmen, and gave this product a new name. Around 1890 the words 'rag' and 'ragtime' began to be applied to what musicians were still calling jigs, just as they had been for more than a hundred years. For a few years 'rag' and 'jig' were interchangeable. One could talk about 'jig piano' or 'rag piano', a 'jig band' or a 'ragtime band'; it meant precisely the same thing.[5] Then 'ragtime' and 'rag' took over from the earlier term, only to be dethroned by 'jazz' twenty years later.

Just how similar these variously named styles were can be seen from the three quotations in Ex. 153. The first is from a 'coon song' of 1886. (On the title page it is called an 'Ethiopian' song, a favourite euphemism of the period.) The second is from a cakewalk of 1894.[6] The third is from the very first published rag, so called, which appeared in 1897. It will be

---

[4] See the examples on pp. 164–7.

[5] The authority for this is Tom Ireland, ragtime clarinettist and associate of Scott Joplin's. See Blesh and Janis, *They All Played Ragtime*, p. 23.

[6] 'Possumala' is a would-be comic mispronunciation of 'Pas Ma La', a popular dance of the period.

Ex. 153

(a) 'Johnny Get your Gun'

(b) 'Possumala Dance'

(c) 'Mississippi Rag'

seen that the style is identical. Everything is the same: rhythm, mode, even the harmony. (The characteristic alternation of tonic and submediant is often found in early ragtime, always with delightful effect. It most probably originated in the improvised fiddle harmonies which went so well with Celtic dance tunes. It is interesting as an early hint of a blurring of the distinction between major and relative minor, later to become important in popular music.)

The actual ragtime craze dated from 1896, when a young Southerner called Ben Harney scored a great success with New York audiences.[7] To

---

[7] Harney's race is doubtful. He used to be described as white, but there is evidence that he was really a mulatto passing as white. See Berlin, *Ragtime*, pp. 24 and 31, n. 14.

this northern, big-city public, his piano playing was far more exciting than anything heard in the coon songs. There is no evidence that there was anything really new in it, however; the innovation consisted, on the contrary, in bringing the city slickers some raw folk music.

Both of Harney's first two hits, 'You've Been a Good Old Wagon but You've Done Broke down' (Ex. 154(a)) and 'Mister Johnson' (Ex. 155) are not merely folk-like, but use actual folk tunes. 'You've Been a Good Old Wagon' is obviously a close relative of 'Mister Frog' (Ex. 154(b)) a song which goes back to about 1880 at least.[8] 'Mister Johnson' is a

Ex. 154

(a) Harney, 'You've Been a Good Old Wagon but You've Done Broke down'

(b) 'Mister Frog'

[8] It is introduced with the sentence: 'Still another variant was given me by Louise Laurense, of Shelbyville, Kentucky, who says that her mother learnt it in her childhood from Negroes in Kentucky.' (Scarborough, *On The Trail of Negro Folk-Songs* (1925), p. 48.) A very similar tune is 'Sugar Babe', in Sharp, *English Folk Songs from the Southern Appalachians*, vol. 2, p. 357. The words can ultimately be traced to the Jacobean 'The Frog Would a-Wooing Ride' (see 'Pretty Polly and Po' Lazarus', p. 194). The alteration in the arrangement of the lines bears out the attribution of black influence.

Ex. 155   Harney, 'Mister Johnson'

T'oth-er   eb'-ning eb' - ry - ting was still,   Oh!   babe,_____   De

moon was climbin' down be-hind de hill, Oh!   babe,____   T'ought eb - ry bo-dy was a

sound a-sleep, But a   old man a John-son was a   on his beat, Oh!   babe.____

member of the same tune family as 'Pretty Polly' (Exx. 18 and 82), and
also very like the bluesy spiritual 'Motherless Children'. In its phrasing it
is half-way between a sixteen- and twelve-bar tune, the third line being
in the process of dropping away; and it is interesting to note that a
similar fate has overtaken 'Mister Frog'. These are folk tunes well on
their way to turning into twelve-bar blues.

Harney's rags were only part of a general folk influx of the time. The
middle classes neither knew nor cared whether they got their Scotch
snaps and pentatonic figures from the blacks or the Irish. The jaunty
'Irish' songs that enjoyed a vogue in the 1890s were confused in their
minds with the 'coon' songs. One of the best, 'The Cat Came Back' is
written in pseudo-Negro dialect:

> Dar was ole Mister Johnson, he had trouble of his own,
> He had an ole yaller cat that wouldn't leave its home;
> He tried eb'rything he knew to keep de cat away,
> Eben send it to the preacher an he tole it for to stay . . .[9]

There is even a song, 'Bedelia' (1903), subtitled 'The Irish Coon Song
Serenade', though the coon element is rather hard to find. (Words by
William Jerome, music by Jean Schwartz, published by Shapiro,
Bernstein and Company—evidently a thoroughly cosmopolitan pro-
duction.)

This early folk ragtime developed in two quite distinct ways. On the
one hand, it was absorbed into parlour music; on the other, it became
more and more genuinely negroid. The year 1896, when Harney
introduced ragtime to New York, was a great time for innovation:
within the space of a year, a New Yorker might have seen his first motor

---

[9] Words and music by Harry S. Miller, 1893. In *Favorite Songs of the Nineties*, pp. 52–4.

car, his first moving picture show, and his first newspaper comic strip—
and heard his first rag. One might say that the twentieth century was
born five years ahead of its time. A year later the first piece explicitly
published as a rag appeared in William Krell's 'Mississippi Rag'
(Ex. 153(c)), described on the title page as 'The First Rag-Time Two-
Step Ever Written, and First Played by KRELL'S ORCHESTRA,
Chicago'. In the same year several other rags appeared in other parts of
the United States, proving the excellent communications of the popular
music trade of the time. It was not until 1899, however, that the real
ragtime mania began.

The great influence behind the piano rags of the 1890s—greater even
than that of the 'jigs'—was the march. There was a vogue for dancing to
actual marches, the dance itself being either the two-step, or, later on, the
cakewalk.[10] Joplin's 'A Breeze from Alabama' (Ex. 119(b)) was described, like 'Mississippi Rag', as a two-step, or rather 'March and Two-
step'. So were many other rags; and if they were not explicitly called
marches, they were often headed, like 'Maple Leaf Rag' (Ex. 158(a)),
'Tempo di marcia', or the equivalent. The touches of folk harmony in the
earliest rags soon faded out, and the rags of the Joplin era are hardly
distinguished in form and harmonic style from contemporary marches.
Nor are ragtime songs distinguished from other popular songs, except by
their syncopated rhythms. As the very word suggests, ragtime was,
initially, a matter of syncopation—'ragged time'—and very little else.

As the black influence made itself felt, however, ragtime came to mean
more than just rhythm, while the rhythms themselves became more
enterprising. In the year after his New York triumph Ben Harney
published his *Rag Time Instructor*, with its raggy version of 'Annie
Laurie' (Ex. 156). At a first glance Harney's syncopating technique
seems laughably simple: just a matter of putting in a quaver rest at the
beginning of every bar. On closer inspection, however, we see that he is
tracing out the rhythms ♩ ♩. ♩ and ♩. ♩ ♩. in the top notes,

Ex. 156

(*a*) Harney, 'Annie Laurie', straight and (*b*) ragged

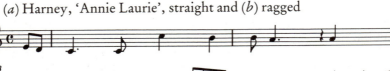

[10] See Lamb, 'March: 19th- and 20th-century Military and Popular Marches', *The New
Grove*, vol. 11, p. 652.

retarded by a half-beat.[11] It was only later that these rhythms, and all their relatives in the 'rumba rhythm' family, began to appear in a straightforward form.

As rhythms became more African, so too did form, with the appearance of the 'break'. In vocal music a break occurs when the voice stops at the end of a phrase and is answered by a snatch of accompaniment. In purely instrumental compositions the bass or high treble does duty for the accompaniment. In spite of its obvious resemblance to African call-and-response patterns, its immediate origin was the 'bass run', common in marches of the Sousa school, like Exx. 157(a) and (b).[12]

Did these bass runs simply take the fancy of black musicians because of an accidental resemblance to the call-and-response pattern, or were they themselves developed by black musicians? After all, there had been black bandsmen since the early nineteenth century. Perhaps a careful

Ex. 157

(a) Sousa, 'Semper Fidelis' (end of first strain, leading back to repeat)

con 8

(b) Sousa, 'The Washington Post' (end of third strain, leading back to repeat)

Tempo marziale

con 8

[11] Compare Harney's remarks on the derivation of such figures from banjo playing on p. 166.
[12] Ex. 157(d) was originally 'Milneberg Joys', from a seaside resort near New Orleans. for another 'break' see Handy's 'Memphis Blues', Ex. 149(d).

(c) James Scott, 'Ragtime Oriole'

Do not play this piece fast

(d) Morton, 'Milenberg Joys'[*]

comparison with European marches of the same period could provide the answer.

RAGTIME AND THE BLUES

The bluesy element in published rags grew steadily with the years.[13] The blue third made its appearance early, though reconciled at first with the classical harmonic system. In the famous 'Maple Leaf Rag', for instance, it appears as part of the flat submediant chord, in a progression straight out of 'The Washington Post' (Ex. 158(a)).[14] By the time of Morton's

Ex. 158

(a) Joplin, 'Maple Leaf Rag'

Tempo di marcia

13 See Berlin, *Ragtime*, pp. 154–60.
14 Two-steps were often danced to 'The Washington Post' (composed 1889; see Ex. 105) so it is quite likely that this very passage was at the back of Joplin's mind when he wrote 'Maple Leaf Rag'. See Lamb, 'March', *The New Grove*, vol. 11, p. 652.

(*b*) Morton, 'King Porter Stomp'*

'King Porter Stomp' (Ex. 158(*b*)), we find it clashing recklessly with the harmonies below.

The twelve-bar blues pattern, already intimated by Harney in 'Mister Johnson', made an isolated appearance in 1904 in a rag entitled 'One o' them Things!' (Ex. 159).[15] Like the publishers later approached by W.C. Handy, the composers of this rag found the twelve-bar pattern too lop-sided for their taste—or feared that their audience might—and therefore turned it into a symmetrical twenty-four-bar scheme, ending first on the dominant and then on the tonic. In spite of this slight anomaly it is clear that they were using an already established harmonic pattern. This piece, behind its urbane and charming ragtime exterior, hides the ancient African end-repeating structure, as can easily be seen if the decorative 'breaks' at the ends of the phrases are omitted, as in Ex. 159(*b*). We then have three phrases, each ending with an identical figure descending to the mediant: the same structure as in a much later 'parlour blues', Bob Dylan's 'Rainy Day Women'.[16]

Ex. 159

(*a*) 'One o' them Things!' (first strain)

[15] This is pointed out in Berlin, *Ragtime*, p. 155 (music quoted on p. 157).
[16] This strongly melodic structure, coupled with the odd title, rather suggests that 'One o' them Things!' was an arrangement of a song. It is tempting to speculate that the recurring figure at the end of each phrase was sung to the words of the title.

(*b*) The basic melody of the same

Eight years after 'One o' them Things!', the first three compositions to be published as blues appeared. Like the rags of 1896, they appeared in different cities. Handy's 'Memphis Blues', by far the most famous of them, is still a rag, though part of it is cast in the twelve-bar blues form. Blues and rags remained, as they had been from the first, inextricably connected.

With the publication of the first blues the materials of the twentieth-century popular composer were complete. Since then popular music has helped itself to various folk styles, taken hints from classical music, and combined existing styles in all sorts of ways. It has striven to maintain a sense of breathless novelty. But it has come up with nothing that, fundamentally, cannot be traced back to 1900 or earlier.

SOME FINAL REFLECTIONS

> I have yet to see any problem, however complicated, which, when
> you looked at it in the right way, did not become still more
> complicated.
>
> Poul Anderson[1]

THE belief in progress has taken some bad knocks since Victorian times,
and nowhere more so than in the arts. It is positively chic nowadays to
admire art that would have been regarded fifty years ago—or far more
recently—as primitive or archaic: to prefer it, in fact, to supposedly
more advanced styles. There is no arguing with such attitudes. By no
reasoning could one prove that classical Greek art, for instance, is better
than archaic Greek art; or the other way round, for that matter. One
could argue that it is more realistic, more polished, more graceful—but
here one is talking, not about vague matters of taste, but about
technique. In the matter of technique, progress is as much a part of the
arts as it is of technology. Well, perhaps 'progress' is rather a loaded term
here. Let us say, instead, 'evolution'. The arts evolve. They get bigger, or
more refined, or more powerful—at any rate, more something, which at
the time is felt to be an improvement. Whether *we* think it is an
improvement is beside the point.

This book has been about just such a process of evolution, or rather
many intimately connected processes. The most obvious examples have
been tune-patterns like the 'Gregory Walker' chord scheme, the twelve-
bar blues, and the thirty-two-bar song. The basis of the pattern is
different in each case: harmonic with Gregory Walker, partially
harmonic with the twelve-bar blues, and mainly a matter of phrase-
rhythms with the thirty-two-bar song. But always the pattern begins
with small, compact tunes and gradually expands until it can get no
bigger. In just the same way the little binary tunes of the late sixteenth
century gradually expand into Baroque dance movements, and then into
the Classical sonata form, until eventually they reach the proportions of
Beethoven's 'Eroica' Symphony.

But one cannot simply blow a musical form up like a balloon. At every
stage of expansion the musical language must change a little to sustain the
form, so that by the time the form reaches its final extent the language is

---

[1] Quoted in Koestler, 'Rhine's Impact on Philosophy', in *Kaleidoscope*, p. 311.

something very different from what it was at the beginning. To sustain the growth of the sixteenth-century chord strings like the *passamezzo antico* or Gregory Walker, composers had to inflate chords into localized cadences; and after these chord strings got as big as they could go, this system of localized cadences continued to develop into the Baroque system of tonality. As sonata form grew out of Baroque dance movements composers came to rely more and more on long-continued stretches on one chord, usually the dominant; and, once again, this device continued to be used after the sonata ceased to be a living form—in Wagner, for instance, and after him in Debussy and even later composers. In similar ways the thirty-two-bar song developed an interesting style of chromatic harmony to sustain interest during its long-drawn-out phrases, and it is quite likely that the blues mode developed partly to support the twelve-bar blues as it got longer and longer; though the origins of the blues are so complex and obscure that I offer this last suggestion with a certain hesitancy.

In short, then, a change of scale also means a change in basic musical resource; in fact, in basic musical syntax. Whether or not they are connected with such a change of scale, there are several such trends, already observable in the nineteenth century, that have continued to grow in the twentieth. The most obvious are:

1. The weakening of the opposition between tonic and dominant. Closely related to this there is a diminishing in importance of the role of harmonic cadences in general. Already early in the nineteenth century it is noticeable that there are fewer and fewer half closes in the waltz, and in the parlour music of the late nineteenth century the distinction between cadences and local modulations is becoming blurred. The half close is likewise rare in the blues (non-existent in the regular twelve-bar form); and in the blues, as we have seen, *harmonic* cadences sometimes disappear altogether, the cadential function being assigned solely to the melody over a static tonic chord.

2. The supplanting in importance of the dominant by the subdominant. This, again, is a feature shared by parlour music and the blues. Both this and the previous tendency continued into the twentieth century.

3. The blurring of the distinction between major and minor, whether 'tonic' or 'relative'. In the blues the distinction between major and minor on the same tonic breaks down completely, and even in parlour music there is a hint of a tendency in this direction. The distinction between relative major and minor is often of the vaguest in folk music, both British and American, and begins to weaken in parlour music too towards the end of the nineteenth century.

4. The increasingly important role of modality in holding the music together. Here again there is a parallel between developments in the

blues and those in parlour music. At the same time as melody develops these modal patterns it becomes uncoupled, so to speak, from harmony. More and more, it comes to be felt that the melody should not reflect the harmony too closely. This also is a tendency that continues into the twentieth century.

5. The increasing emphasis on cross-rhythms.

How does one explain such tendencies? Obviously a full explanation, if such a thing were possible, would be monstrously complicated, but there are certain partial explanations that suggest themselves. To begin with, the simple desire on the part of composers to go one better, either on the works of their competitors or on their own previous efforts. It is extremely difficult to explain why trends *start*, but such an explanation goes a long way towards explaining why they continue. It is not necessary that the process should be conscious—indeed, most of the time it is completely unconscious. The composer exaggerates an admired effect, without necessarily realizing that he is doing so.

The theory of matrices, outlined in chapter 10, may help to elucidate these tendencies a little further. I have already invoked it in connection with the twelve-bar blues; it also casts considerable light on the development of parlour modality. In particular the concepts of bound-upness and at-oddness will help us to understand the appeal of the parlour modes. From the start the essence of the parlour mode was that it was a self-sufficient melodic pattern at odds with the harmony. As the feeling for the modes grew, so the at-oddness increased. But the at-oddness was balanced by the binding effect of these modes. They bound melodies together, they bound harmonies together, and they bound together separate passages in different modes. It was, if you like, a logical step in a process of evolution that had been going on for a thousand years; first the single melodic line, then melodic lines in parallel, then melodic lines at odds with each other but unified by a common harmony, and finally melody and harmony at odds with each other but united in a more complex synthesis.

The word 'evolution' naturally brings to mind biological analogies. And it is true that the arts often behave strikingly like living organisms. But, after all, an art form is not a living thing; it cannot die like an organism or become extinct like a species. The most that can happen to it is to be forgotten, and even that is difficult with modern techniques of notation and recording. Hence the absurdity of statements about 'the breakdown of the major-minor system in the early twentieth century', or the like. The major-minor system is an abstraction. It cannot break down, any more than the multiplication table or Pythagoras's theorem could. The most we can say is that some composers found a way to do without it. The evolutions described in this book are, in fact, a series of discoveries. In essence, they have more in common with, say, the development of the locomotive from 1820 to the present than with the evolution of a species of plant or animal. Of course, the analogy with technological development collapses as soon as we start equating evolution with progress, and progress with improvement. A modern electric locomotive is undoubtedly a vast improvement on an early nineteenth-century steam engine, though it may lack the latter's charm. Who could, nowadays, say the same for a parallel case in the arts?

The above somewhat random remarks hardly claim to account for the development of the popular style. I have not touched on such factors as 'creative fragmentation', or the related process whereby subordinate parts are thrust into prominence; nor on the mutual influence of different cultures, whether African and European, rural and urban, or 'folk' and 'bourgeois'; nor on those class issues by which Marxists set so much store. I have not even touched on the question of why the United States of America has played such a large part in the process. As its title suggests, this chapter is merely a series of reflections—my original plan was to call it 'Conclusions', but the more I thought about the matter, the less there seemed that could be positively concluded.

How is it, for instance, that we find so many parallel lines of development between parlour music and the blues? Quite a few of these parallels can be explained by direct parlour influence on the blues. Recent research has tended to show that there was far more mutual influence between supposedly separate genres—particularly between country and town music, in both Britain and America—than used to be thought. But even allowing for all such possible influence, it still remains a puzzle. The whole development of the popular style, as recounted in these pages, tempts one to invoke a mystical Spirit of History. Though we are entitled to feel awe at the processes of history, this temptation should be sternly resisted. But, though history may not be mystical, it is undeniably mysterious. The hints flung out above only begin to approach its complexity and subtlety. As J. B. S. Haldane said of the universe, it is not only queerer than we suppose, but queerer than we possibly could suppose.[2]

[2] *Possible Worlds*, p. 286.

LIST OF MUSICAL EXAMPLES

No.

by Arthur S. Alberts at Elmina Castle, Gold Coast (now Ghana), in 1949. It appears in conjunction with 'Long John', an American worksong rather similar to 10(*b*); Richard A. Waterman was the first to point out the resemblance.

(*b*) 'Goin' Home' (complete). Transposed down a major third. J. and A. Lomax, *American Ballads and Folk Songs*, pp. 84–5.

11. 'Show Pity, Lord!' (complete). Original pitch. Randolph, *Ozark Folk-songs*, vol. 4, 'Religious Songs and Other Items', p. 70. Sung by Mrs Marie Wilbur, of Pineville, Missouri, in 1927. She said it was popular in Ozark churches in the 1890s.

12. The two-note mode.

13. 'Gwineter Harness in de Mornin' Soon' (complete). Transposed up a fourth. In the original the note in the fourth bar is given as a dotted minim. J. and A. Lomax, *American Ballads and Folk Songs*, p. 47.

14. 'Go 'way f'om mah Window' (complete). Transposed down a fourth. Sandburg, *The American Songbag*, p. 377.

15. Cable's worksong (complete). Transposed down an octave. Cable, 'The Dance in Place Congo', p. 523.

16. (*a*) 'The Maid Freed from the Gallows' (beginning). Transposed down a tone. Smith, *South Carolina Ballads*, p. 144.

(*b*) 'Hangman' (complete). Original pitch. Sandburg, *The American Songbag*, p. 385.

17. 'Way over in the New Buryin' Groun'' (complete). Transposed up a major sixth. Sandburg, *The American Songbag*, p. 473. From the collection of R. W. Gordon; recorded on the Georgia coast.

18. 'Pretty Polly', variant M (complete). Transposed up a fourth. The note at the end of bar 8 is a crotchet in the original. Sharp, *English Folk Songs from the Southern Appalachians*, vol. 1, p. 324. Sung by Mr Jim Samples, of Manchester, Kentucky, in 1917.

19. (*a*) 'Go to Sleep' (complete). Transposed up a fourth. On the Library of Congress Archive of Folk Culture recording *Afro-American Blues and Game Songs*, AFS-L 4. Sung by Harriet McClintock, who was born a slave, in 1940; recorded by John A. and Ruby T. Lomax and Ruby Pickens Tartt.

(*b*) 'Hush-You-Bye' (end). Transposed up a fifth. A. Lomax, *The Penguin Book of American Folk Songs*, p. 59. From the singing of Lomax's Texan mother.

20. (*a*) Blue seventh: 'Freight Train Blues' (end). Transposed up a tone in the original notation. Cohen, *Long Steel Rail*, p. 446. Sung by Clara Smith in 1924.

(*b*) Blue sixth: 'M. and O. Blues' (second line). Transposed up a fifth in the original notation. Titon, *Early Downhome Blues*, p. 95. Sung by Willie Brown in 1930.

21. (*a*) 'Got the Blues, Can't be Satisfied' (second line). Transposed up a major third in the original notation. Titon, *Early Downhome Blues*, p. 81. Sung by Mississippi John Hurt in 1928.

(*b*) 'The Banks of Fordie' (end). Transposed down a fourth. Mother-

No.

well, *Minstrelsy: Ancient and Modern* (1827), no. 26.

22. 'Olúrómbí' (beginning). Pitch as in original notation. The original has a time signature of '24', i.e., counting all the pulses between the double bar-lines. Kubik, 'Àló—Yoruba Story Songs', p. 23.

23. 'City of Refuge' (complete). Transposed down a fifth. White, *American Negro Folk-Songs*, p. 407. Sung by Ed Lloyd.

24. 'Maḍé yi vódú yọ́wé' (beginning). Pitch as in original notation. A drum part has been omitted. Locke and Agbeli, 'A Study of the Drum Language in Adzogbo', p. 38.

25. 'Kuro'i nyẹ mo dea' (beginning). Pitch as in original notation. Nketia, *African Music in Ghana*, p. 71.

26. (*a*) 'Ọnyẹ ampa ara' (beginning). Pitch as in original notation. Turkson, 'Effutu Asafo Music', p. 211.

    (*b*) Tie-shuffling chant (complete). Transposed down a fourth. J. and A. Lomax, *American Ballads and Folk Songs*, p. 15

    (*c*) 'Ọl'ọ́kọ́ d'ẹhìn' (beginning). Pitch as in original notation. The original has a time signature of '24', as in Ex. 22, and the solo is designated 'cantor'. Kubik, 'Àló—Yoruba Story Songs', p. 28.

27. Watutsi song (beginning). Transposed down a minor third. A few irregularly disposed bar-lines in the original have been omitted. Brandel, *The Music of Central Africa*, p. 162.

28. Cornfield holler (beginning). Transposed down a tone. Oliver, *The Story of the Blues*, p. 169. Sung by Thomas Marshall.

29. Keen for a dead child (beginning). Transposed up a tone. On *The Columbia World Library of Folk and Primitive Music: Ireland* (Columbia CSP AKL 4941). Sung by Kitty Gallagher, of Donegal, Ireland, who learnt it from an old woman.

30. 'Run Sinner' (beginning and end). Transposed up a minor third. On *Leadbelly: The Library of Congress Recordings* (Elektra EKL-301/2), side 4, track 2. Sung by Huddie Ledbetter, and recorded by John A. and Alan Lomax.

31. Chanted sermon (extract). Transposed up a minor third. On the Library of Congress Archive of Folk Culture recording *Negro Religious Songs and Services*, AFS-L 10. Recorded on Easter Day, 1934, at Darrington State Farm (a prison farm), Sandy Point, Texas. The preacher was 'Sin-Killer' Griffin.

32. (*a*) Hausa praise song (extract). Transposed up a minor third. A drum part has been omitted. Besmer, 'Hausa Court Music', p. 339, bars 41–4.

    (*b*) Sermon extract. Transposed up a minor third. Rosenberg. *The Art of the American Folk Preacher*, p. 38.

33. (*a*) 'Mkwaze mmodzi' (beginning and end). Transposed down a tone. On *The Music of Africa: Osborn Award, 1958*. Sung by G. Mwale of Nyasaland (now Malawi), to his own accompaniment on the mbira (strictly speaking, the type known as the *sansi*). The transcription is based on suggestions by Andrew Tracey, of the International Library of African Music.

    (*b*) Beginning of the same, in an alternative notation.

No.
34. 'I've Got a Boy Child' (beginning). Transposed up a minor third. On the Library of Congress Archive of Folk Culture recording *Afro-American Blues and Game Songs*, AFS–L 4. Sung by Jim Henry at the State Penitentiary, Parchman, Mississippi, 1937; recorded by John A. Lomax. On the original recording it is called 'I Don't Mind the Weather'.
35. 'Captain Holler Hurry' (beginning). Original pitch. In the original the first three notes of bar 13 are given as a triplet, and the second note of bar 20 is not dotted; probably mistakes for what is given here. Courlander, *Negro Folk Music, U.S.A.*, p. 265.
36. 'Joe Turner' (complete). Original pitch. Sandburg, *The American Songbag*, p. 241.
37. 'Tukhong'ine tulauya' (extract). Transposed down a major third. On *The Music of Africa: Tanganyika Territory*. Sung by P. Mkawa, accompanying himself on the *ligombo* zither, with percussive accompaniment by his son on the gourd of the zither; from the Hehe tribe, Tanganyika Territory (now Tanzania).
38. 'Alberta' (beginning). Transposed up a tone. On *Leadbelly* (Columbia C 30035). Recorded by Huddie Ledbetter in 1935, probably under the supervision of John A. and Alan Lomax (according to a sleeve note).
39. Arap Kapero's song (beginning). Transposed down a semitone. On *The Music of Africa: Kenya*. The cover notes do not give details of the words of this piece, merely describing it as a 'topical song'. From the Nandi tribe of Kenya. The instrument is the *kibugandet* lyre.
40. 'Late Last Night' (beginning). Transposed up a tone. On *The Finest of Folk Bluesmen*. Performed by John Lee Hooker in 1949.
41. 'Chemirocha' (beginning). Transposed up a semitone. On *The Music of Africa: Kenya*. Sung by two young girls of the Kipsigis tribe, Kenya, to the accompaniment of the Chepkong lyre. (The second voice, which supplies a simple ostinato, is omitted.) It seems that they had heard a recording by Jimmy Rodgers, the country and western singer (died 1933) and were so impressed that they composed this praise song in his honour.
42. 'Genuine Negro Jig' (beginning). Original pitch. From a manuscript collection left by Dan Emmet, undated but estimated as from 1845–60. Quoted in Nathan, 'Early Banjo Tunes and American Syncopation', p. 464.
43. 'Susie Q' (beginning). Accompaniment transposed up an augmented fourth, voice transposed down a diminished fifth. The notes in the accompaniment doubling the voice have been omitted. *Solid Gold Rock and Roll*, p. 100 (title given as 'Suzie-Q'). Words and music by Dale Hawkins, Stanley. J. Lewis, and Eleanor Broadwater, 1957.
44. Drum pattern 1.
45. Drum pattern 2.
46. African harp accompaniment pattern (complete). Pitch as in original notation. Kubik, 'Harp Music of the Azande', p. 48.
47. Drum pattern 3.
48. Drum pattern 4.

No.
49. Drum pattern 5.
50.   (*a*) Bach, Partita in E minor, Courante (beginning) with (*b*) the same, in an alternative notation. Transposed up a fourth. In the original notation the two parts appear on separate staves.
51. 'The Reel of Tulloch' (bars 81–4). Transposed up a minor third. *A Curious Collection of Scots Tunes*, pp. 4–5. Published in 1759.
52. 'Marty Inglehart Jig' (complete). Original pitch. *Kendall's Clarinet Instruction Book*, Boston, 1845. By Dan Emmet. Quoted in Nathan, 'Early Banjo Tunes and American Syncopation', p. 465, Ex. 21.
53. 'Soldier, Soldier' (end of tune). Transposed down a minor third. On *The World Library of Folk and Primitive Music: Ireland* (Columbia CSP AKL 4941). Sung by Colme Keane.
54. 'Cripple Creek' (beginning, after some introductory chords). Transposed down a fifth. On *Instrumental Music of the Southern Appalachians* (Tradition Records: TLP 1007). Played by Hobart Smith.
55.   (*a*) 'Tom Brigg's Jig' (extract) with (*b*) the same, in an alternative notation. Transposed down a tone. From a manuscript collection left by Dan Emmet, undated but estimated at from 1845–60. Quoted in Nathan, 'Early Banjo Tunes and American Syncopation', p. 462, Ex. 12.
56.   (*a*) 'Dr. Hekok Jig' (beginning) with (*b*) a blues transformation of the same. Transposed down a fifth. Quoted in Nathan, 'Early Banjo Tunes and American Syncopation', p. 471. Of mid-nineteenth-century origin, though Nathan does not specify the exact source.
57.   (*a*) 'Pea Patch Jig' (extract) with (*b*) a blues transformation of the same. Transposed down a tone. *Kendall's Clarinet Instruction Book*, Boston, 1845. By Dan Emmet. Quoted in Nathan, 'Early Banjo Tunes and American Syncopation', p. 462, Ex. 15.
    (*c*) 'Alberta' (beginning) and (*d*) (near end). See Ex. 38.
58. 'Hilarity Rag' (bars 49–52). Transposed down a semitone. *Classic Piano Rags*, p. 271. By James Scott, 1910.
59.   (*a*) 'Who's Gonna Shoe your Pretty Little Feet?' (beginning), straight and (*b*) the same, jazzed up. Transposed down a tone. The rhythm has been changed from $\frac{3}{4}$ to $\frac{4}{4}$. Adapted from A. Lomax, *The Folk Songs of North America*, p. 216.
60. Charley Patton, 'Pony Blues' (second line). Transposed down a major third. Evans, *Big Road Blues*, p. 147.
61.   (*a*) 'Honky Tonk Women' (second line). Transposed down a fifth. Jagger and Richard, *Rolling Stones: Through the Past Darkly*, p. 2.
    (*b*) 'It's Always You' (beginning). Pitch as in original notation. A Benny Goodman clarinet solo, on the Columbia record 36680. Quoted in Waterman, ' "Hot" Rhythm in Negro Music', p. 32.
62. 'Fanny Blair' (beginning). Transposed down a fifth. Sharp and Marson, *Folk Songs from Somerset*, vol. 5, pp. 43–4.
63. 'Dives and Lazarus' (complete). Transposed down a major third. From the Cecil Sharp manuscript collection. Collected in 1911. Quoted in Bronson, *Traditional Tunes of the Child Ballads*, vol. 2, p. 20.

No.

64. 'Biglitār' (complete). Pitch as in original notation. Fox Strangways, *The Music of Hindostan*, pp. 54–5.

65. (*a*) 'Hangèd I shall be' (English, beginning). Transposed down a tone. Palmer, *The Book of English Country Songs*, p. 107. Sung by 'Shepherd' Taylor, Hickling, Norfolk; collected by E. K. Moeran in 1921.

   (*b*) 'Cradle Song' (Scottish, complete). Transposed down a fifth. Smith, *The Scotish* [sic] *Minstrel*, vol. 1, p. 93; *c*.1821.

66. (*a*) 'Got dem Blues' (beginning). Original pitch. Sandburg, *The American Songbag*, p. 232. Collected by Henry Francis Parks.

   (*b*) 'Get along Home, Cindy' (complete). Transposed down a minor third. Randolph, *Ozark Folksongs*, vol. 3, 'Humorous and Play-Party Songs', p. 376. Contributed by Mrs Rose Wilder Lane, of Mansfield, Missouri, in 1930.

67. (*a*) Praeludium no. xxv from *The Fitzwilliam Virginal Book* (end). Original pitch. Anonymous. Appears in vol. 1, p. 86, of the Breitkopf and Härtel edition.

   (*b*) Purcell, Fantasia no. 7 (beginning), original pitch, *The Works of Henry Purcell*, vol. 31, p. 16. Spelt 'Fantazia' in the original.

   (*c*) Dvořák, String Quartet Op. 34 (beginning). Transposed down a tone. There are slight differences in the bass on repeating.

68. (*a*) Byrd, 'John Come Kiss Me Now' Variations (end of var. 6). Transposed up a fourth. *The Fitzwilliam Virginal Book*, vol. 1, p. 49.

   (*b*) Bach, English Suite in A minor, Bourée II (beginning). Transposed up a minor third.

   (*c*) Handel, Dead March from *Saul* (beginning). Original pitch. Reduction from the full score.

   (*d*) Chopin, Mazurka in G♯ minor/C♯ minor, Op. 6, no. 2 (beginning). Transposed up a diminished fourth.

69. (*a*) 'The Bonny Bunch of Roses' (Scottish folk tune, beginning). Original pitch. Buchan and Hall, *The Scottish Folksinger*, p. 148; originally from Christie, *Traditional Ballad Airs*, 1876.

   (*b*) Purcell, 'A Pastoral Elegy on the Death of Mr. John Playford' (bars 51–3). Original pitch. The original has the voice part and an unfigured bass. *The Works of Henry Purcell*, vol. 25, p. 51.

70. Chuck Berry, 'Sweet Little Sixteen' (beginning). Original pitch. *Solid Gold Rock and Roll*, p. 97, where it appears to the words of 'Surfin' U.S.A.', by Brian Wilson. The original words have been restored from a sound recording.

71. 'Gloria Tibi Trinitas' (complete). Transposed down a tone. Transcribed from Gregorian notation. *Liber Usualis*, p. 914.

72. 'Le Petit Roysin' (complete). Transposed down a tone. Originally notated in breves. A *basse danse* from a Burgundian manuscript of about 1470, in Closson, *Le Manuscrit dit des Basses Danses de la Bibliothèque de Bourgogne*; f. 14r of the original manuscript.

73. (*a*) 'Barbara Allen' (Newfoundland version, complete). Transposed up a fourth. Peacock, *Songs of the Newfoundland Outports*, vol. 3, p. 660, variant F. Sung by William Nash in 1961.

No.

(*b*) Barbara Allen (Appalachian version, complete). Transposed down a major third. On the Library of Congress Archive of Folk Culture recording AFS-F 1. Sung by Rebecca Tarwater, of Rockwood, Tennessee, in 1936. She learnt it from her mother.

(*c*) 'Every Night when the Sun Goes in' (white blues, complete). Transposed down a fifth. The words are those of the refrain. Sharp, *English Folk Songs from the Southern Appalachians*, vol. 2, p. 268. Sung by Mrs Effie Mitchell, of Burnsville, North Carolina, in 1918.

(*d*) 'Blin' Man Stood on de Way an' Cried' (spiritual, complete). Original pitch. The note values have been doubled. J. and A. Lomax, *American Ballads and Folk Songs*, p. 596.

(*e*) 'One Kind Favour' (folk blues, complete). Original pitch, One-chord guitar accompaniment omitted. On the Library of Congress Archive of Folk Culture recording *Afro-American Blues and Game Songs*, AFS-L 4, where it is called 'Two White Horses'. ('One Kind Favour' is the more usual title.) Performed by Smith Casey of Brazoria, Texas, in 1939; recorded by John A. and Ruby T. Lomax.

74.   (*a*) 'Fareweel tae Tarwathie' (complete). Transposed up a fourth. Buchan and Hall, *The Scottish Folksinger*, p. 104. According to a note, 'By George Scroggie; oral version from John Sinclair of Ballater (collected by A. L. Lloyd).'

(*b*) 'Rye Whiskey' (complete). Transposed up a fourth. Randolph, *Ozark Folksongs*, vol. 3, 'Humorous and Play-Party Songs', p. 136. Sung by Miss Billie Baxter, of Argenta, Arkansas, in 1917.

(*c*) 'The Noble Skewball' (complete). Transposed up a fourth. Scarborough, *On the Trail of Negro Folk-Songs*, p. 63.

75.   'Barbro Allen' (complete). Transposed down a minor third. Edmands, 'Songs from the Mountains of North Carolina', p. 132. From Roan Mountain, North Carolina. Quoted in Bronson, *Traditional Tunes of the Child Ballads*, vol. 2, p. 358.

76.   (*a*) 'Tattie Jock' (complete). Transposed down a fifth. The last verse. Buchan and Hall, *The Scottish Folksinger*, pp. 24–5.

(*b*) 'Single Girl' (complete). Transposed down a fifth. Sharp, *English Folk Songs from the Southern Appalachians*, vol. 2, p. 33, variant C. Sung by Alice and Sudie Sloan, of Barbourville, Kentucky, in 1917.

(*c*) 'Josie' (complete). Original pitch. Sandburg, *The American Songbag*, p. 84.

(*d*) 'Frankie' (Mississippi John Hurt version, complete). Transposed down a fifth. Guitar accompaniment omitted. Evans, *Big Road Blues*, p. 45. Recorded by Mississippi John Hurt in 1928.

77.   'Frankie and Albert' (complete). Original pitch. Scarborough, *On the Trail of Negro Folk-Songs*, p. 84.

78.   'I Went to the Hop-Joint' (complete). Transposed up a tone. Ibid., p. 90. In the original the third-last bar is notated | ♪♪♪♪♪|, probably a mistake for my notation.

79.   (*a*) 'Rue the Day' (complete). Pitch as in original notation. Kennedy, *Folksongs of Britain and Ireland*, p. 470. Sung by Lucy Stewart of

No.

Fetterangus, Aberdeenshire, in 1955.

(*b*) 'Sorghum Syrup' (complete). Transposed down a tone. A. Lomax, *The Folk Songs of North America*, p. 255. Sung by Alec Moore, a cowboy, of Austin, Texas.

80. 'Tight like That' (complete). Transposed up a semitone. On *Leadbelly: The Library of Congress Recordings* (Elektra EKL-301/2). Performed by Huddie Ledbetter to his own guitar accompaniment; recorded by John A. and Alan Lomax. Some of the words are unintelligible.

81. 'Long Tall Sally' (complete). Transposed down a fourth. The bass is doubled at the octave below for the first four bars, and is then itself an octave lower for the rest of the piece. The piano doubles the voice, except for the last bar. *A Hundred Golden Oldies*, pp. 136–7. Words and music by Enotris Johnson, Richard Penniman ('Little Richard'), and Robert Blackwell, 1956.

82. 'Pretty Polly', variant T (complete). Transposed down a tone from the original notation. Sharp, *English Folk Songs from the Southern Appalachians*, vol. 1, p. 327. Sung by Mrs Frances Richards, of Callaway, Virginia, in 1918.

83. 'Po' Lazarus' (complete). Transposed down a third. A. Lomax, *The Folk Songs of North America*, p. 567.

84. (*a*) 'The Birmingham Boys' (complete). Pitch as in original notation. Kennedy, *Folksongs of Britain and Ireland*, p. 451. Sung by Harry Cox, of Catfield, Norfolk, in 1953.

(*b*) 'John Henry' (I, complete). Transposed down a tone. Sandburg, *The American Songbag*, p. 24.

(*c*) 'John Henry' (II, complete). Transposed up a minor third. J. and A. Lomax, *American Ballads and Folk Songs*, p. 5.

(*d*) 'John Henry' (knife blues, complete). Transposed down a major third. On *Instrumental Music of the Southern Appalachians* (Tradition Records: TLP 1007). Performed by Etta Baker on the knife (or 'bottleneck') guitar.

85. 'Lady Cassilles Lilt' (complete). Transposed down a major ninth. Some notes are doubled at the octave below in the original. No. 30 in the Skene manuscript (*c.*1620) where it appears as an instrumental piece. Quoted in Bronson, *Traditional Tunes of the Child Ballads*, vol. 3, p. 201.

86. (*a*) Standard blues pattern.

(*b*) Common variant, e.g. 'Long Tall Sally', Ex. 81.

(*c*) The one-chord type, e.g. 'Pretty Polly', Ex. 82.

(*d*) One chord, except for the perfect cadence, e.g. 'Josie', Ex. 76(*c*).

(*e*) The 'Frankie' pattern.

(*f*) The 'Railroad Bill' pattern.

87. (*a*) 'Up and Ware Them A Willie' (beginning). Transposed down a major sixth. Oswald, *The Caledonian Pocket Companion*, vol. 3, p. 1, *c.*1751.

(*b*) 'Jimmy Rose' (complete). Original pitch. Scarborough, *On the Trail of Negro Folk-Songs*, p. 100.

No.
      (*c*) Underlying melodic pattern.
88. 'Darling Nelly Gray' (verse only; chorus omitted). Transposed down a minor third. *Popular Songs of Nineteenth-Century America*, p. 54. By Benjamin Hanby, 1856.
89.   (*a*) Gregory Walker.
      (*b*) The American Gregory Walker.
90. 'Jesse James' (verse only; chorus omitted). Transposed down a fifth. A. Lomax, *The Penguin Book of American Folk Songs*, p. 103.
91.   (*a*) Gregory Walker accompaniment adapted to the twelve-bar blues.
      (*b*) The same, adapted to the 'Railroad Bill' pattern.
92. Football crowd chant.
93. Arab tune (complete). Pitch as in original notation. Fox Strangways, *The Music of Hindostan*, p. 37. Recorded from Arab boatmen landing on the Indian coast.
94. 'Donald MacGillavry' (complete). Transposed up a fourth. Words omitted. Hogg, *Jacobite Relics*, pp. 100–1.
95. Byrd, 'The Woods so Wild' Variations (theme and end). Original pitch. *The Fitzwilliam Virginal Book*, vol. 1, pp. 263 and 266.
96. Boogie-woogie bass.
97. 'Alfa Yaya' (theme). Transposed up a fifth. Coolen, 'The Wolof Xalam Tradition', p. 494. An 'ideal statement' of the theme, built up from bits of the variations.
98. Music-hall tune (complete as quoted). Original pitch. Quoted in Parry, *Style in Musical Art*, p. 118. He does not give the title or source.
99. Mozart, 'Sechs deutsche Tänze', K600, no. 3, Trio (1791) (complete). Transposed up a tone. Reduction of the original score for small orchestra.
100.   (*a*) Schubert, 'Pause' (beginning). Transposed up a tone. No. 12 in the *Schöne Müllerin* song cycle.
      (*b*) Schubert, 'Des Baches Wiegenlied' (beginning). Transposed down a major third. No. 20 in the *Schöne Müllerin* song cycle.
101.   (*a*) Chopin, Scherzo no. 2 in Bb minor/Db (beginning), with (*b*) a later theme (bars 49 ff.), (*c*) beginning of the Trio, and (*d*) end. Transposed down a semitone. Some octave doublings have been omitted from the opening section, and there are some minor variations in rhythm in the second repeat in section (*b*).
102.   (*a*) Chopin, Mazurka in Bb minor, Op. 24, no. 4 (beginning) and (*b*) end. Transposed up a tone.
103. Lanner, 'Terpsichore Waltz' (extract). Original pitch. The bass, marked for double-bass in the original, has been transposed up an octave, and some octave doublings in the treble have been omitted. Reproduced (as 'Terpsichore-Walzer') in *Denkmäler der Tonkunst in Österreich*, vol. 65, p. 7, first half of no. 5.
104. Strauss, 'The Blue Danube' (beginning of main theme). Transposed down a tone.
105. Sousa, 'The Washington Post' (second strain). Transposed down a fifth. *Sousa's Great Marches*, pp. 23–4.

No.

106. Weill, 'Mack the Knife' (beginning). Original pitch. Piano score. The accompaniment doubles the voice except where the voice has half-bar rests. Weill and Brecht, *Die Dreigroschenoper*, p. 7. Original title: 'Moritat vom Mackie Messer'.

107. Mozart, *Die Zauberflöte*, Papageno's glockenspiel tune (just before the chorus 'Das klinget so herrlich, das klinget so schön!' in the finale to the first act). Transposed down an octave and a fifth.

108. (*a*) Chopin, Mazurka in D♭, Op. 30, no. 3 (bars 9–14). Transposed down a semitone.

(*b*) 'Battle Hymn of the Republic' (same tune as 'John Brown's Body'; beginning of verse). Transposed up a tone. *Popular Songs of Nineteenth-Century America*, p. 23. By Julia Ward Howe. Published in 1862. Described on the title-page as 'Adapted to the favorite Melody'.

(*c*) 'Rock-a-bye Baby' (beginning of chorus). Transposed up a tone. *Favorite Songs of the Nineties*, p. 237. By E. I. Canning. Published in 1886.

(*d*) 'I'm Henery the Eighth, I am' (beginning of chorus). Original pitch. Gammond, *Music Hall Song Book*, p. 114. Words and music by Fred Murray and R. P. Weston.

109. Tchaikovsky, Sixth Symphony, first movement (bars 90–3). Transposed down a tone. Composed in 1893.

110. (*a*) 'Oh! Mr. Porter' (chorus). Transposed up a fourth. Garrett, *Sixty Years of British Music Hall*, no. 26. Words by Thomas Le Brunn, music by George Le Brunn, 1893.

(*b*) Tchaikovsky, Second Symphony, last movement (bars 513–28). Original pitch. The bass is doubled at the octave below.

111. 'Champagne Charlie' (beginning of verse). Original pitch. *Popular Songs of Nineteenth-Century America*, p. 48 (though it is of English origin). Words by George Leybourne, music by Alfred Lee, 1867.

112. 'The White Paternoster' (complete). Transposed down a minor third. Baring-Gould, *Songs of the West*, no. 121, where, however, the tune ends on the tonic, not the third, as here. He calls it 'Evening Prayer'.

113. 'Andrew Bardeen' (complete). Original pitch. Randolph, *Ozark Folk-songs*, vol. 1, 'British Ballads and Songs', p. 177. Contributed by Bruce Evans, of Rogersville, Missouri, in 1934; said to be of Kentucky origin.

114. 'Pains in my Fingers' (complete). Original pitch. Scarborough, *On the Trail of Negro Folk-Songs*, p. 167.

115. 'Cowboy's Challenge' (complete). Original pitch. Belden, *Ballads and Folk Songs*, p. 399.

116. (*a*) 'The Golden Victory' (I, beginning). Transposed down a minor third in the original notation. Bronson, *Traditional Tunes of the Child Ballads*, vol. 4, p. 326, no. 33. From the archives of the School of Scottish Studies. Sung by Dodie Chalmers, of Forglen, Banffshire, in 1958. Collected by Hamish Henderson and transcribed by Francis Collinson.

(*b*) 'The Golden Victory' (II, beginning). Transposed up a major third in the original notation. In the original the rhythmic valves of bars 5 and 6 are given as | ♪♪ ♫♫ | ♪ᵧ♫ | . Ibid., pp. 326–7, no. 34. From the

No.

archives of the School of Scottish Studies. Sung by Jeannie Robertson, of Aberdeen, in 1957. Collected by Hamish Henderson and transcribed by James Porter.

117. (*a*) 'Come Ashore Jolly Tar and your Trousers on' (bars 9–16). Transposed down a major third. *A Selection of Scotch, English, Irish and Foreign Airs*, vol. 1, p. 66, 1782.

   (*b*) 'The Cuckoo's Nest' (chorus). Palmer, *The Book of English Country Songs*, p. 155. The compiler writes: 'The melody I have used is from the notebooks of John Clare, a poet who was also an accomplished fiddler, in demand for village merrymakings.'

118. 'Corinna' (complete). Transposed up a fourth. A. Lomax, *The Folk Songs of North America*, p. 588.

119. (*a*) Mozart, String Trio in Eb, first movement (bars 27–30).

   (*b*) Scott Joplin, 'A Breeze from Alabama' (beginning of first strain). Original pitch. Bass transposed up an octave; middle parts omitted. *Scott Joplin: Complete Piano Works*, p. 54. Subtitled 'March and Two-step'. Published in 1902.

120. Mozart, 'Sechs deutsche Tänze', K600, no. 2, Trio (1791) (beginning). Transposed up a fifth.

121. Parlour chords, produced by the divergence of melody and harmony.

122. (*a*) Johann Strauss, 'Wine, Woman, and Song' (no. 4, section in Eb, bars 1–4). Transposed down a minor third. Composed in 1869.

   (*b*) 'The Band Played on' (beginning of chorus). Transposed up a minor third. *Favorite Songs of the Nineties*, p. 18. Words by John F. Palmer, music by Charles B. Ward, 1895.

   (*c*) Johann Strauss, 'Morgenblätter' (no. 2, bar 9–16). Original pitch. Composed in 1864.

   (*d*) Johann Strauss, 'Artist's Life' (bars 3–10). Original pitch. Composed in 1867.

123. Chopin, Waltz in Db, Op. 70, no. 3 (beginning) (1829). Transposed down a semitone.

124. 'Ain't You Coming Back to Old New Hampshire, Molly?' (beginning). Transposed up a fourth. *Song Hits from the Turn of the Century*, p. 2. Words by Robert F. Roden, music by J. F. Helf, 1906.

125. Liszt, 'Liebestraum' no. III (beginning). Transposed up a major third. The second ending to the theme occurs in the section in B major, marked 'Più animato, con passione'. Composed in 1850.

126. 'Sweet Georgia Brown' (first half of chorus). Transposed up a fourth. *A Hundred Best Songs of the 20's and 30's*, p. 77. By Ben Bernie, Maceo Pinkard, and Kenneth Casey, 1925.

127. 'The Holy City' (bars 9–18). Transposed up a tone. *Song Hits from the Turn of the Century*, pp. 102–4. Words by F. E. Weatherly, music by Stephen Adams (real name Michael Maybrick), 1892.

128. 'Daisy Bell' (bars 21–44). Transposed up a fourth. *Favorite Songs of the Nineties*, pp. 66–7. Words and music by Harry Dacre (real name Henry Decker), 1892.

No.

129. 'Day by Day' (beginning of verse). Original pitch. The tie between bars 7 and 8 is missing in the original. *Song Hits from the Turn of the Century*, pp. 46–7. Words and music by Tony Stanford, 1900.

130. 'My Cosey Corner Girl' (bars 25–44). Transposed down a fourth. *Song Hits from the Turn of the Century*, pp. 188–90. Words by C. N. Douglas, music by J. W. Bratton, 1903.

131.   (*a*) 'Cheyenne' (bars 9–16) and (*b*) beginning of chorus. Transposed up a fourth. *Song Hits from the Turn of the Century*, pp. 29 and 32. Words by Harry Williams, music by Egbert Van Alstyne, 1905.

132. Auber, *Fra Diavolo* (Romanza, no. 14, bars 1–6) (1830). Transposed down a fifth.

133. 'Oh! That Gorgonzola Cheese' (second half of introduction). Original pitch. Garrett, *Sixty Years of British Music Hall*, no. 29. Words by F. W. Leigh, music by Harry Champion, 1894.

134.   (*a*) 'I'd Leave ma Happy Home for You' (bars 13–16). Transposed up a fourth. *Song Hits from the Turn of the Century*, p. 121. Words by Will A. Heelan, music by Harry Von Tilzer, 1899.

   (*b*) 'Narcissus' (bars 3–6). Transposed up a major third. *Song Hits from the Turn of the Century*, p. 207. By Ethelbert Nevin (Op. 13, no. 4), 1891.

   (*c*) 'Because' (bars 15–22). Original pitch. *Favorite Songs of the Nineties*, pp. 22–3. Words and music by Guy d'Hardelot (real name Mrs Helen Rhodes). Originally a French *chanson*.

135.   (*a*) Foster, 'My Old Kentucky Home' (chorus). Transposed down a fifth. Copyrighted 1853. Turner and Miall, *The Parlour Song Book*, p. 273.

   (*b*) 'The Sidewalks of New York' (beginning of verse). Transposed down a fifth. *Favorite Songs of the Nineties*, p. 260. By C. B. Lawlor and J. W. Blake, 1894.

136.   (*a*) Cadence 2: 'After the Ball' (bars 25–36). Transposed up a tone. *Favorite Songs of the Nineties*, p. 3. Words and music by Charles K. Harris, 1892.

   (*b*) Cadences 4 and 6: 'In the City of Sighs and Tears' (second half of chorus). Transposed up a fourth. *Song Hits from the Turn of the Century*, p. 136. Words by Andrew B. Sterling, music by Kerry Mills, 1902.

   (*c*) Cadence 5: 'The Dream' (bars 33–41). Transposed down a minor third. Turner and Miall, *The Parlour Song Book*, p. 33. Words by Alfred Bunn, music by M. W. Balfe, from the opera *The Bohemian Girl*, 1843. Also known as 'I Dreamt that I Dwelt in Marble Halls'.

   (*d*) Cadence 5: 'Love Me, and the World is Mine' (bars 9–12). Original pitch. *Song Hits from the Turn of the Century*. p. 155. Words by D. Reed, music by E. R. Ball, 1906.

137. 'I Love a Lassie', (*a*) decorated supertonic: bars 11–14, and (*b*) decorated dominant and tonic: bars 19–24. Original pitch. Gammond, *Music Hall Song Book*, pp. 81–2. By Harry Lauder and Gerald Grafton, 1906.

138. Chromatic decoration within a chord: (*a*) tonic, (*b*) dominant.

139. Chromatic decoration between chords: (*a*) I–V, (*b*) V–I, (*c*) I–IV, (*d*) IV–I, (*e*) II$_\sharp^7$–I.

No.

140.   (*a*) Schubert, String Quintet (beginning). Original pitch. Composed 1828.

    (*b*) Barnby, 'Sweet and Low' (beginning). Transposed up a major third. Turner and Miall, *The Parlour Song Book*, p. 367. Words by Tennyson, music by Sir Joseph Barnby.

    (*c*) 'Buy Me Some Almond Rock' (second half of chorus). Transposed down a tone. Garrett, *Sixty Years of British Music Hall*, no. 25. Words and music by Joseph Tabrar, 1893.

141.   (*a*) Chopin, Waltz in A♭, Op. 34, no. 1 (D♭ theme, first eight bars). Transposed down a semitone.

    (*b*) Liszt, 'Liebestraum' no. III (end). Transposed up a major third. Composed in 1850.

    (*c*) 'An Old Man's Darling' (bars 9–12 of introduction). Transposed down a tone. Garrett, *Sixty Years of British Music Hall*, no. 33. Words and music by Fred Murray and George Everard, 1903.

142. Chopin, Nocturne in C minor, Op. 48, no. 1 (end of first section and beginning of second section). Original pitch. Some octave doublings of the bass have been omitted.

143.   (*a*) 'Sweet Adeline' (introduction). Transposed up a tone. *Favorite Songs of the Nineties*, p. 395. Words by Richard H. Gerard, music by Harry Armstrong, 1903. Full title: 'You're the Flower of my Heart, Sweet Adeline'.

    (*b*) 'Hard Headed Woman' (introduction). Transposed up a tone. *The Compleat Elvis*, p. 92. Words and music by Claude De Metruis, 1958.

144. 'Bill Bailey, Won't You Please Come Home?' (chorus). Transposed down a fifth. There are a few passing chromatic chords that have been omitted from the harmony. *Favorite Songs of the Nineties*, pp. 32–3. Words and music by Hughie Cannon, 1902.

145. Bach, *The Little Music Book of Anna Magdalena Bach*, Musette (bars 11–17). Transposed down a tone.

146.   (*a*) Liszt, Piano Concerto no. 1 (second movement, bars 224–31) (*c.*1840).

    (*b*) Mussorgsky, *Boris Godunov* (beginning of Act III) (1869). Transposed down a major third.

    (*c*) Franck, Symphony in D minor (last movement, bars 7–18) (1888). Transposed down a tone.

147. Mozart, *Don Giovanni*, 'Batti, batti' (no. 13, end of aria). Transposed down a fourth.

148. Mozart, *Così fan tutte*, 'Terzetto' (no. 16, bars 43–56) (1791). Transposed up a fourth.

149.   (*a*) Tchaikovsky, *Swan Lake* (waltz from Act I, Scene 2, bars 19–50)

    (*b*) Ibid. (bars 83–90). Transposed up a minor third.

    (*c*) Handy, 'Memphis Blues' (last strain, bars 7–8). Transposed up a tone. Handy, *Father of the Blues*, p. 105. Published in 1912 but written, according to Handy's account, in 1909.

    (*d*) Ibid. (bars 229–33). Transposed up a tone.

No.
150. (*a*) Beethoven, Piano Sonata in G, Op. 14, no. 2, second movement (beginning of theme) with (*b*) beginning of second variation. Original pitch.
151. Suppé, *Poet and Peasant* Overture (bars 111–25). Transposed up a tone.
152. 'Pompey Ran Away' (complete). Transposed up a fourth. *A Selection of Scotch, English, Irish and Foreign Airs*, published in Glasgow in 1782. Reprinted in facsimile in Epstein, *Sinful Tunes and Spirituals*, p. 122. Subtitled 'Negro Jig'.
153. (*a*) 'Johnny Get your Gun' (beginning of 'Dance'). Transposed down a fourth. *Popular Songs of Nineteenth-Century America*, p. 101. Words and music by Monroe H. Rosenfeld, 1886.
    (*b*) 'Possumala Dance' (beginning of chorus) (1894). Transposed down a fourth. Words and music by Irving Jones, 1894.
    (*c*) 'Mississippi Rag' (bars 19–26) (1897). Transposed down a fourth. The ending is that of the repetition of the theme. *Golden Encyclopaedia of Ragtime*, p. 186, by W.H. Krell, 1897.
154. (*a*) Harney, 'You've Been a Good Old Wagon but You've done Broke down' (Second half of chorus). Transposed down a fifth. Words and music by Ben Harney, 1896.
    (*b*) 'Mister Frog' (complete). Transposed down a fifth. The quaver rest in the second bar is missing in the original, and the underlay of the words at the end has been changed to match the first line. Scarborough, *On the Trail of Negro Folk-Songs*, p. 49.
155. Harney 'Mister Johnson' (beginning). Transposed up a fourth. Words and music by Ben Harney, 1896.
156. (*a*) Harney, 'Annie Laurie' (beginning), straight and (*b*) ragged. Transposed down a tone. Accompanying parts omitted. Ben Harney's *Rag Time Instructor*, Exercise no. 2, 1897.
157. (*a*) Sousa, 'Semper Fidelis' (end of the first strain, leading back to repeat). Original pitch. *Sousa's Great Marches*, p. 11. Published in 1888.
    (*b*) Sousa, 'The Washington Post' (end of third strain, leading back to repeat). Original pitch. Ibid., p. 24. Published in 1889.
    (*c*) James Scott, 'Ragtime Oriole' (bars 9–13). Transposed up a major third. The single notes in the bass are doubled at the octave below. *Classic Piano Rags*, p. 273. Published in 1911.
    (*d*) 'Milenberg Joys' (bars 39–44). Transposed down a minor third. The single notes in the bass are doubled at the octave below. *Golden Encyclopaedia of Ragtime*, p. 65. Copyrighted in 1925 as by 'Leon Roppolo, Paul Mares and "Jelly Roll" Morton', but actually dating from the first decade of the century.
158. (*a*) Joplin, 'Maple Leaf Rag' (end of main theme). Transposed up a major third. *Scott Joplin: Complete Piano Works*, p. 26. Published in 1899.
    (*b*) 'King Porter Stomp' (first half of final sixteen bars). Transposed down a semitone. The single notes in the bass are doubled at the octave below. *Golden Encyclopaedia of Ragtime*, p. 63. Published in 1924, but composed in the 1900s.

No.
159.   (*a*) 'One o' them Things!' (first strain) and (*b*) the basic melody of the
same. Original pitch. Some of the single notes in the bass are doubled at
the octave below. *Ragtime Rarities*, p. 64. By James Chapman and Leroy
Smith, 1904.

WORKS CITED

Akpabot, Samuel Ekpe. 'Functional Music of the Ibibio People of Nigeria'. Dissertation, Michigan State University, 1975.

—— 'Theories on African Music', in *African Arts*, vol. 6, no. 1, autumn 1972, pp. 59–62.

Allen, W. F., C. P. Ware, and L. McKim Garrison (editors). *Slave Songs of the United States*. New York: A. Simpson, 1867.

America's Black Past: A Reader in Afro-American History. Edited by Eric Foner. New York: Harper & Row, 1970.

Ames, David W. 'Igbo and Hausa Musicians: A Comparative Examination', in *Ethnomusicology*, vol. 17, no. 2, May 1973, pp. 250–78.

Bailey, Ben E. 'The Lined-Hymn Tradition in Black Mississippi Churches', in *The Black Perspective in Music*, vol. 6, no. 1, spring 1978, pp. 2–17.

Baines, Anthony. *Woodwind Instruments and their History*. Third edition. London: Faber and Faber, 1967.

Baring-Gould, S., H. Fleetwood Sheppard, and F. W. Bussell (editors). *Songs of the West: Folk Songs of Devon & Cornwall Collected from the Mouths of the People*. Fifth edition. London: Methuen, 1905.

Bear, James A., Jr. (editor). *Jefferson at Monticello*. Charlottesville: University Press of Virginia, 1967.

Bebey, Francis. *African Music: A People's Art*. Translated by Josephine Bennett. London: Harrap, 1975; originally published in French by Horizons de France, 1969.

Beier, Ulli. 'The Talking Drums of the Yoruba', in *African Music*, vol. 1, no. 1, 1954, pp. 29–31.

Belden, H. M. (editor). *Ballads and Folk Songs Collected by the Missouri Folk-Lore Society*. Columbia, Missouri: University of Missouri Press, 1940. University of Missouri Studies, vol. 9, no. 1.

Berlin, Edward A. *Ragtime: A Musical and Cultural History*. Los Angeles: University of California Press, 1980.

Berlin, Ira. *Slaves without Masters: The Free Negro in the Antebellum South*. New York: Pantheon Books, 1974.

—— 'Time, Space, and the Evolution of Afro-American Society on British Mainland North America', in *The American Historical Review*, vol. 85, no. 1, February 1980.

Besmer, Fremont Edward. 'Hausa Court Music in Kano, Nigeria'. Dissertation, Teachers College, Columbia University, 1971.

Blacking, John. 'Problems of Pitch, Pattern and Harmony in the Ocarina Music of the Venda', in *African Music*, vol. 2, no. 2, 1959, pp. 15–23.

Blesh, Rudi, and Harriet Janis. *They All Played Ragtime*. Fourth edition. New York: Oak Publications, 1971; originally published by Knopf, New York, 1950.

Blum, Odette. 'Dance in Ghana', in *Dance Perspectives*, no. 56, winter 1973, whole issue.

The Book of the Piano. Edited by Dominic Gill. Oxford: Phaidon, 1981.

Boulter, Hugh. *Letters Written by His Excellency Hugh Boulter, D.D. Lord Primate of Ireland* . . . Oxford: The Clarendon Press, 1769.

Brandel, Rose. *The Music of Central Africa: An Ethnomusicological Study*. The Hague: Nijhoff, 1961.

Brickell, John. *The Natural History of North Carolina*. Dublin: James Carson for the author, 1737.

Bronson, Bertrand Harris. *The Traditional Tunes of the Child Ballads*. In 4 vols. Princeton, New Jersey: Princeton University Press, 1959, 1962, 1966, 1972.

Broonzy, William. *Big Bill Blues: William Broonzy's Story as Told to Yannick Bruynoghe*. London: Cassell, 1955.

Bruce, J. Collingwood, and John Stokoe. *Northumbrian Minstrelsy: A Collection of the Ballads, Melodies, and Small-Pipe Tunes of Northumbria*. Hatboro, Pennsylvania: Folklore Associates, 1965; facsimile reprint of the original publication by The Society of Antiquaries, Newcastle-Upon-Tyne, 1882.

Bruce, Philip Alexander. *Social Life of Virginia in the Seventeenth Century*. New York: F. Ungar, 1964; originally published 1907.

Bruce-Mitford, Myrtle. 'Rotte (ii)', in *The New Grove*, vol. 16, p. 261.

Buchan, Norman, and Peter Hall (editors). *The Scottish Folksinger: 118 Modern and Traditional Folksongs*. Second edition. Glasgow: Collins, 1978.

Byrd, William. *The Writings of Colonel William Byrd of Westover in Virginia, Esquire*. Edited by John Spencer Bassett. New York: Doubleday, Page & Co., 1901.

Cable, George Washington. 'Creole Slave Songs', in *The Century Magazine*, vol. 31 (new series 9), no. 6, April 1886, pp. 807–28.

—— 'The Dance in Place Congo', in *The Century Magazine*, vol. 31 (new series 9), no. 4, February 1886, pp. 517–32.

Caines, Clement. *The History of the General Council and General Assembly of The Leeward Islands, which were Convened for the Purpose of Investigating and Ameliorating the Condition of the Slaves throughout those Settlements and of Effecting a Gradual Abolition of the Slave Trade*. Basseterre, St. Christopher: Printed by R. Cable, 1804.

Campbell, J. L. (editor), and Francis Collinson (transcriber). *Hebridean Folksongs*. Vols. 2 and 3. Oxford: Oxford University Press, 1977 and 1981.

Carrington, J. F. 'The Musical Dimension of Perception in the Upper Congo, Zaïre', in *African Music*, vol. 5, no. 1, 1971, pp. 46–51.

Chappell, William. *Old English Popular Music*. In 2 vols. New edition, revised by H. Ellis Wooldridge. London: Chappell and Macmillan, 1893.

Chesterton, Gilbert Keith. *Manalive*. London: Thomas Nelson and Sons, 1912.

Chernoff, John Miller. *African Rhythm and African Sensibility: Aesthetics and Social Action in African Musical Idioms*. Chicago: Chicago University Press, 1979.

Child, Francis James. *The English and Scottish Popular Ballads*. In 3 vols. New York: Cooper Square Publishers, 1965; originally published 1882–98.

Christie, William. *Traditional Ballad Airs*. In 2 vols. Edinburgh: Edmonston & Douglas, 1876.

Classic Piano Rags: Complete Original Music for 81 Rags. Selected and with an introduction by Rudi Blesh. New York: Dover Publications, 1973.

Closson, Ernest. *Le Manuscrit dit des Basses Danses de la Bibliothèque de Bourgogne*. Introduction et transcription par E. Closson. Brussels: Société des Bibiophiles et Iconophiles de Belgique, 1912.

Coffin, Tristram P. *The British Traditional Ballad in North America*. Philadelphia: The American Folklore Society, 1950.

Cohen, Norman. *Long Steel Rail: The Railroad in American Folksong*. Music edited by David Cohen. Urbana: University of Illinois Press, 1981. A volume in the *Music in American Life* series.

Collier, James Lincoln. *The Making of Jazz: A Comprehensive History*. London: Macmillan, 1981; originally published by Granada Publishing, 1978.

Collon, Dominique, and Anne Draffkorn Kilmer. 'The Lute in Ancient Mesopotamia', in *Music and Civilisation*, pp. 13–28.

The Compleat Elvis. London: Wise Publications, 1978.

A Concise Historical Account of All the British Colonies in North-America . . . Dublin: Printed for C. Jenkin, 1776.

Cook, Bruce, *Listen to the Blues*. London: Robson Books, 1975.

Cooke, Deryck. *The Language of Music*. London: Oxford University Press, 1959.

Cooke, Peter. 'Heterophony', in *The New Grove*, vol. 8, pp. 537–8.

Coolen, Michael Theodore. 'The Fodet: A Senegambian Origin for the Blues?', in *The Black Perspective in Music*, vol. 10, no. 1, spring 1982, pp. 69–84.

—— 'The Wolof Xalam Tradition of the Senegambia', in *Ethnomusicology*, September 1983, pp. 477–98.

Copper, Bob *A Song for Every Season*. St. Albans: Paladin, 1975; originally published by Heinemann, London, 1971.

Courlander, Harold. *Negro Folk Music, U.S.A*. New York: Columbia University Press, 1963.

—— (editor). *Negro Songs from Alabama*. Second edition, revised and enlarged. New York: Oak Publications, 1963.

Creswell, Nicholas. *Journal of Nicholas Creswell, 1774–1777*. New York: L. MacVeagh, Dial Press, 1924.

Cultural Atlas of Africa. Edited by Jocelyn Murray. Oxford: Phaidon, 1981.

A Curious Collection of Scots Tunes. Edinburgh: R. Bremner, *c*.1759.

Curtin, Philip D. *The Atlantic Slave Trade: A Census*. Madison, Wisconsin: University of Wisconsin Press, 1969.

Donington, Robert. 'Ornaments', in *The New Grove*, vol. 13, pp. 827–67.

Drabkin, William.' "Viennese" Note', in *The New Grove*, vol. 19, p. 741.

Edmands, L. W. 'Songs from the Mountains of North Carolina', in *The Journal of American Folk-Lore*, vol. 6, 1893, pp. 131 ff.

Ekwueme, Lazarus Nnanyelu. 'Analysis and Analytic Techniques in African Music: A Theory of Melodic Scales', in *African Music*, vol. 6, no. 1, 1980, pp. 89–106.

Epstein, Dena J. *Sinful Tunes and Spirituals: Black Folk Music to the Civil War*. Urbana: University of Illinois Press, 1977.

—— 'The Folk Banjo: A Documentary History', in *Ethnomusicology*, vol. 19, no. 3, September 1975, pp. 347–71.

Essays on Music and History in Africa. Edited by Klaus P. Wachsmann. Evanston: Northwestern University Press, 1971.

Evans, David. *Big Road Blues: Tradition and Creativity in the Folk Blues*. Los Angeles: University of California Press, 1982.

——'African Elements in Twentieth-Century United States Black Folk Music', in *Jazz Research*, no. 19, 1978, pp. 85–110.

—— 'Afro-American One-Stringed Instruments', in *Western Folklore*, no. 29, 1970, pp. 229–45.

Fahey, John. *Charley Patton*. London: Studio Vista, 1970.

Farmer, Henry George. *Military Music*. London: Max Parrish, 1950.

Favorite Songs of the Nineties: Complete Original Sheet Music for 89 Songs. Edited by Robert A. Fremont. New York: Dover, 1973.

Ferris, William. 'Racial Repertoires among Blues Performers', in *Ethnomusicology*, vol. 14, no. 3, September 1970, pp. 439–49.

Fiske, Roger. *Scotland in Music: A European Enthusiasm*. Cambridge: Cambridge University Press, 1983.

The Fitzwilliam Virginal Book. Edited by J.A. Fuller Maitland and W. Barclay Squire. New York: Dover Books, 1963; facsimile reprint of the original publication by Breitkopf & Härtel, Leipzig, 1899.

Födermayr, Franz. 'The Arabian Influence in the Tuareg Music', in *African Music*, vol. 4, no. 1, 1966–7, pp. 25–37.

Foster, Pops. *Pops Foster: The Autobiography of a New Orleans Jazzman, as Told to Tom Stoddard*. Los Angeles: University of Los Angeles Press, 1971.

Fox Strangways, Arthur Henry. *The Music of Hindostan*. London: Oxford University Press, 1914.

—— *Cecil Sharp*. In collaboration with Maud Karpeles. Second edition. London: Oxford University Press, 1955; first edition published in 1933.

Franklin, J. H. *The Free Negro in North Carolina, 1790–1860*. Chapel Hill: University of North Carolina Press, 1943.

Gammond, Peter (editor). *Music Hall Song Book: A Collection of 45 of the Best Songs from 1890–1920*. Newton Abbott: David & Charles, and London: EMI Music Publishing, 1975.

Garrett, John M. (editor). *Sixty Years of British Music Hall*. London: Chappell & Co., in association with André Deutsch, 1976.

Golden Encyclopaedia of Ragtime from 1900 to 1974. New York: Charles Hansen, no date.

Gourlay, Kenneth A. 'Long Trumpets of Northern Nigeria—in History and Today', in *African Music*, vol. 6, no. 2, 1982, pp. 48–72.

Grainger, Percy. 'Collecting with the Phonograph', in *The Journal of the Folk-Song Society*, vol. 3, 1908–9.

Green, Archie. *Only a Miner: Studies in Recorded Coal Mining Songs*. Urbana: University of Illinois Press, 1972.

Greig, Gavin. *Last Leaves of Traditional Ballads and Ballad Airs*. Collected in Aberdeenshire by . . . G. Greig, and edited, with an introductory essay, collations, and notes by Alexander Keith. Aberdeen: The Buchan Club, 1925.

Grove's Dictionary of Music and Musicians. Fifth edition. Edited by Eric Blom. In 9 vols. London: Macmillan, 1954.

Gutman, Herbert G. *The Black Family in Slavery and Freedom, 1750–1925*. Oxford: Basil Blackwell, 1976.

Haldane, J. B. S. *Possible Worlds, and Other Essays*. London: Chatto & Windus, 1928.

Hamm, Charles. *Yesterdays: Popular Song in America*. New York: W. W. Norton, 1979.

Handy, W. C. *Father of the Blues: An Autobiography*. Edited by Arna Bontemps. New York: Macmillan, 1941.

—— *St. Louis Blues: Album of Songs and Pictures*. London: Francis Day & Hunter, no date.

Harker, David. *Fakesong: The Manufacture of British 'Folksong', 1700 to the Present Day*. Milton Keynes: Open University Press, 1985.

—— 'Cecil Sharp in Somerset: Some Conclusions', in *Folk Music Journal*, vol. 2, no. 3, 1972, pp. 220–40.

—— 'The Making of the Tyneside Concert Hall', in *Popular Music*, vol. 1, 1981, pp. 27–56.

Harney, Ben. *Ben Harney's Rag Time Instructor*. Chicago: Sol Bloom, 1897.

—— 'Mister Johnson, Turn Me Loose', New York: M. Witmark & Sons, 1896.

—— 'You've Been a Good Old Wagon but You've Done Broke down'. New York: M. Witmark & Sons, 1896.

Hearn, Lafcadio. *Selected Writings*. Edited by Henry Goodman, with an introduction by Malcolm Cowley. New York: The Citadel Press, 1949.

—— 'Levee Life', in the *Cincinnati Commercial*, 17 March, 1876.

Higginson, Thomas Wentworth. 'Negro Spirituals', in *The Atlantic Monthly*, June 1867, pp. 685–94.

The History of Music in Sound. General editor, Gerald Abraham. Vol. 1: *Ancient and Oriental Music*. Edited by Egon Wellesz. London: Oxford University Press, 1957.

Hofstadter, Richard. *America at 1750: A Social Portrait*. New York: Knopf, 1971.

Hogg, James. *The Jacobite Relics of Scotland: Being the Songs, Airs and Legends of the Adherents to the House of Stuart*. Collected and illustrated by J. Hogg. Edinburgh: Blackwood, 1819.

Hopkin, John Barton. 'Jamaican Children's Songs', in *Ethnomusicology*, vol. 28, no. 1, January, 1984, pp. 1–36.

Hornbostel, Erich von. 'African Negro Music', in *Africa: Journal of the International Institute of African Languages and Cultures*, vol. 1, 1928, pp. 30–62.

Howes, Frank. *Folk Music of Britain—and Beyond*. London: Methuen, 1969.

Hughes, Patrick ('Spike'). *Famous Mozart Operas: An Analytical Guide for the Opera-Goer and Armchair Listener*. London: Robert Hale, 1957.

Hugill, Stan. *Sea Shanties*. London: Barrie & Jenkins, 1977.

—— *Shanties from the Seven Seas: Shipboard Work-Songs from the Great Days of Sail*. London: Routledge & Kegan Paul, 1961.

A Hundred Best Songs of the 20's and 30's. New York: Bonanza Books, 1973.

A Hundred Golden Oldies. London: Wise Publications, 1977.

Hungerford, James. *The Old Plantation, and what I Gathered there in an Autumn Month.* New York: Harper & Brothers, 1859.

Hurd, Michael. *The Oxford Junior Companion to Music.* Second edition, based on the original publication by Percy Scholes. London: Oxford University Press, 1979.

Hurston, Zora Neale. *Dust Tracks on a Road.* New York: Hutchinson, 1944.

Jackson, George Pullen. *White and Negro Spirituals: Their Life Span and Kinship.* New York: J.J. Augustin, 1943.

Jagger, Mick, and Keith Richard. *Rolling Stones: Through the Past Darkly (Big Hits vol. 2).* London: Mirage Music, 1969.

Jander, Owen. 'Singing', sections 1–7, in *The New Grove*, vol. 17, pp. 338–46.

Jefferson, Thomas. *Notes on the State of Virginia.* Second American edition. Philadelphia: Mathew Carey, 1794; written 1782, first published 1787.

Jones, A.M. *African Music in Northern Rhodesia and Some Other Places.* Livingstone, Northern Rhodesia (now Zambia): The Rhodes-Livingstone Museum, 1949. No. 4 in the occasional papers of the Rhodes-Livingstone Museum.

—— *Studies in African Music.* In 2 vols. London: Oxford University Press, 1959.

—— 'African Music', in *African Affairs*, vol. 48, 1949, pp. 290–7.

—— 'Luo Music and its Rhythm', in *African Music*, vol. 5, no. 3, 1973–4, pp. 43–54.

Jones, Irving. 'Possumala Dance or My H-O-N-E-Y!' New York: Willis Woodward, 1894.

Joplin, Scott. *Scott Joplin: Complete Piano Works.* Edited by Vera Brodsky Lawrence. Facsimile reprints of the original sheet music. New York: The New York Public Library, 1981.

Kabombo, Robert. 'Some Types of African Songs and How They are Made'. Ch. 3, pp. 14–19, in Jones, *African Music in Northern Rhodesia and Some Other Places.*

Karpeles, Maud. 'The Appalachians, I' and 'The Appalachians, II', chapters in Fox Stangways, *Cecil Sharp.*

Kemble, Frances Anne. *Journal of a Residence on a Georgian Plantation in 1838–1839.* London: Longman, Roberts, & Green, 1863.

Kendall's Clarinet Instruction Book. Boston: Oliver Ditson, 1845.

Kennedy, Peter (editor). *Folksongs of Britain and Ireland.* London: Cassell, 1975.

Kilson, Marion. *Kpele Lala: Ga Religious Songs and Symbols.* Cambridge, Massachusetts: Harvard University Press, 1971.

King, Anthony. 'Employments of the "Standard Pattern" in Yoruba Music', in *African Music*, vol. 2, no. 3, 1960, pp. 51–4.

—— 'Hausa Music', in *The New Grove*, vol. 8, pp. 309–12.

—— 'Nigeria', in *The New Grove*, vol. 13, pp. 235–43.

Kinnard, J., Jr. 'Who are our National Poets?', in *Knickerbocker Magazine*, vol. 26, October 1845.

Kinsley, James (editor). *The Oxford Book of Ballads*. London: Oxford University Press, 1969.

Kirby, Percival R. *The Musical Instruments of the Native Races of South Africa*. London: Oxford University Press, 1934.

—— 'Physical Phenomena which Appear to Have Determined the Bases and Development of an Harmonic Sense among Bushmen, Hottentot and Bantu', in *African Music*, vol. 2, no. 4, 1961, pp. 6–9.

Knight, Roderic C. 'Mandinka Drumming', in *African Arts*, vol. 7, no. 4, summer 1974, pp. 24–35.

Koestler, Arthur. *The Act of Creation*. London: Hutchinson, 1964.

—— 'Rhine's Impact on Philosophy', in *Kaleidoscope* (London: Hutchinson, 1981), pp. 309–12.

Kubik, Gerhard. 'Àló—Yoruba Story Songs', in *African Music*, vol. 4, no. 2, 1968, pp. 10–32.

—— 'Angola', in *The New Grove*, vol. 1, pp. 431–5.

—— 'Ennanga Music', in *African Music*, vol. 4, no. 1, 1966–7, pp. 21–4.

—— 'Harp Music of the Azande and Related Peoples in the Central African Republic', in *African Music*, vol. 3, no. 3, 1964, pp. 37–76.

—— 'Music and Dance', in *Cultural Atlas of Africa*, pp. 90–3.

—— 'The Phenomenon of Inherent Rhythms in East and Central African Instrumental Music', in *African Music*, vol. 3, no. 1, 1962, pp. 33–42.

—— 'The Structure of Kiganda Xylophone Music', in *African Music*, vol. 2, no. 3, 1960, pp. 6–30.

Ladzekpo, S. Kobla, and Hewitt Pantaleoni. 'Takada Drumming', in *African Music*, vol. 4, no. 4, 1970, pp. 6–31.

Lamb, Andrew. 'March: 19th- and 20th-Century Military and Popular Marches', in *The New Grove*, vol. 11, pp. 652–3.

—— 'Quadrille', in *The New Grove*, vol. 15, pp. 489–91.

Lambert, Constant. *Music Ho!: A Study of Music in Decline*. Revised edition. London: Faber and Faber, 1937.

Land, Aubrey C. (editor). *Bases of the Plantation Society*. New York: Harper & Row, 1969.

Lanner, Joseph. *Ländler und Walzer*. Edited by Alfred Ord. Graz: Akademische Druck- u. Verlagsanstalt, 1960. *Denkmäler der Tonkunst in Österreich*: Jg. xxxiii/2–Bd. 65.

The Larousse Encyclopaedia of Music. General editor Geoffrey Hindley. London: Hamlyn, 1971.

The Legacy of Islam. Edited by Sir Thomas Arnold and Alfred Guillaume. First edition. London: Oxford University Press, 1931. Second edition, edited by Joseph Schacht and C. E. Bosworth, London: Oxford University Press, 1974.

The Liber Usualis, with Introduction and Rubrics in English. Edited by the Benedictines of Solesmes. Tournai: Desclée, 1963.

Lloyd, Albert Lancaster. *Folk Song in England*. London: Panther, 1969; originally published by Lawrence & Wishart, London, 1967.

—— 'Hora Lunga', in *The New Grove*, vol. 8, pp. 694–5.

Locke, David. 'Principles of Offbeat Timing and Cross-Rhythm in Southern Eye Dance Drumming', in *Ethnomusicology*, vol. 26, no. 2, May 1982, pp. 217–46.

—— and Godwin Kwasi Agbeli. 'A Study of the Drum Language in Adzogbo', in *The Black Perspective in Music*, vol. 9, no. 1, spring 1981, pp. 25–50.

Lomax, Alan. *Folk Song Style and Culture*. New Brunswick: Transaction Books, 1978; originally published as Publication 88 of the American Association for the Advancement of Science, 1968.

—— (editor). *The Folk Songs of North America in the English Language*. Second edition. London: Cassell, 1963.

—— (editor). *The Penguin Book of American Folk Songs*. Harmondsworth: Penguin, 1964.

Lomax, John A. and Alan (editors). *American Ballads and Folk Songs*. New York: Macmillan, 1934.

—— *Negro Folk Songs as Sung by Lead Belly*. New York: Macmillan, 1936.

Lyttleton, Humphrey. *The Best of Jazz: Basin Street to Harlem*. London: Robson Books, 1978.

MacCormick, Donald (editor). *Hebridean Folksongs: A Collection of Waulking Songs by D. MacCormick in Kilphedir in South Uist in the year 1893 . . .* Completed and edited by J. L. Campbell. Tunes transcribed, from recordings, by Francis Collinson. Oxford: The Clarendon Press, 1969.

Maniates, Maria Rika. 'Street, Cries', in *The New Grove*, vol. 18, pp. 265–6.

Marsh, Richard. *Marsh's Selection, or, Singing for the Million, Containing the Choicest and Best Collection of Admired Patriotic, Comic, Irish, Negro, Temperance, and Sentimental Songs Ever Embodied in One Work*. Three vols. in one. New York: Richard Marsh, 374 Pearl Street, 1854.

Mencken, H. L. *The American Scene: A Reader*. Selected and edited, and with an introduction and commentary, by Huntingdon Cairns. New York: Knopf, 1965.

Morgan, Edmund S. *American Slavery—American Freedom: The Ordeal of Colonial Virginia*. New York: W. W. Norton, 1975.

Morison, Samuel Eliot. *The Oxford History of the American People*. New York: Oxford University Press, 1965.

—— , Henry Steel Commager, and William E. Leuchtenburg. *The Growth of the American Republic*. Seventh edition. New York: Oxford University Press, 1980.

Morley, Thomas, *A Plaine and Easie Introduction to Practicall Musicke*. London: Humfrey Lownes, 1608; originally published by Peter Short, 1597.

Morris, R. O. *Contrapuntal Technique in the Sixteenth Century*. London: Oxford University Press, 1922.

Motherwell, William. *Minstrelsy: Ancient and Modern, with an Historical Introduction and Notes*. Glasgow: Wylie, 1827.

Murphy, Jeannette Robinson. 'The Survival of African Music in America', in *Popular Science Monthly*, September 1899, pp. 660–72.

Music and Civilisation. Edited by T. C. Mitchell. London: British Museum Publications, 1980. The British Museum Yearbook 4.

Nathan, Hans. *Dan Emmett and the Rise of Early Negro Minstrelsy*. Second edition. Norman, Oklahoma: University of Oklahoma Press, 1977.

—— 'Early Banjo Tunes and American Syncopation', in *The Musical Quarterly*, vol. 42., no. 4, October 1956, pp. 455–72; also forms ch. 13 of the above.

The New Grove Dictionary of Music and Musicians. Edited by Stanley Sadie. In

20 vols. London: Macmillan, 1980.

Newman, Ernest. *From the World of Music.* London: John Calder, 1956.

—— 'The World of Music', in *The Sunday Times,* 4 September 1927, p. 5.

Nketia, J. H. Kwabena. *African Music in Ghana: A Survey of Traditional Forms.* Accra: Longmans, 1962.

—— *Folk Songs of Ghana.* Legon, Ghana: Oxford University Press, for the University of Ghana, 1963.

—— *The Music of Africa.* London: Gollancz, 1975.

—— 'Ghana', in *The New Grove,* vol. 7, pp. 326–32.

Nordhoff, Charles. *The Merchant Vessel: A Sailor Boy's Voyages.* New York: Dodd, Mead & Co., 1884.

Northup, Solomon. *Twelve Years a Slave: The Narrative of Solomon Northup, a Citizen of New-York, Kidnapped in Washington City in 1841 and Rescued in 1853, from a Cotton Plantation near the Red River in Louisiana.* Auburn, New York: Derby and Miller, 1853.

Nzewi, Meki. 'The Rhythm of Dance in Igbo Music', in *The Conch,* vol. 3, no. 2, September 1971, pp. 104–8.

Odell, J. S. 'Banjo', in *The New Grove,* vol. 2, pp.118–21.

Odum, Howard W. 'Folk-Song and Folk-Poetry as Found in the Secular Songs of the Southern Negroes', in the *Journal of American Folklore,* vol. 24, July–September 1911, pp. 289 ff.

—— , and Guy B. Johnson. *The Negro and his Songs: A Study of Typical Negro Songs in the South.* Chapel Hill: University of North Carolina Press, 1925.

Oliver, Paul. *Savannah Syncopators: African Retentions in the Blues.* London: Studio Vista, 1970.

—— *Songsters and Saints: Vocal Traditions on Race Records.* Cambridge: Cambridge University Press, 1984.

—— *The Story of the Blues.* London: Barrie & Rockliff, 1969.

Olmsted, Frederick Law. *A Journey in the Back Country.* New York: Mason Brothers, 1860.

—— *A Journey in the Seaboard Slave States in the Years 1853–1854, with Remarks on their Economy . . .* New York: G. P. Putnam's Sons, 1856.

O Lochlainn, Colm (editor). *Irish Street Ballads.* Dublin: At the Sign of the Three Candles, 1939.

Opie, Iona and Peter. *The Lore and Language of Schoolchildren.* Oxford: Oxford University Press, 1959.

—— *The Oxford Dictionary of Nursery Rhymes.* London: Oxford University Press, 1951.

Ord, John (editor). *The Bothy Songs and Ballads of Aberdeen, Banff and Moray, Angus and the Mearns.* Paisley: Alexander Gardner, 1930.

Oswald, James. *The Caledonian Pocket Companion.* London: Printed for the author, *c.*1750–60.

The Oxford English Dictionary. Edited by J. A. H. Murray, H. Bradley, W. A. Craigie, and C. T. Onions. In 12 vols., with a supplement. London: Oxford University Press, 1933.

Palmer, Roy (editor). *The Book of English Country Songs.* London: Music Sales, 1986; originally published as *Everyman's Book of English Country Songs* by Dent, London, 1979.

—— (editor). *The Oxford Book of Sea Songs*. Oxford: Oxford University Press, 1986.

—— (editor). *A Touch on the Times: Songs of Social Change, 1770 to 1914*. Harmondsworth: Penguin Education, 1974.

Pantaleoni, Hewitt. 'Three Principles of Timing in Anlo Dance Drumming', in *African Music*, vol. 5, no. 2, 1972, pp. 50–63.

Parry, Sir Hubert. *The Art of Music*. London: Kegan Paul, 1893.

—— *Style in Musical Art*. London: Macmillan, 1911.

Peacock, Kenneth (editor). *Songs of the Newfoundland Outports*. In 3 vols. Ottawa: The Queen's Printer, 1965. National Museum of Canada Bulletin 197, Anthropological Series 65.

Pearse, James. *A Narrative of the Life of James Pearse . . .* Rutland, Vermont: Printed by W. Fay for the author, 1825.

Ping, Nancy R. 'Black Musical Activities in Antebellum Wilmington, North Carolina', in *The Black Perspective in Music*, vol. 8, no. 2, fall 1980.

Popper, Sir Karl. *The Open Society and its Enemies*. Vol. 2: *The High Tide of Prophecy: Hegel, Marx, and the Aftermath*. Fifth edition. London: Routledge & Kegan Paul, 1966.

Popular Music 1. Folk or Popular? Distinctions, Influences, Continuities. A Yearbook. Edited by Richard Middleton and David Horn. Cambridge: Cambridge University Press, 1981.

Popular Songs of Nineteenth-Century America: Complete Original Sheet Music for 64 Songs. Selected, with an introduction and notes, by Richard Jackson. New York: Dover, 1976.

Purcell, Henry. *The Works of Henry Purcell*. Vols. 25 and 31. London: Novello, 1928 and 1959.

Ragtime Rarities: Complete Original Music for 64 Piano Rags. Selected and with an introduction by Trebor Jay Tichenor. New York: Dover Publications, 1975.

Randolph, Vance (collector and editor). *Ozark Folksongs*. Revised edition, with introduction by W. K. McNeil. In 4 vols. Columbia, Missouri: University of Missouri Press, 1980.

Raper, A. F., and I. de A. Reid. *Sharecroppers All*. Chapel Hill, North Carolina: University of North Carolina Press, 1941.

Ravenel, H.W. 'Recollections of Southern Plantation Life', in *Yale Review*, vol. 25, June 1936.

Ravenscroft, Thomas. *Melismata: Musicall Phansies, fitting the Court, Citie and Countrey Humours*. London: William Stansby, 1611.

Rawley, James A. *The Transatlantic Slave Trade: A History*. New York: W. W. Norton, 1981.

Ridge, Martin, and Ray Allen Billington (editors). *America's Frontier Story: A Documentary History of Westward Expansion*. New York: Holt, Rinehart and Winston, 1969.

Ritchie, Jean. *Folk Songs of the Southern Appalachians as Sung by Jean Ritchie*. New York: Oak Publications, 1965.

Roberts, John Storm. *Black Music of Two Worlds*. London: Allen Lane, 1972.

—— *The Latin Tinge: The Impact of Latin American Music on the United States*. London: Oxford University Press, 1979.

Rose, Willie Lee (editor). *A Documentary History of Slavery in North America*. New York: Oxford University Press, 1976.

Rosen, Charles. *The Classical Style: Haydn, Mozart, Beethoven*. London: Faber and Faber, 1971.

Rosenberg, Bruce A. *The Art of the American Folk Preacher*. New York: Oxford University Press, 1970.

Rosselli, John. *The Opera Industry in Italy from Cimarosa to Verdi: The Role of the Impresario*. Cambridge: Cambridge University Press, 1984.

Roth, Ernst. *The Business of Music: Reflections of a Music Publisher*. London: Cassell, 1969.

Rouget, Gilbert. 'Benin', in *The New Grove*, vol. 2, pp. 487–93.

Rycroft, David K. 'Stylistic Evidence in Nguni Song', in *Essays on Music and History in Africa*, pp. 213–41.

—— 'The Zulu Bow Songs of Princess Magogo', in *African Music*, vol. 5, no. 4, 1975–6, pp. 41–97.

Sachs, Curt. 'The Road to Major', in *The Musical Quarterly*, vol. 29, no. 3, July 1943, pp. 381–404.

Salmen, Walter. 'Towards the Exploration of National Idiosyncrasies in Wandering Song-Tunes', in the *International Folk Music Journal*, vol. 6, 1954, pp. 52–5.

Sandburg, Carl (editor). *The American Songbag*. New York: Harcourt, Brace, 1927.

Sayers, Dorothy L. *Strong Poison*. London: Gollancz, 1930.

Scarborough, Dorothy. *On the Trail of Negro Folk-Songs*. Assisted by Ola Lee Gulledge. Hatboro, Pennsylvania: Folklore Associates, 1963; facsimile reprint of the original publication by Harvard University Press, Cambridge, Massachusetts, 1925.

Scholes, Percy A. *The Oxford Companion to Music*. Ninth edition. London: Oxford University Press, 1955.

Seeger, Charles. 'Folk Music: U.S.A.', in *Grove's Dictionary*, fifth edition, vol. 3, pp. 387–98.

A Selection of Scotch, English, Irish and Foreign Airs, Adapted for the Fife, Violin or German Flute . . . Glasgow: J. Aird, 1782.

Sharp, Cecil. *English Folk-Chanteys*. London: Simpkin, Marshall, Hamilton, Kent & Co., and Taunton: Barnicott and Pearce, 1914.

—— *English Folk Song: Some Conclusions*. Third edition, revised by Maud Karpeles, with an appreciation by Ralph Vaughan Williams. London: Methuen, 1954; first edition published in 1907.

—— and Maud Karpeles. *English Folk Songs from the Southern Appalachians*. In 2 vols. London: Oxford University Press, 1932.

—— and Charles L. Marson. *Folk Songs from Somerset*. In 5 vols. London: Simpkin, Marshall, Hamilton, Kent & Co., and Taunton: Barnicott and Pearce, 1904–9.

Shaw, George Bernard. *Shaw's Music: The Complete Musical Criticism in Three Volumes*. Edited by Dan H. Laurence. London: Max Reinhart, The Bodley Head, 1981.

—— 'The Bach Bi-centenary', in *The Dramatic Review*, 28 March 1885, p. 133.

—— 'Beethoven', in *The Radio Times*, 18 March 1927, pp. 573–84.

—— 'The Popular Musical Union', in *The Star*, 13 April 1889, p. 4.

Skene MS, *c.* 1620. In the National Library of Scotland, Edinburgh, Adv. MS. 5.2.15.

Smith, Reed. *South Carolina Ballads, with a Study of the Traditional Ballad To-day*. Cambridge, Massachusetts: Harvard University Press, 1928.

Smith, Robert Archibald. *The Scotish* [sic] *Minstrel*. In 6 vols. Edinburgh: Purdie, *c.*1820–4.

Solid Gold Rock and Roll. Hialeah, Florida: Screen Gems-Columbia Publications, 1975.

Song Hits from the Turn of the Century: Complete Original Sheet Music for 62 Songs. Edited by Paul Charosh and Robert A. Fremont. New York: Dover Publications, 1975.

The Songs of Scotland. Vol. II: Containing One Hundred and Fifty One songs. Collected and Edited, with new accompaniments, by Myles B. Foster. London: Boosey, no date.

Sousa, John Philip. *Sousa's Great Marches in Piano Transcription: Original Sheet Music of 23 Works by John Philip Sousa*. Selected, with an introduction, by Lester S. Levy. New York: Dover Publications, 1975.

—— 'A Letter from Sousa', in *Etude*, August 1898.

Spence, Keith. *Living Music*. London: Hamish Hamilton, 1979.

Stampp, Kenneth M. *The Peculiar Institution: Slavery in the Ante-Bellum South*. New York: Knopf, 1956.

Stone, Ruth M. 'Liberia', in *The New Grove*, vol. 10, pp. 715–18.

Stravinsky, Igor. *Poetics of Music: In the Form of Six Lessons*. Translated by Arthur Knodel and Ingolf Dahl. Cambridge, Massachusetts: Harvard University Press, 1970. Originally a series of lectures delivered at Harvard in French, *Poétique musicale sous forme de six leçons*.

Sutton, Brett. 'Shape-Note Tune Books and Primitive Hymns', in *Ethnomusicology*, vol. 26, no. 1, January 1982, pp. 11–26.

Temperley, Nicholas. 'The Old Way of Singing: Its Origins and Development', in *The Journal of the American Musicological Society*, fall 1981.

Titon, Jeff Todd. *Early Downhome Blues*. Urbana: University of Illinois Press, 1977. A volume in the *Music in American Life* series.

Tovey, Sir Donald. *Essays in Musical Analysis*. In 7 vols. London: Oxford University Press, 1935.

Tracey, Andrew. 'The Matepe Mbira Music of Rhodesia', in *African Music*, vol. 4, no. 4, 1970, pp. 37–61.

Trimingham, J. Spencer. *A History of Islam in West Africa*. London: Oxford University Press, 1962.

Tuckwell, Barry. *Horn*. London: Macdonald, 1983. A volume in the *Yehudi Menuhin Music Guides* series.

Turkson, Adolphus Acquah Robertson. 'Effutu Asafo Music: A Study of a Traditional Music Style of Ghana with Special Reference to the Role of Tonal Language in Choral Music Involving Structural and Harmonic Analysis'. Dissertation, Northwestern University, 1972.

Turnbull, Jane M. and Marion. *American Photographs*. London: T. C. Newby, 1859.

Turner, Michael R. (editor), and Antony Miall (music editor). *The Parlour Song*

Book: A Casquet of Vocal Games. New York: The Viking Press, 1973.

Van Oven, Cootje. 'Music of Sierra Leone', in *African Arts*, vol. 3, no. 4, summer 1970, pp. 20–7 and 71.

Vaughan Williams, Ralph, and A. L. Lloyd. *The Penguin Book of English Folk Songs.* Harmondsworth: Penguin, 1959.

Venable, W. H. 'Down South before the War: Record of a Ramble to New Orleans in 1858'. Ohio Archaeological and Historical Society, *Publications*, vol. 2, March 1889, pp. 488–513.

Vidal, Tunji. 'Oriki in Traditional Yoruba Music', in *African Arts*, vol. 3, no. 1, autumn 1969, pp. 56–9.

Wachsmann, Klaus, and Peter Cooke. 'Africa', in *The New Grove*, vol. 1, pp. 144–53.

Walker, Ernest. *A History of Music in England.* Second edition. London: Oxford University Press, 1924.

Walsh, Colin (editor). *There Goes that Song Again: One Hundred Years of Popular Song.* London: Elm Tree Books, 1977.

Walvin, James. *Black and White: The Negro and English Society, 1555–1945.* London: Allen Lane, 1973.

Ward, W. E. 'Music in the Gold Coast', *Gold Coast Review*, vol. 3, July–December 1927.

Waterman, Richard A. ' "Hot" Rhythm in Negro Music', in the *Journal of the American Musicological Society*, vol. 1, no. 1, spring 1948, pp. 24–37.

Watson, John Fanning. *Methodist Error: or, Friendly Christian Advice, to those Methodists, who Indulge in Extravagant Religious Emotions and Bodily Exercises. By a Wesleyan Methodist.* Cincinnati: Phillips & Speer, 1819; originally published by D. & E. Fenton, Trenton, New Jersey.

Weelkes, Thomas. *Ayeres or Phantasticke Spirites for Three Voices.* Edited by E. H. Fellowes. London: Stainer and Bell, 1916; originally published in 1608. Vol. 13 of *The English Madrigal School*.

Weill, Kurt, and Bertolt Brecht. *Die Dreigroschenoper.* Vienna: Universal, 1928.

Westrup, J., and F. L. Harrison. *Collins Encyclopaedia of Music.* Second edition, revised by Conrad Wilson. London: Collins, 1976.

White, Newman Ivy. *American Negro Folk-Songs.* Cambridge, Massachusetts: Harvard University Press, 1928.

Wightman, William M. *Life of William Capers, D.D., One of the Bishops of the Methodist Episcopal Church, South; including an Autobiography.* Nashville, Tennessee: Southern Methodist Publishing House, 1859.

Wilson, Colin. *Colin Wilson on Music (Brandy of the Damned).* London: Pan Books, 1967; originally published as *Brandy of the Damned* by John Baker, 1964.

Wiora, Walter, and Wolfgang Suppan. 'Germany: Folk Music', in *The New Grove*, vol. 7, pp. 283–8.

Woodward, C. Vann. *Origins of the New South, 1877–1913.* Reprinted with additions. Baton Rouge, Louisiana: Louisiana State University Press, 1971. Vol. 9 of *A History of the South*.

Zinn, Howard. *A People's History of the United States.* London: Longman, 1980.

GLOSSARY

AMERICAN GREGORY WALKER   An American adaptation of the GREGORY WALKER chord pattern, in which the subdominant chords are replaced with subdominant–tonic progressions.

AT-ODDNESS   Of MATRICES, contrast, divergence. compare BOUND-UPNESS, (Suggested by a passage in R. O. Morris.)

ATONIC   Of a mode, having no tonic.

BOUND-UPNESS   Of MATRICES, interconnectedness, mutual dependence. Compare AT-ODDNESS.

BRITISH   I use this somewhat unpleasant word to mean 'of the British Isles'—that is, including Ireland. In the strict political sense Britain means England, Scotland, and Wales, but the arts make nonesense of political boundaries. This usage is purely a matter of convenience, and I hope no Irishman will be offended by it.

CEILING NOTE   In a MODAL FRAME, the note which is felt to be the top of the mode, though isolated notes may sometimes go above it. See also FLOOR NOTE and CENTRAL NOTE.

CENTRAL NOTE   A note in the middle of a mode around which the other notes of the melody cluster. See also FLOOR NOTE and CEILING NOTE.

CENTRIFUGAL HARMONY   Harmony which begins with the tonic and procedes to outlying chords. Opposed to CENTRIPETAL HARMONY.

CENTRIPETAL HARMONY   Harmony which begins with unstable, outlying chords and then homes in on the tonic, for instance the RAGTIME PROGRESSION. Opposed to CENTRIFUGAL HARMONY.

CHORD-BASED   Describes music where the melody simply conforms to the harmony of the moment, without any sort of MELODIC MODE.

CLASSICAL   In this book the word 'classical' is used more or less in the layman's sense of highbrow, non-popular music. The exact meaning varies with the context, but generally it comprises everything from the early Baroque to the late Romantic. When the word is spelt with a capital letter—'Classical'—it refers to the school of Haydn, Mozart, Beethoven, and their contemporaries.

CLOSED FORM   That which comes to a tonic cadence of some kind at the end. Contrasted with OPEN FORM.

COMPOSER   Includes not only the writer of music, but also the performer where there is an element of improvisation. So also 'composition'.

CO-TONIC   A MELODIC tonic which differs from the harmonic tonic and is equal in importance to it. See also SECONDARY TONIC.

CYCLE   A section of music which is repeated over and over again, with or without variation. Usually each repetition is of equal length, but sometimes the lengths can differ widely. There may be cycles within cycles or cycles beginning at different points (for instance melodic, harmonic, rhythmic) within the same piece of music.

DIALOGUE ACCOMPANIMENT   A type of accompaniment, common in African and Afro-American music, where voice and accompaniment alternate. During the vocal passages the accompaniment either falls completely silent or subsides to some sort of drone.

DROPPING THIRD   See THIRDS, DROPPING and HANGING.

EUROPEAN   Includes those places outside Europe where European culture has been transplanted, for instance, the United States, Australia, Argentina, etc.

FLOOR NOTE   In a MODAL FRAME, the note which is felt to be the bottom of the mode, though isolated notes may sometimes go below it. See also CEILING NOTE and CENTRAL NOTE.

FOCUS, UPPER and LOWER   A localized part of a mode (upper or lower as the case may be) on which the melody dwells for a while. See also MINI-MODE. (Adopted, with a slight change of meaning, from Lazarus Ekueme.)

FOLLOWABILITY   The susceptibility of a section of music to being followed. It varies from those passages which demand to be followed to those which forbid it.

FOUNDATION NOTE   The FLOOR NOTE of a LEVEL.

GREGORY WALKER   The chord string C F C G : C F C–G C. Also known as the *passamezzo moderno*. (Adopted from Thomas Morley.)

HANGING THIRD   See THIRDS, DROPPING and HANGING.

HE, etc.   All masculine pronouns in this book are to be taken as applying equally to the female, except where the context renders this interpretation absurd.

INDIA   As with 'Britain', a cultural rather than a political entity. Includes the present-day Pakistan, Bangladesh, etc.

LADDER OF THIRDS   A type of MODAL FRAME built around thirds superimposed on one another like a ladder. (Adopted from Curt Sachs.)

LEVEL   A temporary MODAL FRAME which is contrasted with another at a different pitch.

LOWER FOCUS   See FOCUS, UPPER and LOWER.

MATRIX   One of the basic patterns that give coherence to a piece of music. Matrices may be elaborate or simple, and the art of composition lies largely in their combination, either simultaneously or successively.

MEDIANT-OCTAVE MODE   A MELODIC MODE spanning an octave between mediant and mediant. See also SUBMEDIANT-OCTAVE MODE and PSEUDO-PHRYGIAN MODE.

MELODIC   As used in the terms MELODIC MODE, MELODIC TRIAD, MELODIC DISSONANCE, etc., this word indicates a pattern independent of the harmony.

MELODIC DISSONANCE   The quality, in a note, of being modally unstable—in other words, attracted to another note in a way that has nothing to do with the harmony.

MELODIC MODE   A pattern giving coherence to a melody independent of the harmony. FLOOR, CEILING, and CENTRAL notes, CO- and SECONDARY TONICS, MELODIC TRIADS, and MELODIC DISSONANCE are all features of melodic modality. Specific melodic modes are the MEDIANT- and SUBMEDIANT-OCTAVES and the PSEUDO-PHRYGIAN.

MELODIC TRIAD   A triad in the melody independent of harmony. Usually the notes are the same as the harmonic tonic triad (tonic-third-fifth), but sixth-tonic-third and third-fifth-seventh are also possible, as are melodic triads built on the dominant or subdominant. The melodic triad is a special case of the NON-HARMONIC ARPEGGIO.

MINI-MODE   Part of a mode which behaves like a small mode in itself. It may, for instance, have its own SECONDARY or CO-TONIC. See also FOCUS, UPPER and LOWER.

MISSED BEAT   A form of syncopation in which a rest is substituted for the beginning of an expected note.

MODAL FRAME   A specialized form of mode in which at least some of the notes have a melodic value independent of the harmony, acting as FLOOR NOTES, SECONDARY TONICS, etc. (see under MELODIC MODE). The modal frame is distinguished from the NOTE FRAME by having a specific tonic.

MODE   A scale with a tonic. See also MODAL FRAME.

NEAR EASTERN   Describes the musical style characteristic of the Islamic empire at its greatest extent: that is, roughly, from Bengal to Morocco, and reaching down into Africa and up into Spain, southern Italy, and the Balkans.

NEUTRAL INTERVALS   Those which fall more or less midway between major and minor.

NON-HARMONIC ARPEGGIO   One which appears in the melody but not the accompanying harmony. The most common type is the MELODIC TRIAD.

NORTH AMERICA   A convenient way of describing the political entity which was the Thirteen Colonies before the American Revolution, and the United States after it.

NOTE FRAME   A MELODIC MODE which either is ATONIC or has an unstable tonic. See also MODAL FRAME.

OPEN FORM   That which does not come to a tonic cadence. It may be rhapsodic, simply spinning the music out indefinitely, or cyclical, in which case every cycle flows into the next. Contrasted with CLOSED FORM.

PARLOUR MODES   Varieties of the major mode that flourished in PARLOUR MUSIC, distinguished by great emphasis on the third, sixth, and seventh of the mode.

PARLOUR MUSIC   EUROPEAN popular or semi-popular nineteenth-century music, distinct from 'folk' music and uncontaminated by highbrow pretensions. So also PARLOUR MODES, harmony, rhythm, etc.

PENDULAR THIRDS   Oscillating notes a third apart. The third varies in its precise extent, but is most typically NEUTRAL. (Adopted from J.H. Nketia.)

PRIMITIVE   As used to describe musical forms or styles (for instance 'the primitive blues', 'primitive harmony') this means merely earlier in point of development—in other words, not necessarily chronologically. There is no pejorative intention.

PSEUDO-PHRYGIAN MODE   A form of the MEDIANT-OCTAVE MODE in which the seventh (of the ordinary major mode) is given special prominence, often in conjunction with the fifth, producing an effect rather like the phrygian mode.

RAGTIME PROGRESSION   The chord-string $(III_\sharp^7)$–$VI_\sharp^7$–$II_\sharp^7$–V7–(I), or a close variant. Typical of ragtime and kindred genres, but actually derived from classical usage. (Adopted from John Fahey.)

RUMBA RHYTHM   The rhythm in which an 8-pulse bar is divided into 3+3+2, or sometimes 3+5. One of the variants of the African STANDARD PATTERN.

SCALE   A pattern of notes, regardless of the weight attached to any of them, for instance which, if any, is the tonic.

SECONDARY TONIC   A MELODIC tonic which differs from the harmonic tonic and is subordinate to it. See also CO-TONIC.

SHIFT   A movement from one LEVEL to another. Distinguished from a *change* of chord.

STANDARD PATTERN   In African music, the division of an 8-pulse pattern (corresponding to the bar of European music) into 3+5 or 5+3, or a 12-pulse pattern into 5+7 or 7+5. The 12-pulse variety is called by A. M. Jones the 'African signature tune'. The RUMBA RHYTHM is a variety of the standard pattern.

SUBMEDIANT-OCTAVE MODE   A MELODIC MODE spanning an octave between submediant and submediant. See also MEDIANT-OCTAVE MODE.

SYNCOPATION   Used in this book for all sorts of cross-rhythms.

THIRDS, DROPPING and HANGING   The two varieties of PENDULAR THIRDS, depending on whether the principal note is the upper one (the HANGING THIRD) or the lower (the DROPPING THIRD).

UPPER FOCUS   See FOCUS, UPPER and LOWER.

INDEX

The page numbers of important references are in **bold** type. *Italics* indicate musical examples, as well as text relevant to them, if confined to the same page. All references to musical examples come at the ends of entries or sub-entries. Works by well-known composers appear under the name of the composer. 'US' refers to both the United States and its colonial predecessors. Odd-looking terms can usually be found explained in the glossary on pp. 319–22.